Macroeconomics and Markets in Developing and Emerging Economies

The book presents and further develops basic principles and concepts in international finance and open economy macroeconomics to make them more relevant for emerging and developing economies (EDEs). The volume emphasises the necessity of greater knowledge of context as populous Asian economies integrate with world markets, as well as the rapidly changing nature of the area due to rethinking after the global financial crisis. It addresses a host of themes, including key issues such as exchange rate economics, macroeconomic policy in an open economy, analytical frameworks for and experience of EDEs after liberalisation, the international financial system, currency and financial crises, continuing risks and regulatory response.

This book will be useful to scholars and researchers of economics, especially in macroeconomics, business and finance and development studies.

Ashima Goyal is Professor at the Indira Gandhi Institute of Development Research, Mumbai, India. She is the author of the book *Developing Economy Macroeconomics: Fresh Perspectives* (1999) as well as numerous research articles and is editor of *Macroeconomics and Markets in India: Good Luck or Good Policy?* (2012), *Handbook of the Indian Economy in the 21st Century: Understanding the Inherent Dynamism* (2014) and *A Concise Handbook of the Indian Economy in the 21st Century* (2015). She was Visiting Fellow at the Economic Growth Centre, Yale University, and a Fulbright Senior Research Fellow at Claremont Graduate University, USA. She won two best research awards at GDN meetings in Tokyo (2000) and Rio de Janeiro (2001), was selected as one of the four most powerful women in economics and a thought leader by *Business Today* (2008) and was the first Professor P. R. Brahmananda Memorial Research Grant awardee (2011) for a study on the *History of Monetary Policy in India since Independence* (2014).

'This [book] is an advanced text on open economy macroeconomics in the context of emerging developing economies by a leading macroeconomist of the country. It provides a valuable New Keynesian perspective, combining forward-looking behaviour and price rigidities with dualism in labour markets.'

V. S. Chitre, *Professor and Director, Indian School of Political Economy, Pune, India*

'With emerging markets in over half of world GDP it is important to incorporate the unique institutional features of these markets into the workhorse analytical frameworks of international macroeconomics, to better understand the past, current and future evolution of the world economy. Ashima Goyal is an expert on these issues and her book is a timely and valuable contribution to the field of international macroeconomics. All students, researchers and practitioners interested in the progress of the world economy will greatly benefit from studying it.'

Gita Gopinath, *John Zwaanstra Professor of International Studies and of Economics, Harvard University, USA*

Macroeconomics and Markets in Developing and Emerging Economies

Ashima Goyal

Routledge
Taylor & Francis Group
LONDON AND NEW YORK

First published 2017
by Routledge
2 Park Square, Milton Park, Abingdon, Oxon OX14 4RN

and by Routledge
711 Third Avenue, New York, NY 10017

Routledge is an imprint of the Taylor & Francis Group, an informa business

© 2017 Ashima Goyal

The right of Ashima Goyal to be identified as author of this work has been asserted by her in accordance with sections 77 and 78 of the Copyright, Designs and Patents Act 1988.

All rights reserved. No part of this book may be reprinted or reproduced or utilised in any form or by any electronic, mechanical, or other means, now known or hereafter invented, including photocopying and recording, or in any information storage or retrieval system, without permission in writing from the publishers.

Trademark notice: Product or corporate names may be trademarks or registered trademarks, and are used only for identification and explanation without intent to infringe.

British Library Cataloguing in Publication Data
A catalogue record for this book is available from the British Library

Library of Congress Cataloging-in-Publication Data
A catalog record has been requested for this book

ISBN: 978-1-138-68881-0 (hbk)
ISBN: 978-1-315-39858-7 (ebk)

Typeset in Sabon
by Apex CoVantage, LLC

To my son, Kovid Goyal

Contents

List of figures	ix
List of tables	xii
List of boxes	xiv
Preface	xv
List of abbreviations	xvii

1	Analytical frameworks and their evolution	1
2	Basic accounting: the balance of payments	28
3	The asset approach to the exchange rate	51
4	Market microstructure of foreign exchange markets	79
5	Purchasing power parity and the exchange rate	107
6	The monetary approach to the exchange rate	123
7	The real exchange rate: beyond monetary theories	140
8	Short-run adjustment: monetary and fiscal policy	154
9	Exchange rate policy	173
10	New open economy macroeconomics	202

viii *Contents*

11 New directions for monetary and fiscal policy 226

12 Structure, stabilisation and structural adjustment 269

13 Currency crises 299

14 The global financial crises and the international
    financial system 330

Index 368

Figures

1.1	Understanding stagflation	6
1.2a	Elastic supply	16
1.2b	Inelastic supply	16
2.1	C smoothing in response to a shock in an open economy	32
2.2	Trade deficit ratios adjusted for oil and gold and current account deficit ratio	34
2.3	India's balance of payments: ratios to GDP	41
2.4	Capital flows in India as ratios to GDP	41
2.5	Debt equity flows (US$ million)	42
2.6	Net primary factor income from abroad as a ratio to GDP	45
2.7	Volatile constituents of capital flows (US$ million)	45
3.1	Equilibrium in the FX market	54
3.2	A fall in R^*	62
3.3a	Payoff from a long position in a rupee forward	70
3.3b	Payoff from a short position in a rupee forward	71
3.4	Profits from (a) call options and (b) put options	72
4.1	FX market turnover (US$ billion)	97
4.2	Entry of noise traders in FX markets	100
6.1	Exchange rate overshooting	127
6.2	Response of each variable to a rise in money supply	130
6.3	The impact of rise in money growth rate when prices are flexible	132
6.4	Response of each variable to a rise in the rate of growth of money supply	133
7.1	Adding PPP to the FX and the money market	145
7.2	Equilibrium in the money and FX market	147
7.3	The current account equated to the capital account	149
7.4	Exchange rate cycles	150

x *Figures*

8.1	Policy under a float	156
8.2	(a) Fiscal and (b) monetary policy under a float	157
8.3	Policy under a fixed exchange rate	158
8.4	(a) Monetary and (b) fiscal policy under a fixed exchange rate	158
8.5	Deriving the FM* curve	159
8.6	Short-run equilibrium	161
8.7	A temporary fall in world demand	161
8.8	A temporary rise in money demand	162
8.9	A permanent rise in G	163
8.10	A permanent rise in M	163
8.11	Fiscal policy when the exchange rate affects prices	164
8.12	The current account balance	168
8.13	The CAB over time	169
9.1	A fixed exchange rate	175
9.2	Monetary policy	176
9.3	A temporary rise in government expenditure	177
9.4	One-time devaluation	177
9.5	Attack on a currency	178
9.6	Automatic stabilisation under fixed exchange rates	179
9.7	Automatic stabilisation under floating exchange rates	180
9.8	Why the impossible trinity rarely holds	182
9.9	Excess returns determined in the local bond market	192
9.10	Sterilised intervention under imperfect substitution in bond	192
9.11	Exchange rate policy in a liquidity trap	197
10.1	A concave and a linear utility function	207
10.2	Monopolistic competition	210
10.3	The response to a monetary shock in an open economy DSGE	217
11.1	Nested structure of production and consumption in a SOEME	235
11.2	Aggregate supply with different slopes	238
11.3	The monetary policy (MP) and inflation adjustment (IA) curves	240
11.4	Aggregate demand and supply	261
12.1	Internal and external balance	279
12.2	Importing inflation	280
12.3	The Swan-Salter model in output space	282
12.4	The Swan diagram: real exchange rate and absorption space	284
12.5	External balance and the labour market	284

Figures   xi

13.1a	Time of attack	303
13.1b	Reserves	303
13.1c	Money supply	303
13.2	*(a)* Low reserves $R = 8$; *(b)* Intermediate reserves $R = 12$	306
13.3	Timeline and equilibria	314
13.4	Rupee and the dollar flows	318
13.5	Equating dollar demand and supply with a flexible exchange rate	319
13.6	Sovereign debt, bailouts and standstills	324

Tables

1.1	Growth, inflation and policy rates	17
1.2	Growth, inflation and policy rates	19
1.3	Rates in new GDP series (base 2011–12)	21
2.1a	India's overall balance of payments (US$ billion)	38
2.1b	Major items of India's balance of payments (US$ billion)	39
2.2	Current and capital accounts of the Indian balance of payments over time	40
2.3	Economic classification of capital inflows into India	43
2.4	Overall international investment position of India (US$ billion)	44
2.5	FDI in China	48
4.1	Comparison of Indian and Australian FX markets	85
4.2	Aspects of the Indian FX market	86
4.3	Policy measures over 2010–14 and effect on rupee (+depreciation, –appreciation)	93
4.4	Rise in cross-border derivatives	98
9.1	CB balance sheet	174
9.2	Exchange rate regimes	183
9.3	Classifying exchange rate regimes in the 1990s	188
11.1	Benchmark calibrations	237
11.2	Monetary policy procedures	245
12.1	Comparison across income categories	271
12.2	Financial sector indicators	273
12.3	Comparative government expenditure and taxes (1993)	276
12.4	India compared to the OECD average (% of GDP)	277
12.5	Comparing types of stabilisation	290
12.6	Comparing Latin America and Asia	294
13.1	Per cent changes in bilateral US$ exchange rates and local currency share prices	308

Tables xiii

13.2	Crises in advanced and emerging economies, 1970–2006	326
14.1	Chinese reserves and savings of US households	335
14.2	Procyclical bank balance sheets	339
14.3	International risk diversification	342

Boxes

2.1	Smoothing consumption in EDEs	32
2.2	Measurement problems in India	35
2.3	The Indian balance of payments	37
2.4	Foreign inflows: components of the capital accounts	42
2.5	Twin deficits and excess demand in India	46
2.6	Comparing Indian and Chinese FDI	47
3.1	The carry trade	61
4.1	Deepening of Indian FX markets	85
4.2	The process of regulatory change in India	88
5.1	The Indian nominal and real effective exchange rate	110
5.2	The Indian state-induced Balassa-Samuelson effect	116
11.1	Evolution of Indian monetary procedures	244
11.2	Monetary transmission channels	250
11.3	Fiscal-monetary interaction concepts	255
11.4	International experience	256
11.5	Monetary-fiscal coordination in India	260
14.1	How banks can become fragile	337

Preface

This book grew out of a course in International Finance I taught at the Indira Gandhi Institute of Development Research (IGIDR) over years when events and analytical frameworks in the area were both in flux, offering great opportunities to learn. And teaching is one of the best ways of learning. The idea of abduction outlined in the first chapter – the evolution of theory with facts – captures the learning process in this area well.

The new material, and the adaption of existing frameworks to context, makes the book more than a textbook. It can be used in many different ways, as a reference book for specialists and an introduction to the area for those who want to understand global developments in international finance, especially as they affect EDEs. In 2014, for the first time, EDEs as a group accounted for more than 50 per cent of global GDP. Understanding them is all the more important as EDEs now impact the globe as a whole. There is, therefore, a greater change of coordinated action that can reduce negative spillovers to and from EDEs and improve global welfare. As 'narrow domestic walls' come down leading more countries towards a 'heaven of freedom', some strengthening as well as new kinds of protection are required.

Most macroeconomic books use too many words. This book has a succinct style that briefly covers a large material. Therefore, it is of smaller size than other books in this area, although it includes many topics omitted in those. But it also requires concentrated and attentive reading. While the primary readers would be students of courses where it could be used, secondary readers include professionals in the area. It is also designed to be flexibly used in different types of courses. Advanced or difficult material is put in starred sections or in appendices. Courses that want to cover key concepts and develop policy intuition could skip such sections, focussing largely on Chapters 2–9, 11 and 14. Readers will have the advantage of rigour, context and

xvi *Preface*

relevance, and can learn to avoid the trap of using frameworks that make it difficult to ask relevant questions.

Parts were tried out on many batches of students and I thank the many whose questions helped sharpen and deepen the exposition. Many research and teaching assistants helped develop the material and Reshma Aguiar provided excellent secretarial support. Parts were presented in conferences, and I thank professional colleagues whose comments added value, as did the Routledge referee. I thank my publishers, especially Shoma Choudhury, for exceptional patience, encouragement and persistence as they waited for the lectures to mature into a book.

The book is dedicated not only to my son Kovid, but also to all my students. Whatever we teach comes back to us multiplied many times.

Ashima Goyal
April 2016

Abbreviations

AD	aggregate demand
AE	advanced economy
AS	aggregate supply
BEPS	base erosion and profit shifting
BIS	Bank of International Settlement
BOP	balance of payments
BR	bank run
BS	Balassa-Samuelson
C	consumption
CA	current account
CAB	current account balance
CAD	current account deficits
CAS	current account surplus
CB	Central Bank
CCIL	Clearing Corporation of India Ltd
CES	constant elasticity of substitution
CIP	covered interest parity
CITR	Consumer Price Inflation Targeting Rule
CPI	consumer price index
CRR	cash reserve ratio
CSO	Central Statistical Organisation
DC	developing country
DITR	domestic inflation targeting rule
DSGE	dynamic stochastic general equilibrium
EB	external balance
ECB	European Central Bank
ECBs	external commercial borrowings
EDEs	emerging and developing economies
EMF	emerging market fund
ERM	exchange rate mechanism

xviii *Abbreviations*

EU	European Union
FD	fiscal deficit
FDI	foreign direct investment
Fed	Federal Reserve
FIIs	Foreign Institutional Investors
FOC	first-order condition
FPI	foreign portfolio investment
FPMA	flexible price monetary approach
FRA	Fiscal Responsibility Act
FSB	Financial Stability Board
FTT	financial transaction tax
FX	foreign exchange
G	government expenditure
GDCF	gross domestic capital formation
GDP	gross domestic product
GDS	gross domestic savings
GFC	global financial crisis
GFCF	gross fixed capital formation
GFD	gross fiscal deficit
GNP	gross national product
GNS	gross national savings
I	investment
IB	internal balance
IBS	international balance sheet
IC	incentive compatibility
IFS	International Financial System
IIC	international illiquidity condition
INR	Indian National Rupee
KAC	Capital Account Convertibility
LCP	local currency pricing
LEIs	legal entity identifiers
LOLR	lender of last resort
LOOP	law of one price
MA	monetary approach
MF	Mundell Fleming
MRS	marginal rate of substitution
MRT	marginal rate of transmission
NAS	National Accounts Statistics
NCI	net capital inflow
NDFs	non-deliverable forwards
NIIP	net international investment position
NKE	new Keynesian economics

Abbreviations xix

NOPL	net open position limits
NRI	non-resident Indian
NT	non-traded
NX	net exports
OCA	optimal currency areas
OMOs	open market operations
OTC	over-the-counter
PPP	purchasing power parity
PTM	pricing to market
QE	quantitative easing
RBC	real business cycle
RBI	Reserve Bank of India
RD	revenue deficit
RE	rational expectations
RW	random walks
SEC	Securities and Exchange Commission
SIFIs	systemically important financial institutions
SLR	statutory liquidity ratio
SME	small and medium enterprises
SOE	small open economy
SOEME	small open emerging market economy
SPMA	sticky price monetary approach
T	traded
UFB	unhedged foreign borrowing
UIP	uncovered interest parity
VAR	vector auto regressions
WPI	wholesale price index

1 Analytical frameworks and their evolution

When facts change, I change my opinion, what do you do, sir?

John Maynard Keynes[1]

1.1 Introduction

Macroeconomics studies an economy as a whole and builds relationships between aggregates. It develops a conceptual framework in which to understand issues like varying rates of inflation and output growth across time periods and countries, and how policy affects these outcomes. Open economy macroeconomics studies the great macroeconomic questions when economies become more open to trade and to movements in financial capital. That is why the field is sometimes called international finance.

There was resurgence in the subject as economies that had been closed after the experience of the Great Depression gradually opened out. There were bursts of growth in hitherto stagnating areas as more countries embraced globalisation, but a number of currency and financial crises also occurred, not only in emerging and developing economies (EDEs) where they were regarded as habitual, but also emanating from an advanced economy (AE) – the United States – and spreading to others such as the United Kingdom and Europe, in what has come to be known as the global financial crisis (GFC). The slowdown that followed proved remarkably persistent. Therefore, old questions of stability became important once again, but new questions also arose, as did new ways of addressing them. There was resurgence in the subject also, as it drew on new tools developed in macroeconomics and in finance.

Freer flows of capital have implications for exchange rate regimes and the effectiveness of macroeconomic policies. For example, in an open economy, domestic interest rates are closely linked to international interest rates through the exchange rate regime; more flexible

2 *Analytical frameworks and their evolution*

exchange rates influence domestic wages and prices; there can be wealth effects through the accumulation of foreign assets.

In recent years, events and analytical frameworks in the area were both in flux. Those developing economies that opened out, reformed and gave markets a greater role came to be known as emerging markets (EMs). By 2014, EDEs as a group accounted for 57 per cent of the world gross domestic product (GDP), up from 46 per cent in 2004, and the IMF included 152 countries in this group. Asia accounts for some of the largest and fastest growing countries, and therefore requires careful study. Crucial simplifications in frontier frameworks of analysis made them more applicable to EDEs, but adaptations were required especially for structural aspects of Asian developing economies, which were neglected even in attempts to adapt modern monetary frameworks to developing economies. For example, *Development Macroeconomics* by Agenor and Montiel (1999), a pioneering macroeconomics textbook for developing economies, is more applicable to Latin America.

Early work on structuralist macroeconomics introduced developing economy features into Keynesian frameworks, but not into the modern forward-looking approach, which is what this book attempts. For example, structuralist macroeconomics often worked with two sectors (Rakshit, 2009). While dualism, especially in labour markets, has persistent macroeconomic outcomes, modern tools of aggregation allow it to be modelled consistently using aggregate demand (AD) and supply curves (Aoki, 2001), as we will see in Chapter 11. The idea that agriculture is supply determined with price adjustment and industry is demand determined is not adequate in a more open economy with freer imports, which will impact prices.[2]

The book presents three types of analytical frameworks, as well as concrete applications, largely based on Indian experience: (1) the simple concept-based frameworks that serve to train and anchor intuition; (2) a more rigourous anchoring framework based on dynamic stochastic general equilibrium (DSGE), which has evolved as a widely used benchmark; and (3) a variety of special models used to analyse specific issues or events, such as currency crises.

The GFC has resulted in a questioning of the DSGE frameworks. These are widely used as a benchmark in open economy macroeconomics. Therefore, this chapter begins with a discussion of appropriate evolution in macroeconomic frameworks, including the DSGE.

In the remainder of the chapter, Section 1.2 examines general methodological principles, or the nature of reasoning in macroeconomics, and develops the centrist position that will be followed in the book. Section 1.3 outlines the new issues and perspectives modern research

Analytical frameworks and their evolution 3

has thrown up in open economy macroeconomics, which will be expanded on in later chapters. Although the general analytical framework remains the same, special questions arise in EDEs. We discuss adaptations that may be required or special models that may need to be built for EDEs in Section 1.4 and illustrate these by applying abductive reasoning to derive the aggregate demand and supply structure, consistent with observed combinations of Indian growth and inflation. Section 1.5 concludes with brief overviews of the book.

1.2 Between deduction and induction

Macroeconomic theories are being constantly surprised by events they are unable to predict, prevent or even understand. The GFC was an illustration of this, as were the stagflation of the 1970s and the unemployment of the Great Depression. None of these could be understood in the prevailing analytical frameworks. Since theoretical modelling gives a causal structure that should hold not only in current, but also in future data sets, this would seem to be a major flaw.

But macroeconomics is intrinsically an empirical relationship between aggregates, and therefore cannot build a watertight deductive universe, as is possible in theories about individual behaviour. These can be deduced from behavioural axioms without reference to facts, although their aim is also to explain real-world behaviour. Macroeconomics has to work with aggregates, distant from individual behaviour, and therefore cannot escape induction, which is ultimately falsifiable. But does this mean it lacks a theoretical foundation?

Macroeconomics does, however, have a non-trivial logical structure in addition to the use of induction. Learning is based on the general methodological principle of abduction, which is a mixture of deduction and induction. There is a substantive role for deduction, while the interplay with induction creates relevance, in a stimulating interaction between analysis and events. Analysis develops in response to puzzling events that cannot be understood in the existing framework. And it defines new concepts and generates facts.

Abductive reasoning is based on both outcomes and analysis. Abduction and induction derive conclusions from outcomes, unlike deduction which derives them from assumed premises. But abduction reasons backwards from the outcome, to deduce the framework with which it is compatible (Goyal, 2016).

Greater generality is a sign of progress. This does not mean that an in-depth analysis of a specific issue is given up, only that all aspects relevant for the question asked are included in the analysis.

4 *Analytical frameworks and their evolution*

For example, Keynesian demand-determined output was a reaction to the failure of classical economics to explain the involuntary unemployment of the Great Depression. But the neglect of the supply side it led to made the stagflation following the 1970s oil shocks a puzzle. This, in turn, led to a reaction away from demand-led theories towards supply-side real business cycle (RBC) DSGE-based theories that made monetary and fiscal policies largely irrelevant. But neglecting these major aspects reduced relevance. Moreover, DSGE models were unable to explain outcomes without adding different kinds of frictions.

The New Keynesian Economics (NKE) School explored the sticky prices and industry structure that allowed demand shocks to be non-neutral, while retaining forward-looking behaviour. This evolution illustrates the response of theory to facts. Similarly, the GFC forced more analysis of the interaction between macroeconomics and finance. But overreaction to recent events, questioning the entire framework, can hurt progressive evolution.

While the focus of the discussion has been on the absence of finance in DSGE models, interesting issues have risen about the impact of financial malfunction on the relative effectiveness of monetary versus fiscal policies and of bringing a macroeconomic view of systemic effects and spillovers to bear on financial regulation. The chapter and the book discuss these issues. While finance has to be added to macroeconomic models, it is equally important to add macroeconomics to finance.

In macroeconomics, stylised facts generate theory, which organises facts. Anomalies generate new theories. There is a chain from analysis to facts to analysis. The methodology is neither deduction nor induction alone, but a combination of the two that Peirce christened abduction:

> The surprising fact, C, is observed,
> But if A were true, C would be a matter of course,
> Hence, there is a reason to suspect A is true
>
> Peirce 5.189, Hoover (1994, p. 301).

Both abduction and induction belong to ampliative inference, which justifies conclusions on the basis of specific outcomes. Explicative inference, by contrast, derives conclusions from assumed premises. This includes deductive logic-based theories, such as classical logic, which starts with a major premise: for example, 'All humans are mortal' includes a minor premise 'I am a human' and deduces to the conclusion 'Therefore I am mortal'. Induction works by accumulating evidence, for example, instances of mortality. But since, without

Analytical frameworks and their evolution 5

deduction from premises, even one counterexample can upset a conclusion, inductive knowledge is temporary. For example, the observation of black swans when the continent of Australia was discovered upset the inductive inference 'all swans are white'. That is why, in econometrics, which is an inductive science, hypothesis can only be falsified. They can never be proved.

Abduction, however, shares features of deduction because it uses critical logic. But it is not deduction. If abduction was only disguised deduction, it would commit the fallacy of affirming the consequence. But it reasons backwards from the consequence. The derivation of Kepler's laws of motion is an example of how abduction works. Kepler observed certain surprising patterns (C). If planetary orbits were elliptical (if A were true), the patterns followed (then C). So, he concluded the orbits were elliptical, deducing backwards from the facts to the framework. Similarly, if a contraction in demand is surprisingly observed to affect output much more than it affects price (if C), such an outcome would be a matter of course if a particular structure of aggregate demand and supply hold (then A). In Section 1.5, we apply such reasoning to derive the structure of Indian aggregate demand and supply.

So, abduction is a weak form of inference. Sense perception is a limiting case of abduction. All ideas start with abduction. It is detective work using facts that do not fit into preconceptions. This is what Sherlock Holmes did when he reasoned that some external factor had silenced it, from the surprising fact that the dog did not bark. Such reasoning explained the anomalous event.

Abduction is more than a Lakatosian defensive heuristic, since conceptual frameworks do change substantially in response to anomalies. But it is less than a Popperian falsification, since an old hypothesis can be modified and need not be discarded. Parts of old frameworks normally need to be retained for more generality. Abduction differs from inductive inference such as used in econometrics, where a hypothesis can only be falsified, never proved to be true, in that a process of deductive thinking develops the framework, which is consistent with facts, but which can be rejected by new facts.

Macroeconomics is criticised for being constantly forced to accommodate new facts. But this is a valid process of scientific discovery, as long as old theoretical frameworks are significantly expanded and explain the new as well as old facts.

For example, the classical framework, in which supply determined output because flexible prices cleared markets, could not explain the involuntary unemployment of the Great Depression. The Keynesian framework, however, explained this since output was demand

6 Analytical frameworks and their evolution

determined; therefore excess supply could persist. So it was accepted and led to the development of new facts – concepts of national accounts. The whole apparatus for measurement of output and its components was a consequence of the framework.

But the focus on aggregate demand (AD) and neglect of aggregate supply (AS) made the stagflation that followed the oil shocks of the early 1970s a puzzle. If output was demand determined, higher growth (y) and inflation (π) should occur together, as higher demand raised output and generated inflationary pressures. In Figure 1.1, where AD and AS curves are drawn in growth and inflation space assuming a positive trend in inflation and in growth rates, the equilibrium π_1, y_1 should shift to π_2, y_2 when demand rises. Since inflation and output both rise, however, this does not explain stagflation. But once aggregate supply is also considered, an upward shift of the AS curve allows a fall in growth and a rise in inflation to occur together. That is, the equilibrium π_1, y_1 shifts to π_2, y_3, a point of lower growth yet higher inflation. Analysing the role of demand explained low growth, but bringing in supply again explained the combination of low growth and high inflation – stagflation. Note, a framework that includes demand and supply is more general.

1.2.1 Progress as more generality

Compared to the early post-Keynes focus on demand, itself a reaction to a sole focus on supply, oil shocks forced more analysis of the supply side, leading to more generality. The theoretical framework

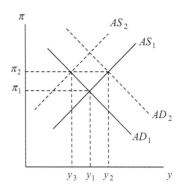

Figure 1.1 Understanding stagflation

Analytical frameworks and their evolution   7

used became more comprehensive also, since the gap between RBC and NKE[3] was smaller compared to that between Keynesians and monetarists – there was some sharing of a richer conceptual apparatus, and agreement that to study aggregate time series, the natural benchmark was optimising over time subject to the general equilibrium of a number of interacting markets. More generality is progress, because a more general model or set of models can address a wider variety of circumstances.[4]

Another example of moving from less to more generality comes from theories of currency crises. In the first-generation crisis models that sought to generalise from the series of crises in Latin America in the 1970s and 1980s, an attack on a currency was the logical culmination of weak macroeconomic policies. Large deficits, and monetary policy that accommodated the deficits, were not consistent with a fixed currency value. But these models ignored the possible complicity of markets in creating crises, and so they were unable to explain the attacks on the British pound in the early days of the exchange rate mechanism (ERM) when macroeconomic fundamentals were not weak. Answers were provided by second-generation models that allowed for multiple equilibria and the possibility that market expectations converge to the attack outcome under intermediate fundamentals. Again, the dialectic between theories and facts improved analytical frameworks by making them more general.

Although the major failures were in financial regulation, the GFC, beginning in 2008, generated a fresh debate on macroeconomic policy. Krugman (2009b) alleged that overuse of mathematics, and return to classical supply-side economics, had led to a forgetting of the basic issues Keynes had highlighted. The efficient markets hypothesis, DSGEs and rational expectations (RE) implied that markets cleared and output was supply-not demand-determined. The crisis had discredited DSGEs. The return to the supply side had been a regression.

The debate exposes the fallacy of extreme positions that do not learn over time from both facts and theories allowing a move to more generality. Cochrane (2009) rightly pointed out that Krugman was neglecting real progress made in using mathematics to clarify, refine, add transparency and think through the consequences of assumptions. But both Cochrane's (2009) and Fama's (2009) arguments validate Krugman's criticism that the Chicago school lacked understanding of even elementary demand-side economics.

Fama, using the basic macroeconomic identity, argued since aggregate savings must always equal investment, the US government spending would not work. It would only reduce government and private

8 *Analytical frameworks and their evolution*

savings, and therefore investment. But this assumes that output is fixed by supply and confuses the distinction between an identity and behaviour. While an identity will always hold, the components may differ, and what they will be depends on behaviour. An argument cannot be just based on an identity without an appropriate theory of behaviour. For example, in a downward spiral, government spending can counter the fall in private demand, thus reducing the fall in output. Private savings would then rise with output. Even if the Chicago School does not believe output can be demand determined, an argument based on an identity alone, which can hold for different outcomes, is logically flawed[5] (Krugman, 2009a).

Thus, a complete reversion to supply-side economics is not helpful, but neither is the neglect of supply. Learning should follow an upward spiral, rather than a swing from one extreme to the other. The implications of abductive thinking for post-GFC monetary policy would be to include financial considerations without sacrificing macroeconomic targets. Flexibility is essential for this. It would suggest that short interest rates, which are the policy instruments, should target inflation and output flexibly. But if the output gap is positive and rates are to be low for extended periods, their effect on raising risk-taking and expanding financial balance sheets needs to be watched and countered with prudential regulations.[6] Similarly, the effect of very high interest rates on a leveraged financial sector, or very low interest rates on excessive risk-taking, should be countered through regulatory measures. The interest rate spread should be an input in policy making. All arms of policy should be coordinated rather than overreliance on any one.

While the focus has been on the absence of finance in DSGE models, interesting issues have risen about the impact of financial malfunction on the relative effectiveness of monetary versus fiscal policies. Supply-side economics does not expect government expenditure (G) or fiscal policy more generally to affect the level of output, since a forward-looking private sector reduces its spending to provide for the higher future taxes required to finance government spending. It views monetary policy as more effective, but even its impact on output is thought to be short term, and in the long run it only affects inflation. Even so, the view that high post-crises debt and fiscal deficits (FDs) due to bailouts constrained expenditure led to overreliance on unconventional monetary policy such as quantitative easing (QE), while neglecting opportunities to use fiscal policy to rebuild infrastructure that could, with interest rates near zero and high unemployment, pay for itself through higher revenues. Moreover, QE, together with lags in agreement and in implementation of financial reforms, created asset

Analytical frameworks and their evolution   9

price bubbles. Indeed it aimed for this as a way to raise wealth and consumption. But the search for yield once more raised pre-GFC-type financial risks. Although the Keynesian position won the post-GFC argument with respect to use of monetary policy, it lost it with respect to use of fiscal policy.[7] The latter was underutilised, while progress in the financial and prudential reforms necessary to reduce risks from QE was slow.

The GFC has also turned attention to systemic risk, which arises from the effect of parts on the whole. General equilibrium is the natural framework in which to analyse such spillovers. Feedback from the whole is an essential part of macroeconomics. This would add a necessary macroeconomic way of thinking to finance.

1.2.2 Accounting for systemic effects

A view of the whole, and of the critical interactions between parts, is a special feature of macroeconomic thinking. But such analysis can become unwieldy if it includes everything; so, macroeconomics requires a modular structure, with modules that can be added as required depending on the question asked. DSGE forms a rigourous and flexible foundation for such a structure. Although all markets are included, a selected module can be developed in more detail, depending on the issue at stake, somewhat like using a magnifying glass, as long as all the relevant modules are included. For example, leaving out either supply or demand will not do, as we saw in the last section, but specific aspects can be highlighted to address the questions asked. A large part of a macroeconomist's skill consists of the ability to select the right framework to address the question posed. Even if the basic framework is correct, emphasising inappropriate aspects can result in errors.

Moreover, the crucial difference between micro- and macromodelling has to be retained. Micromodelling assumptions, such as *ceteris paribus*, are designed to remove spillovers or feedbacks from the whole to the part. Macro modular analysis has to retain these spillovers and feedbacks. As Caballero (2010) argues, it is well worth to give up making welfare statements with the same degree of confidence as in a full micromodel in order to achieve greater empirical realism.

Haldane (2012), like many others, blames the GFC on a loss of the historical memory of many past credit-led crises. This led to a neglect of commercial banks' balance sheets in inflation targeting policy frameworks. Contagion-causing interactions among diverse agents were also neglected in fundamentals-based representative agent DSGE models.

10 *Analytical frameworks and their evolution*

But the criticism applies to a loss of relevant institutional detail and the assumption of market efficiency. Not to tracing macro-outcomes to micro-behaviour in a general equilibrium framework, including necessary feedback, frictions and structural aspects. Neglecting spillovers and systemic effects is the way to invite the next crisis.

In a post-GFC debate on economics (Coyle, 2012), many participants were concerned about a greater reliance on reductive rather than inductive thinking. All wanted to promote empiricism over theory, with economics becoming an empirical study of continuously evolving phenomena. Abductive thinking is the way to include such phenomena in macroeconomic policy frameworks without throwing the baby out with the bath water. Otherwise, there is a danger of economics becoming an ad hoc collection of stories with little connection to each other. To give up theory entirely would also be an overreaction and itself a loss of historical memory.

Deductive logic based on behavioural axioms can be used to some extent since DSGE models individual behaviour. This makes the approach more robust to policy changes – invariant to the Lucas critique. But the aggregation-friendly assumption of identical individuals can be relaxed when the question asked requires it. One natural way to select the necessary disaggregation, or detail, is to ask what sectoral issues affect aggregate outcomes. For example, in an EDE dualism in the labour market and in consumption would be an essential structural feature that must be included. Low per capita incomes imply food has a large share in the consumption basket. Then, food prices may affect aggregate prices and have to be included in a macroeconomic model of such an economy. The Lucas critique that structure changes with policy does not apply to the resulting model because the base in individual maximisation remains, while the additional structural aspects included, such as dualistic labour markets, change slowly.

Forward-looking optimisation itself has to be moderated by various kinds of frictions and imperfections, including those of human psychology, to reproduce outcomes of actual economies. The NKE School systematically includes frictions in DSGE models to add necessary realism, for EDEs deeper structural aspects have to be included. Forward-looking behaviour coexists with slower moving institutions that constrain behaviour. Such an analytical framework is appropriate to include and analyse typical EDEs distortions, which affect the whole. Although their constraints are more numerous and severe and may be different, with such a strategy, analysis is possible in a common language that allows comparison and communication at similar standards of rigour.

Analytical frameworks and their evolution   11

There is progress, also, if theories are refined to make complex structures simpler and useful to policy. The NKE School has reduced DSGE into simple but forward-looking AD and AS curves with clear implications for policy. This has led to an explosion of work on the theory of economic policy. Such aggregative AS and AD curves have also been derived for dualistic EDEs (Goyal, 2011). They can be used to understand Indian growth and inflation, even as they illustrate the use of abduction to extract the relevant framework.

1.3   The open economy

Analysis of the open economy is inherently more complicated than a closed economy. The simplest macro-analytical staple, the IS-LM, must now accommodate the exchange rate. Solow is supposed to have remarked: 'If God intended us to analyze three variables together he would have made the page three-dimensional.' The complexity of multivariable interaction forces analysis of open economies to proceed using variable subsets – somewhat like the two by two entry into Noah's Ark. It also uses a wide set of models. But DSGE provided an organising frame and helped make the subject less of a collection of disparate cases.

Modern open economy macroeconomics has brought many new perspectives, which are emphasised in this book. First is the switch from the dominance of trade to the analysis also of capital flows. This leads to the asset market approach to the exchange rate. The currency of a country becomes an asset: there is arbitrage in response to differential returns and expectations. A floating exchange rate can overshoot to compensate for other prices that are rigid in the short run. Effects can be very different in the short and long run, so sequencing becomes important.

Optimising over time allows intertemporal trade to smooth consumption. A country can borrow today to increase its consumption, running a current account deficit (CAD), which will have to be converted to a surplus in the future to repay accumulated debt. This intertemporal approach shifts attention from the current account, as determined by net imports to the role of macroeconomic policies affecting income, public spending, interest and exchange rates, and therefore savings and investment, which in turn affect the current account.

In DSGE models with frictions, a monetary stimulus has a real effect. In open economy DSGE models, wealth effects from foreign assets accumulated through the current account make impact on the real economy persistent. This is especially so in a small open emerging

12 *Analytical frameworks and their evolution*

market, which is in a catch-up phase, approaching world per capita income levels. Valuation effects on balance sheets become important under freer capital flows and more flexible exchange rates. Industry structure and currency denomination of exports and imports have implications for pass-through of changes in exchange rates.

In the latter part of the 20th century, many economies shifted from a closed import substituting regime to different degrees of openness. This followed the path mature economies had taken, whose opening process started in the 1970s, much after the Great Depression had closed economic borders to allow Keynesian stimuli.

Opening requires a policy gestalt such as recognising the constraint from foreign interest rates on domestic rates; the effect of the exchange rate on wages and intermediate goods costs, and therefore on inflation. Capital flows can relax savings and credit constraints, so that investment exceeds domestic savings. But excessive volatility of capital flows and excessive foreign debt can precipitate currency and financial crises. Crisis proofing requires appropriate macroeconomic policies, including exchange rate regimes, and self-insurance through foreign exchange (FX) reserves in the absence of a supportive global financial architecture. This book will explore all these issues.

1.4 Emerging and developing economies

These questions are all especially important for EDEs and have been under-researched from their perspective. For example, research funds committed to research cancer and cardiac arrests, diseases of prosperous countries, are many times those committed to research on malaria. One reason incorrect advice was given that initially worsened the East Asian crisis was because the under-researched combination of sound government finances with high private leverage was not well understood. Past currency crises in Latin America had originated in weak government finances. But the typical IMF policy advice of belt tightening and raising interest rates was the wrong remedy in countries with a fiscal surplus that faced a demand shock. Their high private debt was vulnerable to rising interest rates. EDEs tend to have weak institutions, imperfections of information, more volatility due to supply and terms of trade shocks, procyclicality of macroeconomic policy and of capital flows and higher risk perceptions (Frankel, 2011).

After the GFC global policy switched to advocate liquidity and demand support, it was effective against shocks from financial market malfunction, fall in trade and fears of contagion. It could be argued that the United States is a different case because of the large global

Analytical frameworks and their evolution 13

spillover of a serious US economic disruption. But in many East European countries also timely, macro-critical, minimum conditionality help made a difference. Unlike in the East Asian crisis when countries were forced to raise interest and exchange rates although this aggravated the burden of high private debt, in East Europe an effort was made to make programmes context sensitive. For example, countries were left free to determine their own exchange rate regimes and sharp depreciations were avoided because of their possible adverse impact given large foreign borrowings. There was probably too little pressure, however, on essential structural changes, such as bank recapitalisation. Greece was given too much credit, conditional on severe austerity, in order to rescue its private creditors. The burden was passed on to Greek tax payers. Austerity did not work, and severe unemployment continued, without the option to switch to its own devalued currency. The threat of Grexit continues to loom over the European Union.

The reasons for flexibilities in these programmes could be their clear origin in a shock external to these countries and IMF learning from the East Asian crisis. But it is possible the involvement of Western European banks explains the speed of response. The one Asian country that went through an IMF program in this period – Pakistan – had to go through the standard severe monetary-fiscal tightening. Interest rates shot up and growth plunged. In neighbouring India, which is the natural comparison, large foreign exchange reserves allowed it to choose its own policies, and it did achieve the second highest growth rate in the world soon after the global crisis. These same agencies had advocated a free float and reduced reserves prior to the crisis, but India's middling through approach served it well. When India did follow the advice to let the exchange rate be market determined, with little intervention, over 2009–11, it led to excessive volatility, a wide current account deficit and a growth slowdown after the 2011 Euro debt crisis. The comparative regional experience suggests Asian countries may have to continue to deal with inappropriate and delayed response unless IMF governance reform gives them real representation.

1.4.1 Crises in emerging and developing economies

Capital imposes stricter financial stability criteria for EDEs. For example, a large current account deficit and a sharp increase in domestic credit are prominent precursors of crises. Therefore, macroeconomic policy has to be more conservative in an open economy. But intelligent adaptation to context is still possible and requires careful research. Questions that are important for EDEs, such as absorption of labour

14 *Analytical frameworks and their evolution*

in higher productivity occupations, policy effectiveness and institutions, capital inflows and reversals, foreign exchange reserves and asset price bubbles are, however, thinly analysed from the perspective of recipients of volatile inflows.

Therefore, using and adapting international tools and methodology to study distinctive structural features of EDEs, their labour markets, financial institutions and role of government are essential. Many examples used in this book are from India. They illustrate the impact of various structural features in shading the answers to the typical questions addressed in open economy macroeconomics. These features include labour endowment, duality, productivity changes, large share of non-traded (NT) goods, limited capital convertibility, but large capital inflows.[8]

International finance is also concerned with the international financial system (IFS) and policy. These encompass issues of countries in relation to each other, micro-regulations, incentives, international institutions such as the IMF and their political economy (Eichengreen, 2006). But international governance and research both neglect issues of importance to EDEs, because the institutional structure was set up by and continues to be dominated by AEs. After a period of rapid growth, EDEs representation in these institutions is much below their economic power.

Indeed, one reason global imbalances grew after the East Asian crisis was Asian countries turning to precautionary holding of large reserves because of a failure to reform the IFS. In the absence of reform to reduce volatility of flows and help them deal with sudden stops, major EDEs had no choice but to accumulate volatile inflows as reserves of foreign currency. This self-insurance was costly but helped them withstand the GFC. The resulting global imbalances were only a minor fraction of the financial leverage lax regulation created.

After the East Asian crisis, there was much more research on debtor moral hazard and crony capitalism in the countries than on herding and excessive leverage as a cause of outflows. While the affected countries largely accepted reform prescriptions, they wanted closing of regulatory gaps such as for hedge funds, which were implicated in the huge capital outflows during the crises. Instead, the US Securities and Exchange Commission (SEC) in a 2004 bargain allowed investment banks higher leverage, removed the net capital rule on borrowing and let investment banks self-regulate based on their own risk models. Oversight windows available were never used even as investment banks reached stratospheric debt to asset ratios of above 30:1. This leverage was partly responsible for massive cross-border flows affecting EDEs.

Analytical frameworks and their evolution 15

The continuing global slowdown after the GFC should lead to more development of alternative perspectives and reform that may reduce the probability of future crises. But for this, more analysis of these questions and a more even spread of power through the globe is required. The latter is happening as the share of EMs in world GDP crossed 50 per cent in 2015. Competitive regional institutions are also being created.

New important questions are always being thrown up for analysis, as growth and resources shift from one region to the other, crises occur and there is pressure to change regulations and IFSs. The analytical structure developed in this book provides a toolkit that is useful to shed light on past issues and to address questions that will surely arise in the future.

Growth-sensitive adjustment is required for EDEs in a catch-up phase. After the GFC, the United States was said to have a large potential output gap since unemployment was at 10 per cent, justifying macroeconomic stimulus. Low productivity employment, however, normally exceeds this figure by a large amount in populous EDEs, although unemployment is poorly measured. One reason belt tightening is advised for EDEs is that overheating, or the attempt to spend more than potential output, is suspected. Calculation of potential output is based on different types of filtering using past data. But if a country is well set on a transition-high growth path with labour mobility and capital flows, a forward-looking measure is needed. The absence of such measures may be one reason the IMF repeatedly under-assessed Indian growth and capacity after Lehman fell. Their predictions of 4–5 per cent growth rates were way below the realised growth rate of 6.7 per cent. Hysteresis, or loss of skills due to prolonged unemployment, is said to have reduced employable labour, and therefore the potential output in the West after the GFC. Faster transitional growth has the converse effect of converting structural unemployment in EDEs into cyclical unemployment, as more types of jobs become available and incentives to acquire skills improve. Imposing standard frameworks to analyse EDE macroeconomics is a failure to reason from context. Abductive reasoning, applied in the next section, helps extract an appropriate framework.

1.4.2   *Using abduction to explain Indian growth and inflation*

There is progress, also, if theories are refined to make complex structures simpler and useful to policy. It has turned out to be possible to reduce DSGE into simple but forward-looking aggregate demand and

16 Analytical frameworks and their evolution

supply with clear implications for policy. This has led to an explosion of work on the theory of economic policy, which we will explore in Chapter 11. Now, we derive the structure of AS and AD from Indian growth and inflation outcomes.

Post-reform growth and inflation showed frequent episodes of either: (1) low growth with high and sticky inflation or (2) lower inflation and higher growth. This is puzzling in the conventional framework of India as a supply-constrained economy, so a rise in demand raises prices (π_2, y_2 in Figure 1.2b) in the standard excess demand explanation for inflation. Then, a policy tightening should reduce inflation, not growth. But in 2008, 2011 and 2013, policy tightening reduced growth while inflation remained sticky – the opposite effect. Even if a vertical AS shifts leftwards or the AS is backward bending at high inflation (Pattanaik and Nadhanael, 2013), a fall in output should precede the demand shock. In addition, the latter should still impact inflation more than growth. But inflation remained high and sticky despite sharply higher policy rates, while growth fell in the quarter immediately following peak rates (Table 1.1).

After high growth and low inflation over 2003–07, Table 1.1 illustrates the many episodes of type (2) that occurred. Monetary tightening raising short rates above 9 per cent in the summer of 2008 precipitated a collapse in industrial output even before the September fall of Lehman. The tightening came after a period of high growth. The economy was feared to be overheating. Inflation, following the international spike in fuel and food, was high. Although interest rates peaked, the wholesale price index (WPI) did not fall until November

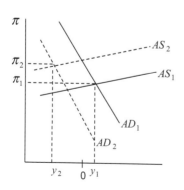 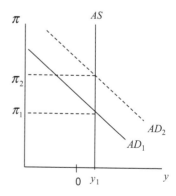

Figure 1.2 (a) Elastic supply   *Figure 1.2 (b)* Inelastic supply

Table 1.1 Growth, inflation and policy rates

	2008–09: Q1–Q4				2009–10: Q1–Q4				2010–11: Q1–Q4				2011–12: Q1–Q4			
	Q1	Q2	Q3	Q4	Q1	Q2	Q3	Q4	Q1	Q2	Q3	Q4	Q1	Q2	Q3	Q4
Growth (Y-o-Y) (%) (constant 2004–05 prices)																
GDP at factor cost	7.9	7.7	5.8	5.9	6.3	8.6	7.3	9.4	8.5	7.6	8.2	9.2	8.0	6.7	6.1	5.3
Manufacturing	7.0	6.6	2.6	1.3	2.0	6.1	11.4	15.2	9.1	6.1	7.8	7.3	7.3	2.9	0.6	−0.3
GFCF/GDP*	33.0	34.8	31.5	32.7	30.4	31.9	30.9	34.5	32.2	34.0	32.3	31.4	33.9	33.4	30.3	30.9
Inflation (Y-o-Y) (%)																
WPI	9.6	12.5	8.6	3.2	0.5	−0.1	5.0	10.2	11.0	9.3	8.9	9.3	9.4	9.7	8.9	7.0
WPI Core	7.1	8.3	6.3	3	0.8	0.2	2.7	5.3	6	5.3	5.2	6.3	7.4	7.9	8	5.9
CPI-IW	7.8	9.0	10.2	9.5	8.9	11.6	13.2	15.1	13.6	10.5	9.3	9.0	8.9	9.2	8.4	7.2
Policy rate																
Overnight (call) money	6.8	9.5	7.8	4.2	3.2	3.2	3.2	3.3	4.2	5.4	6.6	6.8	7	7.8	8.6	8.9

Source: CSO press releases, Reserve Bank of India and updated from Goyal (2012a).

Note: 1.* This row is a ratio not a rate. 2. GFCF: gross fixed capital formations; WPI core excludes commodities; CPI-IW: consumer price index for industrial workers.

18 *Analytical frameworks and their evolution*

when Indian fuel prices fell, while the consumer price index (CPI) remained high.

There was a V-shaped recovery, which also indicates the crisis resulted in demand destruction rather than more intractable destruction of capacity. With the latter, recovery could not have been so fast in response to a sharp end 2008 cut in policy rates. The rise in government consumption, fuelled by an expanding fiscal deficit, compensated for the fall in private consumption and investment and contributed to the quick recovery in 2009. The episode showed that demand is interest inelastic in India and demand affects output. Interest rates affected consumer durable spending, housing demand and so forth. Such an impact has been visible since 1996.

Overstimulus led to growth rising to 9.2 per cent in Q4 2010–11. The tables show only a short lag from policy rates to industry: 2–3 quarters for a sharp fall and 1 quarter for a sharp rise. The crisis response was fast, but the resurgence of inflation before recovery was firmly established that led to policy dilemmas regarding exit. The response to early signs of industrial inflation was delayed due to uncertainties about global recovery. The very large cut in interest rates that had to be reversed then led to too fast a pace of increase in interest rates[9] and to quantitative tightening. The latter contributed to volatility in interest rates and sustained the industrial slowdown.

An even greater collapse in growth occurred – manufacturing actually contracted – after policy rates were raised to 8.5 in October 2011, while inflation remained high and sticky. Similarly, the rise in interest rates to above nine in the summer of 2013, as part of the interest rate defense following US taper-on announcement led outflows, turned industrial growth negative (Table 1.2) while WPI core actually rose, although from low levels. Although core WPI fell from Q4 2011–12, it rose again despite low growth and policy rates that were at their peak since mid-2013.

The sharp resurgence of WPI inflation by Q3 of 2009, although industry had barely recovered, was due to the impact of sustained high CPI and food inflation on wages. The manufacturing price index fell only for a few months and had risen again to its November 2008 value of 203 by April 2009. This can be understood as a cost shock pushing up the elastic AS. For example, the rural unskilled real wage, which had been constant earlier, began to grow from 2007 as food price inflation jumped. Its growth peaked at double digits in 2012, and then it began to fall as food inflation fell below double digits and fiscal contraction reduced the types of government expenditure that had boosted consumption. This reduction in cost-push softened persistent

Table 1.2 Growth, inflation and policy rates

(2004–05 base)	2012–13: Q1–Q4				2013–14: Q1–Q4				2014–15: Q1–Q2	
	Q1	Q2	Q3	Q4	Q1	Q2	Q3	Q4	Q1	Q2
GDP at factor cost	4.5	4.6	4.4	4.4	4.7	5.2	4.6	4.6	5.7	5.3
Manufacturing	–1.1	0	2.5	3	–1.2	1.3	–1.5	–1.4	3.5	0.1
GFCF/GDP*	30.8	31.4	29.2	30.3	32.3	34.2	31.6	31.2	32.7	32.3
Inflation (Y-o-Y) (%)										
WPI	7.5	7.8	7.4	6.7	4.8	6.7	6.9	5.4	5.8	3.9
WPI core	5.3	6.2	5.5	4.7	3.3	2.4	2.8	3.3	3.8	3.5
CPI combined	10.2	9.9	10.1	10.7	9.5	9.7	10.4	8.4	8.1	7.4
CPI core	10.5	8.8	8.6	8.8	8.4	8.6	8.4	8.3	7.9	7.0
Policy rate										
Overnight (call) money	8.3	8.0	8.0	7.9	7.4	9.2	8.5	8.3	8.1	8.0

Source: Calculated from CSO press releases, Reserve Bank of India.

Note: 1.* This row is a ratio not a rate. 2. Core inflation excludes commodities and CPI is the new aggregate CPI to the base 2010.

20 *Analytical frameworks and their evolution*

service sector inflation by Q1 2014–15, so that finally core CPI began to fall by late 2014. While CPI core inflation remained sticky until well into 2014, headline CPI[10] fell below double digits in early 2014, helping reduce the inflationary expectations that enter core CPI inflation. By end 2014, crashing oil prices softened all types of inflation, but especially WPI.

The new GDP series – rebased and with many other changes – show a rise in growth in 2013–14 (Table 1.3 compared to Table 1.2). The series were still controversial since other data, such as credit growth, corporate sales and IIP (a volume index), showed a continuing slowdown. A better corporate database was used with improvements in measurement of informal sector and government activity, and a shift to international concepts and practices, so it may reflect a one-time jump rather than a turnaround in the macroeconomic cycle. Since the series measure value added, growth in value added may reflect the effort by severely pressured firms to save costs, as well as the fall in input costs with oil prices. Even in the new series, there is a slump in growth and in gross fixed capital formation (GFCF) in Q3 after the mid-2013 peak interest rates. The share of gross capital formation in GDP fell from 36.6 in 2012–13 to 32.3 per cent in 2013–14.

For a much larger effect of a demand shock on growth than on inflation, the AS has to be elastic. So, such an AS explains the Indian case where tightening episodes hurt growth more than they reduced inflation. The surprising patterns of growth and inflation (C) are explained if AS has this shape (if A), just as Kepler's patterns came from an elliptical orbit. If AS-AD has the more standard structure of Figure 1.2b, the observed pattern would not follow since a demand contraction would affect inflation more than it would affect growth.

Therefore, abductive reasoning applied to explain the anomalies in the tables suggests a modification of the classical supply-constrained macroeconomic framework with vertical AS to one where the AS is elastic but subject to upward shocks (Figure 1.2a). Policy-induced demand contraction during a supply shock can then explain lower growth and higher inflation, such as π_2, y_2 in Figure 1.2a. A leftward shift of the demand curve along an elastic supply curve, pushed up due to supply shocks or cost creep, results in a high output loss with little effect on inflation, as illustrated in Tables 1.1–1.3 and Figure 1.2a.[11] Periods of higher growth and lower inflation, as in π_1, y_1 in Figure 1.2a, occur when restraints on catch-up growth are reduced during the absence of adverse supply shocks.

What underlying features generate such an AS-AD structure? An aggregate supply, as in Figure 1.2a, is natural in a populous economy

Table 1.3 Rates in new GDP series (base 2011–12)

	2013–14: Q1–Q4				2014–15: Q1–Q4				*% change over previous year 2014–15*
	Q1	*Q2*	*Q3*	*Q4*	*Q1*	*Q2*	*Q3*	*Q4*	
Supply-side break-up of GDP growth									
Gross value added at basic prices	7.2	7.5	6.6	5.3	7.4	8.4	6.8	6.1	7.2
Manufacturing	7.2	3.8	5.9	4.4	8.4	7.9	3.6	8.4	7.1
Public administration	14.4	6.9	9.1	2.4	2.8	7.1	19.7	0.1	7.2
Demand-side break-up of rates of GDP (%)									
Private consumption	58.8	56.9	59.1	55.3	58.5	56.2	57.8	55.5	6.3
Government final expenditure	12.7	13.1	8.7	9.6	12.1	13.2	10.4	8.2	6.6
Gross fixed capital formation	29.8	31.7	30.8	30.7	30.4	30.3	29.6	29.7	4.6
Exports	23.0	27.1	24.3	24.5	23.6	24.5	22.8	20.9	–0.8
Imports	27.6	28.9	25.2	25.0	24.9	26.9	24.3	21.2	–2.1

Source: Calculated from CSO.

22 *Analytical frameworks and their evolution*

undergoing catch-up growth, where structural unemployment is being converted into cyclical unemployment, as new types of jobs appear. Higher productivity releases labour from traditional occupations. Once a populous EDE crosses a critical threshold and high catch-up growth is established, higher labour mobility blurs the distinction between formal and informal sectors. The demographic profile ensures a steady stream of youthful entrants to the work force. Improvements in education supply, and more important, the returns to acquiring an education, ensure that new entrants have adequate skills. Low-skilled and service jobs can absorb new rural migrants. A macroeconomics of the aggregate economy, rather than development theories applied to the informal sector and macroeconomics to the modern sector, becomes both necessary and feasible.

Capital is a produced means of production that can be expanded. Higher per capita income growth with sticky consumption habits and a larger share of earners raises aggregate savings, financial deepening improves intermediation of savings and freer capital inflows complement domestic savings. Therefore, finance becomes less of a constraint.

Labour is taken as the only input into aggregate production in modern macroeconomics (Woodford, 2003), and specific distortions are included. Therefore, it can be a useful framework for EDEs after incorporating the effects of dualistic labour markets. The derived AS would be elastic until surplus labour is fully absorbed and becomes vertical only as the economy matures and capacity constraints raise marginal costs of production.

But poor infrastructure, inadequacies in governance, dependence on oil imports and restrictions on agriculture impart an upward bias to costs. These inefficiencies, distortions and cost shocks tend to push aggregate supply upwards over the entire range rather than only at the margin, as in the L-shaped Keynesian AS. Thus, although the AS is elastic, it is volatile and subject to frequent upward shifts.

While governance failures result in chronic cost rise (Goyal, 2012a), sticky inflation expectations also shift the AS up. The food price-wage cycle is an important mechanism propagating price shocks and creating inflationary expectations, given low per capita incomes and the large share of food in the consumption basket. Over 2007–13, there was a steep rise in nominal and in real wages in response to sharp food inflation (Goyal and Baikar, 2015). Real rural wages were constant before that. Political support also raised wages through minimum wages and employment schemes. If a rise in wages exceeds that in agricultural productivity, prices rise further propagating inflation.

Analytical frameworks and their evolution 23

Political pressure from farmers was normally successful in raising farm support prices, especially if international prices were high.

Sustained inflation, however, requires monetary accommodation. This was absent, so Indian inflation never reached double digits. Although prior to the 1990s monetary policy routinely accommodated a populist rise in deficits, it imposed severe statutory liquidity requirements restricting private credit, and therefore overall money supply growth. After the reforms, discontinuation of ad hoc treasury bills, and other measures of monetary autonomy, prevented automatic financing of deficits. But reforms did not resolve supply-side issues. Government spending continued to be populist, raising hidden and indirect costs. For example, cross-subsidisation of passenger with freight subsidy and a subsidy on diesel shifted freight from the railways to trucks, with a large rise in environment and other resource costs. Monetary tightening, therefore, reduced demand in response to repeated cost shocks, imposing a large output sacrifice. Monetary tightening does reduce inflation expectations but at high output cost. Falling food inflation is more effective. Studies show food inflation has the maximum impact on inflation expectations. Therefore, first best policy requires both monetary and fiscal policy to focus on measures that shift down the AS. If the composition and effectiveness of fiscal expenditure improves, monetary policy can be more accommodative, allowing better monetary-fiscal coordination.

1.5 Concluding remarks and overview of the book

Abductive reasoning is based on both analysis and facts. It explains the evolution of macroeconomic conceptual frameworks as a consequence of shocks that create anomalies. But if a crisis has the effect of over-emphasising one particular aspect, it can neglect relevant issues laying the seeds for the next crisis. This, not the necessary change in macroeconomic frameworks, is the real flaw in macroeconomic thinking. It is not wise to destroy knowledge. Progress requires more generality, which is consistent with a tactical emphasis on a particular aspect, depending on the issue at stake.

A theoretical framework has a causal structure that should be generalisable to situations other than the one in which it was produced. A common criticism of DSGE macroeconomic frameworks is that the modelling of the financial sector is inadequate. But if something is missing, the constructive response is to include it in the analysis if it is important for the question asked. A more comprehensive set of models is an advance since missing aspects are likely to reduce, reducing

24 *Analytical frameworks and their evolution*

the chances of neglecting relevant aspects. Therefore, while an eclectic set of models is used in open economy macroeconomics, DSGE continues to provide a useful benchmark and organising framework.

Many examples of abductive reasoning are given in the chapter. Such reasoning is also used to extract the structure of aggregate demand and supply consistent with the observed negative correlation of inflation and growth in India. If prolonged growth slowdowns do not reduce inflation, it suggests that supply shocks, not excess demand, are causing the inflation. The underlying aggregate supply is elastic but volatile. The lesson for both monetary and fiscal policy is to focus on elements that reduce costs, while avoiding sharp cuts in aggregate demand.

The combination of theory and structure, of logic and facts, is followed throughout the book. Chapter 2 not only develops the foundation of national income accounting and the balance of payments (BOP), but also goes on to introduce the intertemporal approach to the latter. In line with the new emphasis on a currency as an asset, Chapters 3 and 4 cover the asset approach and foreign exchange markets. Chapters 4–9 cover the core short- and long-run theories of exchange rate determination and open economy macroeconomic stabilisation. Chapter 10 covers the canonical small open economy (SOE) DSGE model. Chapter 11 applies it to consider new approaches to monetary and fiscal policy, in a SOE and with adaptations for an EDE. With this basic analytical framework in place, Chapter 12 brings in context. It introduces structural differences in EDEs, develops some models relevant for them, then discusses country experiences and policy options. Chapter 13 presents currency crises and frameworks. Chapter 14 analyses the GFC, in the context of the IFS, ongoing reform, weaknesses and continuing threats such as the Euro debt crisis and global imbalances. There are many boxes illustrating concepts developed for EDEs with Indian experience. The broad themes the book addresses include exchange rate economics, older and new perspectives on macroeconomic policy in an open economy, analytical frameworks for and experience of EDEs after liberalisation, currency and financial crises and the IFS.

Notes

1 https://en.wikiquote.org/wiki/Talk:John_Maynard_Keynes.
2 There are deeper criticisms on the compatibility of the NKE framework with Keynes's own ideas – the latter emphasised uncertainty and instability. I thank a referee for pointing this out. The real world, however, is normally stable. See Goyal and Tripathi (2014) for an argument of how different types of rigidities, rules of behaviour and institutions can create stability.
3 The two are known as freshwater (Chicago, Minnesota) and saltwater (Harvard, MIT, Berkeley) macroeconomics, because of the location of

the universities where the major proponents of New Classical and New Keynesian Macroeconomics, respectively, are. Their convergence then should generate 'brackish' macroeconomics!

4 Rodrick (2014) argues that advance in economics comes from a richer and more relevant set of models, with a better understanding of the conditions in which they apply. The evolution of models used in macroeconomics satisfies these conditions.

5 The Keynesian perspective won the initial battle as coordinated government stimuli reversed the 2008 global crisis that, in the beginning stages, was more severe than the Great Depression on many parameters (see Eichengreen and O'Rourke, 2009). But the persistence of unemployment pointed to supply-side factors, such as financial sector malfunctions and constraints on fiscal spending on infrastructure that needed to be addressed.

6 For example, Blanchard (2011, 2015) made the case for such pragmatism in policy, with macroprudential polices, use of capital controls and foreign exchange market intervention complementing flexible inflation targeting. Incentives created by regulation affect macroeconomic outcomes.

7 Keynes's own view on AD was likely to be inelastic so that shifts in it, due to 'animal spirits' or government expenditure, would have a larger impact.

8 The importance of a detailed knowledge of context cannot be overemphasised. For example, the IPCC, the Nobel Prize – winning international body on climate change, headed by an Indian, made a prediction that Indian glaciers would melt by 2035. This was based on generalisation from studies on international glaciers without local research. An Indian study, with careful documentation, showed melting rates of Himalayan glaciers had not increased. The study was dismissed by the IPCC as schoolboy science, but when the press took up the issue the IPCC's lack of evidence was exposed and its reputation badly damaged.

9 The operative rate went from the reverse repo at 3.25 in March 2010 to the repo at 8.5 by October 2011.

10 Since India did not have a producer price, the WPI was the nearest available giving the quoted price of bulk transactions at a primary stage, which could be the price at the factory gate for manufactured goods. CPI indices were heterogeneous and subject to larger delays; but in 2011, a revised and expanded (base 2010) unified index CPI (combined) became available, with a higher weight of services in the consumption basket.

11 Structural VAR-based tests, time series causality tests, GMM regressions of AD and AS and calibrations in a DSGE model for such an economy. Goyal (2011, 2012a) and Goyal and Tripathi (2015) all support the elastic longer run supply and the dominance of supply shocks. Analysis of the Indian case draws on and extends earlier work (see Goyal, 2012a, 2012b). Even RBI structural VAR-based estimations (e.g. Khundrakpam and Jain, 2012) find monetary policy impacts output first and inflation after about a year. The effect on GDP is 2–3 times greater than that on inflation.

References

Agenor, P. R. and P. J. Montiel. 1999. *Development Macroeconomics*, 2nd edition, Princeton, NJ: Princeton University Press.

26 *Analytical frameworks and their evolution*

Aoki, K. 2001. 'Optimal Monetary Policy Responses to Relative-Price Changes', *Journal of Monetary Economics*, 48: 55–80.

Blanchard, O. 2011. 'The Future of Macroeconomic Policy: Nine Tentative Conclusions', 23 March. Available at www.voxeu.org/index.php?q=node/6262 and www.imf.org/external/np/seminars/eng/2011/res/index.htm (accessed on September 2011).

Blanchard, O. 2015. 'Ten Takeaways from the Rethinking Macro Policy: Progress or Confusion?', 25 May. Available at www.voxeu.org/article/rethinking-macro-policy-ten-takeaways (accessed on June 2015).

Caballero, R. J. 2010. 'Macroeconomics after the Crisis: Time to Deal with the Pretense-of-Knowledge Syndrome', *Journal of Economic Perspectives*, 24(4): 85–102.

Cochrane, John H. 2009. 'How Did Paul Krugman Get It So Wrong?'. Available at http://modeledbehavior.com/2009/09/11/john-cochrane-responds-to-paul-krugman-full-text/ (accessed on June 2010).

Coyle, D. 2012. 'What's the Use of Economics? Introduction to the Vox Debate', 18 September. Available at www.voxeu.org/debates/what-s-use-economics (accessed on May 2013).

Eichengreen, B. 2006. 'A Review of Peter Isard's Globalization and the International Financial System: What's Wrong and What Can Be Done?', *Journal of Economic Literature, American Economic Association*, 44(2): 415–419.

Eichengreen, B. and K. O'Rourke. 2009. 'A Tale of Two Depressions', 1 September. Update available at www.voxeu.org/index.php?q=node/3421 (accessed on June 2010).

Fama, E. F. 2009. 'Bailouts and Stimulus Plans', 13 January. Available at www.dimensional.com/famafrench/2009/01/bailouts-and-stimulus-plans.html (accessed on June 2010).

Frankel, J. 2011. 'Monetary Policy in Emerging Markets', Chapter 25 in B. Friedman and M. Woodford (eds.), *Handbook of Monetary Economics*, Vol. 3B, pp. 1439–1499. North Holland: Elsevier.

Goyal, A. 2011. 'A General Equilibrium Open Economy Model for Emerging Markets: Monetary Policy with a Dualistic Labor Market', *Economic Modelling*, 28(2): 1392–1404.

Goyal, A. 2012a. 'Propagation Mechanisms in Inflation: Governance as Key', Chapter 3 in S. Mahendra Dev (ed.), *India Development Report 2012*, pp. 32–46. New Delhi: IGIDR and Oxford University Press.

Goyal, A. 2012b. 'India's Fiscal and Monetary Framework: Growth in an Opening Economy', *Macroeconomics and Finance in Emerging Market Economies*, 5(1): 108–123 and Chapter 12, in *Macroeconomics and Markets in India: Good Luck or Good Policy?* Ashima Goyal (ed.). Routledge UK, 2012.

Goyal, A. 2016. 'Abductive Reasoning in Macroeconomics', IGIDR working paper no. WP-2016-022. Available at http://www.igidr.ac.in/pdf/publication/WP-2016-022.pdf

Goyal, A. and A. Baikar. 2015. 'Psychology or Cyclicality: Rural Wage and Inflation Dynamics in India', *Economic and Political Weekly*, 50(23): 116–125.

Analytical frameworks and their evolution 27

Goyal, A. and S. Tripathi. 2014. 'Stability and Transitions in Emerging Market Policy Rules', *Indian Economic Review*, 49(2): 69–87.

Goyal, A. and S. Tripathi. 2015. 'Separating Shocks from Cyclicality in Indian Aggregate Supply', *Journal of Asian Economics*, 38: 93–103.

Haldane, A. G. 2012. 'What Have the Economists Ever Done for Us?', 1 October. Available at www.voxeu.org/debates/what-s-use-economics (accessed on August 2013).

Hoover, K. D. 1994. 'Pragmatism, Pragmaticism, and Economic Method', in Roger E. Backhouse (ed.), *New Directions in Economic Methodology*, pp. 286–318. London: Routledge.

Khundrakpam, J. K. and R. Jain. 2012. 'Monetary Policy Transmission in India: A Peep Inside the Black Box', *RBI Working Paper Series No. 11*. Available at www.rbi.org.in/scripts/PublicationsView.aspx?id=14326 (accessed on December 2015).

Krugman, P. 2009a. 'A Dark Age of Macroeconomics (Wonkish)', *New York Times*, January 27. Available at http://krugman.blogs.nytimes.com/2009/01/27/a-dark-age-of-macroeconomics-wonkish (accessed on June 2010).

Krugman, P. 2009b. 'How Did Economists Get It So Wrong', *New York Times*, September 2. Available at www.nytimes.com/2009/09/06/magazine/06Economic-t.html?_r=2& (accessed on June 2010).

Pattanaik, S. and G.V. Nadhanael 2013. 'Why Persistent High Inflation Impedes Growth? An Empirical Assessment of Threshold Level of Inflation for India', *Macroeconomics and Finance in Emerging Market Economies*, 6 (2): 204–220.

Rakshit, M. 2009. *Money and Finance in the Indian Economy, Selected Papers*, Vol. 2, New Delhi: Oxford University Press.

Rodrick, D. 2014. 'What Kind of Social Science Is Economics', April. Available at www.sss.ias.edu/faculty/rodrik/presentations (accessed on 7 April 2015).

Woodford, M. 2003. *Interest and Prices: Foundations of a Theory of Monetary Policy*, New Jersey: Princeton University Press.

2 Basic accounting
The balance of payments

The foundation is unseen, but is often the most important part of the building.

– Anonymous

2.1 Introduction

This chapter explores how the basic macroeconomic identity changes in an open economy, what are the new types of accounts required and how are they designed to support a dynamic perspective where action today affects outcomes over time.

In a closed economy, output produced or value added must equal expenditure on it by final users such as firms who make investment expenditure, consumers and government. This is the basic identity that is the source of national income accounts. Production generates employment and pays out income in equal value.[1] Taking for granted knowledge of basic macroeconomic accounting concepts, such as the difference between production, expenditure and income and treatment of government and taxes, we examine the changes openness requires in the accounts and how the latter facilitate the intertemporal approach.

The remainder of the chapter is structured as follows: Section 2.2 shows how the macroeconomic identity changes in an open economy and why a new set of accounts, the balance of payments (BOP), is required. Section 2.3 develops the intertemporal approach to the BOP. Section 2.4 brings in government and analysis of twin deficits, that is, the relationship between current account and fiscal deficits. Section 2.5 concludes with a brief summary.

2.2 Macroeconomic identities

In an open economy, the aggregate demand equal to supply identity, $Y \equiv C + I + G$, becomes $Y \equiv C + I + G + X - M$. Exports, X, are added to the earlier determinants of aggregate demand: consumption

Basic accounting 29

C, investment I, government expenditure G. Imports M augment domestic output Y, or aggregate supply. The net contribution to aggregate demand of trade is, therefore, net exports (NX) or exports minus imports X – M, since imports satisfy part of demand.

This simple identity already leads to a number of non-obvious insights. First, only net exports add to aggregate demand since imports are a leakage from domestic demand. From a purely accounting point of view, imports have to be subtracted from the RHS of the identity, since they are already included in C, I or G. They have to be removed to get output produced domestically. C + I + G are also known as domestic absorption, which includes imports, and differ from domestic output or production, which excludes imports and includes exports. Second, in this simple identity, X – M is the same as the current account surplus (CAS) of the BOP. X and M each enters the two sides of the current account of the BOP.

An open economy requires a new set of accounts, the BOP, which is the record of a country's foreign transactions and their financing. In the older classification, the BOP had three sub-accounts: the current account, the capital account and the residual showing official financing, including change in reserves. CB interventions directly affect the latter. Transactions recorded in the current account are a part of current income flows, while the capital account records purchases and sales of international assets and other changes in international wealth.

In the new classification widely adopted this century, only non-market activities, or those linked to non-produced, non-financial assets (such as copyrights), resulting in transfers of wealth between countries are recorded in the capital account. The financial account records sales of assets to foreigners and purchases of assets by them. Official reserve transactions are classified in the financial account. The statistical discrepancy is also recorded in the financial account. These changes improved the functional classification of transfers.[2]

In the old classification, the capital account included what is now the financial account. Thus, the current account records income flows while the financial account records changes in wealth that affect balance sheets. But if expenditure exceeds or falls short of income, it will lead to a drawdown or a rise in wealth, so there is a close relationship between the current and the financial account. The latter finances the former.

Returning to the identity, assume, for the time being, there is no income from abroad and no government, then gross domestic product, GDP = C + I + X – M. Net exports are also the trade surplus, in this case equal to the CAS of the BOP, CAS. That is, CAS = X – M = NX. The current account (CA) is in surplus if X > M and in deficit if M > X.

30   Basic accounting

A second definition of the CAS is Income – Absorption $(C + I + G)$. Removing $C + I + G$ from Y gives $X - M$, since subtracting the imports included in $C + I + G$ and the domestic demand from Y leaves only the net external demand.

Substituting savings, S, for GDP – C, in the basic identity gives $S - I = X - M$. Thus, the CAS is also equal to $S - I$. This third way of looking at the CAD shows the financing of the CAD. Items entering $S - I$ enter the financial account of the BOP. This simple relationship is also the source of the modern intertemporal approach to the CA.

2.3   The intertemporal approach

The popular conception of CAS is identified with the net exports of goods and services. The major shift in perspective, the intertemporal approach to the BOP brings, is in making it clear that the CA depends also on macroeconomic factors affecting S and I, not only on trade aspects. While an identity always holds, all these variables adjust to achieve the macroeconomic equilibrium. Attention then shifts from trade elasticities to macro-aggregates and the forward-looking decisions of agents in accumulation and in consumption smoothing over time. If domestic savings exceed investment, this must be reflected in exports exceeding imports and vice versa.[3] But in an EM, global risk rather than domestic conditions affects capital flows, so the capital account is a source of additional volatility. Foreign exchange reserves create a buffer that ensures balance. The monetary and exchange rate policy being followed affects them not only directly, but also indirectly through the impact of these policies on investment and consumption.

The current account affects countries' international asset position over time. For example, if there is a current account deficit, it allows domestic investment to exceed domestic savings, but at the cost of a rise in foreign debt, B. Thus, $CAD = I - S$ would imply rising foreign debt. So, payments on debt would also have to be accounted for. Once debt or income earning foreign assets are involved, we have to bring in the distinction between GDP and gross national product (GNP).

So, another difference to note in an open economy is that between GDP and GNP. The first is output produced within the geographical borders of an economy and the second is that produced by the nationals of the economy, wherever they may reside. GNP is GDP plus net factor income from abroad, primarily from net foreign assets. Since GNP measures the welfare of the citizens of a country, it is the relevant concept to use for consumption and savings decisions. For example, if the country has net foreign debt B, and it must make payments RB

Basic accounting 31

that belong to foreign nationals, then GNP = GDP − RB. Considering only RB is a simplification since a country would receive net income from abroad from many types of assets, and may also receive current and capital transfers (see Box 2.2, for the Indian case).

Rewriting the basic identity as GDP = C + I + X − M and substituting for GDP from GNP = GDP − RB gives GNP + RB = C + I + X − M. This can be rearranged to give GNP − C = I + NX − RB. Since savings must equal the difference between a citizen's income and consumption, GNP − C, we get S − I = NX − RB. The CAD, therefore, gives the change in foreign debt, since CAD = RB + NM = I − S. Both debt repayments and net imports add to a nation's debt if it is running a CAD. If it has a CAS, then the CAS is less than net exports by the amount of net debt repayment, if any. In a steady state, where savings and investments are zero, net exports must be sufficient to pay for any debt servicing, that is RB = NX.

Examining such a steady state in a simple model with perfect foresight helps illustrate the degrees of freedom from the option to borrow abroad. A CAD, which finances investment in excess of savings, adds to a nation's debt. Since current actions affect the future, an intertemporal approach is required. The underlying determinants of the CA lie in the forward-looking decisions of consumers and firms.[4] Consumers' that maximise utility over time would smooth consumption − if necessary, borrowing from abroad to do so. An open economy makes such borrowing possible.

A permanent positive income shock should result in a rise in smoothed consumption, while for a temporary shock savings will also adjust. Fluctuations in savings absorb temporary shocks to income, while permanent shocks should affect foreign borrowing. Forward-looking behaviour also comes from firms' investment decisions, which depend partly on the discounted present value of future profits (or Tobin's q). Investment is the most volatile component of expenditure. Expectations of the future can be particularly volatile in a reforming economy.

If capital markets are complete, a positive multiplicative shock to output will lead to an upward jump to smoothed consumption. Figure 2.1 shows such a shock occurring at time t_0. The figure has net output (GNP − I), and C on the Y-axis, time on the X-axis. Before the shock occurs, there is a steady state where consumption equals output with investment and the current account both equal to zero.

Since consumption jumps up and investment also becomes positive as the shock raises the required level of capital stock, net output GNP − I is now below the new smoothed consumption level C_1. The

32 Basic accounting

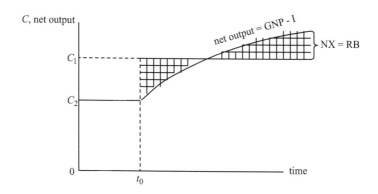

Figure 2.1 C smoothing in response to a shock in an open economy

economy must borrow abroad and it runs a current account deficit, accumulating a foreign debt. Although the debt enables positive investment and higher consumption, it has to be eventually repaid. Therefore, in time, net exports become positive and equal debt repayments RB. GNP – I was first below C_1 in the phase when I was positive. Then, GNP rises above C_1 and GNP – C_1 equals NX = RB, with the CAD and I again zero in the new steady state. The new level of C has to be such that the two shaded areas are equal, so that the economy fully repays the debt accumulated.

Thus, modern theory draws attention to the current and future macroeconomic determinants of the current account.

Box 2.1 Smoothing consumption in EDEs

Figure 2.1 suggests that consumption should rise in a country well established on a transitional higher growth path. But in the Indian case, after reforms that put it on such a path, the savings ratio rose from around 20 per cent to nearly 40 per cent. It is important to remember that the model is only a benchmark that holds under extreme assumptions such as complete markets, one good, perfect foresight and information. Inability to borrow, uncertainty regarding the persistence of growth and failures in the provision of public goods, such as health, education and social security, all suggest domestic savings could rise on a higher growth path. Since a large CAD could increase macroeconomic vulnerability in the absence of perfect capital markets, domestic savings have to also rise to finance investment. Large foreign borrowings are fraught with risk for EMs.

Intertemporal optimisation also suggests the current account should be acyclical, as savings absorbs temporary shocks. This is the stylised fact for most AEs, where the CA is acyclical or mildly procyclical. But in most EDEs, optimal consumption is more volatile and the CA is strongly countercyclical. NX falls in good times as consumption and imports rise. The explanation is shocks are regarded as permanent since trend growth, driven by policy instability, is more volatile. As expected, future income also rises, optimal consumption varies more than income.

In South Asia, however, the CA is procyclical. Correlation of NX/Y with Y is a high positive compared to a high negative for the EDE group and a low negative for AEs. Possible explanations are export-driven growth, especially services export, and remittances, so NX rises with output. As exports rise, they both raise income and reduce the CAD. On the other hand, a sudden collapse of export markets, due to a global shock, reduces income and increases the CAD.

Terms of trade shocks are an alternative explanation. If a deflationary oil price shock raises the import bill for inelastic oil demand, NX would fall as growth falls. This effect may dominate the fall in quantity of oil imports as growth falls, which would tend to make NX countercyclical. Moreover, if oil shocks raise costs, and as a result growth falls, the CAD would rise along with falling growth. Other explanations include repeated transient supply shocks with limits on borrowing for consumption. The CA, then, is a source of shocks rather than serving to smooth domestic demand (Goyal, 2011).

Figure 2.2 shows the large share of oil imports in the Indian CAD. Although the trade deficit was large and negative over 2011–13, it changes to a surplus if oil and gold imports are subtracted from it.

Since policy influences the CA, policy that magnified the negative effect of supply shocks on growth could make NX more procyclical. If higher C, I volatility does not drive income volatility

34 Basic accounting

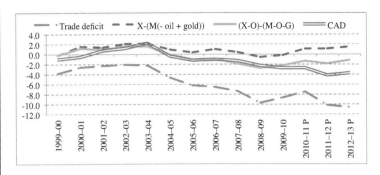

Figure 2.2 Trade deficit ratios adjusted for oil and gold and current account deficit ratio

Source: Calculated with data from the RBI.

but follows it; C and I are not the sources of variation. In line with this analysis, 2011–12, the year of the sharp rise in Indian CAD to 4.2 per cent of GDP, saw both a sharp rise in oil prices and fall in growth. As against this, the CAD was only 1.3 per cent in 2007–08, which was a year of high consumption, investment and output growth.

Undersimplifying assumptions of a low holding of international wealth by domestic residents, a good economy and a rate of discount equal to the international interest rate, a sixth relation for the CA can be derived from the theory of the dynamic CA (Obstfeld and Rogoff, 1995):

$$CA_t = (Y_t - \bar{Y}) - (G_t - \bar{G}) - (I_t - \bar{I}) \tag{2.1}$$

Bars over the variables denote average values. There is a CAD if the expenditure components rise above average values, but a surplus if output rises above its average value. Thus, when government expenditure (G) is above its average level, the CA should go into deficit (become negative), as citizens borrow abroad to smooth their consumption during the period of higher than average government expenditure. But if the increase in government expenditure is regarded as permanent, smoothed consumption should fall, so that the CA is not affected as G and $\bar{G}$ both rise.

Basic accounting 35

Box 2.2 Measurement problems in India

Before 2015, Indian national accounts statistics (NAS) used gross domestic savings (GDS) as if it was gross national savings (GNS). Only the GDS series used to be reported under GNS for India in the IMF database. Despite this, India used the CAD as the measure of capital inflows to derive gross domestic capital formation (GDCF). But the CAD is appropriate with GNS, not with GDS. If GDS is not adjusted for net income from abroad, the concept of net inflows used with it must also not include net income from abroad. The concept of net capital inflows (NCIs) that should be used is the net imports of goods and services, not the CAD.

Balance sheet and CA data were estimated by the Reserve Bank of India (RBI) and output, S, I by the Central Statistical Organisation (CSO). The RBI defined CAS = X – M + NY + NCT, where NY is the net income from abroad and NCT are the net current transfers. The BOP aggregated NY and NCT as part of net invisibles. The National Accounts Statistics (NAS) of the CSO took the CAD as the measure of NCI.

$$NCI = CAD = -(NX + NY + NCT) = NM - NY - NCT$$

But the correct concept of NCI to use with GDS is just the balance of trade, M – X (NM) or the excess of imports over exports of goods and services.

$$GDCF = GDS + NM$$

Only if the substitution is made for GNP will the identity used as the controlling total include NY and NCT:

$$GNS - GDCF = NX + NY + NCT$$

Since NY and NCT add to GNS and subtract from the CAD, they are netted out when GNS and CAD are used to add up to GDCF. Using GDS with the CAD as NCI is not correct. If NM-NCT-NY or CAD is added to GDS instead of NM, it amounts to subtracting the term (NCT + NY). Since measurement of savings is regarded as more robust than that of investment, GDS + NCI from the macroeconomic identity are taken as the controlling total determining GDCF. Since NCT was large and

36 *Basic accounting*

> positive for India while NY was small, negative and reducing (see Table 2.1(b) and Figure 2.6), this procedure reduced the estimate of GDCF (Goyal, 2008).
>
> The NAS switched to the correct identity in 2015, although other data limitations continue. For example, estimates of household physical investment are still used as the estimates of household physical savings. These form part of GNS.

The basic macroeconomic identity reflects flow variables. For example, savings is the share of income, a flow, which is not consumed. The manipulations of this identity to give different measures of the CA are also all flow variables. Therefore, the current account records income flows. But a CAD in any year adds to debt, which is a stock.

While the CA records income flows that are part of current income, the financial accounts record financial flows or acquisition of financial assets that help finance a current account deficit, or else invest a current account surplus, leading to a change in assets. A change in official assets, the reserves of foreign currency held by the Central Bank (CB), is a balancing item. So, a fourth definition of the CAD is the acquisition of domestic assets by foreign residents minus domestic residents' acquisition of foreign assets (including official reserves). The flow of these assets themselves is recorded in the financial account. While the CA records the sales and purchases of goods and services that generate income, the financial account records the sales and purchases of assets that change the stock of wealth. The wealth itself, or the liabilities and asset position of a nation, is recorded in a separate set of accounts known as the international investment position (Table 2.4 gives this for India).

The fundamental equation of the BOP is the current account plus the financial account and capital account must sum to zero or the current and capital account must equal the financial account in the new definition.[5] This follows, since each transaction recorded in the double-entry BOP system generates an offsetting transaction.

In the BOP, receipt from foreigners is a credit and enters with a positive sign; payment to foreigners is a debit and enters with a minus sign. Since it is a double-entry account, each transaction generates one credit and one debit entry. Under barter, imports would equal exports. Otherwise each trade transaction generates a monetary transaction. Actually, four exchanges take place but only the monetary transactions are recorded in the BOP – that is, money paid to or taken from a foreigner. For example, an export by a domestic firm generates a positive

Basic accounting 37

entry in the CA. The foreign exchange received can either be used to buy a foreign good or asset, or sold to the CB. If the CB buys the foreign exchange earned, the rise in reserves invested in foreign securities would be the corresponding negative entry. If the exporter deposits it in his foreign bank account, there is a negative entry in the financial account. This is equivalent to the purchase of an international asset. If the firm uses it to import some intermediate goods, the negative entry now is in the current account.

If the recipient of a payment by an importer deposits it in a bank of the importer's country, it is an export of an asset (the bank deposit), that is, a receipt from foreigners. Therefore, it is a positive capital inflow entering the capital account of the BOP against the negative current account entry for the imports.

The fundamental equation is an identity and cannot in itself imply causality. A rise in inflows does not by itself lead to a CAD, although it finances a CAD.[6] Many types of adjustments can occur. If inflows are absorbed as reserves, the change in reserves not only enters the financial account, but also the balance sheet of the CB as an asset. It leads to a corresponding change in the supply of money – a CB liability – unless the acquisition of reserves is sterilised by the sale of government securities. Without these adjustments, inflows do tend to raise domestic absorption, either directly by appreciating the currency or indirectly by raising domestic demand for non-traded goods and domestic prices. To the extent, capital flows raise investment and capacity prices will need to rise less. As incomes rise, savings (sY) and imports (mY) will also rise, assuming constant propensities. These are a leakage reducing domestic demand and are part of the adjustments that equate $X - M$ to $S - I$, with causality running from exogenous shocks to the demand components I and X to output and prices.

Box 2.3   The Indian balance of payments

Table 2.1a gives the Indian BOP under the old classification for select post-reform years. It shows the current and capital accounts and their components, with more details for the capital account. Payments to foreigners generate negative entries while receipts from foreigners are positive entries. The fundamental equation of the BOP shows the sum of the capital and the current accounts to be zero.

Table 2.1b shows the new classification, distinguishing between the capital and the financial accounts, in quarterly data

Table 2.1a India's overall balance of payments (US$ billions)

	Year	1990–91	2004–05	2005–06	2006–07	2007–08 (PR_)	2008–09 (P)
1	Imports	–27.9	–118.9	–157.1	–190.7	–257.8	–294.6
2	Exports	18.5	85.2	105.2	128.9	166.2	175.2
3	Trade Balance (2–1)	–9.4	–33.7	–51.9	–61.8	–91.6	–119.4
4	Invisibles	–0.2	31.2	42.0	52.2	74.6	89.6
5	Current Account	–9.7	–2.5	–9.9	–9.6	–17.0	–29.8
6	Capital Account						
6.I	*Foreign Investments*	0.1	13.0	15.5	14.8	45.0	3.5
6.II	*Loans*	5.5	10.9	7.9	24.5	41.9	5.0
6.II.i	*External Assistance*	2.2	1.9	1.7	1.8	2.1	2.6
6.II.ii	*Commercial Borrowings*	3.3	5.2	2.5	16.1	22.6	8.2
6.III	*Banking*	0.7	3.9	1.4	1.9	11.8	–3.4
6.IV	*Rupee Debt Service*	–1.2	–0.4	–0.6	–0.2	–0.1	–0.1
6.V	*Other Capital*	1.9	0.7	1.2	4.2	9.5	4.2
6.VI	*Errors and Omissions*	0.1	0.6	–0.5	1.0	1.2	0.6
7	Total Capital (I–VI)	7.2	28.0	25.5	45.2	108.0	9.1
8	Overall Balance (5 + 7)	–2.5	26.2	15.1	36.6	92.2	–20.1
9	Monetary Movement		–26.2	–15.1	–36.6	–92.2	20.1
9a	*IMF Transactions*	1.2	0	0	0	0	0
9b	*Increase (–)/Decrease (+) in Reserves*	1.3	–26.2	–15.1	–36.6	–92.2	20.1
10	Total (a + b)	2.5	–26.2	–15.1	–36.6	–92.2	20.1

Source: RBI Handbook of Statistics, www.rbi.org.in Table 142.

Note: PR: Partially Revised. P: Preliminary

Table 2.1b Major items of India's balance of payments (US$ billion)

	2011–12				2012–13				2013–14
	Q1 (PR)	Q2 (PR)	Q3 (PR)	Q4 (PR)	Q1(PR)	Q2 (PR)	Q3 (PR)	Q4 (PR)	Q1 (P)
1. Goods Exports	78.8	79.6	71.5	80	75	72.6	74.2	84.8	73.9
2. Goods Imports	123.7	124.1	120.1	131.7	118.9	120.4	132.6	130.4	124.4
3. Trade Balance (1–2)	–44.9	–44.5	–48.6	–51.7	–43.8	–47.8	–58.4	–45.6	–50.5
4. Services Exports	33.7	32.3	37.3	37.7	35.8	35	37.1	37.8	36.5
5. Services Imports	17.4	18.3	21.1	20	20.8	18.7	20.4	20.9	19.7
6. Net Services (4–5)	16.3	14	16.1	17.7	15	16.3	16.6	17	16.9
7. Goods and Services Balances (3 + 6)	–28.6	–30.5	–32.4	–34	–28.8	–31.5	–41.7	–28.7	–33.6
8. Primary Income (Net)	–3.6	–4	–3.8	–4.6	–4.9	–5.6	–5.8	–5.2	–4.8
9. Secondary Income (Net)	14.8	15.6	16.2	16.9	16.8	16.1	15.7	15.8	16.7
10. Net Income (8 + 9)	11.2	11.6	12.4	12.3	11.9	10.5	9.9	10.6	11.9
11. Current Account Balance (7 + 10)	–17.4	–18.9	–20.2	–21.7	–16.9	–21	–31.9	–18.1	–21.8
12. Capital Account Balance	–0.3	0.2	0.1	–0.2	–0.2	–0.2	0.02	17.8	20.9
13. Financial Account Balance	18.7	19	20.6	22.4	16.1	21	30.8		
of which: Change in Reserves ([–] increase/[+] decrease)	–5.4	–0.3	12.8	5.7	–0.5	0.2	–0.8	–2.7	0.3
14. Errors and Omissions (11 + 12 – 13)	–0.9	–0.4	–0.5	–0.6	1.1	0.2	1.1	0.3	0.9
As a ratio to GDP									
15. Trade Balance	–9.7	–9.8	–10.6	–10.5	–10.2	–11.4	–12	–9	–11.3
16. Net Services	3.6	3.1	3.5	3.5	3.5	3.9	3.4	3.3	3.8
17. Net Income	2.4	2.6	2.7	2.5	2.8	2.5	2	2.1	2.6
18. Current Account Balance	–3.8	–4.2	–4.3	–4.4	–4	–5	–6.5	–3.6	–4.9
19. Capital and Financial Account, Net (Excl. changes in reserves)	5.2	4.3	1.7	3.3	3.8	4.9	6.5	4	4.6

Source: RBI Macroeconomic and Monetary Developments, various years.

Note: Total of subcomponents may not tally with aggregate due to rounding off.

40 Basic accounting

from 2011, with more detail on items constituting the current account. It also makes the distinction between primary income, which is net income earned by unilateral domestic factors located abroad, and secondary income, or transfers from abroad. Errors and omissions can arise in reconciling the double entries since they come from different sources. The figures show the large increase in the absolute size of India's transactions with the rest of the world over the reform years.

Table 2.2 shows that the current account was relatively stable in the post-reform period, varying between − 3 and + 2.3 as a ratio of GDP (at market prices measured in US$ billion), until after the GFC when it reached a historic low of −6.5 per cent in Q3 2012–13 (Table 2.1b). The trade deficit was very large, but

Table 2.2 Current and capital accounts of the Indian balance of payments over time

	FDI (US $b)	FPI (US $b)	FI total (US $b)	NRI deposits (US $b)	ECBs (US $b)	Change in reserves (Inc-) (US $b)	Current account % of GDP (deficit minus)	capital accounts
1990–91	0.1	0.01	0.1	2.1	2.3	1.3	−3.0	2.3
1991–92	0.1	0.004	0.1	5.8	1.5	−3.4	−0.3	1.5
1992–93	0.3	0.2	0.6	2.2	−0.4	−0.7	−1.7	1.6
1993–94	0.6	3.6	4.2	1.2	0.7	−8.7	−0.4	3.5
1994–95	1.3	3.8	5.1	1.0	1.1	−4.6	−1.0	2.8
1995–96	2.1	2.8	4.9	1.0	1.3	2.9	−1.6	1.3
1996–97	2.8	3.3	6.1	3.3	2.9	−5.8	−1.2	2.9
1997–98	3.6	1.8	5.4	1.2	4.0	−3.9	−1.4	2.5
1998–99	2.5	−0.1	2.4	1.0	4.4	−3.8	−1.0	2.0
1999–2000	2.2	3.0	5.2	1.5	0.3	−6.1	−1.0	2.5
2000–01	4.0	2.8	6.8	2.3	4.3	−5.8	−0.6	1.9
2001–02	6.1	2.0	8.2	2.7	−1.6	−11.8	0.7	1.8
2002–03	5.0	1.0	6.0	3.0	−1.7	−17.0	1.2	2.1
2003–04	4.3	11.4	15.7	3.6	−2.9	−31.4	2.3	2.9
2004–05	6.1	9.3	15.4	−1.0	5.2	−26.2	−0.4	4.1
2005–06	9.0	12.5	21.5	3.7	2.5	−15.1	−1.2	3.1
2006–07	22.8	7.0	29.8	4.3	16.1	−36.6	−1.1	4.9
2007–08	34.4	29.4	63.8	0.2	22.6	−92.2	−1.5	9.2
2008–09	35.2	−13.9	21.3	4.3	8.2	20.1	−2.4	0.6

Source: Calculated with data from www.rbi.org.in.

was partially compensated by a surplus on the invisible items net services and net income flows from abroad.

The capital account, however, showed a steep rise in surpluses with fluctuations peaking at 9.2 as a ratio of GDP in 2007–08. Figure 2.3 shows that the change in reserves was almost a mirror image of the capital account – peak capital flows were largely absorbed in reserves. But after the GFC, inflows were barely sufficient to finance the widening CAD. Since reserves were not drawn down much, there were large fluctuations in the rupee. The current account was largely negative (in deficit), except for a small positive hump in the early 2000s.

Figures 2.4 and 2.5 graph components of the BOP in Indian National Rupee (INR) billion as a percentage of GDP at market prices. Figure 2.4 shows the steady increase in foreign direct

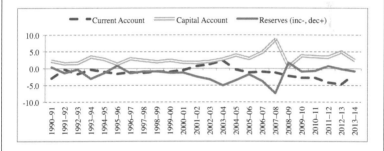

Figure 2.3 India's balance of payments: ratios to GDP
Source: Calculated with data from the RBI.

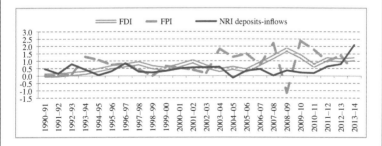

Figure 2.4 Capital flows in India as ratios to GDP
Source: Calculated with data from the RBI.

42 Basic accounting

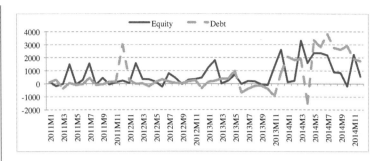

Figure 2.5 Debt equity flows (US$ million)
Source: Calculated with data from the SEBI.

investment (FDI) and the fluctuations in foreign portfolio investment (FPI). A given percentage of GDP implies very different absolute levels of FDI in the later periods, given rapid GDP growth. The absorptive capacity of the economy rose.

Indian reform liberalised equity investment by foreign institutional investors (FIIs) more, while retaining many graduated restrictions on debt inflows.[7] The rationale was that even though equity flows are volatile, they are at least risk sharing, while debt outflows impose a greater burden at bad times. The fluctuations in non-resident Indian (NRI) deposits reflect interest rate arbitrage and periodic regulatory restrictions. External commercial borrowings (ECBs) by domestic firms also reflect these factors (Table 2.2). Restrictions tended to be tightened when there was a surge in aggregate capital inflows, and relaxed in order to finance the CAD when inflows slowed, as during the Euro debt crisis over 2011. Restrictions on outflows by residents were relaxed only very gradually, initially only for current account transactions.

Box 2.4 Foreign inflows: components of the capital accounts

Table 2.3 shows the components of the Indian capital account classified in economic terms. It shows the sharp rise in post-reform volumes, the decline in capital flows on government account and rise in private flows, the relative rise in the share of equity compared to debt flows and the different components of debt

Basic accounting 43

Table 2.3 Economic classification of capital inflows into India

Variable	1990–91	1996–97	2001–02	2003–04	2006–07	2007–08 (PR)	2008–09 (P)
Total Capital Inflows (net) (US$ million) of which: (in per cent)	7,056	12,006	8,551	16,736	45,203	107,993	9,146
Non-Debt Creating Inflows (FDI + FPI)	1.5	51.3	95.2	93.7	65.8	58.9	231.0
Debt Creating Inflows	83.3	61.7	12.3	–6.0	64.2	38.9	87.2
a) External Assistance	31.3	9.2	14.1	–16.5	4.0	1.9	28.9
b) External Commercial Borrowings #	31.9	23.7	–18.6	–17.5	36.4	21.0	75.9
c) Short-term Credits	–9.3	1.2	–9.3	8.5	14.6	15.9	–63.4
d) NRI Deposits $	28.9	27	32.2	21.8	9.6	0.2	46.9
e) Rupee Debt Service	–5.4	–23.3	–6.1	–2.2	–0.4	–0.1	–1.1
Other Capital @	23.1	–75.2	–7.5	12.3	–30.0	2.2	–218.2 (US$ 20 b)

Source: Reserve Bank of India Annual Report 2008–09, Appendix Table 53.

Note: # Refers to medium- and long-term borrowings. $ Includes non-resident (non-repatriable) rupee deposits. @ Includes delayed export receipts, advance payments against imports, loans to non-residents by residents and banking capital.

creating inflows. While domestic interest rates do not affect FDI, relative interest differentials influence debt flows. These, together with changing caps, explain the fluctuations in debt flows. The expected value of the rupee also affects the decision to invest in rupee assets. Leads and lags in remitting export receipts are also affected by the relative returns to holding domestic versus foreign currency assets. These are a major component of other capital. Its large negative percentage share in the year of the GFC

44 Basic accounting

onset (last column) is a function of excess exchange rate volatility in that year. That large negative value (about US$ 20 billion), in turn, explains the positive share of FDI and FPI in that year, although total capital inflows had fallen steeply to about US$ 9 billion.

Over time, capital flows affect international debt. This is available in an account called international investment position that sets out a country's assets and liabilities. The cumulative impact of the period of large inflows is shown in Table 2.4. India's strategic choices in capital account convertibility have the consequence that large shares of the liabilities are in FDI and FPI. The

Table 2.4 Overall international investment position of India (US$ billion)

	September 2009	September 2011	September 2012	September 2013 (PR)	September 2014 (PR)
Assets	375.9	434.7	441.9	436.7	488.6
Direct Investment	76.5	109.1	115.9	120.1	129.5
Reserve Assets	281.3	311.5	294.8	277.2	313.8
Liabilities	482.5	659.6	713.4	736.2	845.4
Direct Investment	159.3	212.9	229.9	218.1	252.2
Portfolio Investment	106	161.5	164.6	171.6	212.3
Equity Securities	85.1	128	125.7	124.3	144.9
Debt Securities	20.9	33.5	39	47.3	67.5
Other Investment	217.1	285.2	318.9	346.5	380.9
Trade Credits	41.9	66.7	76.9	89.6	82.5
Loans	120.7	158	164.8	168.7	176.8
Currency and Deposits	46.7	52.4	67.2	75.2	108.9
Other Liabilities	7.9	8.1	10	13.1	12.8

Source: Press releases, India's International Investment Position, Table 1, www.rbi.org.in.

first is more stable and the second, although volatile, reduces in value if it exits in bad times. Assets largely comprise FX reserves and some outward FDI. The reserves were more than sufficient to cover short-term outflows, particularly since equity outflows would reduce in value during exit. Even so, the rise in the short-term debt component is unhealthy.

Gross positions can be very high as a percentage of GDP, although net positions remain small. Especially for countries with large stocks of international assets, therefore, valuation effects due to changes in exchange rates and stock prices can cause large changes in the net international investment position.[8] So, the current account is not the only cause of the change in a country's wealth.

Figure 2.6 shows that although India's income payments from abroad are negative on account of debt servicing and other net

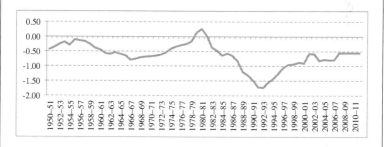

Figure 2.6 Net primary factor income from abroad as a ratio to GDP
Source: Calculated with data from the CSO.

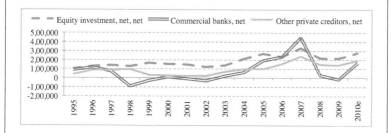

Figure 2.7 Volatile constituents of capital flows (US$ million)
Source: Calculated with data from Institute of International Finance, www.iif.com/.

46 Basic accounting

income flows, they have become less so over the reform period. Global interest rates were low in this period.

Figure 2.7 shows the most volatile cross-border flows around the period of the GFC were interbank flows – India's conservative bank open position limits and restrictions on intermediary flows protected it from volatility on this count, which adversely affected many countries.

2.4 The government and twin deficits

When government is introduced in the macroeconomic identity, a static derivation gives the CAD as the excess of I over S plus the excess of government expenditure over taxes or the fiscal deficit FD.

Adding and subtracting taxes, T, in the GDP identity, $GDP - T - C + T - G - I = X - M$ we get $S = S^P + T - G = I + NX$, where aggregate S is now the sum of private, S^P, and government savings, S^G.

Writing the identity as $S^P = I + CA + G - T$ shows, in an open economy, private savings can be used for domestic investment, acquiring assets from foreigners and for buying government debt. Writing it as $I = S^P + S^G + NM$ shows that either private or government or foreign savings can finance domestic investment. Writing it as $CAD = I - S^P + FD$ shows that private or government excess spending can imply a CAD.

So, if government expenditure exceeds taxes, unless I falls or S rises, the CAD will widen. This is the twin deficits hypothesis, where one deficit increases the probability of another. But a positive FD need not necessarily imply a positive CAD if private savings are high. The twin deficit argument illustrates again the fallacy of arguing from an identity, the mistake that Fama made (see Chapter 1). It needs to be supplemented by a behavioural analysis of the constituent variables before any conclusion can be drawn.

Box 2.5 Twin deficits and excess demand in India

Despite high fiscal deficits, the Indian CAD has averaged about 1 per cent of GDP, except over 2011–13, and there have even been periods when it has been in surplus. Private savings were high enough to compensate for government dissaving.

The distinction between temporary and permanent shocks, changes in taxes and subsidies, moving beyond the one-good assumption to bring in non-traded goods (Baxter, 1995) and incomplete markets can all help to explain the absence of the twin deficits.

Under credible reform and a permanent productivity shock, both C and I should rise and S may rise or fall, depending on the size of the productivity shock and the degree of incompleteness of markets. In India of the 1990s, the adjustments in S and I dominated the rise in G. Even if the rise in output was regarded as permanent, borrowing constraints limited consumption smoothing. Moreover, the rise in government spending took the form of subsidies and transfers to households, which in the reform environment may have been regarded as temporary. In order to smooth consumption over time, savings should rise if subsidies are regarded as temporary. Savings rose, although investment did not rise as much as it could have, suggesting risk aversion, poor credibility of reform and incomplete capital markets.

Since traded goods dominate in I, a rise in I would have required a widening of the CAD. But I was low, and government consumption or subsidies, which fall more on non-tradables, were high. The CAD widened after 2007 when, although investment fell, high inflation reduced financial savings.

Box 2.6 Comparing Indian and Chinese FDI

Entry of FDI was liberalised as part of India's opening out in the early 1990s. But restrictions on ownership shares, negative lists and continued requirements for many state-level clearances all raised costs of entry for FDI. In contrast, China with its centralised decision-making on such issues could offer a red carpet to FDI once the decision to open out had been made. A larger domestic industry may have made India more protective compared to China, which went in for massive FDI-led export growth.

But Table 2.5 shows that the acceleration in FDI into China occurred in the late 1990s, about 20 years after the opening out

48 *Basic accounting*

Table 2.5 FDI in China

In US$ billion	FDI	FDI minus 3 Neighbours
(1)	(2)	(3)
1987	2.7	0.8
1988	3.7	1.3
1989	3.8	1.4
1990	3.8	1.6
1991	4.7	1.5
1992	11.3	2.3
1993	27.8	6.6
1994	34.0	10.2
1995	37.8	4.0
1996	42.1	17.2
1997	52.4	27.1

Source: Chinese data from *China Statistical Yearbook* (1998); Goyal (2004).

Note: In Column 3, the FDI flow to China subtracts that from Hong Kong, Macao and Taiwan.

in 1978. Similarly, FDI into India accelerated and showed peak values in 2007, 20 years after India's opening out (Table 2.2). Chinese rates of growth accelerated in the early 1990s, about 15 years after reform, and India's in the mid-2000s. India is about 10 years behind China.

Both China and India have large billion plus populations, and India could have a similar high catch-up growth. The excess of Chinese over Indian FDI diminishes if the round-tripping between China and its neighbours is adjusted, as in Column 3 of the table. But even in 2013, FDI into India was just US$ 28 billion while China got US$ 124 billion. A concentrated push in 2015, to improve the ease of doing business, aimed to make India more attractive for FDI and showed results. The slogan 'Make in India' was adopted. Early theories of FDI location emphasised cheap labour, ease of entry and political stability, but the Indian and Chinese experience suggests well-established growth, large domestic markets and skilled labour are more potent FDI attractions.

2.5 Summary

This chapter developed the extensions to basic accounting concepts required in an open economy and set out the BOP accounts. It gave multiple definitions of the current account deficit, showing the link between macroeconomic identities and the BOP. It illustrated the BOP concepts with the Indian BOP, demonstrating the different kinds of capital flows and other complexities that can arise in EDEs. Basic concepts such as the difference between stocks and flows, identities and behaviour were emphasised.

The capital account is important, also, for the modern intertemporal approach, the basics of which were developed. The important degrees of freedom to smooth consumption and increase investment in excess of domestic savings were touched upon, as well as the risks of excess capital flow volatility and repayment burdens from foreign borrowing today. The latter affects the country's international wealth and has to be serviced tomorrow.

The cyclicality of the current account, capital flows and of output was examined and the idea of twin deficits developed. Although *ceteris paribus*, a rise in government spending in excess of revenue (the fiscal deficit), would increase the current account deficit, a fiscal deficit need not imply a current account deficit if household savings are large. Aspects of dualism can imply that even twin deficits need not create aggregate excess demand. The concepts were illustrated with the Indian experience.

An integral aspect of intertemporal optimisation is forward-looking behaviour. The future, therefore, affects the present. This is especially the case with assets. Currency becomes an asset, whose value is subject to substantial variations, under a floating exchange rate and a more open capital account. We turn to the asset approach to the exchange rate in the next chapter.

Notes

1 GDP minus depreciation and taxes plus transfers is the income households receive. Secondary incomes, such as gifts and transfers from abroad, are part of a country's income but not of its GDP.
2 The earlier classification puts transactions that affected nations' balance sheets in the current account, which should be a record of current transfers from nations' income. For example, an international asset transfer, such as debt forgiveness, would have earlier entered the current account but was now put in the capital account.
3 The debate on global current account imbalances occurred in the 2000s, since China ran a large current account surplus and the United States a large

50 Basic accounting

deficit. The intertemporal approach suggests that just exchange rate adjustments are not adequate to correct imbalances. Deeper changes are required that would reduce high Chinese savings and increase low US savings.

4 This theory was first worked out, in the context of the large CA deficits that some nations ran in order to smooth consumption, after the oil shocks. See Blanchard and Fisher (Chapter 2) for a formal derivation of consumption smoothing in an open economy. The area is surveyed in Obstfeld and Rogoff (1995), who were instrumental in developing it further.

5 This is the new classification that, for example, the United States adopted in 1999 and India in 2011.

6 To say capital inflows cause a CAD is another example of erroneously imputing behaviour to an identity and was called the theory of immaculate transfer.

7 Capital flows can come in through foreign institution investors (FIIs) or their sub-accounts registered with the regulator. Even in 2011, restrictions on debt were much tighter than on equity flows, although they were liberalised rapidly in this period in order to finance the current account deficit and contribute to infrastructure financing. While an FII could invest up to 10 per cent of the total issued capital of an Indian company, the cap on aggregate debt flows from all FIIs together, which was US\$ 1.55 billion in 2004, reached US\$ 81 billion in 2014. Source: http://investor.sebi.gov.in.

8 The United States lost almost a trillion dollars in this way after the financial crisis in 2008 on a net wealth of above US\$ 20 trillion, although values recovered quickly.

References

Baxter, M. 1995. 'International Trade and Business Cycles', Chapter 35 in G. M. Grossman and K. Rogoff (eds.), *Handbook of International Economics*, Vol. 3, pp. 1801–1864. North Holland, Amsterdam: Elsevier.

Blanchard, O. J. and S. Fischer. 1989. *Macroeconomics*. Cambridge, MA: MIT Press.

Goyal, A. 2008. 'Data and Definitions: Underestimating Savings and Investment in an Open Economy', *Journal of Income and Wealth*, 30(1): 3–10, January–June.

Goyal, A. 2011. 'Exchange Rate Regimes and Macroeconomic Performance in South Asia', Chapter 10 in Raghbendra Jha (ed.), *Routledge Handbook on South Asian Economies*, pp. 143–155. Oxon and New York: Routledge.

Goyal, A. and A. K. Jha. 2004. 'Dictatorship, Democracy and Institutions: Macro Policy in China and India', *Economic and Political Weekly*, 39(42): 4664–4674, October 16.

Obstfeld, M. and K. Rogoff. 1995. 'The Intertemporal Approach to the Current Account', Chapter 34 in G. M. Grossman and K. Rogoff (eds.), *Handbook of International Economics*, Vol. 3, pp. 1731–1799. North Holland, Amsterdam: Elsevier.

3 The asset approach to the exchange rate

Separating the wheat from the chaff requires persistence.

3.1 Introduction

What determines the exchange rate? In later chapters, we will be discussing the traditional macroeconomic fundamentals, but in this chapter we discuss the asset approach to the exchange rate. This is in line with the forward-looking intertemporal approach, which the new open economy macroeconomics has emphasised. It treats currency as an asset and the exchange rate as the price of the asset. Since an asset transfers purchasing power from present to future, its price today depends on the expected future value. As an asset, the exchange rate becomes a jump variable that can change rapidly with a change in expectations. We will see that it can also overcompensate for other sticky macroeconomic prices such as wages and goods prices.

This approach was natural in an era of floating exchange rates, which made it feasible for market-determined currency values to change rapidly. Moreover, free capital mobility in AEs allowed large capital movements in response to differential currency returns. If the demand and supply of a currency determines its price, then this relative demand is dominated by capital flows under free capital mobility. And expectations of future returns affect capital flows. This gave importance to the capital account of the BOP.

Changes in exchange rates can be dramatic. Thus, Oscar Wilde's *The Importance of Being Ernest*, set in the period of float before the World Wars, has a governess warning her sheltered charge:

> Miss Prism: Felicity in my absence you will read your political economy. The Chapter on the fall of the rupee you may omit. It is

52 Asset approach to the exchange rate

too sensational. Even these metallic matters have their melodramatic side.

(Quoted in Corden, 2002)

The structure of the chapter is as follows: Section 3.2 develops the basic concepts underlying the asset view of the exchange rate. Section 3.3 goes on to instruments and activities in FX markets. It also analyses hedging behaviour and why currency risk is not fully hedged. Section 3.4 defines market efficiency and explores tests for market efficiency. Section 3.5 refines the tests and theories, before Section 3.6 summarises and concludes.

3.2 Currency arbitrage

The exchange rate is the price of one currency in terms of another. In this book, we will use the European indirect convention that measures the bilateral nominal exchange rate as units of home currency that can be purchased by a unit of the foreign currency. The Indian exchange rate, therefore, will be written as Rs/$ or INR/US$. With this convention, a rise in the nominal value implies a depreciation or devaluation[1] of the home currency, since more units of the currency can be purchased by a unit of foreign currency. The home currency has lost value, making exports cheaper and imports more expensive. An appreciation has the reverse effect.

For example, only Rs. 1,000 was required to buy US$ 100 worth of goods in the early 1980s, when the Indian exchange rate was Rs. 10 per dollar. But in the 1990s, when the exchange rate reached Rs. 50 per dollar, Rs. 5,000 was required. The effect on the American consumer of Indian goods is exactly the opposite. Indian goods become cheaper – fewer dollars are required to purchase a good worth the same amount of rupees. The exchange rate allows translation of the prices of goods from countries with different currencies into the home currency, enabling a purchase decision to be made. If a nominal exchange rate change does not change domestic prices, it also affects the real or relative prices that enter import or export decisions.

For the BOP, the modern approach shifts the emphasis from the static current account to its financing by capital flows and its affect, therefore, on the international investment position over time. For the exchange rate, it shifts attention from the analysis of exports and imports to the impact of capital flows on the demand and supply of the currency.

Asset approach to the exchange rate   53

3.2.1   Uncovered interest parity

Consider the decision of an investor to hold rupees or dollars. Since interest is earned on holding currency, the relative interest rate also matters, as well as gain or loss on the value of the currency itself. The investor would be indifferent between the two currencies, if the following relationship held:

$$R_t = R_t^* + (S^e - S_t)/S_t \tag{3.1}$$

where R is the Indian interest rate, R^* the US interest rate, S the nominal spot exchange rate in Rs/\$ and S^e its expected value, given by some fundamentals. The equality implies that the rupee return on rupee deposits (LHS) must equal the expected rupee return on dollar deposits (RHS). The latter is approximately equal to the dollar return on dollar deposits plus the expected depreciation of the rupee.

This relationship is the uncovered interest parity (UIP). It says the foreign exchange (FX) market is in equilibrium when the deposits of all currencies, compared in any one currency, offer the same expected rate of return. If not, there would be excess supply or demand for one currency and a shift from the currency giving a lower return. Arbitrage in search of higher returns drives the equilibrium. This is neither an identity nor a behavioural relationship, but a market arbitrage relationship. It implies markets do not leave profit opportunities unutilised. In the process of removing such opportunities, all available information is factored into market prices.

Equation 3.1 is also equivalent to a classic asset return equation, showing that the return to holding a currency is a sum of flow returns and a capital gain or loss. This is equivalent to the return to holding equity as the dividend flow plus capital gain or loss from a rise or fall in the price of the stock. The return to currency is the flow of interest income plus capital gain from any appreciation. Capital loss occurs if there is depreciation.

Figure 3.1 graphs Equation 3.1 in R_t and S_t space and shows how arbitrage leads to equilibrium. The vertical line gives the rupee return on rupee deposits. This return is the domestic interest rate R_1. The expected rupee return on dollar deposits, which graphs the RHS of Equation 3.1, is the downward sloping line. The negative sign of S_t in Equation 3.1 implies the derivative of S_t with respect to R_t is negative – giving the downward slope. The intuition for this is: as the domestic interest rate rises, the spot exchange rate falls (appreciates) giving a negative relationship. At more depreciated rates, the rupee is

54 Asset approach to the exchange rate

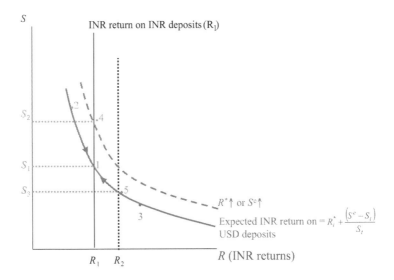

Figure 3.1 Equilibrium in the FX market

expected to appreciate, so expected returns to holding the dollar are relatively low; at a more appreciated rupee, it is expected to depreciate, raising relative returns from dollar holding.

First, consider the solid lines and assume $S^e = S_1$. For the present, shocks studied are assumed to be temporary, so that they do not affect expected exchange rates. Interest rates and expected exchange rates are exogenously given. Consider point 2. This is a disequilibrium point, since expected rupee returns on dollar deposits, $R_t^* + (S^e - S_t)/S_t$, are lower than expected returns on rupee deposits, R_1, creating excess demand for rupees and excess supply of dollars. So, adjustment occurs. Arbitragers would sell dollars and buy rupees, appreciating the rupee until it reaches the equilibrium point 1. Dollar holders have to be offered a higher return to induce them to hold dollars, else they will sell dollars for rupees.

At disequilibrium point 3, expected rupee returns on dollar deposits are higher than on rupee deposits. As the rupee is expected to depreciate, arbitragers would sell rupees and buy dollars, depreciating the rupee to the equilibrium point 1 where there is no excess demand or supply for any currency. The second term of the RHS of Equation 3.1 is positive at point 3, raising returns to holding the dollar. As a jump variable, the exchange rate always adjusts to maintain UIP.

Asset approach to the exchange rate 55

An increase in the interest rate paid on the deposits of any currency would cause that currency to appreciate, to compensate for the interest differential. As the relative price of two assets, the currency changes as the expected returns to the assets change. In Figure 3.1, such shifts are shown as dotted lines. A rise of R_t or rightward shift of the curve raising R_t to R_2 would appreciate the rupee to S_3. An increase in R_t^* raises or shifts out the dollar returns to holding and depreciates the rupee to S_2. At point 4, with unchanged S^e and higher R_t^*, the second term of the RHS of Equation 3.1 is negative, because S_t is expected to appreciate. This compensates for the higher R_t^*, so that UIP holds at the new equilibrium of 4. Similarly, at 5, the expected depreciation from S_3 to S_1 compensates for a higher R_t.

Unless arbitrage is able to reach a point where $S_t^e = S_t$ so $R_t = R_t^*$, a change in the exchange rate has to be expected at the equilibrium point. R_t can equal R_t^* at point 4, only if S^e has changed to S_2, not otherwise. The exchange rate typically is expected to jump to compensate for a policy-induced interest rate differential. That is why a rise in a country's interest rate is expected to strengthen its exchange rate. But, this holds only if expectations remain unchanged.

An exogenous expected depreciation raising S^e to S_2 would also shift expected dollar returns upwards to the dotted line and depreciate the rupee to S_2. Changes in the policy rates or in exchange rate expectations are the shift variables affecting UIP.

3.3   Market efficiency

In a floating regime, with rational expectations, the exchange rate should instantly reflect available information. In an efficient market, all news is factored into market price through the above types of market actions. Since prices fully reflect information, a trader cannot earn excess returns to speculation by taking a position based on private information in an attempt to beat the market. Efficiency does not imply equality of equilibrium expected returns across assets, since risk differs across assets. It also does not imply constancy of equilibrium expected returns over time, since risk can vary over time. It does imply equality of risk-adjusted expected returns across assets.

There are three forms of market efficiency. In the weak form, current price incorporates all information contained in past prices. In the semi-strong form, current price incorporates all publicly available information, including own past prices. This is the form implied by model-based rational expectations (RE). In the strong form, prices reflect all information that can possibly be known. Potential CB

56 *Asset approach to the exchange rate*

intervention implies the third form is not relevant in FX markets, since the CB is unlike other agents and has special information that may not be available to markets.

If markets are risk neutral and efficient, then UIP must hold, since an efficient market does not leave unutilised profit opportunities. These are arbitraged away, implying no arbitrage conditions hold.[2] If the expected exchange rate change equals the interest rate differential so that the gain from holding one currency over another equals the opportunity cost of holding funds in that currency, there are no profits to be made from shifting from one currency to the other.

Arbitrage is not riskless, since future expectations of the exchange rate are involved. No arbitrage will hold only if expectations of the exchange rate turn out to be correct, and an extra premium is not required to cover risk. The activities of speculators will equate futures and forwards to the expected future spot exchange rate, if expectations are unbiased and risk is absent. A tight prior on the expected exchange rate implies risk is low and a diffuse prior that large volatility is possible. The risk premium also depends on preferences.

The pure efficient market hypothesis is a joint hypothesis that traders are endowed with rational expectations and are risk neutral. The efficient market hypothesis reduces to a joint test of equilibrium returns (including risk premia) and of RE, if it is modified to allow for risk. The hypothesis can be tested, as we see below.

3.3.1 *Covered interest parity*

If dollars are bought with rupees in the spot market, but sold at the same time in the one-year forward market, the rupee value of the dollars obtained at the end of the year would be certain. Any exchange risk is laid off or covered. For example, if an importer expecting a dollar payment in six months sells the dollars forward today, he faces no risk from possible depreciation of the rupee in the interim period.

The difference between the forward (F) and spot Re/$ rate (S) is the forward premium, FP. The forward rate is the rate agreed now for an exchange of currencies at a specific future date. The possibility of covered or riskless arbitrage implies the rupee interest rate a currency trader can earn must equal the dollar interest rate plus the FP. This is known as covered interest parity (CIP).

$$R_t = R_t^* + \text{FP} \tag{3.2}$$

Asset approach to the exchange rate 57

With CIP, there is no risk associated with the future. Unlike in UIP, there is no expectations term. Both the spot and forward exchange rates are known at a point in time. If an arbitrage opportunity exists, it is riskless, since the currency exchange takes place at the same time.

$$\text{CIP implies: } \frac{F_t^{(k)}}{S_t} = \frac{1 + R_t}{1 + R_t^*}$$

where $F_t^{(k)}$ is the k – period forward Re/\$ rate, or the rupees to be paid now for a purchase of dollars k periods from now. If CIP does not hold it is because:

$$R_t < \frac{F_t^{(k)}}{S_t}\left(1 + R_t^*\right) - 1 \tag{3.3}$$

Arbitrageurs would borrow rupees for k periods at the low R, sell spot to get $1/S$ dollars, invest them at R^*, while selling dollars forward to get $F_t^{(k)}$ rupees, thus getting an arbitrage profit:

$$\left[\frac{F_t^{(k)}}{S_t}\left(1 + R_t^*\right) - \left(1 + R_t\right)\right] > 0$$

As more rupees are borrowed and sold spot, the rupee depreciates or S_t rises. The money supply falls so R_t rises. R^* falls as dollar buying expands dollar liquidity. The forward rupee–dollar rate $F_t^{(k)}$ falls or the premium on the dollar falls and the forward rupee appreciates, since more dollars are sold forward. All these changes tend to restore equality in (3.3). Disequilibrium pressures and adjustments continue until CIP holds once more. Foreseeing this, rational market participants will not trade at values, such as in (3.3), thus forcing the equality.

CIP is the same as the generic cost of carry rule in futures markets, which states that 'the futures price must equal the spot price plus the cost of carrying the spot commodity forward to the delivery date of the futures contract' (Kolb, 2002, p. 64) to prevent cash and carry or reverse cash and carry arbitrage.

$$F_t^{(k)} = S_t\left(1 + C_t\right)$$

This is CIP with $(1 + C_t) = (1 + R_t)/(1 + R_t^*) \approx (1 + (R_t - R_t^*))$, since the cost of carry, C_t, is 'the difference between the interest rate paid to

58 Asset approach to the exchange rate

borrow funds and the interest earned on investment in foreign funds' (Kolb, 2002, p. 288). No arbitrage is the principle determining futures prices. These are derived from the spot rate given the cost of carry.

The futures prices must lie between no-arbitrage bounds obtained by adding transaction cost, T:

$$S_t (1 - T) (1 + C_t) \leq F_t^{(k)} \leq S_t (1 + T) (1 + C_t)$$

This is an alternative interpretation of CIP. As arbitrageurs act to make these profits and remove profit opportunities, they ensure CIP holds. But much of FX arbitrage is triage trade, seeking to profit from and remove misalignments between cross-currency pairs. Since this triangular arbitrage is intraday, it is independent of interest rates or the cost of carry.

3.3.2   Testing CIP

If CIP holds, that is, markets arbitrage away any riskless opportunity, there should be no risk-free excess profits to be made. It is possible to test this. The logarithmic approximation to CIP is:

$$f_t^{(k)} - s_t = R_t - R_t^* \tag{3.4}$$

where small letters denote log values. Under continuous compounding, CIP can be written as $e^{Rt} = e^{R^*t} \dfrac{F_t^{(k)}}{S_t}$. Taking logs to the base e gives Equation 3.4.

In empirical work, it is usual to take natural logarithms of exchange rates, but not of interest rates. This strategy is a way around Jensen's inequality that generates Siegel's paradox for exchange rates: $1/E(S_t)$ is not the same as $E(1/S_t)$, where E stands for the expectation operator and S_t is the spot exchange rate. That is, expectations of the \$/Rs rate are not the same as the inverse of the expectations of the Rs/\$ rate. This is a problem since in working with exchange rates it should be possible to symmetrically use Rs/\$ or the reverse, without changing the expected value. Taking logs gets around this problem since:

$$\left(E\left[\log_e \frac{1}{S_t} \right] = E\left(-\log_e S_t \right) = -E\left(\log_e S_t \right) \right)$$

Jensen's inequality, on which the paradox is based, arises from non-linearity, so log-linearisation offers a solution. However, $\log_e (1 + R_t) \approx R_t$, since it

Asset approach to the exchange rate 59

can be written as the exponential $\log_e e^{Rt} = R_t \log_e e$ and $\log_e e = 1$. So, while the spot exchange rate is written in logs, logarithms of interest rates are not taken.

Riskless arbitrage implies that CIP must hold between comparable assets, after covering transaction costs. Two approaches to test CIP are first to see if deviations from CIP differ significantly from zero. Second, estimate the regression:

$$f_t^{(k)} - s_t = \alpha + \beta \left(R_t - R_t^* \right) + \mu_t \tag{3.5}$$

If CIP holds, we must have $\alpha = 0$ and $\beta = 1$, while μ_t is random. Considering home and foreign assets, such as Eurocurrency deposits that are comparable in terms of maturity, default, political risk and so forth, tests have found CIP to hold allowing for transaction costs. That is, it holds outside a neutral band of 0.06 per cent per annum from parity in countries without capital controls. Measured deviations from CIP can, therefore, be used as an indirect indicator of capital controls.

Even if the expected coefficient values are obtained in the regression, it implies CIP holds on average, so there may be considerable short-term arbitrage opportunities. Covered interest arbitrage is riskless if all transactions are carried out simultaneously. Modern dealing rooms make this more feasible.

The above tests are for the stylised fact of CIP but not for market efficiency, since that also requires markets to process information effectively to discover the correct value of the spot exchange rate over time.

3.3.3 *Testing market efficiency*

Failure of interest parity would imply the existence of unutilised opportunities to make profits. So, UIP and CIP should hold in efficient markets that effectively process information. These are neither behavioural relationships nor identities, but simple arbitrage relations. However, UIP subsumes expectations of the exchange rate, based on some economic fundamentals. If this information is widely shared and fully factored into market prices, these expectations should be reflected in the forward rate, making it the best predictor of the future spot rate.

Tests for market efficiency use UIP, with CIP substituted in it to replace the expected exchange rate by the forward rate, which is a measured variable. UIP: $R_t = R_t^* + (S^e - S_t)/S_t$ and CIP: $R_t = R_t^* + \mathrm{FP}$ together imply the k period forward rate equals the k period expected spot rate and the forward premium equals expected depreciation: $\mathrm{FP} = (S^e - S_t)/S_t$.

60 *Asset approach to the exchange rate*

Forward premium for a certain maturity k must be linked to expected exchange rate depreciation over the same period k. Writing UIP and CIP in natural logarithms:

$$\text{UIP: } \Delta_k\, s^e_{t+k} = R_t - R^*_t \tag{3.6}$$

where $\Delta_k\, s^e_{t+k}$ is the expected change (Δ) in s ($= \ln S$) over k periods $(s_{t+k} - s_t)$, R_t, R^*_t are nominal interest rates on similar domestic and foreign securities, with k periods to maturity.

$$\text{UIP: } s^e_{t+k} - s_t = R_t - R^*$$

$$\text{CIP: } f^{(k)}_t - s_t = R_t - R^*$$

Removing the interest differential between these two equations gives:

$$s^e_{t+k} - s_t = f^{(k)}_t - s_t \tag{3.7}$$

Or equivalently, the forward rate must equal the market expectation of the future spot rate:

$$s^e_{t+k} = f^{(k)}_t \tag{3.8}$$

Under RE, the actual change in future spot rates should differ from the expected change only by a forecast error. Therefore, given CIP, UIP can be tested by the regression:

$$\Delta_k s_{t+k} = \alpha + \beta\left(f^{(k)}_t - s_t\right) + \eta_{t+k} \tag{3.9}$$

If market efficiency holds, that is, participants have RE and are risk neutral, we must have:

$$\beta = 1 \qquad E\left[\eta_{t+k}\middle|\Omega_t\right] = 0$$

A coefficient of unity and the RE forecast error, uncorrelated with information available at time t, gives back the UIP. It implies that if there is a forward premium on the home currency for the period k, the currency should appreciate over that period. But a large number of regressions yield the stylised fact:

$$\beta = -1$$

This is known as the 'forward discount bias'. From the interest arbitrage conditions, the result implies that with a higher domestic interest

Asset approach to the exchange rate 61

rate differential and a premium on the foreign currency, the domestic currency tends to appreciate over the holding period rather than depreciate, as is required to offset the interest differential.

More precisely, the more the foreign currency is at a premium in the forward market at term k, the less the home currency is predicted to depreciate over the k periods to maturity. The negative coefficient, however, need not imply that FP mispredicts the direction of subsequent change in the spot rate because of the constant term.

Instead of jettisoning market efficiency, the discount bias led to a systematic exploration of other possible explanations for the result. These include removing econometric flaws in the tests, adjusting the expectations hypothesis and collecting better data, and are part of the rigourous evaluation to which science subjects any result before it is accepted.

Box 3.1   The carry trade

The carry trade, which is inherently a bet against the UIP, has become a pervasive feature of global currency markets. Traders borrow in countries with low interest rates and convert the 'funding' currency to invest in high interest rate countries ignoring expected future depreciation of that currency. Carry trade tends to appreciate this 'investment' currency, unlike the prediction of UIP.

As we saw, the cost of carry is the cost of carrying an asset across time or space. For wheat futures, this may be the cost of storing wheat and transporting it to the delivery spot. For currencies, the cost of carry is just the interest differential. Therefore, investment strategies based on this are called the carry trade. Changes in the capital value of the asset that form part of the returns are not included in the cost of carry. Capital gains should cover the cost of carry for UIP to hold.

The currency carry trade plays on interest rate differentials, ignoring potential exchange rate movements, and thus has been described as snatching pennies from in front of a road roller. It is unwound in times of large exchange rate volatilities when it becomes riskier. Although it can give positive returns for long periods, the investment currency can suddenly crash. It tends to be more unstable.

Carry trade and its unwinding helps to explain observed currency movements. The country where borrowing occurs is known as the source and the country where investment occurs is known as the target. For example, prior to the 2008 global crisis, the Yen, the dollar and the Swiss franc, all currencies of countries with low interest rates, were source currencies. Such sourcing meant these currencies steadily depreciated prior to the crisis. Given Japan's near-zero interest rates due to its sustained slowdown, the Yen was a favourite source currency.

As currencies became volatile after the GFC set in, these carry trades were unwound. This provides a partial explanation for the puzzle of why the currency of the country where the crisis originated appreciated. Money returned to the source countries, including to the United States, from the target countries. For example, the Australian dollar, a favourite investment currency, crashed in 2008 and those who had invested just before that date made large losses. The picture was one of steady appreciation above fundamentals, and then a sharp depreciation. As the major source of carry, the Yen saw the most appreciation. As markets stabilised, with bailouts and the coordinated monetary fiscal stimulus, near-zero US interest rates drove a resumption of the dollar carry trade. The dollar depreciated and stock indices rose steeply once more in target EDEs. In early 2010, dollar appreciation due to recovery in the United States outperforming Europe led to some unwinding, and stock indices in EDEs fell.

Why does the carry trade imply UIP does not hold? Suppose $S^e = S_1$ and the domestic interest rate is R_1 (Figure 3.2). Returns to holding the dollar fall, with a fall in R^* from R_1^* to R_2^*. If UIP were to hold, the rupee must jump to a lower value, appreciating

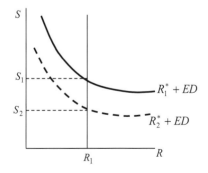

Figure 3.2 A fall in R^*

as capital comes in, so that at the new equilibrium, it is expected to depreciate thus removing arbitrage profits from the relatively higher domestic interest rate. Under rational expectations markets should foresee the future adjustment path and refrain from investing in a currency expected to depreciate. As against this, the experience is of steady rupee appreciation during the period of carry. This is why UIP regressions yield a $\beta = -1$ not 1.

In Figure 3.1, the rupee appreciation, with expected future depreciation, occurs because of a rise in domestic interest rates from R_1 to R_2. In the real world, it must be remembered, a risk premium enters the UIP and there may be uncertainty and divergence of the expected value of the exchange rate. Moreover, as we see in Section 3.5, expectations may not be rational.

*3.4 Explanations for the discount bias[3]

The tests that discovered the forward discount bias were not very robust. A large literature soon developed, aiming to remove possible econometric flaws.

3.4.1 Refining the tests

In the floating exchange rate regimes during which UIP was tested, spot rates were non-stationary and hard to distinguish from random walks (RW). Estimations supported the RW characterisation of floating exchange rates. But if the spot rate was a RW, the estimated value of β would be zero, even if markets were efficient. Under a RW, the best predictor of the future value of the spot rate is simply the current spot rate. RW, together with market efficiency, implies $f_t^{(k)} = s_{t+k}^e = s_t$. As a result, the independent variable in the regression would be near zero, so β would be unidentified. Therefore, a better approach is required to test simple efficiency.

One such approach is to test orthogonality of the forward rate forecast error with reference to a given information set, imposing the restriction $\beta = 1$. The error in forecasting the future spot rate using the current forward rate is $s_{t+k} - f_t^k$, the difference between the future spot rate and the current forward rate for that time period. UIP and CIP together imply $s_{t+k}^e = f_t^k = s_t$. But if $s_{t+k} \neq s_{t+k}^e$ RE would not hold, and there would be a forecast error. The forecast error $s_{t+k} - f_t^k$ is then returned to forward speculation or to taking an open forward position.

64   Asset approach to the exchange rate

That is, it is 'excess return' over the interest differential and predicted depreciation. Excess return is regressed on ψ_t, a vector of variables from the information set Ω_t. If markets are efficient, excess return must not depend systematically on this information.

$$s_{t+k} - f_t^{(k)} = \Gamma\Psi_t + \eta_{t+k} \quad H_0: \Gamma = 0 \tag{3.10}$$

Weak form efficiency is tested using lagged forecast errors in ψ_t. But H_0 is rejected using past price information. Testing semi-strong form efficiency using additional information in ψ_t also rejects H_0 even more strongly, implying all information is not factored into market prices.

More sophisticated econometrics has been applied using cointegration, vector auto regressions (VAR) and error correction models, testing for cross-equation restrictions and correcting for data points finer than the forward contract. While the results do not in general support the forward rate as an unbiased predictor of the future spot rate, there is evidence that forward rates, and the term structure of forward rates, have information useful to forecast future spot rates. This implies fundamental-based models can outperform the RW as predictions of future spot rates. Even so, markets continue to fail efficiency tests in various econometric refinements, of which this section has just given a flavour. Can variations in risk premium explain the failure of market efficiency tests?

3.4.2   Refining UIP: risk

Rejection of the above tests of the market efficiency hypothesis could not only be due to a departure from RE, but they could also be due to risk aversion of market participants, or to both. So far, they have been tested jointly. If agents are risk averse, they would demand a return greater than $R - R^*$ for holding the currency. UIP would now have to be modified to include a risk premium ρ. R must now exceed R^* to cover risk as well as expected depreciation. The risk premium itself could depend on a number of variables, including market liquidity, volatility of exchange rates, country risk and more.

$$R_t - R_t^* = \Delta_k s_{t+k}^e + \rho_t \tag{3.11}$$

Using CIP in the above:

$$fp = f_t^{(k)} - s_t = \Delta_k s_{t+k}^e + \rho_t \tag{3.12}$$

Asset approach to the exchange rate 65

The forward premium now has two parts – expected depreciation and the risk premium. Removing s_t from both sides, Equation 3.12 implies the predictable component of excess returns is just the risk premium: $\left(f_t^{(k)} - s_{t+k}\right)^e = \rho_t.$

If the estimated value of β is less than half or negative, it can be shown (Sarno and Taylor, 2002, p. 19) as $\text{var}\left(\rho_t\right) > \text{var}\left(\Delta_k s_{t+k}^e\right)$, which is the variance of the predictable component exceeds that of expected depreciation itself. This, in turn, implies significant excess returns in FX market, which can be predicted using current information. The time-varying risk premium thus confounds simple efficiency tests.

The above is a partial equilibrium result, since s and R are both exogenous with reference to ρ. A general equilibrium derivation of ρ is possible from the capital asset pricing model, based on maxi-misation of utility over time by the infinitely lived representative consumer.

But for this derived risk premium to explain a significant part of excess returns, the consumer must either have a very large coefficient of risk aversion or consumption must be highly correlated with the exchange rate. If these conditions hold, forward exchange rate positions provide less of a hedge against future variation in consumption. For example, when consumption is low, the exchange rate would also be depreciated. So, the risk premium is high. But in developed economies, since consumption is smooth but the spot rate is volatile, their correlation is low. It is hard, therefore, to explain excess returns or the forecast error in FX markets through the risk premium.

3.4.3 Refining UIP: the expectations hypothesis

Some failure of the expectations component of the joint hypothesis may, therefore, be necessary to explain the rejection of the simple efficient markets hypothesis. We next explore this as a potential source of a failure to make use of arbitrage opportunities.

Rational bubbles

Rational bubbles can occur if multiple RE equilibria exist. Then, excess returns would be non-zero even when agents are risk neutral. A bubble would imply increasing divergence of the exchange rate from its equilibrium value. Agents continue to buy currency that is overvalued in relation to fundamentals, since they expect a continuing bubble to make it profitable to do so.

66   Asset approach to the exchange rate

Such bubbles imply excess volatility of the actual exchange rate relative to the volatility of the exchange rate based on the fundamental solution. Tests confirm the presence of excess volatility, but the tests are conditional on a particular exchange rate model. The tests, however, have econometric problems in the presence of collapsing bubbles that distort the error term in any cointegration estimation of the exchange rate with some measure of fundamentals. Moreover, it is difficult to distinguish between a bubble and expectations of process switching.

Rational learning

If agents are learning about their environment, they may be unable to fully exploit arbitrage opportunities, which become visible in the data ex-post. Since they attach a positive probability to two types of policy regimes, but only one is there in the data, forecast errors would display serial correlation with a non-zero mean,[4] unlike under rational expectations when forecast errors are orthogonal to the information set used and have zero mean.

Peso problem

Another possible explanation is agents may be fully rational and learn instantly, but are uncertain about a future shift in regime. They attach a small probability to a large change, which does not occur in the sample. Developing countries often have persistent forward discounts, although devaluation may not occur (e.g. Mexico in the early 1970s). Peso is the Mexican currency and the problem is named after it.

As in the learning case, the probability of a regime change, which does not occur in the data, implies a skew in the distribution of forecast errors. Once the shift has occurred, the errors disappear. The effects on the forecast errors distribution are similar to rational bubbles, but there is a difference between the two. Rational bubbles occur because of deviation from fundamentals, but peso problems occur because of an expected shift in the fundamentals.

But $\hat{\beta} \simeq -1$ estimated across many countries and periods and persistence of forecast errors implies problems for all the three explanations. Agents cannot forever be learning about a once and for all regime shift. Bubbles and peso problems also are a small sample problem and cannot explain the generally negative estimated values of $\hat{\beta}$.

3.4.4 Using better data

The third refinement of tests is to improve the data sets used. Empirical tests of $\rho > 0$ assume RE and tests of RE assume $\rho = 0$. In testing one leg of the hypothesis the other is assumed to be true. With survey data on s^e, it is possible to test each component of the joint hypothesis. There is, then, no need to impose any assumptions on the expectations formation process of agents in the market.

In the regression:

$$s_{t+k} - s_t = \alpha + \beta \left(f_t^{(k)} - s_t \right) + \eta_{t+k} \tag{3.13}$$

The maintained hypothesis is RE, so $\alpha = 0$, $\beta = 1$ if markets are risk neutral and efficient. But if data on s^e is available, we need not impose any expectational hypothesis and can separately estimate the two components of the forward premium:

$$s_{t+k}^e - s_t = \alpha + \beta^{RE} \left(f_t^{(k)} - s_t \right) + \varepsilon_{1,t+k} \tag{3.14}$$

$$f_t^{(k)} - s_{t+k} = \alpha + \beta^{RP} \left(f_t^{(k)} - s_t \right) + \varepsilon_{2,t+k} \tag{3.15}$$

where $f_t^{(k)} - s_{t+k}$ is the forecast error or excess return from taking an open forward position.

A coefficient of $\beta^{RE} > 0$ implies a forecast error η_{t+k} correlated with the information set Ω_t, and therefore a failure of the RE hypothesis, since RE implies all information should be already incorporated.

The coefficient $\beta^{RP} > 0$ measures time variation in the risk premium and implies excess return or positive forecast error. Therefore, $\beta = 1 - \beta^{RE} - \beta^{RP}$, and if the H_0: $\beta^{RE} = \beta^{RP} = 0$ holds, it would imply markets are efficient.

Frankel and Froot (1987) who first applied this test found $\rho > 0$ but constant; it did not vary with the forward discount bias attributable to systematic expectation errors. The rejection of efficiency was due to the failure of rational expectations since β^{RE} was strongly significant.

Other studies found risk premia to be responsible for the failure of the joint null hypothesis. In general, both risk premia and expectational errors were found to be responsible for the rejection of the simple efficient market hypothesis. It follows there are persistent inefficiencies in information processing, with failures of both rational expectations and risk neutrality.

Micro-level studies, however, tend to find that profit opportunities are arbitraged away. Major arbitrage opportunities do not continue

68 Asset approach to the exchange rate

to exist. So, transaction costs that are not captured at the aggregate level may be responsible for the aggregate efficiency failures recorded. There is evidence (Burnside et al., 2001) that accounting for market microstructure and estimating UIP at the level of the actual transaction, arbitrage opportunities do not persist at the micro level. Different agents and transaction sizes are quoted at different prices in the non-transparent FX market, so that arbitrage gaps maybe a reward for the risk of a sudden unwinding and cannot be closed in reality. The financial literature (Kolb, 2002) suggests observed failures of market forecasting imply variation in risk in these markets.

3.4.5 Exchange rate expectations

Asset approach-based exchange estimations assume RE, but the microstructure literature gives direct measures of expectations. Survey data sets show strong heterogeneity of expectations. There is increasing dispersion at longer forecast horizons with a 'twist', since longer run expectations reverse the direction of shorter run expectations. At longer horizons, fundamentals dominate (Gehrig and Menkhoff, 2005). Static expectations imply the expected change in the exchange rate is zero. Survey data also reject these, since exchange rates are expected to change. But they reject the bandwagon effect that expected change in the spot rate is greater than the most recent change. It follows FX markets are largely stable.

For example, a survey of FX dealers (Cheung et al., 2004) shows that the skew towards technical analysis at shorter horizons is reversed as the length of the horizon is extended. Technical analysis is considered slightly more useful in forecasting trends than fundamental analysis, but significantly more useful in predicting turning points. News related to interest rates is an important fundamental factor. Speculation increases volatility while improving liquidity and efficiency.

A key lesson from efficiency tests also was the heterogeneity of expectations. Can the microstructure of FX markets provide an explanation for these features? We turn to this in the next chapter.

3.5 FX markets: instruments and activities

Interest parity comes about through agents taking positions in markets. They act as hedgers, arbitrageurs or speculators, operating in the spot market or using derivatives such as Forwards, Futures, Swaps or Options (Chance, 1989; Kolb, 2002).

Hedging is reducing an existent risk by eliminating exposure to price movements in an asset. Hedging refers to any contract made in order

Asset approach to the exchange rate 69

to protect the home currency value of a transaction denominated in a foreign currency. The transaction could be an import or an export of goods or a foreign borrowing or a loan. Hedging offsets the exchange risk or removes the exposure to fluctuation in currency value. Creating exposure in the opposite direction removes the effect on profits of currency movement in any one direction. Reducing risk is the dominant motive in hedging.

Speculation and *arbitrage* are fundamentally distinct from hedging, but are often confused with the latter. They occur when the return motive is dominant. Speculation is betting on a predicted one-way price movement. Thus, speculators aim to profit by taking a position in the market. They buy only in order to sell or vice versa. If they believe a currency is going to appreciate, they buy in order to sell the currency in future or take a position using derivative products. It is not linked to reducing risk from an existing transaction, but is rather 'risk-taking attempts to profit from subjective predictions of price movements' (Shiller, 1993). Thus, it is *risk-taking* not *risk-reducing*.

It is sometimes argued that since speculators buy when prices are low and sell when prices are high, rational speculative activity stabilises markets. But this does not always follow since speculators buy when there is a high probability of price appreciation and sell when the probability is low (Hart and Kreps, 1986), and thus can cause cumulative unidirectional movements. Hedging, however, stabilises markets. First, it removes potential shocks to balance sheets that can destabilise the financial system. Second, if hedging is complete at the aggregate level, long and short positions can be matched with less price volatility. Speculation is, however, regarded as contributing to market liquidity.

Arbitrageurs make use of riskless profit opportunities across markets. Their activity ensures that if there are no policy impediments or transaction costs, such opportunities will not persist. Thus, they stabilise markets and improve their functioning. In FX markets, if CIP does not hold between any two currencies, arbitrageurs can make riskless profits.

When currency risk is laid off, the hedging motive is dominant. If such risks are not hedged, it implies a position is taken on future currency values, that is, there is speculation on the future expected exchange rate.

Although there are a number of derivative products available in developed financial markets, hedging can also be accomplished through natural hedges, for example, if an exporter takes a foreign loan. Then, if the home currency depreciates, he will gain in export income but lose as the home currency value of his debt rises, so that his net exposure

70 Asset approach to the exchange rate

is low. This is an example of portfolio diversification. Most long-term hedges are of this costless type. Or he can enter into an insurance contract, in which he pays a certain amount to a foreign party if the home currency appreciates but receives a payment if it depreciates. If the hedging contract is actuarially fair, its expected value is zero, so that currency fluctuation has no systematic effect on profit.

A derivative is a financial instrument that derives its value from underlying more basic variables. Its value changes with the underlying. It also is settled at a future date. The underlying could be an interest rate, security price, commodity price or an index of prices or rates. Here, we consider the spot exchange rate as the basic underlying.

Forwards and swaps are common over-the-counter (OTC) derivatives. A forward contract is an agreement between two parties to buy or sell a foreign currency at a certain specified *delivery price* and *maturity period*. The one who buys takes a *long position* and the seller is in the *short position*. At initiation, the delivery price, D, is chosen to make the value of the forward contract zero to both parties, but if the spot FX rate, S_T, at the maturity T differs from D, there can be positive or negative payoffs. The payoff to the long position is $S_T - D$, since after buying FX at D the investor can sell it at the higher prevailing spot rate. The payoff to the short position is $D - S_T$, since if the spot rate is lower than the delivery price the short investor can buy low at S_T and sell the contracted amount at the higher delivery price D. The figures show how returns from the derivative change with the underlying.

Figure 3.3 shows payoffs from buy and sell positions, respectively, in currency forwards. A forward contract not only removes risk

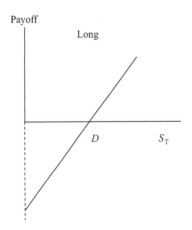

Figure 3.3 (a) Payoff from a long position in a rupee forward

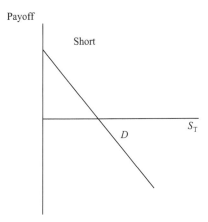

Figure 3.3 (b) Payoff from a short position in a rupee forward

associated with the price of an FX transaction at a future date and thus hedges, but it also can be used to speculate on an expected future change in the spot exchange rate. A futures contract is like a forward, except that it is regularly traded on an exchange, and therefore has certain standardised features. Margin calls that cover possible losses increase when the contract is losing money. If the value in an account falls below the maintenance margin, the exchange will issue a margin call that forces the investor to either liquidate her position in the futures or add more cash to the account.

Another characteristic of a derivative is that it gives exposure to market conditions with little or no initial investment. Since with forwards, money has to be paid only when the actual transaction occurs, it is possible to speculate without current funds, leveraging initial capital manifold. Options leverage funds further, since they confer a right, but not an obligation, to buy or sell foreign currency at a fixed exercise price at any time upto a fixed expiration date. But this option comes at a small initial upfront payment – the *option price*. This is around 2 per cent of the contract price, but can vary with expected profits.

Figure 3.3a shows the profit from a call, that is, a buy option. The holder of a call option will profit from buying the currency only if the spot rate appreciates above E, if that is selected as the exercise or strike price and could make unlimited profits depending on the rise. The call option is then said to be in the money. At E, it is at the money and with a market price below it is out of the money. If the market price remains below E, he would not be able to exercise the option and lose the option price paid. The holder of a put, that is, a sell option, would make profits only if the market rate depreciated below the exercise price E. In that case, it is said to be in the money since he could then buy low and sell high at the fixed exercise price E, making profits after the cost of the option is covered.

With a call option, an importer would be covered against having to pay more than E for foreign currency, while with a put option an exporter would be sure he would not receive less than E, thus hedging currency risk. The option writer, normally a financial institution, also has to cover her risks else she can have unlimited liability. Combinations are possible. For example, buying a call and selling a put is a way to place a collar on a loan rate.

A simple currency swap is a spot sale, together with a forward repurchase of the currency. It can make use of an investment opportunity in another currency for a specified period, reducing two transactions into one, thereby saving broker fees. For example, a swap can transform a loan in one currency into another currency. Both principal and interest payments can be swapped. A swap, therefore, is basically an agreement between two counterparties to exchange future cash flows according to a prearranged formula. It can be regarded as a portfolio of forward contracts, and this correspondence can be used to price a swap. A swap is thus a lower cost and operationally efficient way of achieving a desired cash flow. It allows the two counterparties to borrow according to comparative advantage, and then realise gains from trade through the swap. Part of these gains may be hedging benefits.

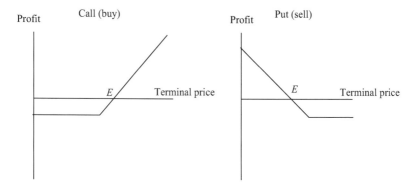

Figure 3.4 Profits from (a) call options and (b) put options

Asset approach to the exchange rate 73

The financial institution warehousing the swaps will also monitor its exposure to different currencies and hedge its risks. Hedging using derivatives has a cost; therefore, a company board normally sets loss limits, after which potential losses will be hedged.

Non-deliverable forwards (NDFs) are types of derivatives for trading in non-convertible or restricted currencies. They mitigate the risk from movements in the non-convertible currency. Since physical delivery is not possible, there is no delivery of the underlying currency. In an NDF contract, generally two parties agree to a cash payment from one party to another at a future date based on the price on that day of some underlying asset, normally a currency pair, as compared to a contractually agreed future price for the same asset. The cash flow is based on the netted difference between the future spot price (e.g. the RBI reference rate in the Indian case) and the contractual price (rupee NDF rate). Generally, the differential amount is settled in a convertible currency like the US dollar (Behera, 2011). So, a party expecting a future dollar inflow can write a contract locking in the current rupee–dollar rate. Then, she will pay the difference in dollars if the rupee depreciates, but recover it if the rupee appreciates. The upside from depreciation is removed as is the downside from a possible appreciation.

The same derivative can be used for hedging or for speculation. For example, a forward contract to buy foreign currency at a fixed rate will benefit an importer if the home currency depreciates, and remove a potential gain if the home currency appreciates, thus smoothing his profits. But a speculator who expects the home currency to appreciate can buy the currency forward at a fixed rate and realise the future gain if it appreciates, thus increasing the volatility of his profits and raising risk. Speculation does contribute to market deepening and volume, but can be counterproductive if it is the dominant transaction type.

To summarise buying and selling currency in the spot market requires an initial cash payment. Forward contracts require no such initial payment, but can lead to a gain or a loss in a future transaction depending on changes in the exchange rate. Forward markets, therefore, provide extra leverage to a speculator in comparison to spot markets. Options increase the leverage further, since they confer a right but not an obligation to make a transaction. For example, an importer who wants to hedge or a speculator who wants to make profits would exercise a call option to buy a foreign currency only if the currency had appreciated above this fixed rate; otherwise he lets the option expire, incurring a fixed cost, which is much lower than the value of the total transaction. The option has an initial cost, but then does not require buying or selling currency either in spot or in the forward market.

74 *Asset approach to the exchange rate*

Among formal instruments available for hedging, retail FX customers tend to use foreign currency options, while banks and commercial traders use swaps and other complex derivatives, as well as options that can continually be custom designed between financial institutions and their clients, and then traded in OTC markets. Standardised derivatives are traded on exchanges. Although futures have grown rapidly and have received a boost from the post-GFC call for more transparency, OTC products still dominate in FX markets. Regulators want these also to shift to exchanges – but that requires customisation, which is difficult.

3.5.1 *Incentives to hedge*

Hedging does not necessarily rise with the availability of more market instruments, since derivatives can be used for speculation, also. *Incentives* have an important role in inducing hedging. Markets, instruments and opportunities, with some restrictions on currency derivatives, existed in East Asia prior to the crisis, yet hedging was inadequate since tightly managed exchange rates reduced incentives to hedge.

Speculation dominates if there are aspects of the financial structure that encourage taking too much risk, such as lowering *liability* for promoters or managers, or if policy, such as *one-way movement* of exchange rates, creates opportunities for speculation. A firm's cost of borrowing is minimised if it is fully hedged so that bankruptcy does not occur. Since creditors normally set interest rates to cover expected default under bankruptcy, the interest rate charged is lower for a fully hedged firm. But if *government guarantees* the loan repayments and covers bankruptcy costs, the incentive to hedge risks disappears (Burnside et al., 2001). Results are similar if laws make it difficult for creditors to recover loans, so bankruptcy costs fall.

If domestic interest rates are high, the high borrowing costs raise the *opportunity cost* of buying hedging instruments. Even if an importer holds a dollar deposit as an informal hedge, he sacrifices potential high domestic interest earnings. Similar considerations affect hedging activities of banks.

Regulatory authorities sometimes put restrictions on derivative products that could facilitate hedging, in order to curb speculation. But with modern technology and regulation, it is possible to distinguish between hedging and speculative foreign exchange market activities. Hedging transactions are charged lower margins on modern exchanges, and their tax treatment also differs. If it is possible to monitor the use of derivatives it is not necessary to ban them.

Asset approach to the exchange rate 75

Caballero and Krishnamurthy (2004) point out thin and segmented capital markets can also reduce hedging. Domestic firms underinsure reversals since because of domestic financial market imperfections they cannot sell insurance to those who need it. Bond issuance (deepening) would allow firms needing external resources to share their revenues with those with access to foreign funds.

Psychological factors also undermine rational hedging decisions. People not only prefer a sure gain, but they also prefer an uncertain outcome with a small probability of a gain to a sure loss. Hedging involves a small sure loss or cost, and without it there is a small probability of a large gain. They are, therefore, willing to forgo hedging and undertake more risk than is rational. But proper 'framing' sensitive to psychological attitudes, emphasising the probability of a large loss, can reduce risk-taking behaviour (Shefrin, 2002). An understanding that concentration on core business makes them more competitive and reduces volatility of profits may make firms more willing hedgers. But it may require 'nudging' from a board-mandated risk strategy and from empowered risk officers. Hedging has an opportunity cost. For example, using futures markets replaces FX risk by cash flow risk as margin money varies. A hedging or risk strategy is, therefore, required. For example, a stop loss can be set so that hedging is triggered when markets move against the firm generating losses for it that go beyond the stop loss.

3.6 Summary

This chapter starts by making precise the bilateral exchange rate that will be used in much of the book. Under mobile capital, equilibrium in FX markets requires not only that the demand and supply for a currency is equal, but also that the deposits of all currencies, compared in any one currency, offer the same expected rate of return. Then, UIP holds. Since an expected value is involved, this arbitrage involves risk. CIP captures the riskless arbitrage possible in FX markets using forward rates. The difference between the forward and spot exchange rate is the forward premium. CIP holds between any two currencies when the interest differential favouring one currency just covers the forward premium on the other currency.

UIP and CIP together define efficiency in FX markets and more generally as the absence of arbitrage opportunities. Since in a floating regime, with rational expectations, all news is instantly factored into the exchange rate, a currency trader should not be able to earn excess returns.

76 *Asset approach to the exchange rate*

The efficient market hypothesis is useful as a benchmark, since it is based on simple market arbitrage. But using it must not blind to possibilities of market failure. Four categories of failure in financial markets are excess volatility and procyclicality (the failure to price risk); asymmetric information; large size implying the entities were too big to fail (TBTF) creating market power; and exclusion of large population categories.

As Turner (2009) pointed out, regulators buying into the efficient market hypothesis created the preconditions for the GFC by relaxing regulation. It was taken for granted that, first, market prices give economic value. Second, market discipline constrains harmful risk-taking. Third, market competition weeds out unproductive innovations. Therefore, it was thought securitised credit would create more liquid, diversified and stable markets. Mathematical models were presumed to provide robust measures of trading risk.

It is necessary, however, to distinguish between risk and uncertainty. The latter is not amenable to mathematical treatment, like risk is. The prior distribution of a high-risk variable may be diffuse with fat tails, but under uncertainty, such as possible black swan or rare unexpected events, a distribution may not even exist. Therefore, although UIP in the sense of no-arbitrage possibilities may hold at the level of individual transactions, the efficiency of markets in aggregate cannot be taken for granted. Appropriate regulation is required to reduce market failures and increase financial stability.

After developing the concepts, the chapter explored a number of ways of defending the failure to find empirical support of the simple market efficiency hypothesis. Market arbitrage is a simple and intuitive idea, and its empirical failure difficult to accept. The process also illustrates the anchoring function of powerful theoretical benchmarks and the systematic relaxation of simplifying assumptions required to apply the benchmarks to reality. But rigourous science is distinguished from Lakatosian defensive heuristics, if instead of accommodating anomalies they lead to substantial change in the theoretical framework generating them. This is the process of abduction or constant learning that builds upon the past instead of discarding it. The major adaption required in FX markets is more complex theories of expectation formation.

The chapter also introduces the instruments used to take positions in FX markets implementing UIP and CIP. It explains derivatives, whose value is based on the underlying FX spot market and the difference between exchange-traded futures and OTC forwards and swaps. OTC derivatives can be custom designed while futures are standardised.

Asset approach to the exchange rate 77

Swaps are the most commonly used FX derivatives, where two currencies are exchanged at some date in the future, then swapped back later.

It also distinguishes between hedging, speculation and arbitrage. The first is laying off currency risk, the second taking a position in a currency and the third utilising opportunities to make profits. It explains why hedging tends to be incomplete and the means to increase it. Instruments in themselves are neutral and can be used for any kind of activity. Derivatives provide leverage, so they can greatly expand speculative activity at reduced risk. Therefore, incentives such as limited volatility of exchange rates and the absence of implicit warranties on the currency level are required to induce more hedging.

In this chapter, the expected exchange rate was taken as given. In subsequent chapters, we will derive the macroeconomic fundamentals determining the equilibrium exchange rate and its expected value.

Notes

1 A currency depreciates in the market, while the government devalues it if it is fixed. Thus, the first term is used for different types of floats, while the second term is used for a fixed exchange rate regime.
2 Robert Lucas put the intuition simply: you do not expect to see five dollar bills lying on the pavement. Someone would pick them up, removing the profit opportunity.
3 * denotes advanced material.
4 In the macroeconomic literature, adaptive expectations gave way to RE, but the huge informational requirements of the latter have led to modifications such as adaptive learning. The latter applies econometric techniques to extract information from noise. An informal characterization of the three approaches is: fools have adaptive expectations since they make systemic errors, while only gods can have RE. In between comes the econometrician, who is an adaptive learner.

References

Behera, H. 2011. 'Onshore and Offshore Market for Indian Rupee: Recent Evidence on Volatility and Shock Spillover', *Macroeconomics and Finance in Emerging Market Economies*, 4(1): 43–55.

Burnside, C., M. Eichenbaum and S. Rebelo. 2001. 'Hedging and Financial Fragility in Fixed Exchange Rate Regimes', *European Economic Review*, 45: 1151–1193.

Caballero, R. and A. Krishnamurthy. 2004. 'Smoothing Sudden Stops', *Journal of Economic Theory*, 119(1): 104–127. 2001. Working paper version. Available at www.nber.org/papers/w8427.

Chance, D. 1989. *An Introduction to Options and Futures*, Orlando, FL: Dryden Press.

78　Asset approach to the exchange rate

Cheung, Y. W., M. D. Chinn and I. W. Marsh. 2004. 'How Do UK-Based Foreign Exchange Dealers Think Their Market Operates?', *International Journal of Finance and Economics*, 9: 289–306. Available at www.ssc.wisc.edu/~mchinn/FXSurveyUK_IJFE.pdf.

Corden, W. M. 2002. *Too Sensational: On the Choice of Exchange Rate Regimes*, Cambridge, MA: MIT Press.

Frankel, J. A. and K. A. Froot. 1987. 'Using Survey Data to Test Standard Propositions Regarding Exchange Rate Expectations', *American Economic Review*, 78: 115–125.

Gehrig, T. and L. Menkhoff. 2005. 'The Rise of Fund Managers in Foreign Exchange: Will Fundamentals Ultimately Dominate?', *The World Economy*, 28(4): 519–540.

Hart, O. D. and D. M. Kreps. 1986. 'Price Destabilising Speculation', *Journal of Political Economy*, 94(5): 927–952.

Kolb, R. W. 2002. *Futures, Options and Swaps*, 4th edition, Oxford, UK: Blackwell Publishing.

Sarno, L. and M. P. Taylor. 2002. *The Economics of Exchange Rates*, Cambridge, UK: Cambridge University Press, p. 19.

Shefrin, H. 2002. *Beyond Greed and Fear: Understanding Behavioral Finance and the Psychology of Investing*, Oxford: Oxford University Press.

Shiller, R. J. 1993. *Creating Institutions for Managing Society's Largest Economic Risks, Clarendon Lectures in Economics*, Oxford: Clarendon Press.

Turner, A. 2009. *The Turner Review: A Regulatory Response to the Global Banking Crisis*, March, UK: Financial Services Authority. Available at www.fsa.gov.uk/pubs/other/turner_review.pdf.

4 Market microstructure of foreign exchange markets

Sound and fury signifying something.

4.1 Introduction

Rapid technological and regulatory changes are profoundly altering FX markets, although special features of these markets are likely to survive. Participant profile and behaviour is also changing, as technology makes it easier for small parties to access markets anytime and anywhere. The chapter reviews these changes, internationally and then domestically. Reforms in Indian markets offer a good case study of the tensions between regulators, markets and technology. The chapter also draws out implications for effective Central Bank (CB) interventions and for exchange rate policy.

The current consensus from many empirical studies is while macro fundamentals determine the exchange rate at long horizons, there are substantial and persistent deviations largely unexplained by these fundamentals. A literature on market microstructure of FX markets, which grew rapidly after seminal work by Lyons (2001), suggests the mechanics of FX trading has important short-run effects on exchange rates. This is a departure from the traditional strategy of treating FX rates as a macroeconomic relative price. It also implies it is not only public information which is relevant for exchange rates.

As the survey data examined in the previous chapter demonstrated, there is considerable heterogeneity in agents' expectations of the future exchange rate. Therefore private information, the transmission of this information and the relation between information flows can play a vital role. Proprietary information is contained in order flows, which are the net of buyer-initiated and seller-initiated orders. Although order flow is a variant of net demand, it is not necessarily equal to zero in equilibrium. Each bank will have knowledge only of its own

80 *Microstructure of foreign exchange markets*

order flow, which it uses to update subjective estimates of the underlying value of the currency.

Order flow is a more precise proxy for expected future fundamentals, since it presents a willingness to back one's beliefs with real money. In specifications that include macro fundamentals and order flow variables, Lyons (2001) reports that order flow is a significant determinant of the exchange rate. It performs better than both standard macroeconomic variables and random walk (RW) forecasts.

It follows FX markets are influenced by a combination of macroeconomic and microeconomic variables. The market microstructure within which they operate, macroeconomic fundamentals and policies affect decisions market agents make. The CB is a special kind of agent with special powers and information. So its actions, including intervention and signalling, also have major effects. The Indian experience confirms this.

Other participants in FX markets include banks, non-bank financial companies, merchants and merchant-brokers. Large banks play the role of market makers, accepting both buy and sell quotes. Merchant transactions were originally restricted to trade and other retail transactions involving foreign currency, but now generate many kinds of transactions due to risk management activities. Sophisticated corporate treasuries also have multiple FX operations.

The remainder of the chapter is structured as follows: Section 4.2 discusses institutional features of FX markets, with a special subsection and boxes on the process of liberalisation and deepening in Indian FX markets. Section 4.3 draws out implications of varying trader information for exchange rate policy. Section 4.4 summarises and concludes. Appendix 4.A.1 gives derivations for the model used in Section 4.3.

4.2   Foreign exchange market: institutional features

Compared to other financial markets, FX markets have unique features.[1] We briefly describe their structure, composition, effects of change in technology and in regulations, then draw out implications for their functioning.

Structure: They are the most liquid markets. Daily market turnover was US$ 5.4 trillion in 2013 (BIS, 2013). But only about 5 per cent of the very large turnover is actually due to customer trade. Decentralised large-volume markets, with many physically separated market makers, interact through the telephone or private networks, not in a centralised market like a stock market. Decentralisation makes FX markets

Microstructure of foreign exchange markets 81

fragmented and less transparent. There is no publicly announced price and no law requiring disclosure of trades. Each broker or market maker only knows own order flows, with no incentive to share the information. Brokers normally accumulate a subset of market makers' limit orders and quote the best buy and sell order from a 'book' they keep of such limit orders. A limit order is an offer to either buy or sell a certain quantity of a currency at a certain bilateral exchange rate.

In a stock market clearing house, each party trades with it – doubling the number of transactions. This is known as 'novation'. The identity of the counterparty does not matter since the clearing house warranties the trade, covering its own risk through margin payments and deposits. But in an FX market, there are many market makers. Market spreads vary to cover the cost of market making, including counterparty risk.[2] Even if the net position is close to zero, credit limits get filled up, unlike in a clearing house, where only the net position is required for settlement.

Banks that are reporting dealers have to be the market makers in a decentralised market, since brokers cannot assess the credit worthiness of clients whose identity may be known only after the deal. The direct FX market is double auction and open bid. That is, two-way prices on both bid and ask are announced to all agents in the market. The brokered market is single auction and limit order. That is, prices are specified only to buy or sell but not both. They are known only to the broker and the party making the offer.

Counterparties, instruments, currencies: Participants are heterogeneous with diverse information sets and reaction speeds; therefore, profit opportunities persist for informed traders. Central banks have a special position. Although in 2013 the interbank market continued to account for the majority of transactions (63%), this share decreased since the 1990s because of the rise of other financial institutions, including groups such as institutional investors, hedge funds (22%) and small non-reporting banks (24%). Sudden shifts in positioning by large hedge funds that have the fastest reaction speeds and operate with high leverage can magnify shocks to FX markets. They implement currency programmes to secure a notional capital value that may be a benchmark risk-free rate.

As the corporate treasury and direct mobile trading FX market grew, traditional brokers were by-passed. But prime brokerage relationships with their clients dominated dealers' trade (16%), with only 3.5 per cent driven by trade with retail customers. Corporate treasuries became sophisticated. Customers changed from passive price takers with emphasis on financing and other banking services

82 *Microstructure of foreign exchange markets*

relating to foreign trade, to foreign investors, corporates availing foreign borrowing or involved in mergers and acquisitions and more. But the share of these non-financial customers in trading fell overall to 9 per cent in 2013.

As the dominant vehicle currency, the US dollar was on one side of 87 per cent of all trades in April 2013. The renminbi, however, became the ninth most traded currency as its turnover grew rapidly to US$ 120 billion. The financial centres of the United Kingdom (with 41%), the United States, Singapore and Japan intermediated 71 per cent of FX trading. Post-GFC bank closures concentrated trading increasingly in the large banks. The 10 most active global traders accounted for 77 per cent of trading volume, of which the top three, Deutsche, Citi and Barclays, were at 40 per cent, according to the 2012 Euro money FX survey.

OTC turnover at about 95 per cent share continued to far exceed turnover on exchanges. In 2013, OTC FX swaps were the most actively traded at 42 per cent, but forwards and options slowed the most rapid growth.

Technology: Although new technologies are causing some change, the majority of transactions continue to be bilateral, occurring in opaque markets without a physical market place. Even so, electronic dealing and brokering systems are giving some amount of virtual centralisation. Electronic Broking System or Reuters D3000, established in 1993, accounted for 85 per cent of interbank trading by the 2000s.

Electronic systems allow netting, lower settlement and counterparty risk, and have operational benefits such as reducing human error. They provide ex ante anonymous limit order bid-ask pricing to dealers and have driven a large increase in liquidity and reduction in transaction costs. The CLS (continuous link settlement) system, used by the majority of the FX market, settles payment instructions relating to underlying FX transactions in 17 major currencies, reducing settlement risk. The share of interdealer trade (39%) fell as increasing concentration allowed dealers to match customer trade on their own books, and investment in IT infrastructure for warehousing risk reduced the need to offload inventory in the interdealer market.

Although voice trading dominates in customer trades, electronic portals are being introduced here, also. Electronic crossing networks that aggregate liquidity pools received a fillip from the GFC. As markets froze, they were successful in finding liquidity where trade could occur without a large impact on price. But electronic systems do not increase the transparency of the FX market, since system governing

Microstructure of foreign exchange markets   83

boards treat electronic order flow as strictly confidential. Information on order flow, therefore, remains divided.

Regulation: It remains to be seen if the regulatory push towards greater transparency after the GFC, which is shifting more OTC trade to exchanges, causes a fundamental change in this market structure. But even the US Dodd-Frank Act that sought to prevent banks' proprietary trading has given exceptions for the spot FX market, thus accepting that the FX market is different. Higher capital requirements and tighter regulations are, however, reducing banks' participation in all markets.

Despite magnified activity, currency markets remained largely stable during the financial crisis of 2008, partly because risk management procedures had been improved after earlier crises. Banks imposed position limits for individual traders and risk capital made available was a function of past performance. Incentives to take risk were reduced because losses reduced traders' risk capital while profits were shared with the bank (Geithner, 2004).

But regulation has to continue to evolve in response to new types of malpractices. Since banks often act as principal to a trade, they buy at the moment the client sells. This conflict of interest gives them an incentive to move rates against their customers. Such behaviour is difficult in a transparent competitive market, since customers getting a poor rate would move elsewhere. But FX markets are not transparent. Collusion further reduces such protection. In 2014, FX traders were caught fixing benchmark rates to suit their own positions. Employees exchanged confidential client information with rival firms in order to trigger orders against their own customers, thus distorting the market. By end 2015, regulators from the United Kingdom, Switzerland and the United States had imposed record fines exceeding US$ 10 billion on six large banks whose weak controls allowed these malpractices. Four had pleaded guilty to felony charges, while others were fined for unsafe practices, wire fraud and electronic misconduct.

Decentralised currency trading with huge volumes scattered across numerous platforms makes it difficult to monitor and identify dubious trades. Solutions being considered include extending the period during which the daily fixed rate is established to make it harder to manipulate. Big data is being used in creative ways to flag unusual activities. Fines reduce the financial incentive to cheat. They also create pressure on management from bank shareholders. Values set by the top management are also important. Traders caught are normally either dismissed or lose their bonus. There are suggestions that higher penalties

84 *Microstructure of foreign exchange markets*

include the risk of a jail sentence. Possible solutions range, therefore, from better monitoring and incentives to strengthening values.

Functioning: More transparency could also be a possible solution. There is some rise in this. More trading on exchanges creates price benchmarks. But is it possible to change the decentralised largely OTC structure of the market with its huge trading volumes? Or does it serve some purpose? Large temporary inventory imbalances generate 'hot potato' trading, as dealers iterate towards their optimal portfolios. Although the share of such interdealer trade is falling, it remains very large. Market makers and dealers do not want to carry inventory overnight – which carries inventory risk – therefore, they quote ask (buy) and bid (sell) spreads such as to get rid of stocks in the day.

Trades are initiated based on macro data and differential order flow information, with the aim of rebalancing portfolios. The information in the order flow sustains trade. The transactions are not all speculative or profit seeking. Although this market structure raises the number of transactions, it is less prone to crashes. A centralised system with too many informed traders may crash as liquidity dries up due to homogeneous views, especially given the few prices quoted.[3] Compared to the large number of quotes in a stock market, prices in an FX market refer only to a few currency pairs, making the FX market more susceptible to herding and explaining its differential structure.

4.2.1 Indian FX markets

Indian FX markets offer an interesting case study of the process of market development. Intra-day trade was first permitted for banks in 1978, but the market really grew after liberalisation,[4] as the Sodhani Committee's (1995) comprehensive blueprint for reform was followed. The Tarapore Committee (2006) also made several recommendations for these markets. Despite major changes in the expansion of turnover and of instruments available for hedging, they were still far behind international markets. The advent of electronic trading and communication platforms reduced transaction costs and risks. The profile of customers changed as capital flows became the prime mover of exchange rates. Rising exchange rate volatility, with a more open capital account, increased FX risks and the requirement for hedging these risks.

The average daily turnover in Indian OTC FX markets, which was about US$ 2.0 billion in 1998, grew to US$ 38 billion in 2007.[5] Growth slowed after the GFC, but even so by April 2010 the daily domestic OTC market turnover was US$ 27 billion and the futures market about US$ 10 billion. So, unlike the global average of 4 per cent, the

Microstructure of foreign exchange markets 85

Indian exchange traded market was about 30 per cent of the domestic market (Mecklai, 2010b). The interbank to merchant turnover ratio halved from 5.2 during 1997–98 to 2.3 during 2007–08, reflecting the growing participation in the merchant segment of the FX market. The spot market remained the most important FX market segment accounting for above 50 per cent of the total turnover. Its share also declined marginally due to a pick-up in the turnover in the derivative segment. Even so, Indian derivative trading remained a small fraction of that in other developing countries such as Mexico or South Korea. Short-term instruments with maturities of less than one year dominated, and activity was concentrated among a few non-public sector banks (IMF, 2008).

Box 4.1   Deepening of Indian FX markets

Table 4.1 shows the rapid deepening of Indian FX markets. The rise in trade and inflows are dwarfed by the large turnover, which itself still remains small even in comparison to a middle-level

Table 4.1 Comparison of Indian and Australian FX markets

US$ billion		Australia			India		
		2001	2007	2013	2001	2007	2013
Daily FX	Amount	54 (54)	176 (220)	182 (462)	3 (3)	38 (24)	31 (53)
turnover	%	3.2	4.1	2.7	0.2	0.9	0.5
Merchandise trade, daily average		0.02	1.1	1.7	0.4	1.5	2.8
FX inflow, daily average		0.02	0.07	0.14	0.02	0.26	0.16

Source: FX turnover calculated from the Bank for International Settlements, various years, for example (BIS, 2007, Table E16, pp. 82, www.bis.org/publ/rpfxf07a.pdf), the International Financial Statistics (IMF, various years).

Note: (1) Foreign inflows are measured as the current account deficit plus reserve gains. (2) Merchandise trade is calculated as exports plus imports of goods and services (absolute values). (3) Domestic FX turnover is on net-gross basis (that is adjusted for local interdealer double counting by subtracting half of the turnover with reporting local dealers). It includes spot, outright forwards and swap transactions. Global INR turnover is given on a net-net basis in brackets. This adjusts for local and cross-border interdealer double counting by subtracting half of the turnover with reporting dealers abroad. BIS (2013) warns turnover for years prior to 2013 may be underreported, especially for EDEs.

86 *Microstructure of foreign exchange markets*

country like Australia. Table 4.2 shows the shares by types of agents and instruments, with domestic market data from the RBI and global INR OTC trade (row 8 onwards) from the BIS. With deepening, there is a sharp fall in the share of RBI

Table 4.2 Aspects of the Indian FX market

	US$ Billion FCY/INR[a]	*2001–02*	*2006–07*	*2012–13*
1	Total domestic spot turnover (sales + purchases)	446.1	1861.4	4525.2
2	Total CB intervention (sales + purchases)	38.6	26.8	29.9
3	2 as % of 1	8.7	1.5	0.7
4	Share of 1 due to interbank (%)	64.5	66.3	73.4
5	Share of 1 due to merchant (%)	35.6	33.7	26.6
6	Total forward as % of total spot	22.5	23.6	24.4
7	Total swap as % of total spot[b]	147.4	77.2	75.1
8	Global total INR spot (for April) (OTC)[c]	1.2	9.0	15.2
9	Share due to RDs (from CB survey) (%)	51.2	63.1	45.2
10	Share due to other financial institutions (%)	9.8	18.4	38.1
11	Share of non-financial institutions (%)	39.1	18.5	16.7
12	Share in total spot of local transactions (%)	94.1	77.2	66.9
13	Share in total spot of cross-border transactions (%)	5.9	22.8	33.1
14	Total domestic FX derivatives as % of total spot (net-gross)	116.8	137.5	102.1
15	Total global INR FX derivatives as % of total spot (net-net)	110.9	134.5	246.5

Note: Items 1–7 were calculated from RBI bulletins. The data were collected for all the months in the given years and summed up. Each year is taken from April to March. Items 8–15 are available in the Central Bank (CB) Surveys (BIS) and refer to net-net daily averages added up across different participants for April 2001, 2007 and 2013, respectively. Items 9–13 and 15 are as percentage to 8, 14 is a percentage of spot in net-gross terms; FCY: Foreign currency; INR: Indian rupees; RDs: Reporting dealers.

a All transactions involve exposure to more than one currency
b Excluding 'tomorrow/next day' transactions
c A swap is considered to be a single transaction in that the two legs are not counted separately. Including 'tomorrow/next day' transactions

Microstructure of foreign exchange markets 87

transactions and some rise in derivative use, although regulatory restraints slowed domestic use after the Euro debt crisis of 2011. Cross-border transactions rose. The share of derivatives is much higher in global INR trade (Table 4.1, row 15), pointing to a large off-shore market. Daily global net-net INR turnover is also higher than domestic FX market turnover (Table 4.1).

The percentage of intervention to interbank turnover fell from 13.4 in 2001–02 to 0.9 in 2006–07, but it was still large compared to that in mature economies. The Bank of Japan intervened successfully in 2011, even with a percentage of 0.2. These figures give the annual intervention percentage. The CB share can be much higher for daily intervention, which tends to be concentrated on a few days. The interbank market remains a large size of the total, but this interbank share is not much higher than the percentage of CB intervention to total turnover. CB intervention, however, affects only domestic markets.

Even so, the derivative segment of the FX market also evolved. Cross-currency derivatives with the rupee as one leg were introduced, with some restrictions, in April 1997. Rupee–FX options were allowed in July 2003. Exchange-traded currency futures were started in 2008.[6] The most widely used derivative instruments were the forwards and FX swaps (rupee–dollar). As elsewhere, FX transactions were mostly OTC structured by banks. But there was user demand for liquid and transparent exchange-traded hedging products, which are easier to regulate. In 2008, the Indian forward market was fairly liquid up to one year. The price movement in the near-term bucket reflected rupee liquidity in the interbank market as well as overnight interest rates, but the six-month and one-year rates were determined also by expected future liquidity. Importers and exporters also influenced the forward markets. Forward rates in a particular segment could differ from other segments due to the excess supply/demand from importers/exporters in that segment.

The NDF OTC market was also growing because of large capital and trade flows, restrictions on FIIs ability to hedge in domestic markets and large spreads between forward, futures and NDF markets. It began with diamond traders using the NDF market for arbitrage.

The Clearing Corporation of India Ltd. (CCIL) set up by the RBI in 2001 settled 90–95 per cent of interbank rupee–dollar transactions. FX trades were settled through multilateral netting, thus saving

88 *Microstructure of foreign exchange markets*

transaction cost. All spot, cash, tomorrow transactions and forward trades were guaranteed for settlement from the trade date reducing FX settlement and counterparty risk. A transparent FX dealing system, FX-Clear, of the CCIL launched in August 2003, decreased settlement risk and gave netting and operational benefits. It facilitated interbank trade through order matching and negotiation mode. Reuter's platform was also available. Swaps and options were essentially interbank transactions and accounted for about 50 per cent of CCIL trade settlement (IMF, 2008).

The RBI moved gradually to eliminate restrictions on FX markets. Historically, the availability of hedging tools against FX risk was limited to entities with direct underlying FX exposures. However, with a larger set of economic agents exposed to FX risk, there was a shift to the concept of 'economic exposure', that is, the effect of exchange rates on a firm's value. There were gradual steps to give greater flexibility to corporates for managing their exposures. For example, it was proposed to permit agents to book forward contracts without production of underlying documents up to an annual limit of US$ 100,000, which could be freely cancelled and rebooked. Cancellation and rebooking of forward contracts and swaps in India were regulated to reduce rupee volatility. There were moves to allow banks to fix their own net open position limits (NOPL) and aggregate gap limits based on their risk appetite and ability to manage exposure, with adequate prudential regulation and supervision to cover systemic risk and prevent excessive leverage. By 2011, while banks boards set the NOPLs, they had to be approved by the RBI.

Box 4.2   The process of regulatory change in India

FX market regulations followed a dynamic process driven by regulatory objectives of market development with stability, as well as demands from and requirements of markets. Some examples of this dialectic are given below over 2002–13, a period with major changes in Indian FX markets.

Since 2002, persons resident in India were allowed to enter into forward contracts on the basis of underlying exposures. Further, exporters and importers were allowed to book forward contracts on the basis of declaration of exposures and based on past performances, subject to specified conditions. Permissions were slowly expanded, with the aim of enabling hedging through the reversal of a real transaction.

The Annual Policy Statement for the Year 2007–08 (paragraphs 142) provided greater flexibility to the small and medium enterprises (SME) sector and resident individuals, further liberalisation of the scope and range of forward contracts, to facilitate such entities to hedge their foreign currency exposures on a dynamic basis. There was a warning that authorised dealer (AD) Category I bank should carry out due diligence regarding 'user appropriateness' and 'suitability' of the forward contracts to the SME customers.

NRIs could now book forward contracts without production of underlying documents up to a limit of US$ 100,000, based on self-declaration. These contracts would normally be on a deliverable basis. However, in case of mismatches in cash flows or other exigencies, the contracts booked under this facility could be cancelled and rebooked. The notional value of the outstanding contracts was not to exceed US$ 100,000 at any time. Further, the contracts were permitted for tenors of up to one year only.

Source: RBI/2007–2008/, A. P. (DIR Series) Circular No. October 10, 2007.

In an interview conducted in September 2007, Mr. Bhaskar Panda – senior vice-president and regional head, treasury advisory group, HDFC Bank – assessed the changes and advocated further reform as follows:

> Customised options have mostly evolved over the past 4–5 years after RBI liberalised its norms. Earlier, a corporate could hedge its risk only for three years; today, they can hedge it for up to 10 years. But the value of the hedge is capped up to the basis of last year's turnover. Banks want this regulation altered to allow booking of forward contracts based on projected performances. Banks mostly trade on Reuters terminal, CCIL and voice brokers. Technology has made a big difference to the level of FX dealing and has helped significantly to increase volumes.

CCIL was guaranteeing forward trades from the date they entered the spot window. But huge outstanding FX exposure and capital requirements still remained. Member banks wanted CCIL to extend guarantee to these trades from trade date itself.

This would imply reduction in bilateral exposure between counterparty members; capital adequacy and balance sheet disclosure would be required only of net exposure in outstanding FX forward trades.

Source: Note on CCIL's website, September 2007.

Despite the GFC, the process of deepening FX markets continued. For example, in 2008–09, futures were allowed and began to trade on exchanges. Further changes proposed in the draft guidelines announced in Paragraph 119 of the Second Quarter Review of Monetary Policy for the Year 2009–10, RBI, included:

1 Importers and exporters with foreign currency exposures in trade transactions, permitted to write covered call and put options both in foreign currency-rupee and cross currency and also to receive premia.
2 AD Category I banks permitted to offer plain vanilla cross-currency options to persons residents in India (other than AD Category I banks), who transform their rupee liability into a foreign currency liability.
3 Given the facilities given in item 1, the facility of zero cost structures/cost reduction structures was to be withdrawn, since these opaque structures were used for speculation on rupee strengthening and imposed large losses on firms in 2008.

Hedging commodity risk on international exchanges was allowed through banks for listed companies on 17 January 2012. Reducing detailed oversight reduces transaction costs for firms, but the regulator still has to mitigate systemic risk. Although the strategy was to move from micro controls to regulating broad patterns, there was some backtracking in times of high volatility. Over 2011–13, there was some reversal in permissions due to global risk-off and excess rupee volatility and FX markets shrank somewhat. FX markets had deepened and the variety of hedging instruments increased, but the concern to increase the share of hedging transactions remained, as the assessment below from a market participant demonstrates:

Daily volumes in the currency futures market crossed US$ 4 billion in just over a year after the launch. But over 70 per cent

Microstructure of foreign exchange markets 91

of the volume traded came from jobbers and day traders. Open positions are an indicator of hedging. Banks and other players that arbitrage the OTC market accounted for another 12–15 per cent. So, the open interest on the market from hedgers and medium-term position takers was only about 12–15 per cent. Compare this to the Chicago Mercantile Exchange, where open interest averaged nearly 95 per cent of a daily volume of about US$ 100 billion a day. For an emerging market currency like the Mexican peso, greater hedging volume takes the ratio of open interest to volume to 300 per cent (Mecklai, 2010a). Since OTC transactions dominate positions in futures markets alone are an insufficient gauge of hedging. But Rathinam and Arora (2011) in a study of the off-balance sheet activities of 15 Indian Scheduled Commercial Banks found that over 97 per cent of notional amounts assigned to derivatives were for trading, not for hedging.

4.2.2 Types of intervention in FX markets

Although its stated position remained, the RBI would act to prevent excess volatility, markets were increasingly allowed to determine INR level (from 2008) and volatility subject to what remained of capital controls that were being reduced under domestic and international pressure. Intervention was temporarily suspended in 2007 at a time of strong inflows that made sterilisation difficult, but resumed in order to accumulate inflows from October after market stabilisation bonds were negotiated for cost sharing with the government.

INR depreciation during the post-Lehman 2008 equity outflows helped share losses, since outflows had to take a write-down in the dollar value of their investment. Even so, the RBI did sell some reserves to support the rupee. Inflows resumed quickly, however, and up to end 2011 were just adequate to finance the CAD. So, there was hardly any intervention in this period. This led to the market misperception that the RBI was unable to intervene in FX markets, aided by statements from the RBI about the large size of India's FX liabilities and potential capital movements relative to reserves. RBI communication of large-scale intervention was not possible since reserves even at 300 billion now just covered India's international liabilities. But, just as policy became increasingly hands off, allowing more market determination of the exchange rate, strong global risk-on risk-off in the period after the GFC created perverse movements in the exchange rate.

92 *Microstructure of foreign exchange markets*

As inflows slowed due to global risk aversion after the Euro debt crisis, market players shorted the rupee and it began to fall steeply, almost reaching 55. An environment of low growth and a rising CAD added to the fragility of FX markets. Measures to further liberalise inflows proved inadequate. So, there was some reversal of liberalisation – restrictions were put on FX markets and intervention resumed. RBI began to sell reserves in November 2011, as the INR spiraled downwards. It also imposed restrictions on markets.

Retrospective taxation in budget 2012 and the Fed's taper announcement in May 2013 all led to outflows requiring RBI action.[7] Policy actions used included administrative measures such as controls, market restrictions, intervention or buying and selling in FX markets, signalling and monetary policy measures such as the classic interest rate defense. Thus, it turned out there were many feasible actions, after all.

Table 4.3, which lists the policy measures taken over 2010–14, attempts to assess their effectiveness by estimating this qualitative and quantitative impact on the exchange rate, that is, did a measure reverse or add to existing market movements and if so, by how much? The table gives the basis points change in the Re/$ rate in the week before and the week after a measure taken. A negative entry implies an appreciation of the INR and a positive entry the reverse.

The table indicates that the most effective measure was the FX swap window[8] announced for oil marketing companies on 28 August 2013. Not only did the INR strengthen substantially, but also it reversed an existing depreciation. The peak value of Re/$ 68 was not regained. The rupee continued to appreciate after that, as other measures were added to the swap window that remained open till end November. Measures that made more FX available, such as the subsidy for banks foreign borrowing or easier ECB, also appreciated the INR. Restrictions on markets, such as reducing position limits, worked only sometimes and total bans were not effective (see also Section 4.2.3).

Raising interest rates to defend the rupee in July 2013 was a total failure. The rupee depreciated from around 60 in July to a low of 68 in August. The 3 per cent rise in short-term rates was aimed at retaining debt flows, since zero open positions already prevented domestic banks from speculating against the rupee.[9] Ten per cent of the US$ 6.6 billion that had come in since 2011 left in June after the May taper-on announcement. Higher short rates did not stop the outflows and by November 40 per cent had left. Already high interest rate spreads and long-term rates rose, hurting the domestic recovery and domestic financial markets, where turnover fell further. Equity inflows, however, continued positive and were a healthy US$ 14 billion over

Table 4.3 Policy measures over 2010–14 and effect on rupee (+depreciation, –appreciation)

Date	Change in Re/$ (week before)	Change in Re/$ (week after)	Policy action
28 December 2010	–0.21	0.03	RBI issues guidelines for OTC FX derivatives and overseas hedging
1 February 2011	0.11	–0.48	Derivatives guidelines applied
15 September 2011	1.82	1.83	Exchange earners foreign currency account and residents foreign currency accounts – liberalisation
15 November 2011	1.19	1.54	Increase in ceiling rate on banks' export credit in foreign currency by 150 basis points
5 December 2011	–0.77	2.18	Speech reinforcing RBI's hands-off policy
15 December 2011	2.79	–1.51	Bank NOPL reduced 75 per cent; free cancellation and rebooking of FX forward contracts disallowed
21 May 2012	1.04	0.90	Netting of positions in currency futures/options with OTC positions disallowed; position limits of banks for currency futures and options reduced
11 September 2012	0.07	–1.18	ECB policy eased
13 May 2013	0.96	0.12	RBI restricts banks' gold imports
22 May 2013	0.89	0.58	Bernanke says Fed may taper QE
20 June 2013	1.43	–0.001	Foreign banks open positions in US$/INR reduced to almost zero
9 July 2013	0.93	–0.71	Any proprietary activity by banks in currency futures banned
10 July 2013	0.72	–0.42	Public sector oil companies directed to buy FX only from one bank (SBI)
23 July 2013	–0.36	1.43	Monetary tightening measures started from 9 July; reduced LAF limit to 0.5 per cent of a bank's own NDTL; banks to maintain a daily minimum CRR balance of 99 per cent; Marginal Standing Facility rate raised to 10.25 and CMR moved up to it from repo of 7.25

(*Continued*)

Table 4.3 (Continued)

Date	Change in Re/$ (week before)	Change in Re/$ (week after)	Policy action
28 August 2013	4.63	–2.32	FX swap window for oil companies (closed end November)
4 September 2013	1.36	–3.24	Window for the banks to swap the fresh FCNR(B) deposits with RBI and increase in banks' overseas borrowing limit with option of swap with RBI
5 September 2013	–2.32	–3.56	Raghuram Rajan's joining speech as RBI governor. Announcement of a BRICS currency pool of US$ 100
18 September 2013	–1.07	–0.92	Fed refrains from QE taper, keeps bond buying at US$ 85 billion
11 November 2013	1.89	–0.74	Participation by SEBI-registered FIIs, Qualified Foreign Investors, long-term investors in credit-enhanced bonds
21 November 2013	–0.63	–0.80	Eased bank's use of swaps in negotiation of loans from international/ multilateral financial institutions
28 January 2014	1.36	–0.54	Fed reduces QE
3 September 2014	0.12	0.37	Relaxation of External Commercial Borrowings (ECB) limits
28 October 2014	–0.13	0.17	Fed ends QE
28 November 2014	–0.13	–0.05	Oil prices plummet as OPEC refuses to cut production

Source: Updated from Goyal (2015).

Microstructure of foreign exchange markets 95

2011–13. Debt flows also revived by September 2013, but this was after short-term rates were reduced somewhat. Of the approximately US\$ 50 billion FII inflows over 2013 and 2014, debt inflows were just a little over half.

Signals that the RBI was unable to intervene and the INR should be left to the markets in 2011 had a large counterproductive impact. Well-designed signals had the desired effect, as with the new RBI governor's joining and speech on 4 September 2013, announcing subsidies for banks raising FX deposits. Fed announcements also impacted the INR. It appreciated after the US Fed's 18 September 2013 postponement of the taper.

The lessons from this experience were the importance of designing policy in line with the current state of capital account convertibility, restraints on debt flows and evolution of markets. Given India's growth prospects and relatively greater reliance on growth-driven equity flows, the interest rate defense was counterproductive and could have been avoided. The value of equity investors' assets decreases with a sharp depreciation, but an ineffective interest rate defense does not help existing equity investors, even as reduced growth harms new entrants. Even debt flows respond to risk premiums determined by overall macroeconomic stability, rather than just to narrow interest differentials.

Under adverse expectation-driven outflows, the market demand and supply for FX will not determine an exchange rate based on fundamentals. Smoothing lumpy foreign currency demand in a thin and fragile FX market is important. Direct provision of FX to oil marketing companies was first used in the mid-1990s.[10] It is a useful way to provide FX reserves to a fragile market without supporting departing capital flows. It also encourages domestic entities to hedge. It showed there are innovative ways of using reserves. Oil companies return the dollars lent. Reserves can be further built up during periods of excessive inflows. Although swaps add exchange rate risk to the RBI's balance sheet, it need not materialise over the short life of the swap if markets are successfully calmed.

In general, intervention must not be one sided and has to be strategic, drawing on CBs superior aggregate market information. Timing is very important and must be based on market intelligence covering net open positions, order flow, bid-ask spreads (when one-sided positions dominate dealers withdraw from supplying liquidity and spreads rise), turnover and share of interbank trades. EDEs typically have less information and more uncertainty, so signaling can be effective. A variety of signals can be used.

96 *Microstructure of foreign exchange markets*

It is only if these polices are not effective that restricting markets may become necessary. But that should be avoided, to the extent possible, since it has adverse side effects. Modelling strategic interaction between differentially informed speculators and the CB, with EDE features included, shows why types of intervention and signalling that are not normally effective may work in FX markets like those in India.[11]

Each party is assumed to make inferences based on the other's behaviour, under shocks that affect information extraction. Conditions for the speculative demand curve to be downward sloping in the spot rate and stable are: first, greater uncertainty about fundamentals; second, if speculators prior on the target; and third, if the CB's weight on the target is small. The first normally holds in an EDE, and the second and third hold if the target is diffuse. So, a CB in an EDE can optimally reveal some information, without announcing an explicit target or revealing its trading tactics. The estimated speculative demand was found to be downward sloping. CB purchase of dollars tended to depreciate the domestic currency and reduce its volatility. Anticipated intervention decreased turnover, so expectations from intervention were stabilising and not perverse. They dampened rupee volatility.

Greater uncertainty about fundamentals makes it more worthwhile for the CB to reveal some information about an exchange rate target. Section 4.3 shows why bounds on exchange rate volatility can reduce entry of poorly informed traders, and thus improve policy autonomy. An EDE is likely to have a larger share of such traders. Market microstructure variables were found to affect intervention efficacy. Since markets form expectations of intervention activity and respond strategically to it, more transparency may reduce the scope for such arbitrage. Estimated strategic market behaviour and model derivations both indicated intervention and signalling to be an effective influence on exchange rates in the Indian context.

The interest rate differential had weak effects on the exchange rate but strong effects on market turnover. With the extant level of controls, the effect of the interest rate on the domestic cycle was stronger than its effect on the exchange rate. The evidence suggests more transparent intervention may effectively influence exchange rates in the Indian context, leaving interest rates to target the domestic cycle. Next, we turn to examining the efficacy of market restrictions in more detail.

4.2.3 *Impact of measures on domestic markets*

The repeated scams and financial mishaps of the 1990s demonstrated the fragility of a controlled system. Therefore, financial reforms towards

Microstructure of foreign exchange markets 97

steady market deepening were undertaken. But the GFC demonstrated the wisdom of India's slow and steady approach to market liberalisation and the necessity of complementary prudential regulation. Action on the INR was not, however, always consistent with these lessons. Sometimes, actions were too hasty and cautious steps forward to deepen domestic markets were reversed, but did not always succeed in reducing rupee volatility.

On 15 December 2011, following volatility in the rupee, the RBI reduced banks NOPL by 75 per cent. This forced MNC banks to close large, long dollar positions. Bank boards did not want to have to report a fine paid to RBI for non-compliance. On representation, the RBI clarified that genuine trade-based positions would be allowed. They also cancelled rebooking of forwards (corporates were shifting hedging band to 55–60, paying the option fee of 2%). These measures to reduce speculation by exporters and banks appreciated the Re/$ from 54.2 to 52.7 (Table 4.3). The rupee was back at 50 within a month.

Adverse tax measures in the March 2012 budget triggered outflows again and the INR again reached 55. Netting of positions in currency futures/options with OTC positions was disallowed and position limits of banks further reduced in May 2012, but the next week saw the INR further depreciate by 0.90. Over June and July 2013, foreign banks open positions in Re/$ was reduced to almost zero and any proprietary activity by banks in currency futures was banned, but depreciation continued.

Figure 4.1 shows various market-restrictive measures reduced market turnover sharply in the currency derivatives markets in exchanges, while total turnover including the dominant OTC FX trading in banks

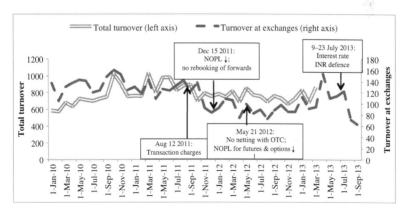

Figure 4.1 FX market turnover (US$ billion)

98 Microstructure of foreign exchange markets

also fell. This suggests OTC and exchange-traded derivatives are complements rather than substitutes. Banks are some of the largest traders on exchanges. Exchanges are thought to be dominated by speculative position taking, since no real underlying is required unlike in the RBI-regulated OTC markets. But in FX markets, worldwide portfolio rebalancing types of transactions between market makers are normally much larger than those based on real exposures. These allow banks, as well as small firms that may not get a good deal at banks, to lay-off risks in futures markets. Futures markets are more transparent and equitable, but expectations play a large role in such markets and can lead to one-way positions. Prudential regulations, therefore, are required.

The other effect of restrictions was offshore markets that grew at the expense of domestic markets. In more open regimes, restricting domestic markets encourages transactions to migrate abroad. Though an accurate assessment of the volumes is difficult, estimated daily INR NDF turnover was around US$ 100 million in 2003–04 and grew substantially since. By April 2013, it exceeded onshore trading. Onshore market affects price discovery in INR NDF market. However, in volatile market conditions, NDF markets influence spot and forward onshore markets. A large spread between INR NDF rate and INR futures/forward rate impacts the spot rates significantly. The INR forward rate is influenced by the movement of INR NDF futures and spot rates with some lag (Behera, 2011). Although such markets create problems for policy, they normally wither away as domestic markets deepen (Ma et al., 2004).

Although it is difficult to measure precisely, BIS (2010 Table E6, 2013 Table 6.3) shows OTC INR turnover (net-gross basis) outside the country rose from 50 per cent (US$ 20.8 billion) in 2010 to 59 per cent (US$ 36.3 billion) in 2013 of the total turnover. Table 4.4 shows

Table 4.4 Rise in cross-border derivatives

	Total outright forwards					
	Domestic: net-gross basis			*Global INR: net-net basis*		
	$ m	*Cross-border %*	*% of spot*	*$ m*	*Cross-border %*	*% of spot*
April 13	3,743	14.64	24.19	24,395	60.43	160.23
April 10	4,895	8.56	36.50	13,620	52.11	100.69

Note: Net-gross basis adjusts for local interdealer double counting. Net-net basis adjusts for local and cross-border interdealer double counting. BIS (2013) warned turnover for years prior to 2013 may be underreported, especially for EDEs.

Microstructure of foreign exchange markets 99

the sharp rise in INR forwards, which include NDF, between 2010 and 2013 when domestic restrictions were imposed. The rise, as well as much higher net-net compared to net-gross value, shows much of the growth was abroad.[12] A rising share of the NDF market is against the objective of developing and deepening domestic markets. Moreover, domestic regulators are unable to influence offshore markets. Using prudential regulations, instead of forbidding transactions, would also have the advantage of not driving markets overseas.

4.2.4 Encouraging hedging

A conviction of possible two-way movement of the exchange rate, large enough to deliver a substantial loss to one-way bets, is a prerequisite for hedging or the laying off of currency exposure. Despite deepening FX markets, the moderate two-way movement within an implicit 5 per cent band seen over 2004–06 was not sufficient to overcome strong expectations of medium-term appreciation given India's high growth rate. In 2007, market expectations of the Re/$ rate had even reached 32. Many corporates borrowed abroad based on such expectations, increasing currency risk. Some had entered into hedging deals, which were actually bets on the value of the Swiss Franc. Many such deals, where Indian banks were often a front for foreign banks, sidestepped existing rules that prevented leverage or underlying risk that exceeded export income. Although firms were not allowed to write options, deals were structured so that, in effect, they were writing options. The deals were so complex that firms sometimes did not understand what risks they were taking. With the volatility in currency markets and steep rupee depreciation in 2008, some firms lost money.

After post-GFC episodes of excess volatility, the rupee was managed and stayed in a tight band of INR/US$ 64–66 over September 2013 – August 2015. Since international interest rates were much lower than Indian rates, firms were again tempted into unhedged foreign borrowing (UFB), although such borrowing, for example, through ECB, remained capped. Even so, gross ECBs worth around US$ 264.4 billion came in from 2001 until Oct 2014. Refinancing makes up a large share of these loans.[13] Not hedging is dangerous since the bulk of the borrowing is by infrastructure firms that do not have any natural hedge such as exports.

Thus, for inducing hedging sufficient flexibility of the exchange rate, along with transparency, clarity, information and strategic use of controls are all required (see Chapter 3). Completing markets will not

100 *Microstructure of foreign exchange markets*

by itself reduce speculation. Availability of more instruments makes it possible to leverage bets on future currency value. Incentives have to be changed and better information provided on fundamentals.

*4.3 FX markets and policy[14]

Well-designed signals can make it possible to use the structure of FX markets, such as varying trader information, to achieve policy objectives of reducing exchange rate volatility. An EDE is likely to have a larger share of poorly informed traders.

Jeanne and Rose (2002) have a model with informed and noise traders (n) in an FX market. The benefit of entry for noise traders rises with excess returns or risk, ρ, but falls with the variance of the spot rate, var (S). But both ρ and var (S) are functions of n. A rise in n lowers ρ since a larger number of traders are demanding the currency, thus spreading risk, but raises var (S) since more traders raise volatility, which reduces entry. But the rise in var (S) itself raises ρ, thus increasing entry. Noise traders, therefore, have two counteracting roles. They both create risk and share risk, making multiple equilibria possible.

This can be shown in a simple diagrammatic device following Goyal (2006). $G(n)$, the function giving the returns to noise trader entry, is graphed against n in Figure 4.2. The two opposing effects of n on $G(n)$ give the curve the shape shown in the Figure (derived in Appendix 4.A.1). At low n, G is high since var (S) is low. It falls as more n share risk reducing ρ. But further entry creates risk raising var (S) and ρ. At high n, G rises again, as the rise in ρ dominates that in var (S).

The lowest dashed curve is the case where fundamentals are strong. Therefore, excess returns are so low that it is not worthwhile for any noise trader to enter. Point O is a stable equilibrium, as is C', on the

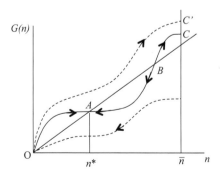

Figure 4.2 Entry of noise traders in FX markets

Microstructure of foreign exchange markets   101

upper dashed curve. On this upper curve, fundamentals are so weak that all the noise traders enter. Multiple equilibria occur, for intermediate fundamentals, when $G(n)$ is such that it cuts the 45 degree line. These are equilibria, since $G = n$ at these points. Point A is stable, since for a small departure from A, net returns are such as to bring entry back to n^*. Point C is also stable. But point B is unstable. Here, the curve cuts the 45 degree line from below.[15] So, a small rise in n raises returns and induces more entry until C is reached. A small fall in n reduces returns and entry until the stable point A is reached.

At C' and C, all noise traders enter. At A, var (S), ρ and, therefore, entry n are all low; at C, var (S) and ρ are both high and maximum entry $\bar{n}$ takes place. Between AB, since $G(n) < n$, entry falls back to n^* at A; between CB, since $G(n) > n$, entry rises and n increases to $\bar{n}$ at C. Therefore, O, A, C and C' are stable equilibria, while B is unstable. It follows that exchange rate volatility can be low if fundamental variance is low, but it can be either high or low for intermediate levels of fundamentals.

Monetary policy can improve welfare if it leads to the selection of low-volatility equilibria. It can do this by committing to var $(S) \leq v$. Then, fewer n enter; this decreases var (S) leading to the selection of the low entry equilibrium A. This is a policy-free lunch, since markets help monetary policy achieve the reduced volatility it had committed to.

A stable exchange rate regime, where policy constrains var (S) to be less than or equal to v, leads to lower entry of noise traders taking the economy to an equilibrium with low exchange rate variance.[16] Although there is a loss of monetary autonomy in adopting the restriction on var (S), the loss is of second order, as the level of noise in the economy is decreased. The monetary policy response function is constrained out of equilibrium, but there is no sacrifice of monetary autonomy in equilibrium.

The proffered objective in the post-GFC period Indian exchange rate volatility was allowed to rise too much, but there were also periods when it was too low. Goyal and Arora (2012) give evidence CB speeches affect the exchange rate, but over the period signals were poorly used. Table 4.3 shows this in 2011, but indicates improvement in 2013.

4.4   Summary

The chapter gives an overview of international and Indian FX markets and discusses market microstructure concepts such as 'order flow', bid-ask spreads, limit order, novation, netting, settlement and counterparty risk, electronic broker and crossing systems, inventory risk and 'hot potato' trading. It also records the very large size of FX transactions and

102 *Microstructure of foreign exchange markets*

the growth and deepening of Indian FX markets aided by steady regulatory changes. OTC and bilateral transactions dominate in FX markets, but it is not yet clear if technological changes and the international post-global crisis regulatory emphasis on transparency will lead to more trading on exchanges. It may be that FX markets are fundamentally different, with a bilateral market structure essential for stability.

Implications of market structure for CB intervention, signalling and exchange rate policy, especially in an EDE, are next explored. Committing to a low exchange rate volatility regime provides something like a free lunch to monetary policy because, as the analysis in the last section shows, entry of noise traders is reduced, which in turn reduces volatility. In an EDE, there tends to be greater uncertainty about fundamentals. This tends to make the speculative demand curve well behaved under strategic interaction between differentially informed speculators and the CB, so that intervention is stabilising. A diffuse exchange rate target and strategic revelation of selected information can be expected, therefore, to be effective. Indian experience supports these conclusions.

Post-GFC experience is used to derive an effectiveness ranking of Indian policy actions influencing the exchange rate at the current state of capital account convertibility. The most effective policy is to address fundamental weaknesses that can trigger adverse expectations, but second, reserves and signalling can be used to smooth market demand and supply keeping the exchange rate within bounds. The efficacy of building up reserves, using them in targeted intervention and of credible communication to markets was clearly demonstrated. Since capital flows do not always match the net import gap, a CB should be ready to close any short-term demand/supply mismatch. Reserves can be built up again during periods of excessive inflows.

Prudential measures such as reducing open positions worked better than a ban on a market or a transaction type. Market restrictions reverse attempts to deepen markets and result in a migration of activity abroad. If they become necessary, therefore, they should be carefully targeted. Even if credit curbs are used, they should apply only to specific commodities such as gold imports. Since these administrative measures reduce one-way positions, a general liquidity squeeze, such as an interest rate defense that hits other markets, should be avoided. EDEs should continue efforts for greater global policy coordination and measures that reduce the financial overleverage that leads to capital flow volatility, even while developing regional safety nets.

After examining short-run and market structure determinants of the exchange rate, we turn, in the next chapter, to long-run determinants of its value.

Appendix 4.A.1
Deriving equilibrium noise trader entry

Equilibrium requires that a constant number of noise traders, n, enter. Noise trader's benefit from entry rises with ρ and fall with var (S). Entry will occur only as long as this benefit exceeds their cost of entry. Equation 4A.1 defines an implicit, smooth twice-differentiable benefit function:

$$B(\rho, \text{var}(S)); \qquad B'[\rho] > 0, \quad B'(\text{var}(S)) < 0 \qquad (4A.1)$$

where a superscript dash indicates a partial derivative. Trader j will enter the market as long as:

$$B(\rho, \text{var}(S)) \geq c_j \qquad (4A.2)$$

But both ρ and var (S) are functions of n. Equilibrium ρ equates demand to supply in the domestic currency security market. It is given by Equation 4A.3, written implicitly as:

$$\rho^* = \rho(\text{var}(S), n); \quad \rho'(\text{var}(S)) > 0, \quad \rho'(n) < 0 \qquad (4A.3)$$

A superscript * denotes an equilibrium value. Similarly, the equation for equilibrium var(S) is written implicitly as:

$$\text{var}(S)^* = \text{var}(S)(n); \quad \text{var}(S)'(n) > 0 \qquad (4A.4)$$

In equilibrium, either all noise traders will enter or none will enter, or some will enter, so that $n \in [0, \bar{n}]$. If B( ) > c_j for all noise traders, all will enter. If B( ) < c_j, no noise trader will enter. In an equilibrium with interior values, Equation 4A.2 will hold with equality, and $\bar{\rho}^*$ and var $(S)^*$ will take critical values such that the marginal noise trader is just indifferent to entering.

104 *Microstructure of foreign exchange markets*

$$B\left(\rho^*, \text{var}(S)^*\right) = c_i \qquad (4A.5)$$

At $\rho < \rho^*$ or var $(S) >$ var $(S)^*$, benefits to entry are lower than at equilibrium, so n will shrink. Since both ρ and var (S) depend on n, a function $G(n)$ can be defined that determines entry: $G\left(\rho\left(\text{var}(S),n\right), \text{var}(S)(n)\right)$. If $n \neq G(n)$, it cannot be an equilibrium. Hence, equilibrium entry is:

$$n^* = G\left(\rho\left(\text{var}(S),n^*\right), \text{var}(S)\left(n^*\right)\right) \qquad (4A.6)$$

If $B( ) > c_j$, then $n < n^*$, noise trader entry will occur and n will rise. Since ρ falls with n but rises with var (S) and var (S) rises with n, multiple equilibria are possible. $G'(\rho) > 0$ and $G'\left(\text{var}(S)\right) < 0$, therefore although $G(n)$ can be high since var (S) is low, it falls with n at low n as ρ also falls and decreases $G(n)$. The risk-sharing function dominates. But at high n, the positive effect of n on var (S), and therefore on ρ will dominate—ρ will rise as risk rises. Hence, $G(n)$ will also rise with n at high n. Therefore, equilibria are possible both at low and at high n. Either a few or a large number of noise traders will enter the FX market. But in each equilibrium, n takes a fixed value given by the function $G(n)$. Noise traders create risk, so var (S) rises, and share risk, so ρ falls with their entry (n). But ρ also rises with var (S), and therefore rises with further entry.

Notes

1 This section is largely based on material in Lyons (2001), Sarno and Taylor (2002), Sager and Taylor (2006), BIS triennial CB surveys and media reports.
2 Counterparties made large losses as currency volatility spiked after Lehman fell in 2008. The risk to market makers inventory caused spreads on quotes to increase from 4 to 16 pips. Trade froze for some transactions.
3 For example, Indian FX futures markets grew rapidly after they were established but were still thin. If a large party came in on the buy side, the sell side would dry up in anticipation of a price rise.
4 This section, unless explicitly mentioned, updates information in Goyal et al. (2009) and Goyal (2015).
5 BIS (2007) notes this was the fastest rate of growth amongst all world FX markets, although the 72 per cent rate of growth of world FX market activity between 2004 and 2007 was also the fastest. In the next three years, growth was 19 per cent but rose to 35 per cent over 2010–13. BIS measures only OTC market turnover, however.
6 In the absence of full rupee convertibility, a future contract could not result in the delivery of foreign currency. It was netted out in rupees, reducing its usefulness for hedging.

Microstructure of foreign exchange markets   105

7 After zero intervention from January, monthly net purchases in $ million were 10,678 over 2007:10–2008:10. This switched to net sales of 1,505 over 2008:11–2009:4, as outflows intensified under the GFC. Average intervention was near zero at monthly net purchases of 285 over 2009:05–2011:10. But 2011:10–2013:07 saw heavy monthly net sales of 8,580.

8 By entering into fixed tenor sell/buy $/Re swaps through designated banks, the RBI effectively lent dollars against rupees, with the transaction to be reversed in the future as the companies returned the dollars.

9 The net open position measures risks due to a bank's mix of buy and sell positions in different currencies. It is measured by the higher of net buy or net sell positions across all currencies. A zero open position means a bank cannot have foreign currency assets exceed foreign currency liabilities in its balance sheet or have an unsettled buy position in foreign currency. This reduces selling pressure on the rupee coming from banks.

10 I thank Dr. Y. V. Reddy for this point.

11 This analysis is based on Goyal et al. (2009).

12 It is noteworthy that the relative size of forwards in net-net and net-gross global GBP trade in the United Kingdom is reversed for the United Kingdom, which is the deepest FX market. In April 2013, the net-gross was at US$ 309 billion was much larger than net-net at US$ 69 billion. The reason is large trade in international currencies taking place domestically. FX trade in the United Kingdom is very large in currencies other than the GBP, including the INR. It follows a large share of transactions involving the INR occurring abroad. Relative turnover sizes for other EDEs are like that for India.

13 For example, of the US$ 2.8 billion that came in October 2014, 28 per cent was for refinancing.

14 * denotes advanced material.

15 The style of proof is similar to the well-known Keynesian cross where the AD line cuts the 45 degree AS line from above in a stable equilibrium. The intuition is similar in the fixed point theorems used in general equilibrium theory. The proof following Goyal (2006), a major simplification of that used in Jeanne and Rose (2002), is given in the Appendix.

16 Higher entry of noise traders was illustrated by the large-scale shorting of the INR in December 2011, after the CB's communications were taken to imply it would not intervene to support the rupee.

References

Behera, H. 2011. 'Onshore and Offshore Market for Indian Rupee: Recent Evidence on Volatility and Shock Spillover', *Macroeconomics and Finance in Emerging Market Economies*, 4(1): 43–55.

BIS (Bank of International Settlements). 2013. 'Triennial Central Bank Survey of Foreign Exchange and Derivatives Market Activity in 2013'. December, and earlier reports. Available at www.bis.org/publ/rpfx13.htm.

Geithner, T. J. 2004. 'Hedge Funds and Their Implications for the Financial System', *Federal Reserve Bank of New York*. Available at www.newyorkfed.org/newsevents/speeches/2004/gei041117.html.

Goyal, A. 2006. 'Exchange Rate Regimes: Middling Through', *Global Economic Review*, 35(2): 153–176, June.

106 *Microstructure of foreign exchange markets*

Goyal, A. 2015. 'External Shocks', Chapter 3 in S. Mahendra Dev (ed.), *India Development Report 2015*, pp. 36–51. New Delhi: IGIDR and Oxford University Press. Earlier version available at www.igidr.ac.in/pdf/publication/WP-2014-046.pdf.

Goyal, A. and S. Arora. 2012. 'The Indian Exchange Rate and Central Bank Action: An EGARCH Analysis', *Journal of Asian Economics*, 23(1), February: 60–72.

Goyal, A., R. A. Nair and A. Samantaraya. 2009. 'Monetary Policy, Forex Markets, and Feedback under Uncertainty in an Opening Economy', *Development Research Group, Department of Economic Analysis and Policy*, Mumbai, Study No. 32. Available at http://rbidocs.rbi.org.in/rdocs/Publications/PDFs/DRGMP030909.pdf.

IMF (International Monetary Fund). 2008. 'India: Selected Issues', *IMF Country Report No. 08/52*, January. Washington: IMF.

Jeanne, O. and A. K. Rose. 2002. 'Noise Trading and Exchange Rate Regimes', *The Quarterly Journal of Economics*, 117(469): 537–570.

Lyons, R. K. 2001. *The Microstructure Approach to Exchange Rates*, Cambridge, MA: MIT Press.

Ma, G., C. Ho and R. N. McCauley. 2004. 'The Markets for Non-Deliverable Forwards in Asian Currencies', *BIS Quarterly Review*: 81–94, June.

Mecklai, J. 2010a. 'Market Maniac: Bringing Hedgers to the Futures Market', *Business Standard*, January 8. Available at www.business-standard.com/article/opinion/jamal-mecklai-bringing-hedgers-to-the-futures-market-110010800002_1.html.

Mecklai, J. 2010b. 'Market Maniac: The OTC-FX Market – Falling behind the Curve', *Business Standard*, October 1. Available at www.business-standard.com/article/opinion/jamal-mecklai-otc-fx-market-falling-behind-the-curve-110100100093_1.html.

Rathinam, F. X. and D. Arora. 2011. 'OTC Derivatives Markets in India: Recent Regulatory Initiatives and Open Issues for Market Stability and Development', *Macroeconomics and Finance in Emerging Market Economies*, 4(2): 235–261, September. Available at www.tandfonline.com/doi/pdf/10.1080/17520843.2011.580571.

RBI (Reserve Bank of India). 1995. *Report of the Expert Group on Foreign Exchange Markets in India*, Chairman: Sodhani. June. Mumbai: RBI.

Sager, M. J. and M. P. Taylor. 2006. 'Under the Microscope: The Structure of the Foreign Exchange Market', *International Journal of Finance and Economics*, 11: 81–95.

Sarno, L. and M. P. Taylor. 2002. *The Economics of Exchange Rates*, Cambridge, UK: Cambridge University Press.

Tarapore, S. S. 2006. 'Report of the Committee on Fuller Capital Account Convertibility', *Reserve Bank of India: Mumbai*.

5 Purchasing power parity and the exchange rate

Water finds its own level.

5.1 Introduction

In Chapter 4, we took the expected nominal exchange rate to be given exogenously. In this chapter, we begin to examine more carefully what determines equilibrium real, and therefore expected nominal exchange rates.

Trade arbitrage between any two countries should lead to a nominal exchange rate that is proportional to the relative price levels of the two countries. This is known as the purchasing power parity (PPP) nominal exchange rate. PPP, thus, links the nominal exchange rate to relative price levels. It implies the bilateral exchange rate between two countries is the ratio of their price levels. The concept has been known for centuries, although it was given its modern name by Gustav Cassel in 1918.[1] Although there is little empirical support for PPP, it serves as a benchmark and is a major component especially of the monetary theories of the exchange rate.

In this chapter, we explain absolute and relative PPP and the underlying law of one price (LOOP). Then, we survey some of the empirical tests of these theories, before turning to reasons why they may fail to hold.

The remainder of the chapter is structured as follows: Section 5.2 derives PPP and its variants from trade arbitrage. Section 5.3 reports on tests of trade arbitrage and Section 5.4 on why PPP is difficult to establish empirically, before Section 5.5 concludes with a summary of the chapter contents. Appendix 5.A.1 has a formal derivation of the Balassa-Samuelson (BS) result on why the real exchange rate is more appreciated in richer countries.

108 *Purchasing power parity and exchange rate*

5.2 Trade arbitrage

Just as arbitrage determines equilibrium under UIP, trade arbitrage affects the real equilibrium value of a currency. PPP exchange rate between two currencies is the rate, which would equate the two relevant national price levels if they were expressed in a common currency. That is, the purchasing power of a unit of one currency would be the same in both economies. Since there is no difference between domestic and international purchasing power, parity holds. Under trade arbitrage, a good should have the same price in the same currency in different countries, so that no opportunity for trade arbitrage is left. This is expected to give the value of the nominal exchange rate in the long run. The real exchange rate is then obtained by deflating the nominal exchange rate by relative prices, since this gives the relative price of the foreign good basket in terms of the domestic basket. The real exchange rate is the relative price of two output baskets.

Trade arbitrage implies:

$$S_t P_t^* = P_t \tag{5.1}$$

P_t is the domestic and P_t^* the international price level. If $P_t > S_t P_t^*$, trade arbitrage should occur, and as imports increase domestic supply, P_t should fall removing the arbitrage opportunity.

If small letters denote natural logs, Equation 5.1 can be written in levels and in logarithms, respectively, as:

$$S_t = P_t / P_t^* \text{ or } s_t = p_t - p_t^* \tag{5.2}$$

That is, the bilateral nominal exchange rate is the ratio of the price levels of the two countries. If Equation 5.2 holds, it implies the real exchange rate Q_t must be unity, as can be seen by substituting Equation 5.2 in Equation 5.3 or by deriving Q_t from Equation 5.1:

$$Q_t = \frac{S_t P_t^*}{P_t} = 1 \tag{5.3}$$

If the nominal exchange rate is the price of one currency in terms of the other, the real exchange rate is the nominal exchange rate adjusted for relative national price-level differences (Sarno and Taylor, 2002, p. 51). That is, it is the relative purchasing power of one country relative to another. Q_t written in logs would be:

$$q_t \equiv s_t - p_t + p_t^* \tag{5.4}$$

Purchasing power parity and exchange rate 109

If absolute PPP holds, the real exchange rate must equal unity, and since log 1 = 0, so q_t must equal zero. It is free of units, since the Re/$ cancels out between the nominal exchange rate and the two price levels. If the nominal exchange rate is the ratio of two price levels, the real exchange rate is that ratio free of units. PPP provides an anchor for the long-run value of the real exchange rate. It serves as a benchmark for comparison of national currencies to determine their overvaluation or undervaluation.

$Q \neq 1$ implies a deviation from absolute PPP. 'Relative PPP' is said to hold when the rate of depreciation of one currency relative to the other equals the difference in aggregate price inflation between the two countries. This implies a constant Q or constant deviation from PPP, so the real exchange rate does not change. Differentiating Equation 5.4 gives the change in nominal exchange rate. This is determined by inflation differentials when Q is constant, so relative PPP holds. Although the nominal exchange rate no longer equals the relative price, its rate of change equals the inflation differential. The currency of the country with the higher inflation would depreciate under relative PPP.

$$\dot{s}_t = \pi_t - \pi_t^* \tag{5.5}$$

Multilateral nominal and real effective exchange rates are defined as trade weighted exchange rates, with the real exchange rate corrected for inflation differentials. Box 5.1 shows how the Indian NEER and REER are calculated.

Law of one price: Trade arbitrage actually occurs at the level of individual goods. This is the basis of the LOOP. In frictionless markets, if goods are perfect substitutes, arbitrage should equate prices in the same currency for each good i, i running from 1 to n.

$$P_{i,t} = S_t P_{i,t}^* \qquad i = 1, 2 \ldots n$$

Summing over i goods then gives the PPP relation as a weighted average. The weights are based on a typical consumption basket and sum to one.

$$\sum_{i=1}^{N} \alpha_i P_{i,t} = S_t \sum_{i=1}^{N} \alpha_i P_{i,t}^*$$
$$\sum_{i=1}^{N} \alpha_i = 1$$

If relative PPP holds, so that depreciation equals the difference in aggregate inflation between the two countries, then the relationship

110 *Purchasing power parity and exchange rate*

between changing nominal exchange rates and prices at the level of the individual good are given by:

$$\frac{P^*_{i,t+1}S_{t+1}}{P_{i,t+1}} = \frac{P^*_{i,t}S_t}{P_{i,t}} \qquad i = 1, 2, \ldots n$$

Box 5.1 The Indian nominal and real effective exchange rate

In this chapter, we work with bilateral exchange rates, but any country trades with a large number of countries, so multilateral exchange rates are the relevant ones. In India, effective exchange rates are defined as a weighted average of bilateral exchange rates with its major trading partners. They are reported with both 36 and 6 country weights.

The six-currency trade-based NEER and REER are constructed on a daily as well as monthly basis. The currencies chosen are US dollar, euro, pound sterling, Japanese yen, renminbi and Hong Kong dollar.

NEER is the weighted geometric average of the bilateral nominal exchange rates of the home currency in terms of foreign currencies. The formula is:

$$NEER = \prod_{i=1}^{6} (e/e_i)^{w_i}$$

REER is the weighted average of NEER adjusted by the ratio of domestic inflation rate to foreign inflation rates. The formula is:

$$REER = \prod_{i=1}^{6} [(e/e_i)(P/P_i)]^{w_i}$$

where

e: Exchange rate of rupee against a numeraire (SDRs; i.e. SDRs per rupee; in index form)

e_i: Exchange rate of currency i against the numeraire (SDRs; i.e. SDRs per currency i)

(i = US dollar, euro, pound sterling, Japanese yen, renminbi, Hong Kong dollar)

Purchasing power parity and exchange rate 111

W_i: Weights attached to currency/country i in the index as a function of bilateral trade

P: India's WPI (in index form)

P_i: CPI of country i (in index form)

With this convention, a rise in the NEER or the REER is an appreciation and vice versa, since SDR is the numerator. In 2014, the CPI began to be used for India's price level, and P in the formula as a new broad-based index became available. But since CPI exceeded WPI over 2007–15, the REER calculated using CPI was more appreciated. The CPI is more relevant for the REER as a measure of the purchasing power of a currency, but WPI has a larger share of traded goods.

5.3   Testing LOOP and PPP[2]

Extensive econometric tests of LOOP and PPP reject both during the floating rate regimes, when markets were free to drive exchange rates towards equilibrium. Deviations from LOOP are highly volatile. Volatility of relative prices is considerably lower than the volatility of nominal exchange rates. A simple test of PPP is to estimate $s_t = \alpha + \beta p_t + \beta^* p_t^* + \mu_t$ to test the hypotheses H_0: $\beta = 1$, $\beta^* = -1$, which if satisfied implies absolute PPP. That β and β^* are equal and of opposite signs is known as the symmetry condition, and that they respectively take the values of unity and minus unity is known as the proportionality condition. If the variables are taken in first differences, it is a test of relative PPP.

These simple tests reject PPP. But there are problems in these estimations. For example, dynamics are missing. It is necessary to distinguish between the short and the long run.

Both s_t and price levels are endogenous; so, instrument variables are required. If both s_t and p_t/p_t^* are non-stationary, the regression becomes spurious, the residuals are not stationary and bias in estimated standard errors makes statistical inference invalid. Time series methods are required.

A first step is to test for the existence of a unit root in the real exchange rate. The condition for PPP is that q_t or 'equilibrium error' from PPP is stationary over time. If not, S_t and relative price P_t/P_t^* will permanently tend to diverge. The next step is to test for cointegration

112 *Purchasing power parity and exchange rate*

using the Johansen method. A linear combination of any non-stationary series, integrated of the same order, is cointegrated if a linear combination of the two is stationary. Cointegration of S_t and relative prices will imply PPP holds in the long run. But even if stationarity of q_t holds in the long term, as is necessary for PPP, short-run dynamics can exist that allows q_t to vary.

There are other refinements: for example, using long spans to increase the power of the tests. Working with panel data is one way to increase the span, which is otherwise restricted by the length of floating rate regimes. But since the null hypothesis taken is of unit root (joint non-stationarity) in all the real exchange rates, probability of rejection is high if even one of the series is stationary. But this cannot be taken as supporting PPP in all the countries.

Some evidence has been found of non-linear mean reversion to fundamentals in the long run, with adjustment being faster further from equilibrium and for large shocks, but slowing down in a narrow band around the equilibrium. Disagreement about equilibrium values may allow chartist or trend following behaviour to dominate in the short run or for small shocks, giving rise to a unit root in the data. As the deviation from fundamentals becomes large, there is greater consensus about the direction of movement towards fundamentals. So, even though the exchange rate does not follow a RW, deviations from PPP can last long.[3]

Apart from non-linear adjustment, another source of upward bias in the estimation of the half-life of real exchange rate deviations is if the length of time between observed data points exceeds the frequency at which the exchange rate adjusts. Evidence supporting PPP is more when WPI rather than CPI or even the GDP deflator is used, since the first has a smaller share of non-tradables that are not subject to trade arbitrage. The next section explores the reasons why trade arbitrage may not occur.

5.4   Failures of trade arbitrage

There are many reasons why trade arbitrage can be expected to be incomplete. First, the real world is not frictionless – transaction costs are not zero. Rogoff (1996) comes to the conclusion that the answer to what he calls the PPP puzzle must lie in factors like transaction costs and other barriers that prevent perfect trade integration. This is, however, an ad hoc explanation. Transaction costs themselves need to be explained.

Deviations from LOOP are expected because of tariffs, transport costs and the border effect. The border effect adds on to real

Purchasing power parity and exchange rate 113

transaction costs. Two equidistant locations are likely to have lower price differentials if they are in the same country. A physical border has been found in itself to increase the volatility and persistence of price differentials. For example, catalogues on international airlines typically have prices printed in many currencies. Menu costs of printing catalogues means they are not changed frequently. As exchange rates change, the prices diverge much beyond currency conversion costs without provoking a switch to the cheapest currency – a pure example of the border effect despite zero distance. There are also psychological factors, such as comfort, in using own currency despite perceptible arbitrage differences.

Second, PPP is obtained by aggregation from LOOP, so the average can differ if price index weights differ across countries and also shift over time. Since inflation data in different countries are based on different commodity baskets, trade arbitrage cannot offset these official inflation differentials.

Third, product differentiation allows producers to act as discriminating monopolists and vary prices in geographically separated markets according to the elasticity of demand. Pricing to market (PTM) or local currency pricing (LCP) reduces the pass through of changes in the nominal exchange rate. Producer or exporter currency pricing implies import prices would move one to one with the domestic exchange rate, so that pass through is complete. This may be true for commodities, which tend to be priced in dollars, but manufactured products demonstrate considerable stability in local prices. PTM may occur also because of menu costs faced by firms in changing prices and switching costs for consumers in shifting to other products, implying an adjustment time for exchange rate pass through, so that effects would differ in the short and long term.

A more recent literature (Gopinath et al., 2010) makes the firm's choice of currency for invoicing endogenous. When exporting firms set prices in the foreign markets, they face the choice of either invoicing in their own country's currency, importer's currency, or in the reserve currency.[4] Invoice choice is a microeconomic decision, but it has significant macroeconomic impacts due to the pass through of exchange rate changes. If exporting firms invoice in the importer's currency, zero pass through is expected, while full pass through is expected if the invoicing is based on exporter's currency or in hard currencies. LCP is said to exist when domestic prices of imported goods do not respond to changes in the exchange rates, while producer currency pricing is said to exist when imported goods respond to exchange rate changes. If import prices do not rise, there is no impact on aggregate prices and domestic inflation.

114 *Purchasing power parity and exchange rate*

If a firm desires low exchange rate passes through in the short run, it resorts to LCP. The pass through is incomplete when both markups and prices adjust less than proportionately to exchange rate changes. The degree to which the markups are adjusted to exchange rate changes is the degree to which the firms follow PTM. A firm faces stiff competition in international markets if its goods are close substitutes to those of its competitors. Then, it is more likely to price the commodity in the importer's currency, thus reducing pass through but raising both its profits and the consumer's welfare. If hard or reserve currency use is the norm, this option becomes less likely.

Fourth, price impulses impinge heterogeneously across the various goods and services in an economy. Trade arbitrage affects the prices of traded goods, but not directly those of non-traded goods. The CPI has a significant non-traded component, so the WPI is used in tests of PPP.

A major reason for the failure of PPP is the dominance of non-tradable goods in the consumption basket. These include difficult to transport goods such as services. Any good for which the transport cost is large in relation to the production cost becomes difficult to trade. Traded goods are largely manufactured goods, agricultural products, raw materials and services traded through the Internet. Non-tariff barriers can make some of these also non-traded goods. Expensive services, such as medical, construction, hospitality and entertainment, reduce purchasing power in any country. Domestic demand and supply determine the prices of such goods and they are part of the country's price level.

Fifth, since the relative price of non-traded services is lower in developing countries, the nominal exchange rate calculated as the ratio of such prices (the PPP rate) is typically much more appreciated (Q_t lower) compared to the actual exchange rate.[5] If $S_t P_t^* > P_t$, the purchasing power of the home country is higher at home than it is abroad or Q_t is > 1 since $S_t > P_t / P_t^*$. That is, the PPP nominal exchange rate P_t / P_t^* is less than S_t, so the currency is overvalued in the sense it can buy more at home than it can abroad.

Purchasing power of any currency falls at home when its non-traded goods prices rise. To the extent traded goods prices are equalised, the real exchange rate changes largely with changes in non-traded goods relative prices.

Working with these relative prices, the BS effect offers a useful explanation for a lower average price level or higher domestic real purchasing power of the currency in EDEs. Since the real exchange rate is the relative international price level across two countries, it explains deviations of the real exchange rate from

Purchasing power parity and exchange rate   115

PPP. The deviation is explained using international productivity differences across traded and non-traded sectors. Wages are equalised across traded and non-traded goods in each country. Productivity is higher in both sectors in the rich country compared to the poor country. But the productivity gap is higher in tradables than in non-tradables. So, wages in the non-tradable sector will exceed productivity in that sector in the rich country. Relative prices of non-tradables will rise and the price level, which is the average of the two sectors, will be pushed up in the rich country. This explains why AE currencies can buy less in PPP terms.[6] The BS result is derived using log differentiation of sectoral marginal productivity conditions in Appendix 5.A.1. A large number of empirical studies have found some support for the result.[7]

The Bhagwati-Kravis-Lipsey effect provides an alternative explanation. This is based on higher capital compared to labour endowments in richer countries together with greater labour intensity in the non-tradable sector. The first means the average wage level is higher and the second that non-tradable prices are higher because of relatively expensive labour in richer countries giving them a higher price level.

Relative PPP was a reasonable approximation of stylised facts averaged over long periods, prior to the period of floating exchange rates, but after that, the volatility of nominal exchange rates has generally exceeded that of price levels. Price ratios tend to be more stable than nominal exchange rates. Relative PPP, therefore, is of limited use even as a characterisation of long-run stylised facts, although there is some evidence of non-linear convergence to thresholds.

But, even if after econometric and other refinements it was possible to provide some support for PPP, thus reducing the first PPP puzzle, there is a second puzzle. Although there is mean reversion, the half-life of PPP deviations is about 3–5 years. Since real (taste, technology) shocks are not volatile enough to account for observed deviations, it follows nominal shocks must be large and persistent. Nominal shocks do have persistent effects on real variables, but the current consensus is the effect of nominal shocks lasts only as long as wage and price stickiness lasts, which is much less than 3–5 years.

The consensus, so far, is that monetary shocks have significant but transitory effects. VAR-based studies used to identify shocks suggest both nominal and real shocks explain nominal and real exchange rate movements in AEs, but their relative importance varies over studies. There are few studies for EDEs, but the consensus is that real exchange rates in such countries are largely driven by real shocks. The BS effect can cause predictable departures from PPP, also, over the long run.

116 *Purchasing power parity and exchange rate*

So, further work is required to unravel relative contribution of nominal exchange rate and nominal price ratios to changes in q_t in EDEs to find stronger evidence for the non-traded goods prices BS effect and labour market changes with development and to examine the effect of official exchange rate intervention and the relative impact of monetary and fiscal policy, including government demand for non-tradable goods.

Box 5.2 The Indian state-induced Balassa-Samuelson effect

India has a highly segmented labour market, so the BS assumption of wage equalisation does not hold. It also has large unemployment in different labour market segments. Large numbers of unskilled labour, since even in 2015 53 per cent of the population depended on agriculture, were thought to keep wages low in the subsistence category. Growth in real wages for rural unskilled male labourers was often negative before September 2007, but became positive after that. Although output growth rates fell, real wages rose sharply. Nominal wage growth far exceeded that in the relevant CPI. Real wage growth peaked at 12.5 per cent in January 2012.[8]

Goyal and Baikar (2015) estimated dynamic panel regressions using data on state-level monthly wages for rural unskilled labour. This is just the category targeted for schemes such as MGNREGS. It also has a high share of food in its consumption basket. WPI food inflation and the fiscal deficit were found to have the most consistently significant effect on rural unskilled wage inflation. A large share of government expenditure in rural areas went to construction. The MGNREGS may have raised the wages of the subsistence segment, especially since state governments competed with each other to raise minimum wages as the Centre was footing part of the bill. A dummy variable for the years MGNREGS spread through the country, however, came in with the wrong sign. But announcement of a steep rise as part of indexation of MGNREGS wages in 2011 significantly raised rural wages. The indexation was also partly a response to high food inflation. There may have been overcorrection to food price peaks, in the setting of MGNREGS wages. Special circumstances of repeated food price peaks and large government

Purchasing power parity and exchange rate 117

spending drove an unusually sharp rise in real wages, so that real wage growth could soften if these conditions did not persist. It did indeed begin to fall by 2012.

The BS result requires the productivity differential between traded and non-traded goods sectors to be higher in AEs compared to EDEs. So, inflation in EDEs is often attributed to the catch-up process, where productivity in traded goods starts growing faster than that in non-traded goods and wage equalisation causes inflation. But Indian inflation over 2008–15 is better explained by wages growing at a productivity growth relatively higher in non-traded goods compared to that in traded goods (dominated by agriculture), while nominal shocks triggered deviations from equilibrium and adjustments that sustained inflation (Goyal, 2014). This framework retains the BS ranking of relatively higher productivity in traded goods in AEs and is consistent with a lack of domestic reforms that reduced productivity in traded goods. The latter are also more dependent on physical infrastructure where bottlenecks remain.

Exchange rate volatility was high in this period as a consequence of risk-on risk-off capital flows following the GFC. As the real exchange rate deviated from the level required for external balance, it therefore lead to further nominal depreciation. But as this leads to a deviation from the level compatible with a real wage target in terms of food prices, it can sustain inflation. Nominal wages rise in response to a nominal depreciation. Thus, the exchange rate is trapped in a region of continuous inflationary pressure.

Exchange rate policy can abort external price shocks that can otherwise set off a wage-price spiral. In the longer term, of course, improvements in productivity are required that remove the shortfalls in actual from target wages and the gaps between target and equilibrium real exchange rates that otherwise tend to sustain inflation.

A possible solution to persistent wage inflation is a real exchange rate appreciation. A nominal appreciation is the best way of achieving any required real appreciation. In its absence, inflation achieves the same effect with much higher social cost. Since nominal appreciation was resisted, India did end up having much higher inflation than the rest of the world over the years 2007–12. So, the BS affect does contribute to explain Indian inflation, but with a peculiar Indian twist. A forced version of the BS held in India, with the wage differential narrowed by government

118 *Purchasing power parity and exchange rate*

action, while productivity rose more in non-traded goods. Since monetary shocks have persistent real effects in the presence of real wage rigidities, macroeconomic policies have a critical role.

5.5 Summary

This chapter introduced some key building blocks of the monetary approach (MA) to open economy macroeconomics. Just as UIP was derived from arbitrage across assets offering different returns, trade arbitrage implies that a good priced in the same currency should cost the same in two different countries. This is the LOOP. The same principle, expressed in average price levels, is PPP.

PPP has powerful implications for the nominal and the real exchange rates. It implies that the bilateral nominal exchange is the ratio of the price levels of the two countries and the bilateral real exchange rate is the ratio of the two price levels expressed in the same currency. If PPP holds, the real exchange rate must be unity. If the latter is a constant not equal to unity, it implies the rate of depreciation of one currency relative to the other equals the difference in aggregate price inflation between the two countries. Then, relative PPP holds.

A series of econometric tests and their successive refinements, however, have not been able to establish PPP or its weaker versions in the floating rate regime. While real exchange rates were generally stable in the pre-Bretton Woods fixed exchange rate regimes, the belief in continuous PPP that characterised the monetary theories that dominated in the switch to floating exchange rates could not be empirically supported. Exchange rates were highly volatile while relative prices were less so. But unit-root tests require a long data span which was missing, so the rejection of PPP was also questionable. There is some evidence supporting non-linear reversion to PPP, but disaggregated tests of LOOP also find failures depending on industry structure and the currency of denomination.

There are a number of reasons trade arbitrage may fail. These include aggregation problems, transaction costs, tariff and non-tariff barriers, industry structure and the presence of non-tradable goods. This chapter explores these, in particular the BS effect, which explains why price levels are lower in poorer countries or their real exchange rate is more depreciated. With a rise in per capita income levels, therefore, the real exchange rate would tend to appreciate in such countries. With an understanding of PPP, we can turn to the MA in the next chapter.

Appendix 5.A.1
The Balassa-Samuelson effect

Assume smooth CRS production functions for both traded, T, and non-traded goods N, with different total factor productivities A for the two goods. Output Y is a function of labour L and capital K. The derivation is adapted from Obstfeld and Rogoff (1996, p. 210).

$$Y_T = A_T F(K_T, L_T) \tag{5A.1}$$

$$Y_N = A_N G(K_N, L_N) \tag{5A.2}$$

Total labour supply is employed in the production of the two goods:

$$L = L_T + L_N$$

The price of traded goods is taken as the numeraire:

$$p = p_N; p_T = 1$$

So, p is also the relative price p_N / p_T.

Price and productivity variables are transformed as:

$$\hat{X} \equiv d\log X = dX / X$$

Thus, a hat over a variable denotes a logarithmic derivative giving the percentage rate of change. Labour cost per unit output is:

$$\mu_{LT} \equiv wL_T / Y_T; \mu_{LN} = wL_N / pY_N \tag{5A.3}$$

Y_T is nominal tradable goods output, since p_T is normalised to unity, and w is nominal wages. CRS production functions imply the

120 *Purchasing power parity and exchange rate*

pricing equations can be obtained by maximising profit subject to the technology:

$$0 = \mu_{LT}\hat{w} - \hat{A}_T \tag{5A.4}$$

$$\hat{p} = \mu_{LN}\hat{w} - \hat{A}_N \tag{5A.5}$$

The growth in wages is equated over the two sectors and given by:

$$\hat{w} = \frac{\hat{A}_T}{\mu_{LT}} = \frac{\hat{P}_N + \hat{A}_N}{\mu_{LN}}.$$

Substituting for $\hat{w}$ in (5A.5) from (5A.4):

$$\hat{p} = \frac{\mu_{LN}}{\mu_{LT}}\hat{A}_T - \hat{A}_N \tag{5A.6}$$

The other country has identical production functions, but factor productivities A_T^*, A_N^* are different. In addition:

p: Home price of non-tradables in terms of tradables

p^*: Foreign price of non-tradables in terms of tradables

Therefore, if there is PPP in traded goods so their price is unity in both countries, price levels, given by a weighted average of traded and non-traded goods prices, are:

$$P = (1)^{\gamma}(p)^{1-\gamma} = p^{1-\gamma}; \qquad P^* = (1)^{\gamma}(p^*)^{1-\gamma} = (p^*)^{1-\gamma}$$

P for each country is a geometric weighted mean of tradable and non-tradable goods prices, with weight $1 - \gamma$ for non-tradable prices, and tradables as the numeraire having a common price of 1 in both countries. Therefore, foreign (AE) to home (EDE) price-level ratio or the real exchange rate depends only on the relative price of non-tradables (since S is normalised to unity):

$$\frac{P^*}{P} = \left(\frac{p^*}{p}\right)^{1-\gamma} \tag{5A.7}$$

It is the real exchange rate, since it is free of units. Log differentiating Equation 5A.7 and using Equation 5A.6:

$$\hat{P}^* - \hat{P} = (1-\gamma)(\hat{p}^* - \hat{p}) = (1-\gamma)\left[\frac{\mu_{LN}}{\mu_{LT}}\left(\hat{A}_T^* - \hat{A}_T\right) - \left(\hat{A}_N^* - \hat{A}_N\right)\right] \tag{5A.8}$$

Purchasing power parity and exchange rate   121

The share of labour in non-tradable goods μ_{LN} is assumed to exceed the share of labour in tradable goods. That is, $\mu_{LN} > \mu_{LT}$ or non-tradables are more labour intensive. Then, $\frac{\mu_{LN}}{\mu_{LT}} \geq 1$, the labour share ratio is greater than one.

If the foreign (AE) productivity growth gap is higher in tradable compared to non-tradable goods, the foreign price level will be higher. That is, if $\hat{A}_T^* - \hat{A}_T > A_N^* - \hat{A}_N < 0$ (or the richer [AE] country's productivity advantage in T is relatively greater than in N), $\hat{P}^* > \hat{P}$ or the home (EDE) country's real exchange rate ($Q = P^*/P$) is depreciated, exceeding unity.

While the productivity gap is lower in N, productivity is normally much higher in T, so richer countries have a real appreciation. The BS effect also implies that price levels tend to rise with real per capita income, as the productivity gap between foreign and home countries in tradables shrinks.

Notes

1 See Froot and Rogoff (1995) and Taylor and Taylor (2004) for a review of the concept of PPP and debates about it, and Taylor (2002) for a historical perspective.
2 * denotes advanced material.
3 See Sarno and Taylor (2002) for a more detailed survey of empirical tests of PPP.
4 The exception is the United States where the reserve currency is the local currency. Since the majority of US imports are priced in dollars, there is little pass through of dollar depreciation. For a country like India, 86 per cent of whose imports are priced in dollars, rupee depreciation raises import prices.
5 For example, the *Economist*'s famous Big Mac PPP exchange rate calculated as a ratio of the price of a similar burger in New Delhi and in New York would give a value of 30 INR/US$ in 2014 compared to the nominal exchange rate which was almost double. If the price of a burger in New Delhi, P_t, is Rs. 60 and that in New York, P_t^*, the PPP nominal Re/$ rate P_t/P_t^* is US$ 2. If $S_t = 60$ instead of the PPP value of 30, $Q_t = S_t P_t/P_t^* = 2$ instead of unity. The rupee's purchasing power is higher in India. The real exchange rate is depreciated, as it can buy less in the United States than it can in India. The burger index would typically exceed the nominal exchange rate in countries such as Japan or Germany.
6 Just differences in aggregate productivity would not explain changes in relative prices, since higher productivity in one country would allow it to absorb higher wages without rising price levels. The real exchange rate then would not be affected.
7 See Ito et al. (1999), Choudhri et al. (2005) and Lothian and Taylor (2008). Lee and Tang (2007) study the effect of productivity on real exchange rates.
8 After real rural unskilled wage growth around zero over 2004–08, these wages (deflated by CPI rural labour indices) grew at 7 per cent from November 2010 to October 2012.

122 *Purchasing power parity and exchange rate*

References

Choudhri, E. U. and M. S. Khan. 2005. 'Real Exchange Rates in Developing Countries: Are Balassa-Samuelson Effects Present?', *IMF Staff Papers*, 52(3): 387–409. Available at www.imf.org/external/pubs/ft/staffp/2005/04/pdf/choudhri.pdf.

Froot, K. A. and K. Rogoff. 1995. 'Perspectives on PPP and Long-Run Real Exchange Rates', Chapter 32 in G. M. Grossman and K. Rogoff (eds.), *Handbook of International Economics*, 1st edition, Vol. 3, pp. 1647–1688. North Holland, Amsterdam: Elsevier.

Gopinath, G., O. Itskhoki and R. Rigobon. 2010. 'Currency Choice and Exchange Rate Pass Through', *American Economic Review*, 100(1): 304–336.

Goyal, A. 2014. 'Purchasing Power Parity, Wages and Inflation in Emerging Markets', *Foreign Trade Review*, 49(4): 327–347.

Goyal, A. and A. Baikar. 2015. 'Psychology or Cyclicality: Rural Wage and Inflation Dynamics in India', *Economic and Political Weekly*, 50(23): 116–125.

Ito, T., P. Isard and S. Symansky. 1999. 'Economic Growth and Real Exchange Rate: An Overview of the Balassa-Samuelson Hypothesis in Asia', in Takatoshi Ito and Anne O. Krueger (eds.), *Changes in Exchange Rates in Rapidly Developing Countries: Theory, Practice, and Policy Issues: NBER-EASE*, Vol. 7, pp. 109–132. Chicago: University of Chicago Press. Available at http://www.nber.org/chapters/c8616.pdf.

Lee, J. and M. K. Tang. 2007. 'Does Productivity Growth Appreciate the Real Exchange Rate?', *Review of International Economics*, 15(1): 164–187. Blackwell Publishing.

Lothian, J. R. and M. P. Taylor. 2008. 'Real Exchange Rates over the Past Two Centuries: How Important is the Harrod-Balassa-Samuelson Effect', *Economic Journal Royal Economic Society*, 118(532): 1742–1763, October.

Obstfeld, M. and K. Rogoff. 1996. *Foundations of International Macroeconomics*, Cambridge, MA: MIT Press.

Rogoff, K. 1996. 'The Purchasing Power Parity Puzzle', *Journal of Economic Literature*, 34: 647–688, June.

Sarno, L. and M. P. Taylor. 2002. *The Economics of Exchange Rates*, Cambridge, UK: Cambridge University Press.

Taylor, A. M. 2002. 'A Century of Purchasing-Power Parity', *The Review of Economics and Statistics*, 84(1): 139–150, February.

Taylor, A. M. and M. P. Taylor. 2004. 'The Purchasing Power Parity Debate', *Journal of Economic Perspectives, American Economic Association*, 18(4): 135–158, Fall.

6 The monetary approach to the exchange rate

Steam escapes from any vent.

6.1 Introduction

Purchasing power parity (PPP) is an important component of the monetary approach (MA) in which relative money supplies are the fundamentals determining the nominal exchange rate. A key component of the MA is the money market equilibrium, which determines the nominal interest rates, thus endogenising another variable we have so far taken as given. The MA to the exchange rate can be divided into the flexible price monetary approach (FPMA) and the sticky price monetary approach (SPMA). FPMA is the standard MA. The asset price approach to the determination of exchange rates, explored in Chapter 3, plays a major part in the SPMA. The FPMA is presented in addition to the SPMA, and the very different behaviour of the interest rate under the SPMA compared to the FPMA is drawn out.

In floating exchange rate regimes, the exchange rate, as an asset price, is a jump variable that can change rapidly. The combination of highly flexible exchange rates with sticky goods market prices was the foundation of modern open economy macroeconomics. Dornbusch (1976), in a seminal paper, showed how the exchange rate could overshoot its fundamental value under a monetary shock to compensate for slow adjustment in goods prices. In translating this base to the idiom of modern macroeconomics, Obstfeld and Rogoff (1996) attempted a comprehensive unification of the scattered field of open economy macroeconomics. They provided microfoundations for the Dornbusch result, starting with the representative forward-looking consumer of modern macroeconomics and working out the consequences of monetary shocks under sticky and flexible prices. Sticky prices are a basis for Keynesian-type real effects of monetary shocks.

124   *Monetary approach to the exchange rate*

While monetary shocks can have real effects in the Dornbusch model, these are only temporary, lasting as long as prices are sticky. Therefore, this is also known as the SPMA – it continues to have similar long-term results as the MA. The real effects of monetary shocks do not persist into the long term. In the modern open economy approach, however, monetary shocks can have persistent effects because of wealth creation through the BOP.

Dornbusch's paper had a major impact also, because it explained some new facts: the excess volatility observed in exchange rates as many developed countries shifted to floating regimes. Changes in nominal exchange rates far exceeded those in relative prices. The asset approach was also relevant because of the increasing role returns from holding currencies played as currency values began to vary.

In this chapter, we develop the basic intuition of the overshooting result given its importance. We also examine the determinants of the domestic interest rate and exchange rate expectations, thus making endogenous more of the variables taken as given in the analysis of UIP. Money affects exchange rate expectations, since the exchange rate is the ratio of nominal price levels.

The full simultaneous determination of output, prices, exchange and interest rates in two countries is complicated. So, we proceed step by step. In this chapter, the MA is developed first under sticky, and then under flexible prices. Non-monetary influences on the exchange rate are taken up in the chapters to follow. The assumption maintained in this chapter – that output is given – is then relaxed.

The structure of the chapter is as follows: Section 6.2 introduces the MA to the exchange rate. Section 6.3 is on the SPMA and demonstrates overshooting of the exchange rate. Section 6.4 turns to the FPMA, before Section 6.5 concludes. Appendix 6.A.1 demonstrates rational bubbles can exist in the exchange rate, even under the stringent assumptions of the MA.

6.2   Monetary approach to the exchange rate

The MA defines the exchange rate as the relative price of two monies, which are determined by the demand and supply of money.

Absolute PPP or perfect trade arbitrage is one component of this approach. Another is money market equilibrium. Prices are assumed to be perfectly flexible, so markets are always in equilibrium. The canonical MA is the FPMA.

The MA makes strong assumptions of perfect markets. Underlying it is an implicit market-clearing general equilibrium system with

Monetary approach to the exchange rate 125

six markets. Goods market equilibrium is brought about by flexible prices, flexible wages clear the labour market and flexible exchange rates clear the FX market. R_t is determined in the money (fourth) market. Under perfect substitutability, domestic and foreign bonds collapse to one market, forming the nth (fifth) market that must clear in a general equilibrium when the other $n - 1$ markets clear. The money market equilibrium, therefore, brings about the equilibrium in the full system through the adjustment of R_t^1.

The MA models the exchange rate in terms of the relative supply of and demand for two monies. The money market equation equates the supply and demand for home country real balances:

$$\frac{M_t^S}{P_t} = M^d \left(R_t, Y_t \right) \tag{6.1}$$

There is a similar equilibrium for the foreign country. These can be written in logarithms for the domestic and the foreign country, respectively, as:

$$m_t = p_t + ky_t - \theta R_t \tag{6.2}$$

$$m_t^* = p_t^* + k^* y_t^* - \theta^* R_t^* \tag{6.3}$$

Superscript* denotes the foreign country. Since log real exchange rate $q_t = 0$, absolute PPP can be written in logarithms as:

$$s_t = p_t - p_t^* \tag{6.4}$$

Subtracting Equation 6.3 and Equation 6.2 and using Equation 6.4 gives the fundamental equation of the MA:

$$s_t = \left(m_t - m_t^* \right) - \left(ky_t - k^* y_t^* \right) + \left(\theta R_t - \theta^* R_t^* \right) \tag{6.5}$$

Let $k = k^*$ and $\theta = \theta^*$, that is, the income and interest rate semi-elasticities are equal in the two countries, and substitute from UIP for the interest rate differential, to get:

$$s = \left(m_t - m_t^* \right) - k \left(y_t - y_t^* \right) + \theta \dot{s}_{t+1}^e \tag{6.6}$$

That is, the nominal exchange rate will depreciate with a rise in relative money supply or with expected depreciation, but appreciate if relative output rises. Under the strong assumptions of the MA, output and interest rates will always be at their full employment equilibrium

126 *Monetary approach to the exchange rate*

levels, so that changes in relative money supplies affect the nominal exchange rate.

Despite the extreme assumptions of the MA, the value of the nominal exchange rate is still not uniquely tied down, since the rational bubbles, discussed in Chapter 2, can occur affecting expected and therefore actual S_t. An extraneous component that satisfies the dynamic process of the exchange rate can be sustained by an appropriate belief structure. Because exchange rate expectations enter Equation 6.6, self-fulfilling deviations of the exchange rate from its fundamental determinants are possible. Appendix A.6.1 derives this explicitly.

The next section develops the famous overshooting result of the SPMA and shows how the interest rate can have a very different effect on the exchange rate compared to that in the FPMA. A higher nominal interest rate differential leads to depreciation in the FPMA, but can lead to appreciation in the SPMA, as we see below.

6.3 Sticky price monetary approach: the asset market and overshooting

Chapter 3 analysed the no-arbitrage equilibrium in FX markets under UIP, in which the returns to holding different currency deposits are equated in the same currency. We now bring in the money markets, which determine the returns to holding domestic currency, that is, we endogenise R_t. Either it can be regarded as determined by the money market equilibrium where the demand for money equals its supply, or as set by the CB, which adjusts money supply to achieve its target R_t.

Figure 6.1 graphs the FX market in the first and the money market in the second quadrant.[1] In the latter, real money demand or liquidity preference for real money balances, M_t/P_t, falls as the opportunity cost of holding money, R, rises. Real money demand rises with output, as more money is required for transactions. If money supply rises, individuals seek to get rid of an excess supply of money balances by lending to others or by buying interest-yielding assets such as bonds; the first reduces loan rates. The second raises the price of bonds, reducing bond yields (interest rates). Falling interest rates raise demand for real liquidity until equilibrium is restored. The economy as a whole cannot reduce money holdings. Under excess demand for money balances, the opposite adjustment would take place as bonds are sold and loans are taken.

If the monetary authority targets the interest rate, a fall in short-term policy rates would induce a market portfolio shift towards bonds, as

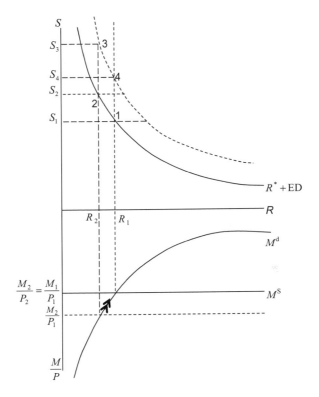

Figure 6.1 Exchange rate overshooting

their prices would be expected to rise. This would release liquidity for rising money demand. Loan demand would rise as interest rates fall. Primary liquidity injections from the CB would support the increase in money and loan demand as interest rates fall.

Given output Y_t and the supply of real money balances, R_t is determined, which in turn determines the FX market equilibrium. Equilibrium in the money markets requires that money demand equals supply, that is, Equation 6.1 is satisfied. This is graphed in Figure 6.1. The initial equilibrium has M_1 and P_1 determining real money balances or money supply. The real balance line is horizontal, since the price level is given exogenously. Where the line cuts the money demand curve, the money market clears and determines the nominal interest rate R_1. This is the return to holding domestic money balances, and equating this to the return from holding foreign balances in the FX market determines

128   *Monetary approach to the exchange rate*

the nominal exchange rate S_1. Thus, money supply affects the exchange rate. A similar analysis determines R_t^* in the foreign money market. With this apparatus, we can consider the effect of a temporary and a permanent monetary shock.

Temporary monetary shock: We start from equilibrium, where the expected value of S_t is S_1. Output, prices and exchange rate expectations are given. The money market equilibrium determines the interest rate. Since prices are sticky, if a monetary shock raises money supply M_1 to M_2, real money balances rise. As a result, the rate of interest falls, making holding dollars more attractive. The exchange rate depreciates to S_2 at point 2 to maintain UIP, so that capital outflows stop. This is the final outcome of a temporary rise in money supply and is reversed with the fall in money supply back to M_1. Since the shock is temporary, the analysis is restricted to the short run. But if the rise in money supply is permanent, the outcome differs.

Permanent monetary shock: Prices adjust fully to a permanent shock in the long run, when the interest rate and output are at their full employment levels. Then, R_t equals the productivity of capital or the consumer discount rate;[2] then, the money market equilibrium 6.1 determines the price level as proportional to the money supply.

Prices may be sticky in the short run, but a rise in money supply raises inflationary expectations as demand rises. Workers who expect prices to rise bargain for higher wages today; producers think they will be able to pass on price increases in the future. Prices of agricultural goods, metals and petroleum products are flexible even in the short run. As these rise, raw material costs are raised.

As these factors work out over time, a permanent increase in the money supply causes a long-run proportional rise in the price level. Since the exchange rate is the domestic currency price of foreign currency, it must also rise proportional to the money supply. If the exchange rate is the relative price of two monies, the fundamental determinant of the nominal exchange rate is the relative money supply under the MA. But since S_t is a flexible asset price, its value adjusts in the short run itself.

Permanent shock short-run impact: A permanent rise in money supply from M_1 to M_2 will, therefore, raise the expected value of S_t proportionally to the change in money in the short run itself. Therefore, the vertical distance between the solid and the dashed curve in Figure 6.1 equals the change in nominal money supply. Output is assumed to be at full employment, so prices are expected to change proportionally to any change in nominal money supply in the long run.

Monetary approach to the exchange rate 129

Since prices are sticky, taking time to adjust, the real money balances rise in the short run and the rate of interest falls. With a temporary rise in M_t, the exchange rate had depreciated to point 2 to maintain UIP. But now with a permanent rise S_t^e, the expected value of the exchange rate also rises. The expected return to holding foreign currency shifts up and the exchange rate depreciates to S_3 at point 3. Long-run expectations affect the current value of S_t, and it can adjust instantly as the floating exchange rate is a jump variable.

Long-run impact: This, however, is not the final equilibrium. Over time, goods prices will rise from P_1 to P_2. This will continue until real money balances are back at their original position, and R_t rises back to R_1, giving the final equilibrium exchange rate as S_4 at point 4. The exchange rate overshoots its final equilibrium position.

At point 4 as at point 1, $R_t = R_t^*$ again and the expected depreciation or appreciation is zero once more. Figure 6.2 shows the time lines of adjustment to the monetary shock occurring at time t_0. R_t falls immediately and S_t jumps up, then each comes back to its final equilibrium as the price level slowly rises, bringing money balances back to their original level. After all adjustments are over, the rise in the exchange rate S_1 to S_4 is equal to that in prices P_1 to P_2 and to that in nominal money supply M_1 to M_2. In the final equilibrium, the rise in S_t and P_t is proportional to that in M_t, but initially S_t rises more than proportionately – that is, it overshoots. Figure 6.2 shows how after the initial jump the asset prices R_t and S_t adjust slowly back to the final equilibrium along with P_t. The immediate impact of the rise in M_t is on the assets prices R_t and S_t. Then, as P_t slowly rises, they adjust along with real balances. R_t and real balances return to original levels, while the depreciation of S_t is reduced.

Why does overshooting occur? Sticky prices imply a rise in real money balances as M_t rises, so R_t must fall to maintain money market equilibrium. After R_t falls, to satisfy UIP, the exchange rate must be expected to appreciate. The only way this is possible is for it to depreciate so much initially that it has to appreciate to reach its final equilibrium.

While the fundamental trigger for overshooting is the sticky prices that prevent immediate adjustment of prices to a rise in money supply, other reasons are the capital mobility that requires a jump in the asset price to satisfy UIP, when currency is treated as an asset; the floating exchange rate regime that makes currency prices so flexible they can register changed long-run expectations and compensate for sticky goods prices. The combination of sticky and jump variables leads to

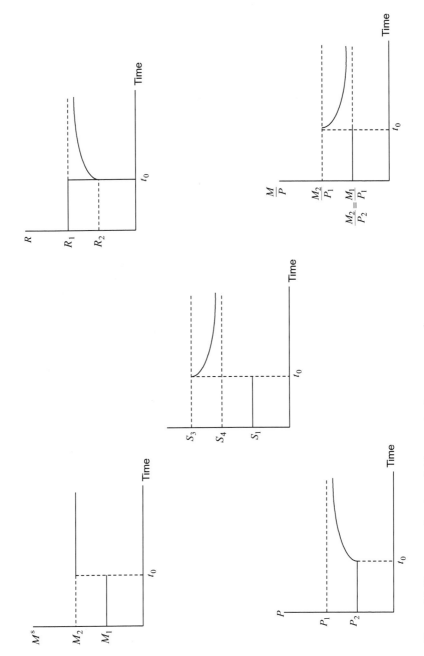

Figure 6.2 Response of each variable to a rise in money supply

Monetary approach to the exchange rate 131

this outcome. The jump variables overshoot due to slack created by the slowness of the sticky variables to adjust.

Overshooting would not occur if prices were perfectly flexible. Indeed, it does not occur in the flexible price monetary model, as we see in the next section. The result was first worked out in a sticky price monetary model due to Dornbusch (1976). In the abductive tradition of macroeconomics, Dornbusch's paper was written in the 1970s when mature countries had shifted to floating exchange rate regimes, which turned out to be highly volatile, not in the earlier fixed exchange rate period. It responded to the new stylised facts of volatility in floating exchange rates, much exceeding that in prices.

Outcomes in the SPMA differ from those in the pure MA of Section 6.2. Equation 6.5 of the MA implies that the exchange rate depreciates with a rise in money supply and in interest rates. But in the SPMA, a rise in money supply leads to a fall in interest rates and a depreciation. The difference occurs because under flexible goods market prices a rise in money supply growth raises inflation and nominal interest rates. This is the Fisher effect. Under sticky prices, however, interest rates fall with a rise in money supply.

6.4 The flexible price monetary approach

In a closed economy, the Fisher effect implies that the nominal interest rate must equal the real interest rate plus expected inflation, that is, the nominal interest rate must rise with expected inflation. In an open economy, the Fisher effect implies a relationship between nominal interest rate differentials and inflation differentials.

If PPP or relative PPP holds so the real exchange rate does not change, then the bilateral nominal exchange rate must change to cover the inflation differential between the two countries. Differentiating the definition of the real exchange rate with respect to time and taking expectations gives:

$$\dot{s}_t^e = \pi_t^e - \pi_t^{*e} \tag{6.7}$$

In addition, from UIP, we have that the interest differential must cover expected depreciation:

$$\dot{s}_t^e = R_t - R_t^* \tag{6.8}$$

132 Monetary approach to the exchange rate

Substituting out expected change in the nominal exchange rate between the two equations gives:

$$R_t - R_t^* = \pi_t^e - \pi_t^{*e} \tag{6.9}$$

This is the open economy version of the Fisher effect, saying that a country with higher expected inflation would have a higher nominal interest rate. Countries with higher rates of inflation over longer periods of time do tend to have higher nominal rates of interest, and inflation is associated with a growth in money supply.

We next consider the effect of a rise in the growth rate of money supply, under the perfectly flexible goods market prices of the MA. In this case, a one-time jump in money supply is not interesting since it would have no effect except a proportional jump in prices. But with a rise in the growth rate of money supply, the interest rate, inflation and depreciation all rise. Unlike in the sticky price case, we have a rise in interest rates associated with depreciation. Figures 6.3 and 6.4 give details of the process.

Our familiar two quadrants in Figure 6.3 show the instantaneous effect of the announcement of a higher rate of growth in money supply in t_0, while Figure 6.4 shows the time lines. In Figure 6.4, the higher

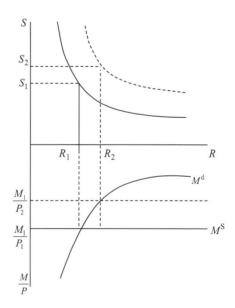

Figure 6.3 The impact of rise in money growth rate when prices are flexible

Monetary approach to the exchange rate 133

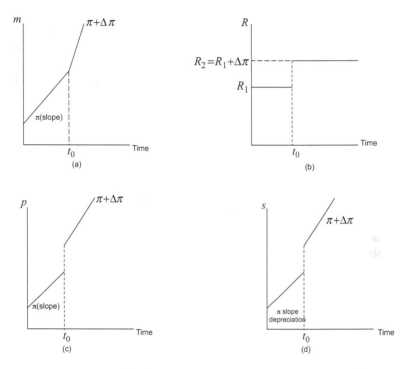

Figure 6.4 Response of each variable to a rise in the rate of growth of money supply

expected rate of inflation, in line with the higher rate of money supply growth, must raise the nominal interest rate from the Fisher effect. The new rate of inflation and depreciation is the same as the new higher rate of money supply growth. The log-linear lines of Figure 6.4 show this higher and equivalent slope after t_0. The vertical axes are in log scales so the slopes show the rates of growth. R_1 was matched to the old rate of inflation, and the new R_t must be matched to the new higher rate of inflation from the Fisher effect, that is $R_2 = r + \pi_t^e$, where $\pi_t^e = \pi_t + \Delta \pi_t$.

Current money supply is unchanged, since the higher growth of money is expected in the future. Even so, in Figure 6.3, R_t rises since the price level jumps up in anticipation, thus reducing real money balances. Expected inflation accounts for the rise in the price level from P_1 to P_2 at t_0, although M_t remains unchanged at M_1. Similarly, higher money supply growth implies the fundamentals determining the

134 *Monetary approach to the exchange rate*

exchange rate have changed, so it is expected to depreciate. The returns to foreign balance holders rise relatively, the returns curve shifts outwards and the exchange rate also jumps up from S_1 to S_2. The rise in R_t reduces money demand, equating it to the reduced money supply.

Thus, while in the SPMA, a fall in the interest rate was associated with depreciation, in the FPMA a rise in the interest rate is associated with depreciation. A rise in money supply can raise real balances because of sticky prices in the SPMA. It cannot do so in the FPMA because of the assumption of flexible goods prices. The change in R_t in the FPMA comes from expected inflation due to the growth in money supply. In the SPMA a rise in money supply lowers interest rates. In the FPMA, it raises them as expected inflation rises.

The FPMA is the same as the pure MA, where a rise in R_t reduces demand for money (Eq. 6.5), thereby raising net money supply and depreciating the exchange rate. The SPMA is an aberration in that sticky prices allow money supply to affect real variables – but only in the short run. The difference between sticky and flexible prices is at the heart of the real effect of a monetary stimulus.

In the long run, however, as prices adjust or for large and sustained changes in money supply, the SPMA gives the same result as the MA. Money becomes a veil affecting only nominal variables. With a sustained rise in money supply, inflationary expectations raise the interest rate so the rise in money supply cannot lower interest rates. The MA illustrates Freidman's famous dictum: in the long run, inflation is always and everywhere a monetary phenomenon. And PPP, combined with MA, ensures that so is the nominal exchange rate.

6.5 Summary

To develop the MA to the exchange rate, we added the money market to the analysis of the FX market developed in earlier chapters. This determined the nominal interest rate, which was taken as given in Chapter 2. The second exogenous variable endogenised in this chapter was the expected nominal exchange rate. To do this, we drew upon PPP developed in Chapter 5. This gives the nominal exchange rate as the ratio of domestic and foreign price levels. Under assumptions of full market clearing and flexible prices, this relative price level depends only upon relative money supplies.

Apart from the MA to exchange rate determination, the chapter also developed its variants – the fixed and flexible price monetary approaches. The first demonstrated exchange rate overshooting – how a monetary shock can lead to excess volatility in exchange rates, which as flexible asset prices compensate for sticky goods market prices, coming back to equilibrium values as goods prices slowly adjust.

The FPMA drew upon the UIP and an open economy version of the Fisher's effect, whereby expected inflation raises nominal interest rates. Therefore, in this case, a rise in interest rates was associated with monetary shock-induced depreciation – the opposite result held under sticky prices, where a rise in money supply lowered the interest rate. Since prices also adjusted instantaneously now, along with the exchange rate, there was no overshooting.

In the SPMA, money affects real variables – but in the short run and for limited changes. In the long run, as in the MA and FPMA, money affects only prices, and the nominal exchange rate is the price of money.

For an EDE, overshooting adds to the volatility, due to thin markets, in moving to a floating exchange rate regime.

*Appendix A.6.1[3]
Rational bubbles

We can rewrite the basic equation for the monetary approach as[4]:

$$s_t = \left(m_t - m_t^*\right) - k\left(y_t - y_t^*\right) + \theta\left(E_t s_{t+1} - s_t\right)$$

And transform it as:

$$s_t = \left(1 + \theta\right)^{-1}\left[\left(m_t - m_t^*\right) - k\left(y_t - y_t^*\right) + \theta E_t s_{t+1}\right] \tag{6A.1}$$

Equation 6A.1 can be written in the generic form 6A.2 that clearly shows the basic structure of Equation 6A.1. This shows that the spot exchange rate is determined by its discounted expected future value and the fundamentals that determine it. Such an equation can apply to any asset. For example, a stock price would depend on its expected future price and the dividend it earned.

$$s_t = \lambda E_t s_{t+1} + v_t \tag{6A.2}$$

$$\lambda = \frac{\theta}{1+\theta} < 1 \tag{6A.3}$$

Since future values are involved, we need to get the RE solution. In order to do so, we first lead one period to write the equation for s_{t+1} as:

$$s_{t+1} = \left(1 + \theta\right)^{-1} E_t\left[\left(m_{t+1} - m_{t+1}^*\right) - k\left(y_{t+1} - y_{t+1}^*\right) + \theta s_{t+2}\right]$$

Substituting in s_t gives:

$$s_t = \left(1 + \theta\right)^{-1}\left[\left(m_t - m_t^*\right) - k\left(y_1 - y_t^*\right) + \theta\left(1 + \theta\right)^{-1} E_t\left[\left(m_{t+1} - m_{t+1}^*\right)\right.\right.$$
$$\left.\left. - k\left(y_{t+1} - y_{t+1}^*\right) + \theta s_{t+2}\right]\right]$$

Monetary approach to the exchange rate 137

Continuing the process and collecting terms, we get the solution:

$$\tilde{s}_t = (1+\theta)^{-1} \sum_{i=0}^{\infty} \left(\frac{\theta}{1+\theta}\right)^i E_t\left[(m_{t+i} - m^*_{t+i}) - k(y_{t+i} - y^*_{t+i})\right] + \frac{\theta s_\infty}{1+\theta}$$

The solution can be written as a generic function of the present discounted value of monetary and output fundamentals, v:

$$\tilde{s}_t = \sum_{i=0}^{\infty} \lambda^i E_t v_{t+i} \tag{6A.4}$$

But 6A.4 is only one solution. We show Equation 6A.2 can have multiple rational solutions, including a bubble term B_t:

$$s_t = \tilde{s}_t + B_t \tag{6A.5}$$

We can find conditions on B_t such that it is a rational bubble. Lead Equation 6A.5 one period and take expectations given information at time t:

$$E_t s_{t+1} = E_t \tilde{s}_{t+1} + E_t B_{t+1} \tag{6A.6}$$

Replace s_t and s_{t+1} in Equations 6A.2 from 6A.5 and 6A.6:

$$\tilde{s}_t + B_t = \lambda E_t \tilde{s}_{t+1} + \lambda E_t B_{t+1} + v_t$$

From the definition of $\tilde{s}$ in Equation 6A.2, that is $\left[\text{since } \tilde{s}_t = \lambda E_t \tilde{s}_{t+1} + v_t\right]$, these terms cancel out, giving:

$$B_t = \lambda E_t B_{t+1} \tag{6A.7}$$

Any B that satisfies Equation 6A.7 also satisfies the generic form Equation 6A.2, since it follows the same dynamic process as the exchange rate, consistent with its fundamentals.

Since $\lambda < 1$:

$$E_t\left[B_{t+1}\right] = \frac{1}{\lambda} B_t = \begin{cases} + \infty \text{ if } B_t > 0 \\ - \infty \text{ if } B_t < 0 \end{cases}$$

The bubble would tend to become too large or too small. But a possible belief structure that could sustain an RE bubble is one where there

138 *Monetary approach to the exchange rate*

is some probability of the bubble continuing and some probability of it bursting:

$$B_t = \begin{cases} (\pi\lambda)^{-1} B_{t-1} & \text{with prob. } \pi \\ \\ 0 & \text{with prob. } 1 - \pi \end{cases}$$

$$B_t = \frac{1}{\pi\lambda}\pi B_{t-1} + (1-\pi)0$$

$$B_t = \frac{1}{\lambda}B_{t-1}$$

or

$$B_{t-1} = \lambda B$$

That is, the expected bubble is replaced with an actual path. With a certain probability, traders expect the bubble to continue, and with one minus that probability expects it to collapse, yielding a sustained bubble that can be independent of fundamentals but satisfies the dynamic process associated with fundamentals. The asymmetry of the probability distribution sustaining the bubble implies the rational expectation forecast error will also be skewed confounding tests of rational expectation.

With regard to the fundamental determinants of the spot exchange rate, expectations of high m_{t+i} would imply s^e_{t+i} is expected to depreciate and high y_{t+i} would imply s^e_{t+i} is expected to appreciate, as money supply is absorbed in transaction demand. A risk premium can also distort the exchange rate. A risk premium, however, differs from a rational bubble. The latter also differs from overshooting, which is a process of adjustment to fundamentals, while a bubble is a deviation from fundamentals. Overshooting requires sticky goods prices, while a bubble can occur even with flexible prices. It can also occur with sticky prices and enhance the overshooting.

Notes

1 Krugman et al. (2014) use such diagrams.
2 This is the technology or preferences that the new classical approach to macroeconomics considers as the deep determinants of macroeconomic outcomes.
3 *denotes advanced material.
4 This proof is adapted from Sarno and Taylor (2002) and Blanchard and Fischer (1989).

References

Blanchard O. J. and S. Fischer. 1989. *Macroeconomics*, Cambridge, MA: MIT Press.

Dornbusch, R. 1976. 'Expectations and Exchange Rate Dynamics', *The Journal of Political Economy*, 84(6): 1161–1176, December.

Krugman, P. R., M. Obstfeld and M. Melitz. 2014. *International Economics: Theory and Policy*, 10th edition, Delhi: Pearson Education.

Obstfeld, M. and K. Rogoff. 1996. *Foundations of International Macroeconomics*, Cambridge, MA: MIT Press.

Sarno, L. and M. P. Taylor. 2002. *The Economics of Exchange Rates*, Cambridge, UK: Cambridge University Press.

7 The real exchange rate
Beyond monetary theories

Can money be the measure of all things?

7.1 Introduction

The monetary approach gives a simple and clear benchmark for the real exchange rate. If perfect trade arbitrage implies PPP exists, the nominal exchange rate is a ratio of price levels, so the real exchange rate that deflates the nominal exchange rate by the same price levels must be unity. Trade arbitrage is an essential part of the monetary approach since it fits in with the underlying philosophy of well-functioning markets.

But the assumptions underlying the monetary approach are extreme. Moreover, there is only limited empirical support for PPP. So, in this chapter, we explore what other factors determine the real exchange rate. If the real exchange rate is not tied to PPP, then the non-monetary factors that affect it would affect nominal variables such as the price level, the nominal interest and exchange rate, also. Not only can monetary variables have real effects, but real variables also affect monetary variables. Broader determinants of the real exchange rate can be classified into those affecting relative demands and supplies of a country's products.

The real exchange rate affects trade. So, adjustment may occur in it, either through changes in the nominal exchange rate or in price levels, in response to BOP pressures. If demands and supplies of traded goods and services are equal, the current account must be balanced. Alternatively, allowing for financing of temporary excess demand through the capital account, an equilibrium real exchange rate is such that it ensures a sustainable CAD, conditional on sustainable values of other macroeconomic variables also. That is, internal and external balance should hold over time. For example, if the CAD is large, the

Beyond monetary theories   141

required adjustment could occur as capital outflows force depreciation under a floating exchange rate. Capital flows could be responding to fundamentals such as demands and supplies,[1] or to global trends, fashions or changes in risk preference. The latter type of behaviour is especially prevalent in an EDE. In the literature, therefore, estimation of equilibrium real exchange rates includes, apart from relative prices, variables affecting relative demands and supply and the CAD such as growth, productivity and interest rate differentials.[2]

In addition, factors, such as rising standards of living, will affect the real exchange rate in an EDE. There is also an inverse relation between the real exchange rate and the real wage, which is part of the adjustment to PPP in an EDE. If there is a real wage target, it implies a real exchange target. We show that a gap between this and the equilibrium exchange rate can sustain inflation.

These factors capture other influences that help to determine an equilibrium real exchange rate, apart from market-based trade arbitrage. These non-monetary factors form part of the fundamentals that affect nominal exchange rates. Traders must then include shocks to all these variables in taking market positions that affect the nominal exchange rate.

The structure of the chapter is as follows: Section 7.2 presents some broader determinants of the real exchange rate. Section 7.3 explores alterations in the monetary approach when the real exchange rate can vary and Section 7.4 the relationship between real wages and the real exchange rate, before Section 7.5 concludes.

7.2   Real exchange rate: broader determinants

The real exchange rate deflates the nominal exchange rate by the price levels of the two countries.[3] It can be understood as the relative price of the representative baskets of each of the two countries goods and services measured in the same currency, giving therefore the relative price of foreign goods in terms of domestic goods. The problem is that the average price level is difficult to define even in one country, and even more so across two and more countries, so that the real exchange rate can be calculated in many different ways.

Rather than assuming perfect trade arbitrage and identical baskets, we now allow the composition of the two baskets to differ, depending on income levels and preferences in the two countries. For example, the Indian basket would have a higher share of food. The rupee–dollar real exchange rate $Q_t = S_t P_t^* / P_t$ then is the $ price of the US basket converted into rupees and divided by the rupee value of the typical

142   *Beyond monetary theories*

basket consumed in India. Since quantities are the opposite of prices, this gives the Indian basket a US basket can command. A rise in Q_t means the US basket can command more of the Indian basket – there is a real depreciation of the rupee. The purchasing power of the US basket rises in India.

$$Q_t = \frac{\text{Re value of US basket}}{\text{Re value of Indian basket}} = \text{Indian baskets per US basket}$$

A rise in world relative demand for Indian products would raise the rupee value of the Indian basket relative to the US basket. Q_t would fall, that is, the rupee would appreciate against the dollar in real terms.

A rise in the relative supply of Indian products, perhaps due to a rise in productivity, would lower the relative value of Indian goods through a real depreciation. Q_t would rise, that is, the rupee would depreciate against the dollar in real terms.

The BS effect showed that the general price level tends to be lower in an EDE, so that the real exchange rate tends to exceed unity.[4] If per capita income levels rose, so would the price level, and the real exchange rate would appreciate, through the working of the BS effect.

Since these are real effects, they are independent of the money supply. These real effects occur independently of monetary variables even if prices are ultimately determined by the money supply.

7.3   The monetary approach when the real exchange rate can vary

If Q_t can change, the results of the MA have to be modified. If Q_t varies, it follows that the long-run nominal exchange rates also depend on factors other than just nominal money supplies. Since:

$$S_t = Q_t \times \frac{P_t}{P_t^*}$$

S_t is now affected by factors changing Q_t as well as nominal factors affecting price levels. The factors affecting S_t can, therefore, be classified as:

1   As in the previous chapter, both a rise in money supply and its rate of growth affect P_t, and therefore S_t. Since in the long run, a rise in money supply affects only price levels and a change in the relative

Beyond monetary theories 143

growth of money supply affects inflation, but not real output or a relative price such as the real exchange rate, only S_t changes with change in money supply or its growth rate.

2 But non-monetary changes will also now affect S_t. For example, the expected appreciation in the real exchange rate through the BS effect, as standards of living rise in an EDE, would appreciate nominal exchange rates.

3 A change in relative world demand for Indian products will now affect S_t through the resulting change in Q_t. Such a change affects only Q_t or the relative price of Indian output; it does not affect the absolute level of Indian prices, if the latter are considered as purely monetary variables. As Q_t appreciates so would S_t.

4 A rise in relative Indian output supply compared to US supply, would raise (depreciate) Q_t, and therefore S_t. But it would also raise transaction demand for money, and therefore Indian price levels would fall, so the net effect on S_t could be in either direction – it could appreciate or depreciate.

The canonical MA assumes output is at full employment and preferences and technology determine the real interest rate. But if the real exchange rate can change, a positive real interest differential can exist across countries – that is, changes in the real exchange rate affect the real interest rate.

7.3.1 Real UIP

If the real exchange rate can change, even relative PPP does not hold. In that case, interest rate differentials need not equal inflation differentials and real interest rates can differ across countries. Another type of interest parity, real UIP can be derived.

Differentiating q_t with respect to time, using its definition, and taking expectations:

$$\dot{q}_t^e = \dot{s}_t^e + \pi_t^{*e} - \pi_t^e \tag{7.1}$$

UIP gives:

$$\dot{s}_t^e = R_t - R_t^*$$

Substituting for $\dot{s}_t^e$ in Equation 7.1 using UIP gives:

$$\dot{q}_t^e = R_t - R_t^* + \pi_t^{*e} - \pi_t^e \tag{7.2}$$

144   *Beyond monetary theories*

This can be written as:

$$R_t - R_t^* = \pi_t^e - \pi_t^{*e} + \dot{q}_t^e \qquad (7.2)'$$

Equation 7.2' shows the home nominal interest rate can be below the foreign interest rate, or a positive interest differential can be reduced to the extent a real appreciation is expected.

The Fisher effect Equation 7.3 says, given the expected real interest rate, r_t, the nominal interest rate rises one to one with expected inflation:

$$R_t = r_t + \pi_t^e \qquad (7.3)$$

Substituting Equation 7.3 and its equivalent for the other country in Equation 7.2 gives real UIP:

$$\dot{q}_t^e = r_t^e - r_t^{*e} \qquad (7.4)$$

Since these are expected real interest rates and not quoted on any market unlike UIP, they do not, however, generate arbitrage opportunities for market participants.

7.4   Modifications in FPMA when real rates can vary

Next, we add PPP to the FX and money market equilibrium to demonstrate the role of the real exchange rate in affecting fundamentals determining the expected nominal exchange rate and to demonstrate how, when there are deviations from PPP, the results of the FPMA, derived in the previous chapter, are modified.

7.4.1   *Emerging and developing economies and changes in real exchange rates*

In an EDE, Q_t is normally greater than one, as its price level is relatively lower. Q_t can be expected to appreciate and fall towards unity on the transition catch-up path. This process implies the exchange rate may not depreciate with a higher rate of money growth.

The two LHS quadrants and the dotted lines in Figure 7.1 tell such a story. The bottom LHS quadrant adds PPP to the familiar FX and money market equilibria depicted on the RHS in quadrants I and II. The solid curve is a rectangular hyperbola showing the relationship between P_t and S_t given P_t^* and money supply M_t, such that $S_t P_t^* = P_t$,

Beyond monetary theories 145

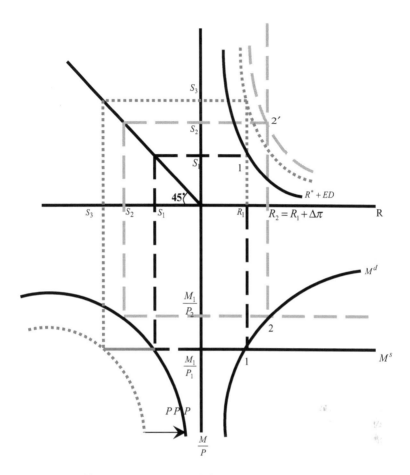

Figure 7.1 Adding PPP to the FX and the money market

or PPP is satisfied. The dotted PPP curve for an EDE lies below the solid curve, since the price level is lower in such an EDE.

The 45 degree line in the fourth quadrant maps the exchange rate into itself. The PPP hyperbola links the price level to the exchange rate. The exchange rate is more depreciated at a higher price level. The dashed lines indicate the starting position for an AE, while the light dashed lines indicate its final position after a rise in the rate of growth of money. Since the price level jumps up, real money balances fall, the interest rate rises to reflect expected inflation, so the FX market curve shifts up and expected depreciation leads to actual depreciation.

146 *Beyond monetary theories*

The dotted line represents an EDE where $Q_t > 1$ gives the higher dotted hyperbola. If higher money growth coincides with a higher growth phase, although output or money supply has not yet changed in period 1, the expected productivity improvements combined with the BS effect will shift down the dotted hyperbola and the returns to holding dollars. As the dotted line approaches the solid hyperbola, there is no jump in prices due to the higher money growth because of the nominal exchange rate appreciation. In subsequent periods, the higher money growth may be absorbed in higher income growth.

But for an AE where the dashed solid lines are the initial state, the FPMA result of the previous chapter holds. A rise in the growth rate of money leads to a shift to the light dashed lines, as the price level jumps up. The exchange rate is expected to depreciate at the new higher growth rate of money, and the nominal interest rate rises.

In an EDE, however, if real appreciation accompanies higher money growth, the dotted curve shifts towards the PPP line. Then, the expected depreciation could actually fall from the dotted line to the solid line. The price level need not jump and reduce money balances and the nominal interest rate need not rise. Then, interest rates would not rise with higher money growth, and S_t would appreciate from S_3 towards S_1. The equilibrium for the EDE shifts from the dotted line to the solid line of the earlier AE equilibrium in the FX market quadrant. The reasons the FPMA results do not hold are that higher output growth absorbs higher money growth, and expected nominal depreciation is reversed because of real appreciation as standards of living rise.

Thus, the MA is a useful benchmark, but several riders have to be kept in mind. We just saw that, in the MA, a rise in money supply depreciates the exchange rate. But this conclusion can be reversed in an EDE that is in a phase of high growth and productivity improvement, so that prices do not rise proportional to money supply.

Consider a permanent rise in money supply as shown in Figure 7.2. The exchange rate should depreciate from S^1 to S^2 and further, as expected depreciation rises with a fall in the interest rate from R^1 to R^2. But assume output is rising at the same time from Y^1 to Y^2, then S^1 and R^1 would stay unchanged. Without the rise in money supply, R_t would have risen to R^3 and S appreciated to S^3. If productivity changes, as discussed in Figure 7.1, are leading to a real appreciation, then the return to holding dollars shifts downwards, S_t appreciates to S^3 and R_t falls to R^4. A rise in money supply has been accompanied by an appreciation and a fall in the interest rate. Caution is, therefore, necessary in any straightforward application of the MA, especially to an EDE.

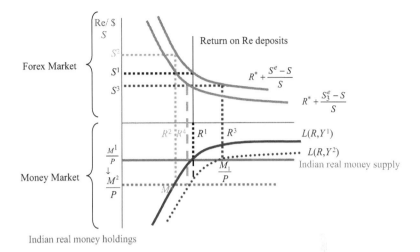

Figure 7.2 Equilibrium in the money and FX market

There are other characteristics of EDEs that interact with real exchange rates and their changes over time. We consider two such issues below. First, EDEs often have CADs, which have implications for sustainable real exchange rates. Second, inflation tends to be higher in EDEs, and the interaction between real wages and real exchange rates is one of the factors that propagate it.

*7.5 Real wages and the real exchange rate[5]

If other kinds of macroeconomic misalignments rather than PPP deviations drive changes in the real exchange rate, it should be measured in ways that capture these adjustments. Since an EDE is small in external markets and takes import and export prices as given, the internal real exchange rate measured as the ratio of traded to non-traded is the only one that can adjust and that affects the incentives of domestic agents to consume and produce. While the standard REER calculation uses the CPI, this is more contaminated with foreign goods prices that cannot respond to domestic actions. Using produce prices for partner countries allows the numerator of Q_t measured as $P_{T,t}/P_{N,t}$ to measure pure foreign traded goods less contaminated by domestic goods prices (Montiel, 2003). In this section, we define Q_t as $P_{T,t}/P_{N,t}$.

148 *Beyond monetary theories*

The real exchange rate is also inversely related to the real wage rate, and this can have interesting consequences as the model below (Goyal, 2010, 2014) brings out. In an EDE with labour near subsistence, employers may want to pay efficiency wages in the medium term, leading to a real wage target:

$$\bar{w} = \frac{W_t}{P_t} \tag{7.5}$$

Nominal wages, W_t, are raised in line with the CPI, P_t, to maintain a real wage target. Lags in the adjustment of wages and prices, which affect the adjustment of the actual real exchange rate, Q_t, are omitted in order to simplify.

P_t is a weighted average of traded and NT goods prices. The weights are given by respective consumption shares, such that $0 < \delta < 1$.

$$P_t = (eP_{Tt}^*)^\delta P_{Nt}^{(1-\delta)} \tag{7.6}$$

Perfect trade arbitrage ensures that traded goods prices are given by world prices multiplied by the nominal exchange rate. The prices of NT goods are set as a markup on wages after correcting for labour productivity, β_N, where m is the profit share.

$$P_{Nt} = \left(\frac{\beta_N}{(1-m)}\right) W_t \tag{7.7}$$

If Equation 7.6 is substituted in Equation 7.5, and W substituted out by using Equation 7.7, we can solve for the value of the real exchange rate (Q_t defined as $S_t P_{T,t}/P_{N,t}$) that satisfies the wage-price relations Equations 7.5–7.7 and call it Q_w or the target level of the real exchange rate. It is the target level because it satisfies the real wage target Equation 7.5.

$$Q_w = \left[\left(\frac{\beta_N}{1-m}\right)\bar{w}_t\right]^{-\frac{1}{\delta}} \tag{7.8}$$

If a devaluation leads to $Q_t > Q_w$, it implies that real wages are below the target value, because the domestic price level is higher than that warranted by the wage target. Therefore, W_t will rise, but from Equation 7.7, P_{Nt} will also rise, and finally, from Equation 7.6, so will P_t. As this sparks another rise in W, there will be continual inflation, π will be above its steady-state value, as long as $Q_t > Q_w$. In a steady state, therefore, Q_t must equal Q_w.

Since PPP does not hold in an EDE, and it may be borrowing from abroad, and the share and price of non-traded goods are changing with productivity as the country develops, an alternative relevant concept of the equilibrium real exchange rate, $\tilde{Q}$, is that determined by equating the current account of the BOP (the net imports or NM curve at full capacity output or internal balance) to a sustainable capital account (the excess of investment over saving, $I_t - S_t$, or capital inflows).[6] Since I_t and S_t are forward looking, they need to be derived from intertemporal optimisation by a representative consumer with money in the utility function (Goyal, 2006). This ensures feasible consumption smoothing and that debt cannot be accumulated forever. This optimisation should drive the changes in relative demands that affect exchange rates (Section 7.2) and induce inflows.

Before an economy becomes mature, imports will exceed exports and will be financed by net inflows; later on, an excess of exports will finance repayments or other outflows. The NM curve (Figure 7.3) is downward sloping; as the real exchange rate appreciates, net imports rise. It also shifts up as income (Y_t) rises. The $I_t - S_t$ curve is vertical[7] and shifts outward as income rises. The intersection of the two curves is the point of internal and external balance and therefore gives $\tilde{Q}$ (point A in Figures 7.3 and 7.4). Monetary, exchange rate and reserve accumulation policy affect the position of the $I_t - S_t$ curve. Thus, $\tilde{Q}$ is conditional on other macroeconomic variables[8] and is at equilibrium when they are at sustainable levels.

At low levels of productivity, $\tilde{Q}$ can exceed Q_w, giving rise to sustained inflation. Figure 7.2 depicts such a possibility and gives the relation between the equilibrium, actual and target real exchange rate.

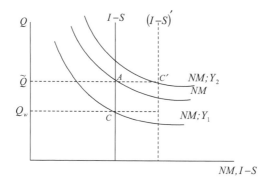

Figure 7.3 The current account equated to the capital account

150 *Beyond monetary theories*

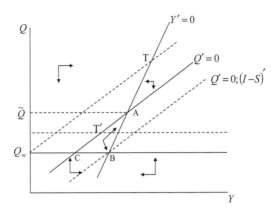

Figure 7.4 Exchange rate cycles

The horizontal line at Q_w graphs Equation 7.8 or the level of Q_t satisfying the real wage target. The $Q' = 0$ ($Y' = 0$) curve graphs the combination of Q_t and output, Y_t that yield external (internal) equilibrium. As net exports rise with Q_t, the demand stimulus raises output, so that the $Y' = 0$ curve, which depicts points where the goods market clears must slope upwards. The $Q' = 0$ curve, which is derived from the equilibrium points of Figure 7.4, as Y_t varies, must also slope upwards. But the slope of the $Y' = 0$ curve will be steeper. This is necessary for stability. Otherwise, as Q_t rises to equate the demand and supply of foreign exchange, it will stimulate further rise in Y_t.

The market-clearing variable for the goods market is Y_t and for the foreign exchange market is Q_t. Below the $Q' = 0$ curve there is excess demand for foreign exchange and Q_t will rise. Above the $Y' = 0$ curve aggregate excess demand is positive and Y_t will rise. The arrows show the direction of motion in the triangle ABC. Since the target wage is not attained, wages and prices rise in an attempt to reach Q_w. But there is also excess demand for goods and foreign exchange. Equilibria are overdetermined in the region ABC. Since the system does not settle down, the inflation continues.

If inflation is positive because the economy is in the region ABC, and money supply is decreased in order to lower it, nominal and real interest rate rise, the equilibrium real exchange depreciates, while since Q_t still exceeds Q_w inflation continues, so that Q_t itself appreciates. The latter, together with the depreciation of $\tilde{Q}$, increases the distance between Q_t and $\tilde{Q}$, and therefore the expected depreciation of Q_t.

Proposition 1: If $Q_t > Q_w$, then further rounds of inflation occur causing cycles of real appreciation and depreciation.

Beyond monetary theories 151

Proof: If the level of Q_t equilibrating $Y' = 0$ and $Q' = 0$ curves is $\tilde{Q}$ and it exceeds Q_w, Q_t will tend to rise to reach a sustainable BOP. Any $Q_t < \tilde{Q}$ requires a real depreciation for this. Capital outflows that shift the $Q' = 0$ upwards when the CAD rises can induce such a depreciation of Q_t. But if $Q_t > Q_w$, then P_t is higher than that required by the wage target. Since the minimum wage is not attained, wages rise in an attempt to reach $\bar{w}$. But as costs rise, so does P_N, pushing Q_t back towards Q_w. A rise of Q_t to $\tilde{Q}$ again will sustain the process and inflation will continue.

The horizontal line at Q_w in Figure 7.4 shows the level of Q_t satisfying the real wage target. The level equilibrating the BOP is $\tilde{Q}$. If $\tilde{Q}$ exceeds Q_w, there exists a triangular region ABC in Figure 7.4, within which there is unemployment and a CAD. If $\tilde{Q}$ exceeds Q_w, Q_t will be in the region ABC and inflation will continue. The arrows show the direction of motion. Inflation is too high if $Q_t > Q_w$ and the CAD is too large if $\tilde{Q} > Q_t$. Nominal depreciation to improve the CAD will raise prices and spark another rise in w_t. For the system to settle down, it must be that $Q_t = Q_w = \tilde{Q}$.

Output is demand determined below the internal balance schedule $Y' = 0$ and limited by available labour supply above it. Since a rise in absorption, such as a rise in government expenditure, makes the CAD worse, a possible equilibrium is around C in Figure 7.4 with large unemployment. Trying to achieve external equilibrium, with limits on relative price adjustment, can generate unemployment. But even with unemployment, there is inflation. So, the AS derived for such an economy would be flat because of unemployment, but subject to upward shifts because of the wage price spiral.

Even if Q_w rises with labour productivity to the line through T', a reduced triangle can still exist, or other shocks can raise $\tilde{Q}$ to T, if $Q' = 0$ shifts up, keeping the economy within the inflationary triangle. For example, a fall in global demand shifts both the schedules in Figure 7.4 upwards, raising $\tilde{Q}$. A rise in capital flows shifting $I_t - S_t$ and the $Q' = 0$ outwards can close the triangle, allowing wages to rise. Imports rise and are financed through the inflows. But the inflows may lead to too large a widening of the CAD, which is risky since it can trigger a reversal. So, the safest way to close the triangle is to raise labour productivity allowing Q_w to rise towards $\tilde{Q}$.

7.6 Conclusion

This chapter defines the bilateral real exchange rate as the relative value of typical consumption baskets across two countries and then considers broader determinants of the real exchange rate such as world

152 *Beyond monetary theories*

relative demands and supplies. The implication is that non-monetary factors also affect nominal exchange rates.

Potential changes in real exchange rates can modify some other typical outcomes of the MA such as the depreciation associated with a monetary shock. The fundamental factors and shocks to these factors that traders factor in when taking positions in FX markets include output growth, global demand, domestic development and standards of living as well as monetary factors. All these are priced into the nominal exchange rate under flexible market determined regimes.

Real interest rates can vary across countries, as long as real interest parity is satisfied.

Since trade arbitrage does not push the real exchange rate to unity, and the real exchange rate affects trade, the relevant concept of equilibrium real exchange rate is that consistent with internal balance and a sustainable current account of the BOP.

A real exchange rate implies a real wage rate, with real appreciation being associated with higher real wages. Therefore, a target real wage out of alignment with the real exchange rate may lead to sustained inflation, in ineffective attempts to reach the wage target.

After developing the fundamentals, from which there are short-run deviations, but which influence expectations even in the short run, the next chapter turns to the relative short-run impact of monetary and fiscal policy in an open economy.

Notes

1 If this was so, capital flows would cause adjustment in exchange rates in line with fundamentals.
2 See Edwards and Savastano (2000) and Montiel (2003) for a survey on the estimation of equilibrium real exchange rates in EDEs.
3 Sections 7.2–7.4 modify and adapt material in Krugman et al. (2014).
4 A country with a nominal exchange rate overvalued in PPP terms normally has a depreciated real exchange rate. Higher purchasing power at home goes together with lower purchasing power outside the country.
5 * denotes advanced material.
6 This is consistent with Montiel's (2003) definition: 'The traditional definition of the "equilibrium" real exchange rate is that it is the value . . . that is simultaneously consistent with internal and EB, conditioned on sustainable values of exogenous and policy variables' (p. 316).
7 Both I_t and S_t can be influenced by Q_t. If the stimulus to I from real depreciation of the exchange rate exceeds that to S_t, the $I_t - S_t$ curve will have a positive slope; this will not change the results qualitatively.
8 This follows not only from Keynesian investment and savings functions, but also from intertemporal optimisation in an open economy. See Blanchard and Fischer (1989), Chapter 2, and Goyal (2006).

References

Blanchard, O. J. and S. Fischer. 1989. *Macroeconomics*, Cambridge, MA: MIT Press.

Edwards, S. and M. A. Savastano. 2000. 'Exchange Rates in Emerging Economies: What Do We Know? What Do We Need to Know?', Chapter 13 in Anne Kreuger (ed.), *Economic Policy Reform*. Chicago: University of Chicago Press. Earlier version available at www.nber.org/papers/w7228.

Goyal, A. 2006. 'Transitional Exchange Rate Policy in a Low Per Capita Income Country', *ICFAI Journal of Monetary Economics*, 4(3): 37–56, August.

Goyal, A. 2010. 'Inflationary Pressures in South Asia', *Asia-Pacific Development Journal*, 17(2): 1–42, December.

Goyal, A. 2014. 'Purchasing Power Parity, Wages and Inflation in Emerging Markets', *Foreign Trade Review*, 49(4): 327–347.

Krugman, P. R., M. Obstfeld and M. Melitz. 2014. *International Economics: Theory and Policy*, 10th edition, Delhi: Pearson Education.

Montiel, P. J. 2003. *Macroeconomics in Emerging Markets*, Cambridge, UK: Cambridge University Press.

8 Short-run adjustment
Monetary and fiscal policy

She who can should do.

8.1 Introduction

So far, output was taken as given. In the long run, it is determined by technology, preferences and fully employed resources. But in the short run, if goods market prices are sticky, output must adjust to bring about equilibrium. Since goods prices do not adjust instantly to clear markets, aggregate demand determines output. In this chapter, we introduce the goods market. While output becomes endogenous, the price level is fixed in the short run.

In an open economy with perfect capital mobility, however, the role of the exchange rate has to be taken into account even in short-run Keynesian analysis. The long run we have developed in the earlier chapters also affects the short run, since expectations of fundamental values affect short-run values of variables such as the exchange rate. These will, however, be affected by the many types of variables, discussed in the previous chapter, not only by the monetary variables. If forward-looking behaviour is modeled, it is necessary to distinguish between temporary and permanent changes. In the former expectations will not be affected and in the latter they would. The expected exchange rate, which was exogenous in our early analysis, now becomes endogenous.

After briefly reviewing the mechanics of short-run output determination, we set up the canonical perfect capital mobility Mundell Fleming (MF) model and assess short-run stabilisation in the open economy. In the MF model, the relative effectiveness of monetary and fiscal policy depends on the exchange rate regime. But this assumes static expectations, so the effect of the long run on the short run is absent. If non-static expectations or some flexibility in prices are allowed, results are moderated.

Short-run adjustment 155

The MF model is a powerful benchmark for open economy macroeconomics, because of the clarity, symmetry and simplicity of its result. Therefore, its results, such as the impossible trinity – that autonomous monetary policy is not possible with a fixed exchange rate and perfect capital mobility – are well internalised and often quoted. But it is a simplification based on strict assumptions, and therefore almost never holds in the real world. The assumptions are systematically relaxed and their effects examined in this chapter. In addition to non-static expectations, we also examine FX market equilibrium under floating exchange rates, when some prices are flexible in the short run. This is the way a benchmark should be used rather than expecting to find it in the data. Alternatively, deviations from the benchmarks, often found in the data, set up puzzles to be explained.

The frameworks developed[1] are used to assess the relative effectiveness of monetary and fiscal policy for stabilisation in response to temporary and permanent shocks, before concluding with some discussion of the limitations of and historical experience with fiscal and monetary policy. Assessment of their relation evolved over time. For example, fixed exchange rates fitted well with Keynesian sticky prices and led to an emphasis on fiscal policy in a closed economy. In general, to the extent the long run affects the short run, degrees of freedom for short-run policy are reduced.

The remainder of the chapter is structured as follows: Section 8.2 examines the relative effectiveness of fiscal and monetary policy under static exchange rate expectations, while Section 8.3 extends the analysis to non-static exchange rate expectations. Section 8.4 turns to an assessment of fiscal and monetary policy, and Section 8.5 assesses the effect of the exchange rate on the current account before Section 8.6 summarises and concludes.

8.2 Relative effectiveness of fiscal and monetary policy

If shocks cause output to deviate from full employment values, can macroeconomic policy bring output back to optimal values? And if so, which policy is more effective?

These fundamental stabilisation issues are taken up in this section.

8.2.1 Output market equilibrium

Output is demand determined in the short run. The components of aggregate demand are consumption (C), investment (I), government expenditure (G) and net exports (NX). Consumption rises with output,

156 Short-run adjustment

net of taxation T, investment falls with the real interest rate and NX rises as real depreciation encourages exports and falls as higher domestic income raises imports.

The open economy demand equals supply identity and becomes an equilibrium condition determining output, once the underlying determinants of demand or expenditure E are added. The signs below give the direction of the effect:

$$E_t = C(\underset{+}{Y_t - T_t}) + I(\underset{-}{R_t - \pi_t^e}) + \underset{+}{G_t} + NX\left(\underset{+}{\frac{S_t P_t^*}{P_t}}, \underset{-}{Y_t - T_t}\right) \qquad (8.1)$$

This can be written as:

$$Y_t = E\left(\underset{+}{Y_t}, \underset{-}{R_t - \pi_t^e}, \underset{+}{G_t}, \underset{-}{T_t}, \frac{S_t P_t^*}{P_t}\right) \qquad (8.2)$$

In addition to the causal variables shown for the components of aggregate demand, output (Y) can also affect investment (I) and the real interest rate ($R - \pi^e$) affects consumption (C). The real interest rate is the nominal interest rate minus expected inflation. The real exchange rate affects NX, and therefore the current account. Since prices are sticky, it is changes in the nominal exchange rate that immediately affect the real exchange rate. Exogenous shifts in prices would also change the real exchange rate.

Depreciation raises aggregate demand and output shifting up the goods market E curve in E and Y space.[2] So, goods market equilibrium requires S_t and Y_t to rise together – the IS* curve, in S and Y space, along which the goods market is in equilibrium, slopes upwards (Figure 8.1).

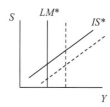

Figure 8.1 Policy under a float

8.2.2 Mundell Fleming model

First consider a floating exchange rate. If exchange rate expectations are static, the UIP reduces to $R_t = R_t^*$ under perfect mobility. The famous MF model, which gives the relative effectiveness of fiscal and monetary policy in an open economy, for this case is governed by the three equations below:

$$R_t = R_t^* \tag{8.3}$$

Substituting Equation 8.3 in the money and goods market equilibrium, respectively, gives:

$$\frac{M_t^S}{P_t} = M^d\left(R_t^*, Y_t\right) \tag{8.4}$$

$$Y_t = E\left(R_t^* - \pi_t^*, Y_t, G_t, T_t, S_t P_t / P_t^*\right) \tag{8.5}$$

The assumptions made are perfect capital mobility, sticky prices and static exchange rate expectations.[3] Figure 8.1 shows the equilibrium in S and Y space. The LM* and IS* curves are derived from Equations 8.4 and 8.5, which have $R_t = R_t^*$ substituted in them. Total differentiation of these equations gives the slopes in S and Y space.[4] The LM* curve showing money market equilibrium is vertical since S_t does not enter Equation 8.4. Y_t is not affected by S_t. Money supply, given $R_t = R_t^*$, determines the position of the curve or the level of Y_t. Therefore, monetary policy is effective, but fiscal policy that shifts the IS* curve along the vertical LM* curve is ineffective.

The IS-LM curves in R_t and Y_t space (Figure 8.2) explain the mechanics underlying this result. A rise in G_t shifts out the IS curve, but this raises R_t above R_t^*, capital flows in, the exchange rate appreciates and

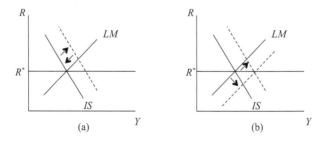

Figure 8.2 (a) Fiscal and (b) monetary policy under a float

as export demand falls the IS curve shifts back. This adjustment will continue until it is back in its original position, thus making fiscal policy ineffective.

An increase in money supply (M), however, will shift out the LM curve. This lowers R_t below R_t^*, capital flows out, the exchange rate depreciates and as export demand rises the IS curve shifts outwards. This adjustment will continue until the rise in demand is sufficient to raise R_t to R_t^*. Monetary policy is thus effective.

Under a floating exchange rate, adjustment is driven by capital flows due to interest rate arbitrage. These change the exchange rate. But if the exchange rate is fixed, the capital flows change reserves and the money supply. This now becomes the source of automatic adjustment. As Figure 8.3 shows, money supply is tied to the fixed exchange rate. The money market equilibrium degenerates into a horizontal line at that rate. Shifts in IS* are now effective in stabilisation. For example, an outward shift with a rise in G_t would raise output.

Figure 8.4 explains why. A rise in M_t shifts out the LM curve, but this lowers R_t below R_t^*, capital flows out and the exchange rate tends to depreciate. But since the CB is committed to a fixed exchange rate, it must buy the domestic currency being sold by the exiting traders. Selling dollars for rupees absorbs rupees and decreases M_t. This adjustment will continue until the LM curve is back in its original position, thus making monetary policy ineffective.

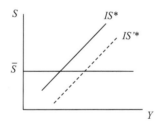

Figure 8.3 Policy under a fixed exchange rate

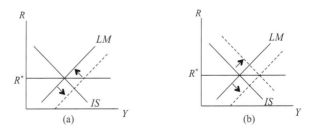

Figure 8.4 (a) Monetary and (b) fiscal policy under a fixed exchange rate

A rise in G_t shifts out the IS curve, but this raises R_t above R_t^*, capital flows in, so that the exchange rate tends to appreciate. But since the CB is committed to a fixed exchange rate, it must buy foreign currency, thus increasing its FX reserves. As it buys dollars with domestic currency, it injects rupees and M_t increases. This adjustment will continue until the LM curve shifts out sufficiently to lower R_t to R_t^*. Fiscal policy is thus effective, being supported by an automatic monetary accommodation.

8.3 Relative effectiveness of policy: non-static exchange rate expectations

Now, consider non-static exchange rate expectations. Fundamentals determine the latter. Since the expected exchange rate can differ from the current exchange rate, expected depreciation or appreciation drives a wedge between domestic and FX rates. So, UIP has to be considered along with the money market equilibrium. In S, Y space the IS* curve remains as derived above, but we derive a new curve, FM*, giving the combination of S_t and Y_t at which the FX and money markets are in equilibrium. Analogous to the LM*, which gives the money market equilibrium in S and Y space, this is FM*, since it gives the equilibrium in the FX and money market together in the S and Y space.

To derive the relation between S_t and Y_t, giving the FM* schedule, consider a rise in Y_t in Figure 8.5, which depicts UIP in the FX market

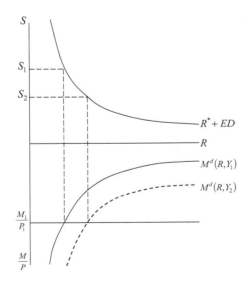

Figure 8.5 Deriving the FM* curve

160 *Short-run adjustment*

above and the money market equilibrium below. As money demand rises with Y_t, so does the interest rate. Since the rise in Y_t absorbs money balances, R_t must rise to keep the money market in equilibrium. Since returns to holding domestic currency rises, S_t must appreciate. An appreciation is consistent with UIP, since the higher interest rate covers the expected depreciation back to the expected exchange rate S_1. Therefore, a rise in Y_t is associated with an appreciation of the currency. The FM* schedule must slope downwards.

Factors increasing net domestic money supply and reducing the demand for rupee assets would shift out the FM* schedule, while factors reducing net domestic money supply or raising the returns to holding rupee assets would tend to appreciate S and shift out FM*.

The specific factors causing the FM* schedule to shift are, therefore, those affecting the money and FX markets, respectively:

1 A rise in money supply shifts FM* out, since it depreciates S_t for every Y_t.
2 A rise in P_t reduces real money balances, raises R_t and appreciates S_t for every Y_t, so the FM* schedule shifts down.
3 If money demand (M^d) falls, this has the same effect as a rise in money supply, shifting the FM* schedule upwards. Net money supply rises, R_t falls and S_t depreciates (rises).
4 If S_t^e rises, or FX participants expect the future value of the rupee to be lower, the relative return to holding dollars rises, so the rupee must depreciate as holders shift to dollars – the FM* curve shifts out.
5 A rise in R_t^* has the same effect as 3, since the returns to holding dollars rise.

In summary, the changes causing the FM* curve to shift outwards are $M_t\uparrow, P_t\downarrow, M_t^d\downarrow, R_t^*\uparrow, S_t^e\uparrow$. Changes in the opposite direction would cause it to shift inwards. A rise in Y_t^* or fall in M_t^* would also raise R_t^*.

The short-run equilibrium of the economy (assuming P_t sticky) must satisfy all three markets; thus it must lie on the intersection of the IS* and FM* curves. Figure 8.6 shows the response from a position of disequilibrium. At a point below both curves, there is excess supply in the goods market since Y_t exceeds its goods market equilibrium value and S_t is appreciated below values that would equilibrate the goods market. There is excess supply of domestic currency since there is an expected depreciation. At higher Y_t, reduced net money supply has raised interest rates and appreciated the currency. Since capital is mobile and asset prices can jump, S_t depreciates immediately to a point on the FM* curve

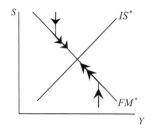

Figure 8.6 Short-run equilibrium

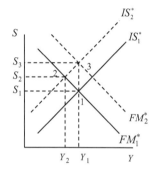

Figure 8.7 A temporary fall in world demand

to reach FX market equilibrium, and then steady adjustment occurs along the FM* to remove the goods market disequilibrium. S_t depreciates as a fall in Y_t reduces money demand and interest rates. Firms reduce production because inventories have built up. In the upper quadrant, similarly excess demand for both domestic currency and goods leads to a jump to reach the FM* curve, and then further appreciation along it. FX market equilibrium needs to hold, but gradual adjustment can occur along the IS* curve to bring about goods market equilibrium.

8.3.1 Stabilisation of a temporary shock

The apparatus developed can now be used to examine the relative effectiveness of monetary and fiscal policy for short-run stabilisation.

Temporary shocks: Remember P_t^* and R_t^* are exogenous, P_t is fixed in short run and S_t^e does not change since the shock is temporary. A temporary fall in world demand would shift the IS* curve upwards. With an unchanged FM* curve, output would fall from Y_1 to Y_2 (Figure 8.7).

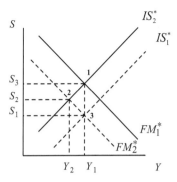

Figure 8.8 A temporary rise in money demand

Among alternative stabilisation policies, a rise in money supply would shift out the FM* curve until Y rises once more to Y_1, but the rise in money supply would also depreciate the exchange rate to S_3. Fiscal policy or a rise in G_t would also raise Y_t, but it would be accompanied by an appreciation as the IS* curve shifted downwards. Thus, unlike the MF model, under floating exchange rates, non-static exchange rate expectations allow fiscal policy also to be an effective stabilisation tool. A rise in R_t above R_t^* and an appreciation due to a G_t rise is consistent with UIP because of an expected future depreciation. This allows $R_t > R_t^*$ and some fiscal stimulus to continue without inviting inflows.[5] In the MF model, these inflows persist until the original demand stimulus is reversed. But since appreciation with a fiscal stimulus reduces demand while depreciation under a rise in money supply increases it, monetary policy remains a more effective stabilisation tool for an adverse demand shock.

Figure 8.8 shows the working of similar stabilisation options to restore output to its original level after a temporary rise in money demand shifts the FM* curve downwards. The options are a rise in money supply to restore the FM* curve back to its original level, or a rise in G_t or cut in taxes, shifting out IS*. Both stabilise output, but the first depreciates the exchange rate while the second appreciates it, making the first more effective.

8.3.2 Permanent shocks

Under a permanent shock, however, fiscal policy is ineffective, as in the MF model. The reason is that the expected exchange rate also changes if the shock is permanent. Starting from an equilibrium where $R_t = R_t^*$ and expected depreciation is zero, Figure 8.9 shows that under a

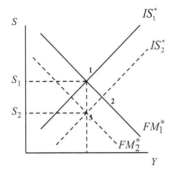

Figure 8.9 A permanent rise in G

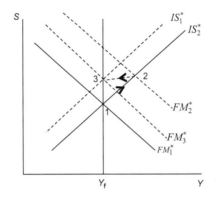

Figure 8.10 A permanent rise in M

permanent rise in G_t, expected appreciation would shift the FM* curve downward, keeping output unchanged.

A permanent rise in money supply would also raise expected depreciation, so that the FM* curve would shift out more than for an equivalent temporary shock. Y_t would rise in the short run and the exchange rate would depreciate.

But neither monetary nor fiscal policy can, in the long run, raise output above the full employment level. If demand exceeds the full employment level, Y_f, prices will rise shifting the FM* curve downwards, as real money balances fall, and the IS* curve leftwards, as demand for domestic goods falls, until they intersect with output at the level of Y_f. Thus, the exchange rate will overshoot, or its initial depreciation will exceed its final level, since it will appreciate from point 2 to point 3 (Figure 8.10). But the overshooting is less than that

164 Short-run adjustment

in Chapter 6, since here Y_t can also adjust to absorb some of the excess money balances.

The general point is that forward-looking behaviour under permanent shocks reduces the effectiveness of macroeconomic policy.

8.3.3 Fiscal policy and some short-run price flexibility

Fiscal policy is effective not only under non-static expectations, but there are also other factors that can increase its effectiveness. Consider the case of some short-run price flexibility and static exchange rate expectations. In the earlier section, we saw how the MF results are modified when the assumption of static exchange rate expectations are relaxed, so that UIP holds rather than $R_t = R_t^*$. In this section, we let consumer prices be a function of the exchange rate, and find a similar modification of the MF results.

Equation 8.6 shows log consumer prices, p_t^c, to be a weighted average of log foreign $(s_t + p_t^*)$ and domestic prices p_t, where σ is the weight of foreign goods in the consumption basket.

$$p_t^c = \sigma\left(s_t + p_t^*\right) + (1-\sigma)p_t \tag{8.6}$$

Normalising foreign and domestic prices at unity, so that $p_t^* = p_t = 0$, p_t^c reduces to σs. Then, substituting for price in the money market equilibrium, Equation 8.4 makes it a function of S_t (as in Eq. 8.7), so that LM* is no longer a vertical line but is negatively sloped:

$$m_t = \sigma s_t + k y_t - \theta R_t \tag{8.7}$$

If $\sigma = 0$, LM* becomes a vertical line, but if $\sigma > 0$ it implies the derivative of money demand with respect to the exchange rate exceeds zero $(M_s^d > 0)$ so LM* has a negative slope[6] (Figure 8.11) like FM*. The

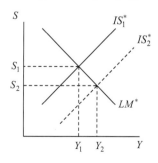

Figure 8.11 Fiscal policy when the exchange rate affects prices

Short-run adjustment 165

slope allows fiscal policy to be effective in stabilisation, just like it is effective with FM*. Appreciation lowers domestic prices, raising real money balances. The MF model is the limiting case of such more general cases.

The results on the relative effectiveness of monetary and fiscal policy are specific to the models and assumptions under which they were derived. In applying them to an actual situation, it is necessary to make a judgement on which assumptions are appropriate. For EDEs in particular, the assumption of fluctuations around a full employment level may not be appropriate, so that both monetary and fiscal policy can have persistent effects as they contribute to maintaining higher trend growth. Even at the global level, this has become obvious as most economies have underperformed relative to potential over 2008–15, which is a longer period than any short run. Macroeconomic policy failures have contributed to this deviation.

8.4   Limits of macroeconomic stabilisation

Stabilisation is never perfect or complete. Although the above analysis is able to clearly specify the policy to be used in response to a particular shock, there are limitations in actual policy making. It is easier to say what should have been done ex-post rather than to act under many types of uncertainties.

For example, it is difficult to clearly identify a shock, its type and source, and therefore which policy to use. Under simultaneous shocks, each may require opposite responses. Consider a simultaneous external adverse cost and demand shock, the first calls for an appreciation, but the second calls for depreciation. There may be trade-offs between objectives such as encouraging growth and reducing inflation. Market imperfections may vitiate the working of policy. Aggregate policy may have varying impacts on different sectors. The lags in monetary policy are said to be long and variable. But fiscal lags can be larger than monetary. The response time, especially, is much longer, especially for expenditure. It is easier to change interest rates than it is to get legislatures to pass a new tax expenditure package. Implementation lags are also long, and there can be large leakages, depending on administrative capacity.

The 1950s were the period when Keynesian ideas dominated. Especially following the Great Depression, government expenditure was thought to be the dominant macroeconomic tool. Money, following Keynes, was regarded as having limited impact on the real sector because of the liquidity trap and low demand elasticities. In a closed economy with fixed exchange rates, fiscal policy was more effective.

166 *Short-run adjustment*

With the development of rational expectations and the resurgence of the supply side, Ricardian equivalence-type arguments suggested private actions would counter fiscal policy. For example, if government spent more, taxpayers foreseeing a rise in future taxes would save more. This would reduce the effect of government spending on demand. Long lags and political constraints on fiscal policy were also being recognised as weakening fiscal policy. Markets were dominating governments and price adjustments were dominating quantity adjustments, once again. While the original Keynesian position had been that fiscal policy was generally more effective than monetary policy, the New Keynesian view was that interest rates were effective in closing the output gap, given wage and price rigidities, except in extreme liquidity traps. Overall, monetary policy came to be regarded as the more potent stabilisation tool (Blanchard et al., 2010).

Under globalisation and financial innovations, interest rate effects on domestic expenditures become significant. Deeper financial markets spread effects more widely. These markets are very sensitive to interest rates. Forward-looking behaviour becomes more important and markets try to guess the CB's response to uncertainty and to shocks. Thus, transparency became a major issue. Forward-looking monetary policy can reduce lags. For example, if prices are sticky, a rapid initial policy response to inflation prevents inflationary expectations being factored into these sticky prices, and therefore reduces the length and output cost of disinflation. To the extent agents become more forward looking, trade-offs reduce since excess demand can be removed without output loss. This modern approach to macroeconomic policy is explored in more detail in Chapter 11.

Under temporary supply shocks that are more common in EDEs, policy can act on the supply curve to reduce costs and the output cost of a demand squeeze. For example, while the interest rate channel works through widening the output gap, and then influencing price setting, the exchange rate directly affects consumer prices and intermediate commodity prices. Such flexible asset prices lower monetary policy transmission lags. Typically, monetary policy is more effective in reducing a boom than in reversing a bust, because of a preference for liquidity in bad times and prices that are sticky downwards.

Just as the depression era gave rise to Keynesian government expenditure-based policies, there was a revival of such policies after the GFC and the freezing of credit markets. But large government debt in AEs, after banking sector rescues, restrained the use of fiscal policy, leading to an overuse of monetary policy through near-zero interest rates and large liquidity injections through quantitative easing (QE) programmes. The early QE did moderate the slowdown and forestall another great depression, but it created risks by raising asset prices, motivating competitive currency depreciation and leading to surges and reversals of capital flows to EDEs. Ongoing rethinking on macro-economic policy in the post-GFC era (Blanchard, 2015) emphasises the complementary role of financial regulation.

If, however, CBs are not independent they can be subject to political pressure. This can force them to use surprise inflation to reduce real wages, and therefore unemployment, leading to what is known as the inflation bias. Inflation is chronically high without much gain in output. This idea led to a lot of work on analysis of institutions and strengthening the autonomy of the CB. In populous low per capita income countries, such as India, however, political pressure works rather to reduce inflation even at high output cost, because of inflation sensitivity in the absence of widespread wage indexation (Goyal, 2014).

Political pressures also vitiate fiscal policy. Thus, governments typically spend more in an election year, giving rise to a political business cycle working against successful stabilisation. Frequent elections may reinforce a short-term outlook, whereby the welfare of future generations is neglected, resulting in the accumulation of too much debt. In EDEs, populist transfers may take precedence over building long-term physical and human capital for sustainable development.

Ideally, both fiscal and monetary policy should be countercyclical, but lags in implementation and impact can make them procyclical. The lack of space can not only be a problem, especially in EDEs, but also in AEs as public debt shot up after the financial sector rescues of the GFC. Large fiscal and current account deficits can make it difficult to provide fiscal or monetary stimuli, even if they are required.

Given the limitations of fiscal and monetary policies, an independent but supportive exchange rate policy can be an added instrument. This is explored in the next chapter.

At the zero lower bound, the major effect of QE-type monetary expansion is on the exchange rate, but exchange rate policy refers to policies other than changes in money supply that also affect exchange rates.

8.5 The effect of the exchange rate on the current account

The floating exchange rate affects exports and imports, and therefore the current account balance (CAB). Figure 8.12 gives the combination of S and Y at which the CAB equals some sustainable level. It is

168 Short-run adjustment

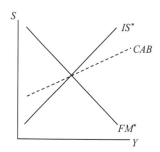

Figure 8.12 The current account balance

upward sloping, but the slope is less than that of IS* because the current account is more responsive than the goods market to a change in S_t, therefore requiring less of a rise in S_t to reach balance. A rise in output raises imports and requires a depreciation to stimulate exports and keep the current account in balance, so the upward slope. Since part of the demand boost from exports leaks into savings and imports, a larger change in S_t is required to equilibrate the goods market compared to that required for the current account.

A fiscal stimulus that shifts down the IS* will deteriorate the CA. A monetary stimulus that shifts up the FM* will initially improve the CA. The CAB drawn in Figure 8.12 assumes the CA improves with a rise in S. But imports and exports have to be sufficiently responsive to price changes for depreciation to be able to improve the current account. That is, on differentiating the CA written in local currency, with respect to S, it must exceed zero:[7]

$$CA = X - SM \qquad (8.8)$$

$$\frac{\delta CA}{\delta S} = \frac{\delta X}{\delta S} - M - S\frac{\delta M}{\delta S} > 0 \qquad (8.9)$$

Dividing by M:

$$= \frac{1}{M}\frac{\delta X}{\delta S} - 1 - \frac{S}{M}\frac{\delta M}{\delta S} > 0$$

If the CA is fully balanced $X = SM$ or $\frac{1}{M} = \frac{S}{X}$. Substituting this above:

$$= \frac{S}{X}\frac{\delta X}{\delta S} - 1 - \frac{S}{M}\frac{\delta M}{\delta S} > 0$$

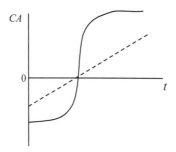

Figure 8.13 The CAB over time

Since η_M has a negative sign:

$$= \eta_X + \eta_M > 1 \tag{8.10}$$

This is the Marshall-Lerner condition. It must be satisfied for the CA to improve with depreciation.

Improvement of the CA may take time. Since export and import volumes tend to be precontracted, the immediate effect of a depreciation may only be a rise in the rupee value of imports while the rupee value of exports is unchanged, leading to a deterioration of the current account. Thus, the CAS takes the shape of a J-curve (Figure 8.13). In most countries, the Marshall-Lerner condition is satisfied only after a year, when this adjustment is complete and the CA starts to improve. If a monetary expansion, therefore, is not stabilising in the short run, it may require overshooting of interest, and therefore exchange rates in responding to the domestic cycle, thus adding to volatility.

It also depends on the degree of pass through of exchange rate changes. We have assumed P_t and P_t^* to be sticky so that import prices $S_t P_t^*$ change with S_t, implying the pass through is unity. Exporters are assumed to denominate exports in domestic currency. To the extent monopolistically competitive export firms follow PTM, they may not change local prices even if S_t changes. This factor is not important for the commodity trade, where pass through is direct. Pass through is low also if trade is invoiced in local currency, so that it is generally lower for the United States (see Chapter 5).

Since for an EDE imports are often priced in dollars and exports in foreign currency, the initial impact of depreciation only raises the import bill. The CAD deteriorates. If exporters have less market power, they may not be able to get the higher domestic currency prices required to stimulate export supply, even in the long run.

170 *Short-run adjustment*

If the pass through from depreciation to domestic prices is high, inflation appreciates the real exchange rate and real depreciation is limited. The pass through tends to be higher for commodities such as oil, which are contracted in dollar prices, and for differentiated goods imports such as high-quality capital goods, for which competition is limited. These dominate the Indian import basket. It is also higher in times of high inflation, for large spikes and persistent changes in the exchange rate since menu costs of price change are then exceeded (Ghosh and Rajan, 2007). Mallick and Marques (2008) also find the pass through to import prices to be high in India.

A price through of less than unity moderates the J-curve (Figure 8.13) to the dashed curve. The initial value effect is less, but then so are future volume adjustments. In a high-inflation country, where P_t also changes in the short run, Q_t changes less with S_t, with a correspondingly lower effect on trade. All these factors reduce the effect of the real exchange rate on the CA, especially in the short run. For a high-inflation country dependent on dollar-denominated imports, the immediate impact of a nominal depreciation is likely to be a rise in inflation and real appreciation.

The real exchange rate affects the CA, but reverse causality also holds and varies over time. Although a fiscal deficit may cause a CAD and a real appreciation in the short run, in the long run, as CADs reduce wealth of domestic consumers, relative demand for home goods will decrease causing a real depreciation. Domestic consumers tend to consume a larger share of domestic goods compared to foreign goods.

8.6 Summary

This chapter shows how, if prices are sticky, output is demand determined in the short run. Under perfect capital mobility and static exchange rate expectations, results from the Mundell-Fleming (MF) model are that monetary policy is effective for stabilisation in response to shocks, but fiscal policy is not under floating exchange rates. The relative policy effectiveness reverses under fixed exchange rates.

Under non-static expectations or some flexibility in prices, fiscal policy regains some effectiveness but only in the short run and for temporary shocks. Long-run effects are reduced because forward-looking behaviour reduces the effectiveness of policy that tries to go against fundamentals.

Historical experience with fiscal and monetary policy brings in more complexities. Assessment of their relative effectiveness has changed over time. There are problems in identifying shocks and political complications. Although the evolution of theory tended to downplay the

Short-run adjustment 171

contribution of macroeconomic policy, the experience of the GFC has again emphasised its importance. Policy also has to factor in the effect of the exchange rate on the current account. For a depreciation to reduce, a current account deficit, trade and supply elasticities and pass through of the change in exchange rates have to be high.

The next chapter turns to management of the exchange rate, from an outright fix to varying degrees of intervention, and in what circumstances exchange rate policy can complement monetary and fiscal policy.

Notes

1 These follow those in standard textbooks such as by Romer (1996), Sarno and Taylor (2002) and Krugman et al. (2014), but are adapted to EDEs.
2 This assumes the Marshall-Lerner condition is satisfied or the elasticities of export and import are high enough so that the volume effect is larger than the value effect. The latter raises the domestic cost of a given volume of imports.
3 As a referee pointed out, if capital flows are exogenous as they tend to be in an EM, this adds an additional equation to the MF, which can make the policy equations redundant (Patnaik, 2015, ch.1). Something else, perhaps capital controls, is then required to regain policy autonomy.
4 The slopes can be derived by total differentiation of Equations 8.4 and 8.5, respectively, w.r.t S. They are: $\left.\dfrac{dY_t}{dS_t}\right|_{LM^*} = -\dfrac{M_S^d}{M_Y^d} = 0,\ \left.\dfrac{dY_t}{dS_t}\right|_{IS^*} = \dfrac{E_S}{1-E_Y} > 0$ where the subscripts give the partial derivatives of the money demand and expenditure function.
5 Compared to the MF model, adjustment does not continue until IS goes back to its original position because expected depreciation allows $R_t > R_t^*$. This is also the reason the FM* is negatively sloped compared to the vertical LM*. Substituting from UIP in M^d for R_t gives a positive partial derivative for M_s from the negative R_t and negative S_t effect. At low S_t, R_t will be high to cover expected depreciation, requiring high Y_t to clear the money market.
6 The slope $\left.\left(\dfrac{ds_t}{dy_t}\right)\right|_{LM^*} = -\dfrac{m_y}{m_s} = -\dfrac{k}{\sigma} < 0$ since the partial derivative of money with respect to s_t is now not zero, but is positive.
7 As a simplification, $P = P^* = 1$ in this derivation. That is, prices are fixed. The derivation using the real exchange rate Q instead of S gives a Q_2/Q_1 term pre-multiplying η_M. The term can be ignored if the change in the real exchange rate is small.

References

Blanchard, O. 2015. 'Ten Takeaways from the Rethinking Macro Policy: Progress or Confusion?', 25 May. Available at www.voxeu.org/article/rethinking-macro-policy-ten-takeaways (accessed on June 2015).

172 *Short-run adjustment*

Blanchard, O., G. D'Aricca and P. Mauro. 2010. 'Rethinking Monetary Policy', *International Monetary Fund*. Available at www.imf.org/external/pubs/ft/spn/2010/spn1003.pdf (accessed on January 2014).

Ghosh, A. and R. S. Rajan. 2007. 'Exchange Rate Pass Through in Asia: What Does the Literature Tell Us?', *Asian Pacific Economic Literature*, 21(2): 13–28.

Goyal, A. 2014. *History of Monetary Policy in India since Independence, Springer Briefs in Economics*, New Delhi: Springer.

Krugman, P. R., M. Obstfeld and M. Melitz. 2014. *International Economics: Theory and Policy*, 10th edition, New Delhi: Pearson Education.

Mallick, S. and H. Marques. 2008. 'Pass-Through of Exchange Rate and Tariffs into Import Process of India: Currency Depreciation versus Import Liberalization', *Review of International Economics*, 16(4): 765–782.

Patnaik, P. 2015. *ICSSR Research Surveys and Explorations: Economics*, Vol. 3, New Delhi: Oxford University Press.

Romer, D. 1996. *Advanced Macroeconomics*, Singapore: McGraw-Hill Companies Inc.

Sarno, L. and M. P. Taylor. 2002. *The Economics of Exchange Rates*, Cambridge, UK: Cambridge University Press.

9 Exchange rate policy

There can be many routes to a goal.

9.1 Introduction

Monetary and fiscal policies themselves affect the exchange rate. In the previous chapter, changes in the money supply and through that the interest rate changed the exchange rate. A fixed or a floating exchange rate has implication for monetary policy and for the relative effectiveness of fiscal and monetary policy – we saw this in the MF model. In this chapter, we first examine the kind of CB interventions required to fix the exchange rate. Second, we extend the analysis of relative policy effectiveness under non-static exchange rate expectations to the case of a fixed exchange rate. Results revolve around the credibility of the fix and are the same as the MF, regardless of permanent or temporary shocks, if the fix is credible. Otherwise, the country can involuntarily loose FX reserves, approaching a crisis situation. Devaluation becomes a new policy option under fixed exchange rates. We also explore the shocks for which there is automatic adjustment under fixed and floating exchange rates.

We extend the analysis to the case of imperfect substitutability between domestic and foreign assets and to varying degrees of fixity – that is, to alternative exchange rate regimes. Finally, we examine if sterilised CB intervention in FX markets, which does not change the money supply, and signalling can affect the exchange rate. This would allow some independence in exchange rate policy from monetary policy.[1] We also see how the exchange rate and macroeconomic policies affect the current account of the BOP.

Without perfect capital mobility or a perfectly fixed exchange rate, there are degrees of freedom for monetary policy. A trade-off is possible between domestic objectives and exchange rate stability.

174 *Exchange rate policy*

For example, a monetary expansion may be required for the domestic cycle, but money supply may have to be reduced to mitigate the resulting depreciation. To the extent there are other ways of influencing the exchange rate independently of monetary and fiscal policy – the trade-off is reduced, thus making monetary and fiscal policy more effective.

The remainder of the chapter is structured as follows: Section 9.2 analyses the CB balance sheet, stabilisation and credibility under a fixed exchange rates. Section 9.3 compares automatic stabilisation under fixed and flexible exchange rates. Section 9.4 moves on to the range of intermediate exchange rate regimes. Section 9.5 outlines the MA to the BOP; Section 9.6 discusses the portfolio balance channel of intervention; Section 9.7 CB intervention; and Section 9.8 signalling. Section 9.9 analyses the contribution of exchange rate policy under a liquidity trap, before Section 9.10 concludes with a summary.

9.2 Fixed exchange rates

Money supply affects the exchange rate and CB intervention in the FX market affects the money supply. To see why and how, we set up a hypothetical CB balance sheet. The balance sheet, shown in Table 9.1, has foreign currency reserves F and domestic government bonds A as assets. Its liabilities are currency holdings of the public C and deposits D from commercial banks, with the CB's net worth N as a balancing item. If N is constant, change in assets must equal that in liabilities.

Each time the CB buys an asset, it pays for it by creating money – its liability. A positive F implies that the CB is intervening in the FX market. Under a pure float, the exchange rate is determined by the market demand for and supply of FX. There is no intervention from the CB. To maintain a fixed exchange rate, however, it may have to buy or sell F to remove any excess demand or supply for the currency at that rate. But this will change its liabilities, and therefore the money supply. For

Table 9.1 CB balance sheet

Assets	Liabilities
A	C
F	D
	N

example, a purchase of US$ 100, if paid for in rupees, would increase C by the same amount.

But a fixed exchange rate also requires a fixed level of money supply. So, a dollar purchase may have to be sterilised to keep money supply the same. Sterilised intervention occurs if the CB matches a rise in F with an equal fall in A, so that money supply remains unchanged. Sterilised intervention, therefore, is a swap of domestic for foreign assets.

Under perfect capital mobility, the level of the fixed exchange rate uniquely determines the money supply. We saw this in the MF model, and now see this through the interaction of the FX and money market in Figure 9.1. If the exchange rate is credibly fixed at S^0, this is the expected exchange rate. Then, R_t must equal R_t^* from UIP for FX market equilibrium, and money market equilibrium requires money supply to equal whatever is the demand at that interest rate. The CB must intervene to maintain FX market equilibrium. Given the fixed exchange rate S^0 in quadrant I (at 1), the money supply gets determined in quadrant II (at 2).

For S^0 to remain credibly fixed, the interest rate R_t must continue to equal R_t^*. Now, consider a rise in income. Transaction demand for money rises and the money demand curve shifts downwards. The fall in net money supply will tend to appreciate the exchange rate to point 3' in quadrant I and raise R_t above R_t^*. To prevent this, given

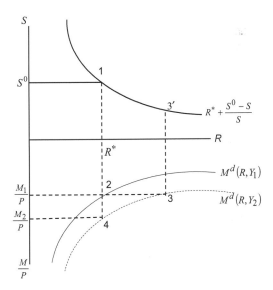

Figure 9.1 A fixed exchange rate

its commitment to the fixed exchange rate, the CB must increase the money supply to M_2 to match the increased money demand. This would happen automatically, as the CB bought the foreign currency flowing in due to the rise in R_t, thus injecting rupees and increasing the money supply. At point 4, R_t is back at R_t^* and S is at S^0.

Consider an attempt at raising money supply. R_t would fall and the rupee depreciates as traders sold rupees (bought dollars), since the relative return to holding dollar assets has risen. So, the CB must buy rupees (sell dollars) to prevent the depreciation. As a result, the money supply falls. Thus, a fixed exchange rate ties the money supply. If devaluation is expected or the country risk premium rises, then money supply has to fall as the CB buys rupees to support the exchange rate, selling dollars to those who want to take out foreign currency. R_t rises to cover the expected devaluation.[2]

Since money supply is tied to maintaining the exchange rate, monetary autonomy is lost. Thus, monetary policy becomes ineffective as in the MF model. Figure 9.2 shows that, since a monetary stimulus through a purchase of domestic assets would tend to depreciate the exchange rate as it shifted the FM* curve rightward, the CB must sell foreign assets to prevent the depreciation. But this would reduce the money supply and bring the FM* curve back to its original position so that Y_t returns to Y_1.

Fiscal policy, however, becomes more effective than under floating exchange rates. Figure 9.3 shows that monetary policy must accommodate a fiscal stimulus to prevent the exchange rate from appreciating. As Y_t rises, the rise in money demand tends to raise R_t. The inflows that result appreciate S_t. To prevent this, the CB must buy foreign assets. As it pays for these, money supply rises. So, a rightward shift of the FM* curve matches the rightward shift of the IS* curve. As a result, income increases to Y_3 higher than the Y_2 possible under flexible exchange rates.

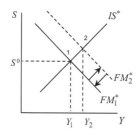

Figure 9.2 Monetary policy

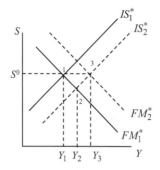

Figure 9.3 A temporary rise in government expenditure

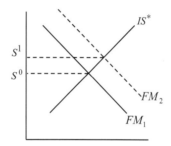

Figure 9.4 One-time devaluation

If S^0 is credibly fixed and anchors expectations even in the long run, there is no difference between the short-run effect of policy responses to temporary or to permanent shocks.

Apart from monetary and fiscal policies, an additional stabilisation policy now becomes available – a devaluation or revaluation of the exchange rate. To do so, a CB only has to announce that it is willing to buy or sell any amount of foreign currency at the new rate.

In Figure 9.4, the first step is the announcement of devaluation. This raises output as exports rise, and money supply expands to accommodate the rise in output. Devaluation is normally accompanied by a rise in FX reserves, since the preceding expectation of devaluation, which leads to a reserve outflow, is reversed. The rise in reserves itself raises money supply, as the CB buys foreign assets. Therefore, devaluation is a way of stimulating output and raising reserves. A CB may, however, be forced to devalue if it is losing reserves rapidly.

178 *Exchange rate policy*

But, as in the flexible exchange rate case, a macro stimulus cannot sustain output above the full employment level in the long run. Under excess demand, the price level would rise. This would, over time, reduce real money balances, shifting the FM* curve leftward, and cause a real appreciation shifting the IS* curve also leftward, until the two intersect at Y_f. Thus, equilibrating flexibility in the real exchange rate is achieved through changes in the price level even without flexibility of the nominal exchange rate. But an adjustment of the nominal exchange rate normally achieves the required real change faster and with lower cost, since goods prices are sticky.

If the nominal exchange rate is fixed at a level incompatible with fundamentals, such as the fiscal deficit, it cannot be credibly sustained. In that case, markets expect devaluation. The return from holding foreign assets shifts up in Figure 9.5. If the CB maintains its commitment to the earlier level of the exchange rate, it must raise the domestic interest rate to cover not only the international interest rate, but also the expected devaluation. The equilibrium combination shifts from point 1 to point 2 in the figure. Unless UIP is satisfied in this way, speculators will exit the domestic currency. The CB will lose reserves, as it sells foreign currency to satisfy the demand for it. Money supply will fall with the reserve loss until domestic interest rates reach the required level.

A currency attack has similar features. A loss of reserves and sharp rise in domestic interest rates normally accompany such an attack.

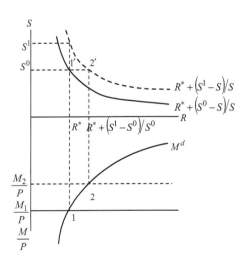

Figure 9.5 Attack on a currency

The key point is CBs lose reserves involuntarily, not by choice. Market expectations drive the reserve loss and fall in money supply. A fixed exchange rate is susceptible to such a loss of market confidence.

9.3 Automatic stabilisation under fixed and flexible exchange rates

Commitment to a fixed exchange rate makes monetary policy not only ineffective in open capital markets, but it also implies that money supply adjusts automatically to any shock originating in money markets. Thus, there is automatic stabilisation for such shocks. For example, in Figure 9.6, if money demand rises, the exchange rate tends to appreciate with the rise in R_t. To maintain the fixed exchange rate, the CB must buy the foreign currency that flows in, thus raising FX reserves and the money supply. Thus, money supply adjusts to the rise in money demand so that a fall in output is averted.

Under a floating exchange rate, fiscal policy is less effective in open capital markets, because of the appreciation that partly counters the demand stimulus. But exchange rate flexibility implies automatic stabilisation in response to goods market shocks, since the exchange rate adjusts in the right direction after such a shock. For example, in Figure 9.7, if world demand falls, the IS* curve shifts left. But the exchange rate depreciates, partly countering the fall in demand. Output falls only to Y_2 from Y_1. Without the depreciation, it would have fallen further to Y_3.

Floating exchange rates, however, aggravate a monetary shock. For example, a rise in money demand would lead to an appreciation,

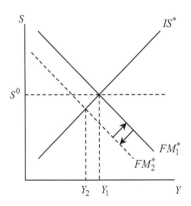

Figure 9.6 Automatic stabilisation under fixed exchange rates

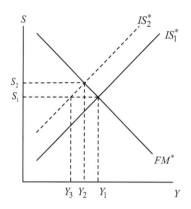

Figure 9.7 Automatic stabilisation under floating exchange rates

worsening the fall in demand if the exchange rate was floating (Figure 9.6). Just as fixed exchange rates would aggravate a demand shock (Figure 9.7), output would fall to Y_3 if the exchange rate were fixed. Where there is policy autonomy, there is no automatic adjustment.

Therefore, the modern monetary policy practice is to combine an interest rate instrument with floating exchange rates and an inflation target. Such an instrument rule neutralises a money demand shock compensating for unstable money demand. There was a higher incidence of monetary shocks as more close money substitutes developed with financial deepening. Automatic stabilisation was required for more frequent monetary shocks. Flexible exchange rates help adjust to goods market and terms of trade shocks, compensating for sticky goods market prices. The inflation target provides the nominal anchor for prices, even if the price of the currency is changing. This combination, therefore, allows automatic adjustment of money supply as well as automatic response to demand shocks, along with a nominal anchor.

But exchange rate volatility can be excessive. In the presence of uncertain fundamentals, a bubble can develop in assets, including the currency, taking them far from fundamentals and requiring CB intervention to prick the asset bubble and maintain stability. This is especially so for EDEs with thin FX markets subject to volatile and procyclical cross-border capital movements. FII investments lose value from a sharp depreciation, while excess volatility also hurts trade. EDEs also tend to have more supply shocks. Oil price rise hurt oil importers, while a fall in commodity prices hurt exporters. Some exchange rate management

Exchange rate policy   181

can help mitigate this complex of shocks, as can fiscal policy targeted to the supply side. The post-GFC period, in particular, has brought out these flaws – excessive response to commodity price shocks, excessive exchange rate volatility and neglect of asset bubbles – in inflation targeting and made it clear that inflation targeting must be flexible in EDEs and be complemented by some management of exchange rates (Frankel, 2011).

One of the aims of a fixed exchange rate is often to impose discipline on macroeconomic policy. There is a loss of monetary autonomy, but a fixed exchange rate was not able to impose the fiscal discipline required for macroeconomic stability. Periodic crises and devaluations occurred before the break-up of the Bretton Woods system, when countries had fixed exchange rates. Even after AEs had shifted to floating rates, with the demise of the gold exchange standard in the 1970s, many EDEs continued with variants of fixed exchange rates. Latin American countries, many of which had lax fiscal regimes, suffered repeated crises in the 1980s. Some flexibility in exchange rates is essential.

One type of supply-side stabilisation that flexible rates make possible is neutralising the impact of a shock to international prices, or compensating for sticky domestic prices. This is not automatic, however, and requires FX intervention. Since the real exchange rate, $Q_t = S_t P_t^* / P_t$, affects aggregate demand, a rise in P_t^* implies a real depreciation that raises demand, which over time will raise domestic prices. But since goods prices are normally sticky, especially in a downward direction, the adjustment through domestic prices takes a long time to work out. Flexible exchange rates are an antidote to sticky goods market prices. A fall in S_t can neutralise the rise in P_t^* and abort any incipient inflationary effect.[3] P_t^* may also more directly raise domestic prices, especially if the price of major intermediate goods imports such as oil is more flexible. So, EDEs subject to volatile commodity prices require flexible and not floating exchange rates. To the extent alternative means of managing the exchange rate are available, appreciation in response to a rise in import prices need not imply a rise in interest rates and overall monetary tightening.

9.4   Exchange rate regimes and stabilisation

Since few countries are either a pure float or a pure fix, the decision on the exchange rate regime to be followed can itself give varying degrees of autonomy for monetary and fiscal policy.

The triangle diagram (Figure 9.8), originally due to Frankel, shows three points – a closed capital account on top, gradually opening

182 *Exchange rate policy*

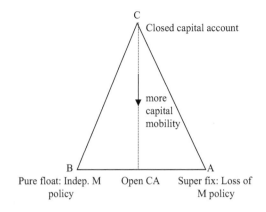

Figure 9.8 Why the impossible trinity rarely holds

towards the base. The two points of the base represent a pure float and pure fix, respectively. Only at the point of a pure fix with a fully open capital account is there no independence of monetary policy. This is the famous trilemma: perfect capital mobility, a fixed exchange rate and autonomous monetary policy cannot be found together. But everywhere else, there is a varying degree of monetary policy independence. Since no country is at the point of the trilemma, most countries have some monetary independence. Greater capital account openness does generate some loss of independence, but this can be partially compensated by moving to more flexibility in exchange rates.

Exchange rate policy itself generates policy options. Table 9.2 shows the varieties of exchange rate regimes and their effects, including on macroeconomic policies and key episodes associated with them. A pure fix is high on credibility, since the CBs ability to create surprise inflation is severely circumscribed, but it is low on flexibility. This can make even constitutionally mandated fixes difficult to sustain.[4] Fiscal policy is more effective with a fixed exchange rate, but excessive deficit financing can result in a crisis. Responsiveness to real shocks is reduced under a fix, as is the ability to compensate for sticky wages and prices through the exchange rate.

There can be a fine and a coarse classification of exchange rate regimes. Table 9.3 shows the difference between the official de jure classification and the de facto classification by various researchers based on actual outcomes. The official classification which countries give to the IMF is biased towards greater flexibility, while outcomes suggest

Table 9.2 Exchange rate regimes

Regime	Features	Benefits	Shortcomings	Some episodes
1. Free Float	Value of currency freely determined in the market. Actual and expected changes in demand/supply of assets and goods reflected in exchange rate changes.	Changes in nominal exchange rate shoulder bulk of adjustment to foreign and domestic shocks. Automatic adjustment to demand shocks. High international reserves not required. Monetary policy is effective.	High nominal (and real) exchange rate volatility may distort resource allocation. Monetary policy requires nominal anchors different from the exchange rate; scope for discretion and inflation bias may be large.	Virtually no country has a pure float. The United States, Switzerland (and maybe Japan) come close.
2. 'Dirty' Float	Sporadic central bank interventions in FX market. Modes and frequency of intervention and objectives guiding the intervention vary. Active intervention (sterilised and non-sterilised) results in changes in international reserves. Indirect intervention (through changes in interest rates, liquidity and other financial instruments) does not result in changes in reserves.	Same as in a free float, except that higher international reserves may be needed. Dampens 'excessive' fluctuations of exchange rates.	Lack of transparency of central bank behaviour may introduce too much uncertainty. Effects of intervention are typically short-lived (even when intended as a signal) and may be destabilising.	Many AEs and some EMs have adopted this regime – Canada, Australia (maybe Japan). Mexico adopted a system similar to this following the 1994–95 crisis. A dirty float could be thought of as a managed float with wide bands, with the (undisclosed) position of the bands providing the criterion for intervention.

(*Continued*)

Table 9.2 (Continued)

Regime	Features	Benefits	Shortcomings	Some episodes
3. Floating within a Band (Target Zone)	The nominal exchange rate is allowed to fluctuate (somewhat freely) within a band. The centre of the band is a *fixed rate*, either in terms of one currency or in terms of a basket of currencies. The width of the band varies (in the ERM it was originally ± 2.25%). Some band systems are the result of cooperative arrangements, others are unilateral.	System combines the benefits of some flexibility with some credibility. Key parameters (bands, mid-point) help guide the public's expectations. Changes in the nominal rate within the bands help absorb shocks to fundamentals.	If band is too narrow or domestic macroeconomic policies are not consistent, the system can be destabilising and prone to speculative attacks. Selecting the width of the band is not trivial. Systems that allow for the possibility of realignment of the bands and central parity weaken the credibility afforded by the regime.	ERM of the European Monetary System. The ERM crisis of 1992–93 showed the system can be subject to severe speculative pressures and even collapse, when currencies become misaligned and central banks are hesitant to defend the bands.
4. Sliding Band	There is no commitment to maintain the central parity 'indefinitely'. It is clear that the central parity will be adjusted periodically (e.g. due to competitiveness considerations). The system is an adaptation of the band regime to high-inflation economies.	The system allows countries with an ongoing rate of inflation higher than the world inflation to adopt a band without it leading to severe real appreciation.	The fact that the timing and size of central parity adjustments are unknown introduces considerable uncertainty, which often leads to high interest rate volatility. As in the case of the standard band system, it is difficult to choose the appropriate width for the band.	Israel had a system similar to this from early 1989 to December 1991. The uncertainty and volatility associated with this system makes it less attractive than other alternatives, such as the crawling band.

5. Crawling Band	A band system, whereby the central parity crawls over time. Different rules can be used to determine the rate of crawl. The two most common are backward-looking crawl (e.g. based on past inflation differentials) and forward-looking crawl (e.g. based on the expected or target rate of inflation).	System allows high inflation countries to adopt a band system without having to undertake (large) stepwise adjustments of the central parity.	Choosing the criteria for setting the rate of crawl entails serious risks. A backward-looking approach can introduce considerable inflationary inertia into the system. A forward-looking approach that sets the 'wrong' inflation target can produce overvaluation and give rise to speculative pressures.	Israel in December 1991. Chile had a widening band system from 1986 to mid-1998. Italy also between 1979 and 1991. Venezuela in July 1996–February 2002 had a very credible crawling band, which effectively controlled the evolution of the Bolivar/US$ exchange rate.
6. Crawling Peg	The nominal exchange rate is adjusted periodically according to a set of indicators (usually lagged inflation differentials) and is not allowed to fluctuate beyond a narrow range (say, 2%). One variant of the system consists of adjusting the nominal rate by a preannounced rate set deliberately below ongoing inflation (known as a 'tablita' regime).	Allows high-inflation countries to avoid severe real exchange rate overvaluation. The 'tablita' helps to guide the public's expectations and buys a limited amount of credibility	A pure backward-looking crawling peg (where the nominal rate is mechanically adjusted according to past inflation differentials) introduces inflationary inertia and may eventually cause monetary policy to lose its role as nominal anchor. Equilibrium changes in the real exchange rate are difficult to accommodate. A 'tablita' system will not last if fiscal and income policies are not supportive.	The 1960s and 1970s in Chile, Colombia and Brazil. Used longest in Colombia, leading to a higher degree of inflationary inertia.

(*Continued*)

Table 9.2 (Continued)

Regime	Features	Benefits	Shortcomings	Some episodes
7. Fixed but Adjustable Exchange Rate	The nominal exchange rate is fixed, but the central bank is not obliged to maintain the parity indefinitely. No tight constraints are imposed on the monetary and fiscal authorities, who can follow, if they so decide, policies that are inconsistent with preserving parity. Adjustments of the parity (devaluations) are a powerful policy instrument.	Provides macroeconomic discipline by maintaining tradable good prices in line with foreign price, reduces uncertainty. The built-in 'escape clause' provides some flexibility. Since money supply is tied to the exchange rate, there is automatic adjustment to monetary shocks. Fiscal policy is effective.	Realignments – devaluations under this system have typically been large and disruptive introducing uncertainty and inflationary pressures rather than smooth and orderly events. If supplemented by the right institutions (e.g. an independent central bank), the time inconsistency problems embedded in the system could be moderated.	Bretton Woods system held much of the 20th century. Most developing countries held on to (variants of) it after the formal collapse of the Bretton Woods agreement in 1973. Many EMs continued to subscribe to this system de facto (e.g. Mexico 1993, Thailand 1997), if not de jure, even after the collapse of Bretton Woods system.
8. Currency Board	Strict fixed exchange rate system, with institutional (legal and even constitutional) constraints on monetary policy and no scope for altering the parity. The monetary authority only can issue domestic money when it is fully backed by inflows of FX.	The system maximises credibility and reduces problems of 'time inconsistency'.	The system increases credibility but reduces flexibility. Large external shocks cannot be accommodated through exchange rate changes, but have to be fully absorbed by changes in domestic unemployment, prices and economic activity. The central bank loses its role as lender of last resort.	Small countries have had systems of this type, but have often been forced to abandon the regime when faced with major external shocks. In 2010, Hong Kong and Estonia had currency boards. Bulgaria had quasi-currency boards' arrangements. Argentina abandoned its currency board in January 2002 after a severe recession.

9. 'Full Dollarisation'	Generic name given to an extreme form of a currency board system, where the country gives up completely its monetary autonomy by adopting another country's currency.	Credibility is maximised under this regime. Monetary authorities have, in theory, no scope for 'surprising' the public.	As in the currency board, the system is long on credibility but lacks flexibility. Adverse external shocks have to be absorbed fully by the real economy. The central bank loses its role as lender of last resort. A non-trivial shortcoming of this system is that it is usually resisted on political and national grounds. Also, the rules of the game can be changed under extreme circumstances.	There are few historical episodes of full dollarisation. A regime similar to this has worked relatively well in Panama. However, the case of Liberia unmasked a serious shortcoming of this type of system: when faced with an emergency (civil war), politicians decided to change the rules of the game and issued a national currency.
10. Monetary Union	A currency union normally also aims to build a single market in a constitutional legal process that should be impossible to reverse. Economic and monetary union normally requires three phases: coordinating economic policy, achieving economic convergence (i.e. economic cycles broadly in step) and culminating with the adoption of a common currency. But to sustain, it also requires a fiscal and banking union.	Reduction in exchange risk, equalisation of interest rates, decline in relative price variability and general increase in economic efficiency likely to accompany unification.	The strongest argument against monetary union is the diversity of the economies involved. Problems emerge when economies with different economic structures, efficiency, productivity and inflation are integrated under a single currency. Or when a large shock has to be handled without monetary or exchange rate flexibility. Clever accounting can escape preconditions on debt and deficits. The year 2010 revealed this for Greece, forcing a rescue to prevent a costly Eurozone break-up, despite no-bailout provisions in the treaty.	European Union members adopted the Euro as their sole legal tender since 1 January 2002. Initially, there were 12 countries, with later expansion. The global financial crisis of 2008 impacted the Eurozone severely and tested its cohesiveness. The strengthening Euro hurt competitiveness; the absence of monetary autonomy was a drag. The CIS and CEE countries suffered from reversals of inflows from MNC banks that occurred in the run-up to joining the Eurozone.

Source: Adapted from the literature.

Table 9.3 Classifying exchange rate regimes in the 1990s

Country	IMF	Levi-Yeyati and Sturzenegger (2005) January–December 1996	Grier and Grier (2001) January–February 1997	Reinhart and Rogoff (2004)	Bubula and Okter-Robe (2002) 1996
Argentina	Pegged to $	Fix	Peg	Currency board	Currency board
Brazil	MF	Dirty/CP	Peg	June 1995–January 1999 preannounced CB/dual	Forward-looking CB
Chile	MF (±10%) weight $ = 45%	Float	Peg	de facto CB (+5%)/dual MF	Backward-looking CB
China	MF	NA	Peg	January 1994–December 2001 de facto peg	Fixed peg to a single currency
Colombia	MF	Float	Float	January 1994–June 1999 de facto CB (+ 5%)	Backward-looking crawling peg
Egypt	MF	NA	NA	de facto peg/multiple rate	Horizontal band
Hong Kong	Peg to Dollar	Fix	NA	Currency board	Currency board
Hungary	MF	NA	Float	May 1994–January 1999 de facto CB (±2%)	Backward-looking CP
India	Indep Float	Float	Peg	July 1995–December 2001 de facto CP	Tightly managed float
Indonesia	MF	Dirty/CP	Peg	November 1978–July 1997 de facto CP	Backward-looking CB
South Korea	MF	Fix	Peg	December 1995–November 1997 de facto CP	Tightly managed float

Malaysia	MF	Dirty float/CP	Peg	September 1975–July 1997 de facto moving band	Tightly managed float
Mexico	Indep Float	Dirty float	Float	December 1994–March 1996 free falling/free float	Independent float
Pakistan	MF	Float	NA	May 1994–July 1998 de facto CP/parallel MF	Fixed peg to a single currency
Peru	Indep Float	Float	NA	November 1993–March 1999 de facto CB (±2%)	Other managed float
Philippines	Indep Float	Fix	Peg	September 1995–June 1997 de facto peg	Fixed peg to a single currency
South Africa	Indep Float	Float	Float	March 1995–December 2001 free float	Other managed float
Singapore	MF	Dirty float/CP	Peg	June 1973–November 1998 de facto moving band (±2%)	Tightly managed float
Sri Lanka	MF	Dirty float/CP	–	95m3–98m2 preannounced CB ± 2%	Backward-looking CB
Thailand	Pegged to composite	NA	Peg	March 1978–July 1997 de facto peg	Fixed peg to a basket
Turkey	MF	Float	Float	May 1984–January 1998 free falling/MF	Forward-looking CB
Venezuela	MF	Dirty float/CP	Float	July 1996–July 1997 preannounced CB	Backward-looking CP

Source: Derived from the literature.

Note: CB: Crawling band; CP: Crawling peg; MF: Managed float

190   *Exchange rate policy*

that different types of intervention actually occur. For example, Chinese currency was officially given as a managed float in the period while researchers found it to be some variant of a peg.

9.5   Monetary approach to the current account

In Chapter 2, the intertemporal approach to the current account was developed. This involved a shift from trade to macro determinants of the current account. The section above developed the effect of Q_t on the trade balance of the CA. There is also a MA to the CA, which brings out the effect of the money market on the CA. Note that money supply is determined by CB assets, F_t and A_t:

$$M_t^s = \mu\left(F_t + A_t\right)$$

$$\frac{M_t^s}{P_t} = M^d\left(R_t, Y_t\right)$$

Substituting for money supply in the money market equilibrium relation and solving for FX reserves, F_t, and then considering a change in the reserves, gives the final Equation 9.1.

$$F_t = \left(1/\mu\right)\left(P_t M^d\left(R_t, Y_t\right)\right) - A_t$$

$$\Delta F_t = \left(1/\mu\right)\Delta\left(P_t M^d\left(R_t, Y_t\right)\right) - \Delta A_t \tag{9.1}$$

Adjustment is through the impact of money market changes on the interest rate, and therefore on reserves. A rise in money demand would raise interest rates and reserves, and given A_t, raise money supply. But a negative income shock by reducing money demand would lower interest rates and reduce reserves, suggesting that money supply should be tightened to improve the BOP. But that would be exactly the wrong response. Therefore, like the automatic stabilisation under fixed exchange rates, where money supply responds to fixed S_t, this works for shocks originating in the money market, but can have perverse effects for output market shocks.

Since monetary theories build in the assumption of perfect market clearing, they are only satisfactory if output markets are always at full employment. Moreover, in EDEs, a large fraction of inflows are attracted by growth rates and not interest differentials.

Relative money supplies affect the exchange rate, as the MA explains, and the interest rate affects it through the arbitrage as in the UIP. These are the direct instruments of monetary policy. The CB has other ways of

Exchange rate policy 191

affecting the exchange rate, apart from through changes in the money supply. One is through direct intervention in the FX market, involving the buying and selling currency. Since buying foreign currency increases the domestic money supply, intervention affects the exchange rate by changing the money supply. But most CBs sterilise their intervention operations by selling equivalent domestic assets. Even so, there is evidence that sterilised intervention itself affects the exchange rate. Signals or announcements from the CB, sometimes associated with different exchange rate regimes, complement these. Different types of restrictions on the capital account give the CB an additional lever of control. Capital mobility is imperfect also, if domestic and foreign assets are not perfect substitutes. We explore these alternative policy tools in Sections 9.6–9.8.

9.6 Portfolio balance channel of intervention

Intervention affects the exchange rate if it changes the money supply. In this section, however, we show how even sterilised intervention can affect the exchange rate. If domestic and foreign bonds are not perfect substitutes, a risk premium is introduced in the UIP. The exchange rate then can be changed, even with no change in the money supply. If assets are perfect substitutes, their relative quantities do not matter. But if they are not, a change in their relative price can change the portfolio of assets held. Since risk also matters now, this becomes a case of less than perfect capital mobility. The economy is at a point above the base of Frankel's triangle, so there is some independence for monetary policy.

Risk premium or excess return from investing in government bonds denominated in local currency is:

$$\rho_t = R_t - R_t^* - \dot{s}_t^e \tag{9.2}$$

Bond demand is a rising function of this excess return.

$$B_t^d = B_t^d\left(\rho_t\right) \tag{9.3}$$

The net market supply of government bonds is minus the amount A_t held by the CB:

$$B_t^s = B_t - A_t \tag{9.4}$$

Market clearing in the bond market determines the risk premium. The excess return required for the market to hold bonds rises with the

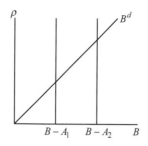

Figure 9.9 Excess returns determined in the local bond market

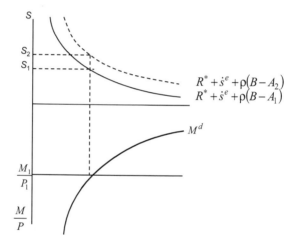

Figure 9.10 Sterilised intervention under imperfect substitution in bond

relative net supply of government bonds; therefore, it rises if the CB holds fewer bonds. For example, when $A_2 < A_1$ in Figure 9.9.

It follows that by changing its bond holding, the CB can change the exchange rate even if money supply does not change, as the return to holding foreign bonds shifts with the risk premium (Figure 9.10).

The above was a simple example of the more general portfolio balance approach due initially to Tobin. It broadens the MA, allowing the exchange rate to be determined by the demand for and supply of financial assets. Wealth enters demand functions and changes in the current account affect wealth. Long-run stock adjustment or balance has to allow for these changes in wealth. Individuals rebalance portfolios

Exchange rate policy   193

based on risk and return. Since return is not the only consideration in holding a particular currency, domestic and foreign assets become imperfect substitutes.

The simple model may not be appropriate for an EDE where the risk premium depends largely on other factors, including political stability. EDE risk premium is a function of country risk that falls with larger FX reserves, since the probability of a currency attack and forced depreciation falls. This model implies that risk will rise as F_t rises and A_t falls. But India, for example, saw risk premium fall over 2004–07 as F_t rose. Moreover, the government debt market was repressed in this period, with domestic financial institutions as captive customers. Since foreign and private holders were limited, so was the effect of switching between domestic and foreign bonds. Although segments with near perfect capital mobility were large in absolute terms, many restrictions continued. Domestic residents could not hold foreign bonds, and there were limits to foreign participation in debt markets.

9.7   CB intervention

CBs follow an active exchange rate policy, except under a pure float. This need not be implemented only through changing the money supply or the interest rate. Where there is a liquid FX market, CBs can influence the exchange rate by participating in it. They buy and sell FX, thus intervening in FX markets. There are a number of reasons for such CB intervention (Sarno and Taylor, 2002).

First, a wrong exchange rate can persist, because of perverse market expectations, or markets can persistently deviate from fundamentals. We saw in Chapter 3 that rational bubbles can occur in FX markets, even under strict MA. Deviations from fundamentals can also occur due to the peso problem and due to chartist or trend following behaviour.[5]

Speculative market activity is supposed to lead to a fundamental driven price, since speculators must buy when low and sell when high in order to make profits. But destabilising speculation can occur under stop loss trading rules. In such a case, buying when others are expected to keep buying makes profits.

The asset approach shifts the perspective to the currency as an asset. Then, the CB has a choice either bursting a bubble if it forms or preventing an asset bubble from forming.

The CB may have superior information justifying its intervention. Markets may reinforce its actions if they understand and agree with them or they may act against the CB. Thus, the credibility of the CB's actions is important.

194 *Exchange rate policy*

We have also seen that, under sticky goods market prices, a floating exchange rate can overshoot its fundamental value, again justifying CB intervention.

Even if markets are self-correcting after a shock, the adjustment could take a long time. Therefore, smoothing the adjustment process could be another justification for CB intervention. An example is using the exchange rate channel of monetary transmission to abort the inflationary process after an external price shock. In EDEs, if markets are thin, smoothing large currency-demand shocks can be helpful, as in the case of the oil company swaps used effectively in India in 2013.

But the CB could also intervene wrongly, for example, in holding a nominal exchange rate peg even as the real rate departs from its equilibrium value. The market view, as expounded by Miller (1997), is that markets know more as they pool the information of so many agents. Private traders would not trade unless they make profits, and they normally do so at the expense of the CB, making the CB a patsy whose intervention sets it up to make losses.[6] In this view, intervention cannot affect the exchange rate.

Empirical work, however, supports the effectiveness of intervention. It has shown intervention works best when it is announced and coordinated[7] (Dominguez and Frankel, 1993). The time of intervention also matters, with the most impact at times of high market liquidity. But surprisingly, most CB intervention is secret. Reasons for secret intervention include intervention undertaken for portfolio adjustment rather than to affect the exchange rate. Or, at times intervention is inconsistent with other macroeconomic policies. In the United States, the Treasury is responsible for exchange rate policy, reducing coordination with other monetary policy objectives.

But the most important reason for secrecy is probably a fear of loss of face. The large volume of FX market transactions make CB interventions only a drop in the ocean. Commitment to a particular rate may be risky, since if the CB is not believed it would lose reserves. Many CBs have been brought to their knees in an attempt to act against market beliefs. But secrecy is not a zero one choice. For example, the direction of intervention may be revealed but not the quantity. The section below examines the varieties of signals possible.

Different types of intervention are feasible under a managed float, allowing the money supply to adjust to the domestic cycle. Under a pure fix, only sterilised intervention is possible. There are two ways sterilised intervention can also affect S, apart from through the money supply – first, through the portfolio balance effect; second,

Exchange rate policy 195

through signalling, including information on future monetary and fiscal policy.

9.8 Signalling

If intervention is indeed a drop in the ocean, more than the quantity of CB transactions, it is the signal of intent that could work. Signalling would not affect exchange rates in perfect markets with perfect foresight and unique equilibria. Four features that can make it work, and are pervasive in real world economies, are nonstationarity, learning, the absence of unique RE and the presence of asymmetric information. The signal has, however, to be credible. It has to be consistent with fundamentals. Profitability of the action contributes to the credibility of a signal, although this is not essential for a taxpayer-backed CB. For example, in the portfolio balance effect of Section 9.6, while a fall in government securities raises risk and depreciates S the rise in foreign securities that accompanies this bolsters depreciation expectations, since the CB would gain from a valuation effects on its reserves. Similarly, a sale of reserves may credibly signal a domestic appreciation from a planned monetary tightening.

Use of signalling follows the rethink in the last decade on the more general issue of CB communication. Blinder et al. (2008), in a survey of the issue, start with quotes from Brunner and then from Bernanke, highlighting the move to greater transparency over time.[8] A central banker was earlier expected to be a discreet master of the art of speaking and yet saying nothing, but a major task for the modern CB is to guide market expectations. After the rational expectations revolution, only unanticipated monetary shocks were thought to affect outcomes, surprise was the essence. But with the realisation that multiple rational expectations equilibria are possible, guiding expectations became a valuable CB function.

CB communication either creates news or reduces noise – that is, it increases the predictability of CB actions. Both are expected to raise the signal to noise ratio, reduce financial market volatility and lead to better monetary policy outcomes. Then, CB pronouncements influence expectations and so move asset prices.

Empirical tests have supported the above by showing that CBs are able to move interest rates with less open market operations (OMOs), thus improving the cost effectiveness of policy. The yield curve has been found to predict policy changes, thus supporting greater predictability of CB actions.[9] Similarly, signalling enables the CB to move exchange rates with less intervention. A signal can focus exchange

196 *Exchange rate policy*

rate expectations, even if intervention is a small part of the market. If a signal substitutes for interest rate changes, it frees the interest rate to target the domestic cycle.

Signalling is, of course, not a panacea. Unguarded communication can cause mayhem in markets. Communication can degenerate to cacophony without some restraints.[10] Moreover, there are many types of signals – for example, an FX market intervention may convey the price at which intervention will occur but not the amount.

There may be an optimal degree of transparency, determined partly by limits to digestion of information. One useful rule is not to communicate if own signal is noisy. Internal deliberations in CBs are normally kept secret; there is a period of purdah before each policy meeting. Communication must be skillful but can vary from the crystal clear (e.g. announcing a target) to the cryptic. Markets give a different weight to CB words, depending on who has uttered them. For example, speeches get higher weight compared to fleeting high-frequency remarks.

The case for obfuscation was based on the theoretical presumption linked to perfect markets that only unanticipated money matters. If goods market prices are sticky, as the NKE school assumes and evidence supports, the real interest rate can change, and money has real effects through this channel. Another reason for non-transparency could be if the public does not precisely know the CB's preferences, and this gives a strategic advantage to be utilised, for example, in surprise inflations. A third argument against transparency is possible excessive coordination of expectations in following the CB's signals so that market information is lost.

After the GFC, there was some rethink on CB predictability. But transparency is not the same thing as committing to a particular action. Any announcement of a future action is conditional on external events. Potential responses to potential shocks should also be communicated. Two-way movement and surprise could, therefore, occur through shocks. Any price should not be fixed for too long to allow price discovery, prevent deviations from equilibrium values and one-way speculative positions.[11] Forward market guidance that is time dependent, such as used after the GFC, can involve too strong a commitment independent of data.

9.9   A peg as a solution to a liquidity trap

When interest rates are so low that everyone believes they must increase, a liquidity trap can occur. Under such conditions, shifting to bonds creates an expected capital loss, so preference for liquidity increases. Any addition to money supply is then held rather than used to purchase assets. As a result, the bond price and the interest rate, which is the inverse of the price, cannot change and monetary policy is ineffective in stabilisation.

Given an expected exchange rate, UIP fixes the nominal value of the exchange rate in a liquidity trap. If R_t cannot change, neither can the nominal exchange rate. Money demand is low at low Y_t. If net money supply is high so that R_t is driven to zero, the FM curve has a flat stretch in S and Y space (Figure 9.9). The value of S_t on this stretch can be solved from UIP, given $R_t = 0$ in the money market.[12]

$$R_t = 0 = R_t^* + (S_t^e - S_t)/S_t$$
$$S_t = \frac{S_t^e}{1 - R_t^*} \tag{9.5}$$

Any rise in money supply would just elongate the horizontal stretch and be unable to affect R_t, S_t or Y_t. Monetary policy becomes ineffective. Japan was trapped in this situation after its financial crash in the 1980s. Post-liberalisation in the early 1980s, firms borrowed abroad, the Yen appreciated, banks lent indiscriminately to real estate, but eventually the bubble burst. With monetary policy less effective, overuse of fiscal policy led to its debt GDP ratio reaching 200 per cent; so, fiscal policy was also constrained.

Suggested solutions included a rise in money supply that should create expected inflation, thus shifting up the horizontal stretch. But given the conservative reputation of the Bank of Japan, inflation was not credible. An alternative, based on an independent exchange rate

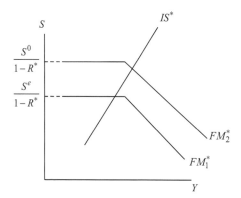

Figure 9.11 Exchange rate policy in a liquidity trap

198   Exchange rate policy

policy, was for the BOJ to shift to a pegged exchange rate and peg the currency at a more depreciated level S^0. Now, output would rise along the upward rising IS*, so stabilisation is achieved.[13]

9.10   Summary

After studying the mechanics of fixing an exchange rate, this chapter explores deviations from pure MAs, and in particular deviations relevant for and applicable to EDEs. These caveats need to be kept in mind because the MA works best for small deviations from full employment, but in EDEs the deviations can be substantial and persistent.

For an EDE, changes in output and productivity add to the degrees of freedom for monetary policy that come from intermediate exchange rate regimes and less than full capital account convertibility. For example, real interest parity implies the real interest rate can be below international rates in an EDE, if the real exchange rate is appreciating. Relative PPP is relaxed to the extent non-monetary factors affect the real interest rate. Monetary tightening can increase reserves only to the extent inflows are sensitive to interest differentials, but growth rates attract equity flows.

In the absence of a perfect float, there is room for active exchange rate policy. Fiscal policy is more effective under a fixed exchange rate, but excessive deficits can destroy the credibility of the fix, forcing devaluation and could even create crisis-like situations. There is automatic adjustment to monetary shocks under fixed exchange rates, but aggravation of a shock to the goods market. Equivalently, the MA to BOP gives the correct policy response under a monetary shock, but makes matters worse under a goods market shock. Nominal fixity does not mean the real exchange rate is fixed, however, and it will change slowly as wages and prices adjust.

Without perfect capital mobility or a perfectly fixed exchange rate, there are degrees of freedom for monetary policy. Floating exchange rates make monetary policy more effective, allow automatic adjustment to demand shocks, can compensate for delays in wage and price adjustment that could lead to deviation from equilibrium rates and abort the inflationary effect of border price changes. Some of these advantages are also available from different degrees of flexibility in the varying exchange rate regimes that lie between a pure float and a pure fix. Flexible inflation targeting provides the advantages of a nominal anchor with automatic adjustment to money demand shocks, while flexible exchange rates respond to demand and external shocks.

Exchange rate policy 199

But how does policy affect the exchange rate? While changes in money supply and the interest rates affect the nominal exchange rate, sterilised CB intervention in FX markets, which does not change the money supply, can also change the exchange rate when substitutability between domestic and foreign assets is imperfect. Different types of intervention in FX markets, signalling and capital controls give exchange rate policy some independence from money supply. For example, after a temporary adverse supply shock, a monetary expansion is required to sustain the domestic cycle, but an appreciation would reduce the inflationary pass through from border prices. If intervention or signalling can achieve the appreciation, money supply may not have to be reduced to appreciate the exchange rate.

The next chapter gives an introduction to the new open economy macroeconomics and sees how deriving policy from optimising foundations changes the results on fiscal and monetary policy and on exchange rate overshooting.

Notes

1 Some texts (e.g., Montiel, 2003) prefer to call only non-monetary action affecting exchange rates, exchange rate policy.
2 See Krugman et al. (2014). It is also possible that money supply fall leads to an expected devaluation if output falls as R_t rises.
3 We have noted that there are persistent deviations from the PPP real exchange rate under floating rates, since nominal rates show excessive volatility driven by FX market arbitrage decisions while volatility in prices is much lower. But with restricted capital account convertibility, a float can be managed to keep the real exchange rate closer to equilibrium, as S_t can compensate but not overcompensate for sticky prices.
4 When large Greek deficits were discovered in 2010, questions rose about the survival of the Euro. Although successive bailouts were put together, it was not clear that Greece would be able to repay its debts, despite painful austerity, without the option of depreciating its currency. Its debts were largely socialised, in that foreign banks had been repaid, with the debt held by the Eurozone and the IMF. In 2015, it almost became the first AE to default on repayments due to the IMF.
5 Chartists who follow past trends are like turkeys bred for Christmas. The break in trend is a surprise for them – they find being fed in the past is no guarantee of future feeding.
6 Understandably, market players hold this opinion, but regulators hold the opposite. One market player said markets players believe they are God. In this clash of the titans, the relative power of each side is affected by the prevailing pro- or anti-market philosophy.
7 G-7 coordination and transparency successfully depreciated the dollar during the Plaza Accord of 1985.
8 Indian Central Bankers show a similar progression. While Dr. Rangarajan

200 *Exchange rate policy*

was guarded with the press in the 1990s, Dr. Jalan held regular press meetings in the new century. Dr. Reddy, who followed Dr. Jalan, occasionally practiced what he called the 'open mouth policy'. Dr. Subbarao, who took office in 2008, made a focussed attempt to improve RBI communication.

9 A large empirical literature has also estimated the vector of signals, the direct effects on expectations measured through survey data, the effect on interest rates, exchange rates and stock prices.

10 Dr. Bernanke, in his first year as Fed Chairman, had what he admitted was a lapse of judgement. After becoming chairman on 1 February 2006, he had raised the possibility of the Fed pausing in its two-year, credit-tightening campaign, in a congressional appearance on 27 April. Stocks rallied that day. But on 1 May, CNBC reported that Bernanke had told CNBC anchor Maria Bartiromo that investors had misinterpreted his recent congressional remarks as an indication the Fed was nearly done raising rates – stock markets tanked. In response to a Senate enquiry, Bernanke committed to make future communications with the public and with the market entirely through regular and formal channels. In an address to FX dealers in Goa, Dr. Reddy expressed unhappiness with the value of the exchange rate. This sparked off unprecedented volatility.

11 Goyal and Arora (2013) found communication channels to have potential in India, but they were not used effectively.

12 If R_t was negative it would be subtracted from the denominator of Equation 9.5, further increasing depreciation. Unless, as was the experience when Japan tried to implement negative interest rates in 2016, global risk aversion rose, and Japan's safe-haven status led to inflows and an appreciation of the Yen.

13 As a Japanese commentator remarked, the problem was the world would not let Japan fix its exchange rate, since there was deep suspicion of the trade-enhancing effect of any devaluation. It was only in 2013 that, following the United States and the United Kingdom example, the BOJ undertook a sufficiently large expansion of its balance sheet that the Yen began to depreciate substantially. It had fallen 33 per cent against the dollar by mid-2015.

References

Blinder, A. S., M. Ehrmann, M. Fratzscher, J. D. Haan and D. J. Jansen. 2008. 'Central Bank Communication and Monetary Policy: A Survey of Theory and Evidence', *Journal of Economic Literature*, 46(4): 910–945. Available at www.nber.org/papers/w13932.pdf?new_window=1.

Bubula, A. and I. Okter-Robe. 2002. 'The Evolution of Exchange Rate Regimes since 1990: Evidence from Defacto Policies', *IMF Working Papers, No. 02/155*. Available at https://www.imf.org/external/pubs/ft/wp/2002/wp02155.pdf.

Dominguez, K. M. and J. A. Frankel. 1993. *Does Foreign Exchange Intervention Work?*, Washington, DC: Institute for International Economics.

Frankel, J. 2011. 'Monetary Policy in Emerging Markets', Chapter 25 in B. Friedman and M. Woodford (eds.), *Handbook of Monetary Economics*, Vol. 3B, pp. 1439–1499. North Holland, Amsterdam: Elsevier.

Exchange rate policy 201

Goyal, A. and S. Arora. 2013. 'Inferring India's Potential Growth and Policy Stance', *Journal of Quantitative Economics*, 11(1 and 2): 60–83, January–July.

Grier, K. B. and R. M. Grier. 2001. 'Exchange Rate Regimes and the Cross-Country Distribution of the 1997 Financial Crisis', *Economic Inquiry, Western Economic Association International*, 39(1): 139–148, January.

Krugman, P. R., M. Obstfeld and M. Melitz. 2014. *International Economics: Theory and Policy*, 10th edition, Delhi: Pearson Education.

Levy-Yeyati, E. and F. Sturzenegger. 2005. 'Classifying Exchange Rate Regimes: Deeds vs. Words', *European Economic Review*, Elsevier, 49(6): 1603–1635, August.

Miller, M. 1997. 'Risk and Return on Futures Contracts: A Chicago View', Chapter 10 in Merton Miller (ed.), *Merton Miller on Derivatives*, pp. 92–100. New York: John Wiley & Sons, Inc.

Montiel, P. J. 2003. *Macroeconomics in Emerging Markets*, Cambridge: UK: Cambridge University Press.

Reinhart, C. and K. S. Rogoff. 2004. 'The Modern History of Exchange Rate Arrangements: A Reinterpretation', *The Quarterly Journal of Economics*, 119(1): 1–48.

Sarno, L. and M. P. Taylor, 2002. *The Economics of Exchange Rates*, p. 19, Cambridge, UK: Cambridge University Press.

10 New open economy macroeconomics

Progress sometimes involves pain.

10.1 Introduction

DSGE models are a natural benchmark in macroeconomics, since an economy is a general equilibrium of all the constituent markets running over time and subject to shocks. But an economy is much more complex than any model could be. So, a model has to be an abstraction. It is useful if it is able to isolate core issues. The canonical DSGE model seeks to explain fluctuations from shocks to preferences or technology, when representative agents with rational expectations optimise over time in perfect markets. The Keynesian behavioural consumption function with a constant marginal propensity to consume gives way to the first-order condition (FOC) from intertemporal utility maximisation. There are new insights from forward-looking behaviour, which were not there in the earlier models with static expectations.[1]

The parameters of behavioural functions are subject to the Lucas critique – they are not stable to policy regime changes when agents are forward looking. Parameters, derived from preferences and technology, however, are stable. Smaller models also give results closer to theory and are less of a black box compared to large macroeconometric models.

DSGE models led to a shift in estimation approaches, with greater use of calibration and simulation. The problem, however, was to reproduce the functioning of actual economies. The real shocks with money neutrality that characterised the RBC approach required ad hoc lags and other adjustments to get even close to reproducing data moments.

NKE, while sharing the intertemporal optimising approach, sought to build in various kinds of imperfections and to find rigorous micro-foundations for them. Frictions introduced included monopolistic competition and different types of price rigidities.

Although many scholars carried out similar exercises, Obstfeld and Rogoff (1996) wrote a book extending this macroeconomic approach to the open economy. In doing so, they sought to provide a unifying framework for the diverse field of international finance, and to include more general macroeconomic questions in it, in addition to its emphasis on cross-border flows. Since their work led to the rapid development of the field of new open economy macroeconomics, this chapter presents a simplified version of their model. Their work also can be regarded as a rigourous version of the Dornbusch (1976) overshooting model, as they acknowledge. Just as Dornbusch modelled the effect of sticky prices in a monetary model, Obstfeld and Rogoff model the effect of sticky prices in an open economy DSGE. Indeed, they regard themselves as providing the microfoundations for Dornbusch's framework of analysis. The forward-looking approach moderates some of Dornbusch's results, validates others and adds new insights.

The new open economy macroeconomics can be characterised by product variety and monopolistic competition, plus the intertemporal approach to the current account, which generates the dynamic evolution of the current account and debt. Microfoundations make welfare analysis possible, while incorporating frictions valid for the question and context makes for greater realism. This approach is useful for EDEs, which have many types of frictions. For example, DSGE models lay great emphasis on productivity shocks, but these are likely to be more persistent in EDEs. The approach, therefore, needs to be adapted suitably.

The negatives of DSGE are the analytical complexity and the sensitivity of results to the precise specifications of preferences, technology and rigidities. But there are no ad hoc implicit assumptions, and benchmarks make careful analysis of the effect of assumptions possible. Besides, it is possible to choose context relevant assumptions.

This approach provides workhorse models and an organising frame for open economy macroeconomic analysis, where the major questions in the area can be systematically addressed. In this approach, monetary shocks have unusual persistent real effects because of induced short-run wealth accumulation via the current account.

In assessing fiscal policy, the forward-looking consumer will anticipate the future effect of current government policy; so, for example, an unanticipated permanent increase in government expenditure will have no real effect. Individual savings will rise to cover an expected future rise in taxes. This Ricardian equivalence does not hold for temporary stabilisation policy, which can have real effects. For example, since a wartime rise in government spending is expected to reverse,

204 New open economy macroeconomics

savings do not compensate for the rise, so real interest rates typically rise during wars.

Keynesian results on international transmission of macroeconomic policies are also reversed in this approach. While in the Mundell-Fleming and Dornbusch models, one country's stimulus was normally at another country's expense, here depending on consumption elasticities, both countries could benefit. Other questions that can be addressed include exchange rate regimes and sources of CA imbalance.

As this area developed and matured, modelling conventions and structures have been refined and established. We start by developing an understanding of these in Section 2 before going on to the seminal open economy macroeconomics model in Section 3. Section 4 overviews the literature, before Section 5 summarises and concludes. Two Appendices give some derivations.

10.2   The building blocks

Over the years, the models and their components have been refined and simplified. Since the building blocks have become standard and are repeated in various models, it is useful to grasp them first. We emphasise their economic interpretation.

Among the modelling refinements, which have enabled rich microfoundations to be consistent with tractable macro aggregates, is the use of constant elasticity of substitution (CES) aggregation. CES functional forms have the advantage of being log-linear, which allows considerable simplification. The use of agents distributed along a unit line makes the average also the total. Taxation in these models is often lump sum because that does not disturb the marginal equilibrium conditions. These modelling tricks are either non-injurious abstractions or increase relevance.

10.2.1   Intertemporal optimisation

The representative household[2] maximises the discounted present value of the sum of expected utility from the present to infinity, where β is the discount factor:

$$E_0 \sum_{t=0}^{\infty} \beta^t U\left(C_t, N_t\right) \tag{10.1}$$

Subject to a sequence of flow budget constraints for $t = 0, 1, 2 \ldots$ given by:

$$P_t C_t + Q_t B_t \leq B_{t-1} + W_t N_t - T_t \tag{10.2}$$

New open economy macroeconomics 205

Consumption, C_t, gives positive utility while there is disutility from the labour hours, N_t, required to earn the income to consume. The utility function is continuous and twice differentiable. Consumption plus current savings must equal assets from past accumulation B_{t-1}, plus wage income $W_t N_t$, net of taxation T_t. All savings are assumed to be held in bonds. B_t is quantity of one-period, nominal riskless discount bonds purchased in period t and maturing in period $t + 1$. Each bond pays one unit of money at maturity, and its price is Q_t and gross yield R_t $(Q_t = R_t^{-1})$ and i_t is the interest rate. The household takes as given the price of the good, the wage rate and the price of bonds.

The representative household is subject to a solvency constraint that prevents it from engaging in Ponzi-type schemes. The expected value of wealth or borrowing must be zero in the terminal period:

$$\lim_{T \to \infty} E_t \left\{ B_T \right\} \leq 0 \text{ for all } t \tag{10.3}$$

Optimal consumption and labour supply

The first optimality condition, the consumption Euler, implied by the maximisation of Equation 10.1 subject to Equation 10.2 is:

$$R^{-1} = Q_t = \beta_t E_t \left\{ \frac{U_{c,t+1}}{U_{c,t}} \frac{P_t}{P_{t+1}} \right\} \tag{10.4}$$

The second optimality condition is the labour-leisure FOC Equation 10.5:

$$-\frac{U_{N,t}}{U_{C,t}} = \frac{W_t}{P_t} \tag{10.5}$$

To derive the consumption Euler, write the budget constraint as:

$$C_t = \frac{B_{t-1}}{P_t} - \frac{B_t}{P_t R_t} + \frac{W_t}{P_t} N_t - \frac{T_t}{P_t}$$

Substitute in Equation 10.1 and consider the relevant terms with B_t. The utility summation runs to infinity, and the budget constraint has B with two time subscripts. So, B_{t-1} in the budget constraint will become B_t in time period $t + 1$, giving:

$$U \left(\cdots \frac{-B_t}{R_t P_t} \cdots \right) + \beta_t E_t U \left(\cdots \frac{B_t}{P_{t+1}} \cdots \right) \cdots \cdots \tag{10.6}$$

206 *New open economy macroeconomics*

Differentiating w.r.t. B_t gives the consumption Euler. The derivation is with respect to B_t, since these savings enable the smoothing of consumption:[3]

$$U_{C,t}\left(\frac{-1}{R_t P_t}\right) + \beta_t E_t U_{C,t+1}\left(\frac{1}{P_{t+1}}\right) = 0$$

$$\beta_t E_t\left(\frac{U_{C,t+1}}{P_{t+1}}\right) = \frac{1}{R_t}\left(\frac{U_{C,t}}{P_t}\right) \tag{10.7}$$

If $U(C_t)$ is the logarithmic utility function ($\ln C_t$), which is separable in its arguments, doing the derivation gives:

$$\frac{\beta_t}{E_t P_{t+1} C_{t+1}} = \frac{1}{P_t C_t R_t} \tag{10.8}$$

$$\frac{\beta_t P_t C_t}{E_t P_{t+1} C_{t+1}} = \frac{1}{1+i_t} \tag{10.9}$$

Simple variational proof

The Euler can be obtained even without calculus. Consider the impact on expected utility at time t of a reallocation of consumption between periods t and $t+1$, while keeping consumption in any period other than t and $t+1$ and hours worked (in all periods) unchanged. If the household is optimising, it must be the case that:

$$U_{c,t} dC_t + \beta E_t\left\{U_{c,t+1} dC_{t+1}\right\} = 0 \tag{10.10}$$

For any pair (dC_t, dC_{t+1}) satisfying

$$P_{t+1} dC_{t+1} = -\frac{P_t}{Q_t} dC_t = -R_t P_t dC_t \tag{10.11}$$

where the latter equation determines the increase in consumption expenditure in period $t+1$ made possible by the additional savings $-P_t dC_t$ allocated into one-period bonds. Combining the two previous equations yields the intertemporal optimality condition Equation 10.5.

To understand the labour-leisure FOC, consider the impact on utility of a small departure in period t, from the household's optimal plan: increase in consumption dC_t and an increase in hours dN_t, everything else unchanged. If the plan was optimal, it must be the case that:

$$U_{C,t} dC_t + U_{N,t} dN_t = 0 \tag{10.12}$$

For any pair (dC_t, dNt) satisfying the budget constraint, that is:

$$P_t dC_t = W_t dN_t \qquad (10.13)$$

If not, it would be possible to raise utility by increasing (or decreasing) consumption and hours. This would contradict the assumption that the household is on an optimal plan. Combining both equations gives the optimality condition Equation 10.5.

Interpretations of the Euler equation

To further understand the FOC Equation 10.4, consider the curvature of the utility function or elasticity of marginal utility (MU) with respect to consumption, that is, $\dfrac{C_t U''(C_t)}{U'(C_t)}$. This, in turn, can be related to the intertemporal elasticity of substitution between two points of time s and t:

$$\gamma(C_t) \equiv -\frac{U'(C_s)/U'(C_t)}{C_s/C_t} \frac{d(C_s/C_t)}{d[U'(C_s)/U'(C_t)]} \qquad (10.14)$$

The limit of the above, as $s \to t$ is $\gamma(C_t) = \dfrac{-U'(C_t)}{U''(C_t)C_t}$. This is the inverse of the negative of elasticity of MU. The intertemporal elasticity of substitution is very large if utility is linear. Then, the elasticity of MU is low and the coefficient of relative risk aversion (RRA) is low since $\text{RRA} = \dfrac{1}{\gamma(C_t)}$, $-\dfrac{U''(C_t)C_t}{U'(C_t)} = -$ elasticity of MU. The latter is large for a highly curved utility function (shown in Figure 10.1). High risk aversion, therefore, means a low intertemporal elasticity of substitution.

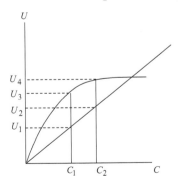

Figure 10.1 A concave and a linear utility function

208 New open economy macroeconomics

With a linear utility function, γ is high and RRA is low, so a rise in consumption from C_1 to C_2 gives a large rise in utility from U_1 to U_2 (Figure 10.1). The elasticity of MU is low and constant since the slope is constant. With high risk aversion, the utility function is highly curved. Then, the same rise in consumption from C_1 to C_2 gives a much lower rise in utility $U_4 U_3$. The reason is consumers with higher risk aversion discount future consumption more.

An example of a utility function

A commonly used specific utility function, belonging to the CES family, is the constant relative risk aversion or CRRA utility function. Considering only one argument, C_t, this takes the form:

$$U(C_t) = \frac{C_t^{1-\sigma}}{1-\sigma} \quad \sigma > 0, \sigma \neq 1$$
$$= \ln C_t \quad \text{for } \sigma = 1$$

Its CES is $\gamma = \frac{1}{\sigma}$, the inverse of the negative of the elasticity of MU, $-\sigma$, and the inverse of the constant coefficient of risk aversion, σ.

We have already seen that if $U(C_t) = \ln C_t$, the condition for optimal consumption reduces to:

$$\frac{C_t}{E_t C_{t+1}} = \frac{1}{1+i_t}$$

where the discount factor and inflation are also 0. Since $1 + f'(k_t) = R_t$ or $f'(k_t) = i_t$, where $f'(k_t)$ is the marginal product of capital, this has the interpretation that for consumption between time t and $t + 1$, the marginal rate of substitution (MRS) between consumption today and tomorrow equals the marginal rate of transformation (MRT) from production. If MRT > MRS, saving more in order to increase future consumption would raise welfare.[4]

Where consumption is constant, the Euler condition gives the golden rule condition $f'(k^*_t) = 1/\beta$, which gives the optimal capital stock k^* that maximises steady-state consumption. The golden rule is that the marginal product of capital must equal the discount rate (or rate of time preference plus the rate of growth of population, if it is positive). The discount rate is the inverse of β, since β is the discount factor.

As the interest rate increases, the substitution effect makes C_{t+1} more attractive so C_t decreases. The income effect, or rise in wealth from a rise in interest rates with positive savings, makes more consumption possible

New open economy macroeconomics   209

in both periods – C_t and C_{t+1} increase. If $\gamma = 1$, the two effects cancel out so that the interest rate does not affect consumption.

FOCs: Bringing in the labour argument, the CES utility takes the form:

$$U(C_t, N_t) = \frac{C_t^{1-\sigma}}{1-\sigma} - \frac{N_t^{1+\varphi}}{1+\varphi}$$

The consumers' optimality conditions, Equations 10.4 and 10.5, now became Equations 10.15 and 10.16 for the specific CES form of the utility function:

$$R^{-1} = Q_t = \beta E_t \left\{ \left(\frac{C_{t+1}}{C_t} \right)^{-\sigma} \frac{P_t}{P_{t+1}} \right\} \tag{10.15}$$

$$\frac{W_t}{P_t} = \frac{N_t^{\phi}}{C_t^{-\sigma}} = C_t^{\sigma} N_t^{\varphi} \tag{10.16}$$

Equation 10.16 can be written in log-linear form as:

$$w_t - p_t = \sigma c_t + \varphi n_t \tag{10.17}$$

where lower case letters denote the natural logs of the corresponding variable (i.e. $x_t \equiv \log X_t$). This is a competitive labour supply schedule, determining the quantity of labour supplied, n_t, as a function of the real wage, given the MU of consumption (which under the assumptions is a function only of consumption).

Monopolistic competition gives valid microfoundations for macroeconomics. Firms' decisions are modelled, capturing aspects of industry structure, innovation and diversity, yet avoiding complications from positive profits in the aggregation. Since output is less than optimal, there is scope for macroeconomic stabilisation – policy can improve welfare. Appendix A.10.1 formally derives aggregate supply under monopolistic competition.[5]

Figure 10.2 illustrates how monopolistic competition combines zero profits with output at less than its optimal value. Product diversity means each product is unique and faces a downward sloping demand curve (DD_{MC}), so the producer has some market power. But competition due to free entry drives profits to zero. The downward sloping demand curve is tangent to the average cost curve, but not at the point of minimum cost, as with the demand curve under perfect competition DD_{PC}. Therefore, output produced under monopolistic competition (Q_{MC}) is less than that under perfect competition (Q_{PC}).

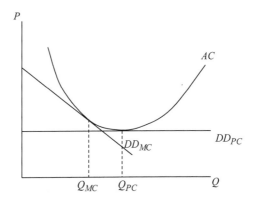

Figure 10.2 Monopolistic competition

Equation 10.15 can be written in log-linear form as (see Appendix A.10.2):

$$c_t = E_t\{c_{t+1}\} - \frac{1}{\sigma}(i_t - E_t\{\pi_{t+1}\} - \rho) \qquad (10.18)$$

where $\rho \equiv -\log \beta = \beta^{-1} - 1$, $\pi_{t+1} \equiv p_{t+1} - p_t$ is the rate of inflation between t and $t + 1$ and $p_t \equiv \log P_t$. The nominal interest rate i_t corresponds to the log of the gross yield on the one period bond, defined as $Q_t \equiv (1 + \text{yield})^{-1}$, since $Q = R_t^{-1}$ and $R_t = $ gross yield, $i_t \equiv -\log Q_t \equiv \log R_t$. Note that $i_t = \log(1 + \text{yield}_t) \simeq \text{yield}_t$, where the latter approximation will be accurate as long as the nominal yield is 'small'; ρ can be interpreted as the discount rate of the household, from the steady state where constant consumption implies $\beta(1 + \overline{\text{yield}}) = 1$.

*10.3 The two-country open economy macroeconomics model[6]

Obstfeld and Rogoff (1996) put the static, closed sticky price monopolistic competition model in an analytically tractable, dynamic, open two-country framework.[7]

There is a continuum of individual monopolistic producers $z \in [0, 1]$, each produces a single differentiated good indexed by z. Home producers $\in [0, n]$ and foreign producers $\in [n, 1]$. There is no investment, labour supply is elastic and all agents have symmetric preferences and constraints. The elasticity of intertemporal substitution is assumed to be unity and the elasticity of disutility from labour is taken to be two.

New open economy macroeconomics 211

The representative consumer – producer $j \in [0, 1]$ maximises the separable utility function:

$$U_t^j = \sum_{s=t}^{\infty} \beta^{s-t} \left[\log C_s^j + \chi \log \frac{M_s^j}{P_s} - \frac{\kappa}{2} y_s (j)^2 \right] \tag{10.19}$$

Utility, U_t, increases with the discounted present value of consumption, C_t, and money balances M_t/P_t, but decreases with work effort put in to produce output y_t.

To derive the third term in Equation 10.19 for labour disutility, consider disutility from effort (l) to be $-\phi l$; l enters the production function $y = A l^\alpha$, where $\alpha = 1/2$. Substituting from the production function and with $\kappa = \dfrac{2\phi}{A^{\frac{1}{\alpha}}}$ gives disutility from effort that enters Equation 10.19. If productivity A rises, κ would fall.

C is a real consumption index:

$$C = \left[\int_0^1 C^j (z)^{\frac{\theta-1}{\theta}} dz \right]^{\frac{\theta}{\theta-1}} \tag{10.20}$$

where $\theta > 1$ is the price elasticity of demand faced by each monopolist. There is a consumption-based price index corresponding to Equation 10.20. Let $p(z)$ be the home currency price of good z. Then, the home money price level is:

$$P = \left[\int_0^1 p(z)^{1-\theta} dz \right]^{\frac{1}{1-\theta}} \tag{10.21}$$

P gives the lowest possible cost, measured in units of good 1, of purchasing a unit of C and is obtained by minimising:

$$\underset{c(z)}{Min} \; Z = \int_0^1 p(z)c(z)dz \; s.t \left[\int_0^1 c(z)^{\frac{\theta-1}{\theta}} dz \right]^{\frac{\theta}{\theta-1}} = 1$$

We proceed to derive individual demands and aggregate them to get world demand, substituting out endogenous variables in the objective function in order to reduce them to y_t, M_t, C_t for the jth individual.

A home individual's demand for z (Eq. 10.22) is obtained by maximising C subject to the nominal budget constraint $\int_0^1 p(z)c(z)dz = Z$, where Z is any fixed nominal expenditure on goods:

$$Max \; L = \left[\int_0^1 c(z)^{\frac{\theta-1}{\theta}} dz \right]^{\frac{\theta}{\theta-1}} + \lambda \left[Z - \int_0^1 p(z)c(z)dz \right]$$

212 New open economy macroeconomics

$$c^j(z) = \left[\frac{p(z)}{P}\right]^{-\theta} C^j \text{ for individual } j \tag{10.22}$$

where P is the minimum cost of one unit of composite consumption.

By symmetry, the foreign agent's demand is:

$$c^{*j}(z) = \left[\frac{p^*(z)}{P^*}\right]^{-\theta} C^{*j} \tag{10.23}$$

The government budget constraint is:

$$G_t = \tau_t + \frac{M_t - M_{t-1}}{P_t} \tag{10.24}$$

If $G_t = 0$, it implies all seignorage revenue is given to the public in the form of transfers. If $G_t = G_t^* = 0$,

Aggregate global consumption is:

$$C^w = \int_0^n C^j dj + \int_n^1 C^{*j} dj = nC + (1-n)C^* \tag{10.25}$$

where we drop superscripts and impose symmetry to simplify.[8] The function of government is preserved, but there effectively is no government.

The assumption of no impediments or costs to trade between countries implies LOOP holds for each good Z:

$$p(z) = Sp^*(z) \tag{10.26}$$

Because of LOOP, P can be written as:

$$P = \left[\int_0^1 p(z)^{1-\theta} dz\right]^{\frac{1}{1-\theta}} = \left[\int_0^n p(z)^{1-\theta} dz + \int_n^1 \left[Sp^*(z)\right]^{1-\theta} dz\right]^{\frac{1}{1-\theta}} \tag{10.27}$$

Since $0 \ldots n$ is produced in the home country and $n \ldots 1$ in the foreign country, so P^* is:

$$P^* = \left[\int_0^1 p^*(z)^{1-\theta} dz\right]^{\frac{1}{1-\theta}} = \left[\int_0^n \left[p(z)/S\right]^{1-\theta} dz + \int_n^1 \left[p^*(z)\right]^{1-\theta} dz\right]^{\frac{1}{1-\theta}} \tag{10.28}$$

Equations 10.26 and 10.27 imply home and foreign CPIs are related by PPP, giving consumption-based PPP:

$$P = SP^* \tag{10.29}$$

New open economy macroeconomics 213

PPP follows, since commodity baskets and preferences are taken to be identical across countries. Relative prices of individual goods are not constant and changes in the terms of trade or relative prices of tradable goods play a large role. LOOP and PPP imply $\frac{p(z)}{P} = \frac{p^*(z)}{P^*}$ for any good z.

Using world consumption C^w, and integrating demand for good z across all agents (i.e. taking a population weighted average of home, 10.22, and foreign, 10.23, demands), gives total world demand for good z:

$$y^d(z) = \left[\frac{p(z)}{P}\right]^{-\theta} C^w \tag{10.30}$$

This is the demand curve facing each monopolist.

We assume an integrated world capital market in which both countries can borrow and lend, but the only internationally traded asset is a riskless real bond denominated in the composite consumption good.

The period (dynamic) *budget constraint for a representative home individual j*, in nominal terms, can be written as:

$$P_t B_{t+1}^j + M_t^j = P_t(1+r_t)B_t^j + M_{t-1}^j + p_t(j)y_t(j) - P_t C_t^j - P_t \tau_t \tag{10.31}$$

We can substitute out $P_t(j)$ in the income term using world demand Equation 10.30. Individual j is the sole producer of output $y_t(j)$ because of product differentiation, so $p_t(j)$ is not the same for all j. We replace the endogenous $p_t(j)$ by P_t, the price level. C_t^W and y_t are also taken as given by agents from Equation 10.30. Then, we substitute for $p_t(j)$ in the budget constraint, divide by P_t and rewrite it to solve for C_t^j. Substituting the latter in the utility function sets up the maximand for unconstrained maximisation:

$$\max_{y(j),M^j,B^j} U_t^j = \sum_{s=t}^{\alpha} \beta^{s-t} \left\{ \log\left[(1+r_s)B_s^j + \frac{M_{s-1}^j}{P_s} + y_s(j)^{\frac{\theta-1}{\theta}}\left(C_s^w\right)^{\frac{1}{\theta}} - \tau_s - B_{s+1}^j - \frac{M_s^j}{P_s}\right] + \chi \log\left(\frac{M_s^j}{P_s}\right) - \frac{\kappa}{2}y_s(j)^2 \right\} \tag{10.32}$$

To get optimal consumption, differentiate Equation 10.32 with respect to B_{t+1}^j, using $s = t$ and $s = t + 1$, since B_{t+1} terms enter those two periods. As in the maximisation (Eq. 10.6) earlier, we get the standard Euler:

$$C_{t+1} = \beta(1+r_{t+1})C_t \tag{10.33}$$

214 New open economy macroeconomics

To get the labour-leisure trade-off differentiate the objective function (Eq. 10.32) with respect to $y_t(j)$:

$$y_t^{\frac{\theta+1}{\theta}} = \frac{\theta-1}{\theta\kappa}\left(C_t^w\right)^{\frac{1}{\theta}}\frac{1}{C_t} \tag{10.34}$$

This says the cost in MU terms, of producing an extra unit of output (implicitly due to foregone leisure), equals the MU from consuming the added revenue that an extra unit of output brings.

Finally, to get optimal real money balance holding, we need to differentiate Equation 10.32 with respect to M_t^j. The nominal interest rate i_t has to be brought in. The relationship between nominal and real interest rates (the Fisher effect in discrete time) is:

$$1+i_{t+1} = \frac{P_{t+1}}{P_t}\left(1+r_{t+1}\right)$$

The Euler condition for a nominal bond is:

$$u'(C_t) = \beta_t E_t\left\{\left(1+i_{t+1}\right)\frac{P_t}{P_{t+1}}u'(C_{t+1})\right\}$$

The first two terms in the bracket give ex-post gross real return for bonds. The required FOC follows by equating this to the stochastic Euler equation for money:

$$\frac{M_t}{P_t} = \chi C_t\left(\frac{1+i_{t+1}}{i_{t+1}}\right) \tag{10.35}$$

Equation 10.35 equates the MRS of consumption for the services of real money balances to the consumption opportunity cost of holding real money balances (the nominal interest rate). Indices denoting agent j have been dropped in the FOCs.

The three FOCs and the transversality condition (Eq. 10.36) characterise equilibrium.

$$\lim_{T\to\infty} R_{t,t+T}\left(B_{t+T+1} + \frac{M_{t+T}}{P_{t+T}}\right) = 0 \tag{10.36}$$

In the limit, either wealth or its return must be zero in order to maximise C_t. This ensures an agent cannot be indefinitely indebted.

New open economy macroeconomics 215

For a closed-form solution, we need to linearise around a steady state (indicated by overbars). From the consumption Euler (Eq. 10.33), in a steady-state $\overline{C} = \beta(1+\overline{r})\overline{C}$. Since $\beta(1+\overline{r}) = 1$, we have $\overline{r} = \dfrac{1-\beta}{\beta} \equiv \delta$, where δ is the rate of time preference.

In the special case where initial foreign assets $\overline{B}_0 = 0$, a symmetric equilibrium holds characterised by:

$$\overline{C}_0 = \overline{C}_0^* = \overline{y}_0 = \overline{y}_0^* = \overline{C}_0^w$$

Our assumption of a unit line allows the individuals' consumption to equal aggregate consumption. Then, substituting $y_t = C_t^w = C_t = \overline{y}$ in FOC (Eq. 10.34), which gives the individuals' choice of output y_t, we can solve for the steady-state output:

$$\overline{y}_0 = \overline{y}_0^* = \left(\frac{\theta-1}{\theta\kappa}\right)^{\frac{1}{2}}$$

Because prices are flexible, this output is independent of monetary factors. If a planner were to maximise the utility of consumption net of the cost of leisure given up, her maximand would be:

$$\max_{y}\left(\log y - \frac{\kappa}{2}y^2\right)$$

This has the FOC: $\dfrac{1}{y} = \kappa y$ or $y^2 = \dfrac{1}{\kappa}$

As θ approaches $\propto$, implying goods become perfect substitutes, market-determined steady-state output y_0 approaches the planner's optimal output y, above. Global output is suboptimally low in a decentralised equilibrium, since y is higher, that is:

$$y = \left(\frac{1}{\kappa}\right)^{\frac{1}{2}} > \left(\frac{\theta-1}{\theta\kappa}\right)^{\frac{1}{2}} = \overline{y}_0$$

Monopolistic producers do not capture all the benefits of increasing their output. This coordination failure lowers output. Policy intervention can, therefore, raise welfare.

In order to solve the impact of policy shocks, we log-linearise the equations of the model around the steady state. For example, taking logs and differentiating FOC Equation 10.34 gives:

216 *New open economy macroeconomics*

$$(\theta+1)\hat{y}_t = \hat{C}_t^W - \theta\hat{C}_t$$

$$\text{where} \quad \hat{C} = \frac{dC_t}{\overline{C}_0}$$

Thus, we need to solve for steady-state variables and 10 short-run variables, or deviation from the steady state $\hat{C}, \hat{C}^*, \hat{y}, \hat{y}^*, \hat{P}, \hat{P}^*, \hat{E}, \hat{C}^w, \hat{r}$ and $d\overline{F}$ (change in current account) in response to a monetary shock. Barred variables denote the long run or steady state, while hatted variables denote deviations from the steady state. Solving gives the result that with flexible prices the classical invariance of the real economy with respect to monetary factors holds. Therefore, monetary policy has no impact on real variables. Typically, some types of sticky prices are required for such an impact of policy. Obstfeld and Rogoff (1996) make the sticky price assumption that prices are set one period in advance and they can be adjusted fully after one period.

The model's symmetry can be exploited to get differences between home and foreign variables, further reducing the number of variables to two equations. Subtracting foreign from domestic counterpart equations, using the Euler and PPP equations, gives the money market equilibrium MM:

$$\hat{\varepsilon} = \left(\hat{M} - \hat{M}^*\right) - \left(\hat{C} - \hat{C}^*\right)$$

where the percentage change in domestic consumption relative to international is $\hat{C} - \hat{C}^*$, $\hat{\varepsilon}$ is the percentage change in exchange rate and $\hat{M} - \hat{M}^*$ is the relative percentage increase in home money supply.

MM is analogous to the MA, but money demand is a function of C, not y here. C functions as the scale variable affecting the transaction demand for money. The exchange rate depreciates with a rise in M and appreciates with a rise in C, which increases money demand. As an asset price, it remains capable of instant adjustment.

The short-run labour-leisure trade-off equations do not bind, since the current account allows income and expenditure to differ. Steady-state consumption differentials derived from short-run equations and net international investment positions (NIIP), which link short- and long-run systems, give the GG curve.

$$\hat{\varepsilon} = \frac{\overline{r}(1+\theta)+2\theta}{\overline{r}(\theta^2-1)}\left(\hat{C} - \hat{C}^*\right)$$

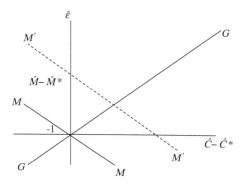

Figure 10.3 The response to a monetary shock in an open economy DSGE

Home consumption can rise relative to foreign only if the exchange rate depreciates, so that home producers increase output. The GG, therefore, slopes upward in Figure 10.3.

The MM curve has a negative slope, since money demand rises with C. When $\hat{C} = \hat{C}^*$ at the origin $\hat{\varepsilon} = \hat{M} - \hat{M}^*$, a permanent unanticipated relative home money supply shock shifts MM up to M'M'. Relative consumption changes affect the exchange rate by changing money demand. Equilibrium is at the intersection of the two curves.

The exchange rate depreciates, but by less than the increase in M. The exchange rate depreciation is smaller if θ is large, so firms have less monopoly power. If goods are close substitutes, a small change in the exchange rate implies a large effect on demand, so the exchange rate effect of a money supply increase is smaller. As θ approaches ∞, GG becomes horizontal and an M shock does not affect the exchange rate at all. In any case, there is no overshooting – the exchange rate rises less than the money supply. Even in the long run, ε increase is less than proportional to the M increase; ε equals long-run value $\bar{\varepsilon}$ for a permanent money shock.

Since y rises, the country runs a CAS to smooth C. Part of the y increase is saved. There is some substitution into leisure, a fall in home goods supply and an improvement in the terms of trade. So, the rise in C, y and the real exchange rate imply less ε increase is required compared to the flexible price case. The steady-state rise in wealth increases leisure. Since the initial level of output is too low (because of imperfect competition), the demand-driven increase in y^w, due to the home M increase, raises welfare in both countries. That home agents

218 *New open economy macroeconomics*

produce more does not raise their relative utility level, since the extra revenue is exactly cancelled out by the increase in work effort.

Two new fundamental results are obtained, though the effects may not be large. First, there are persistent effects of monetary shocks, so money supply can be non-neutral. Second, depreciation can have non-zero sum effects, benefitting both countries.

10.4 Extensions

DSGE models may be stylised, but they can serve as an economic laboratory where the effects of alternative assumptions can be examined. Although outcomes are assumption dependent, the trick is to include the details necessary to answer the question being examined. There is now a large literature that builds in different aspects and examines their effect on outcomes. The answers have the advantage of a consistent inclusion of general equilibrium interactions. For example, including financial markets in DSGE models after the GFC could give an estimate of the direct effect plus indirect spillovers of new types of financial regulations.

Alternative *institutional* assumptions can be made. For example, the SOE structure is more relevant for most economies since their international transactions are too small to affect international prices, which they take as given. Then, a distinction can be made between traded (T) and non-traded (NT) goods. For example, in an early paper, Hau (2000) found that the overshooting effect returns with a large NT sector, since the exchange rate now affects only a small share of goods and so must change more. Sticky wages combine in interesting ways with price rigidities. Different types of nominal-real rigidities and price staggering assumptions and the effect of PTM are explored. Obstfeld and Rogoff prefer exporter good pricing, since LCM or PTM tends to be short term and is not so relevant except for the United States. If there is PTM, flexible exchange rate is better since there is less pass through and volatility.

Different assumptions are made regarding preferences and technology, financial market structure, capital, risk, trading frictions. The effects of imposing different *functional forms* for the utility functions are explored. Higher elasticities imply a higher impact on the current account, but this leads to multiple steady states, which are difficult to handle, so unit elasticities tend to be imposed. The perfect capital markets assumption is used as a way to shut down current account adjustments, which are difficult to handle analytically since they lead to multiple steady states. But these are especially important in the catch-up paths EDEs follow. Ghironi (2000) finds omitting these can result in large errors. For EDEs handling capital flows and investment, variation in risk premium is especially important.

New open economy macroeconomics 219

There are DSGEs being developed for EDEs that are capable of reproducing EDE business cycles. We will discuss some of these in the next two chapters. In one of the earliest such studies, Neumeyer and Perri (2005) decompose the real interest rate into an international rate and a country risk component. The presence of working capital amplifies the effects of fundamental shocks to country risk. The model generates business cycles that are more volatile than in AEs. Consumption volatility exceeds that of output. Net exports are strongly countercyclical. Real interest rates are also countercyclical and lead the cycle. All this matches Argentine data. The effect of country risk on Argentine output volatility is found to be nine times larger than that of international rates.

DSGE models have given rise to a large empirical literature. The main strategy, as in the above case, is to match unconditional moments from the model with the data. But in open economies, the unconditional variances of S and Q are infected by considerable market noise, unrelated to fundamentals.

VAR-based evidence is also used. Impulse responses help evaluate the performance of model in describing the economy's response to macroeconomic shocks. Monetary shocks are largely found to move the real exchange rate in a manner that is qualitatively consistent with the model predictions. But appropriate identification restrictions are an issue, as is testing for the effect of real shocks, for example, on Q.

Empirical strategies also test the implications of these models. For example, Romer (1993) tests the hypothesis that since an open economy gains less from surprise inflation as demand leaks abroad, inflation should fall in such economies. He finds empirical support after controlling for openness and country size. But openness can also increase vulnerability to external price shocks – controls for these are also required.

The optimisation approach provides a benchmark that cannot be fully satisfied in the real world, which has major frictions. Therefore, it has generated what are known as 'puzzles' in international finance. Analysing and explaining these has been an active source of research.

Six major such puzzles are first, the trade home bias. That is, countries consume too much of their own products, given the options available from trade in an open economy. Second is the high correlation of domestic savings and investment, given the option in an open economy of financing domestic investment with foreign savings or vice versa. Third is the equity home bias. Typical portfolios are not sufficiently globally diversified, containing too large a share of home equity. The fourth is that consumption correlation is too low across countries, implying that consumption risk is not adequately diversified given opportunities to do so in a global financial market. Fifth is the PPP puzzle or the failure of trade arbitrage. Rogoff's (1996) preferred

220 *New open economy macroeconomics*

explanation for all these is higher transaction costs for any type of cross-border interaction. For example, threshold barriers reflecting sunk costs of international arbitrage imply firms wait for large opportunities before acting to remove trade arbitrage. Trade and transaction costs drive wedge between borrowers and lenders.

A sixth set of puzzles concerning exchange rates and FX markets is the more general exchange rate disconnect. Currency values are only weakly related to macroeconomic aggregates, except perhaps in the long run. Included in these are a range of issues, such as volatile exchange rates subject to discontinuous jumps, short-run drifts and long-run swings, forward discount bias, profitable speculation and the impact of extrapolative versus recursive expectations on exchange rate behaviour. Manifestations of these anomalies are the huge volume of FX market transactions[9] and the currency and financial crises a wide range of countries have had to deal with.

10.5   Summary

This chapter developed the basic building blocks of the intertemporal optimising approach and their economic intuition, in order to derive aggregate consumption and labour supply in an open economy. It, then, obtained the impact of a monetary shock on the relative exchange rate and output in a two-country DSGE model.

There are basic differences compared to earlier results in short-run macromodels. First, there is no overshooting – the exchange rate depreciation is less than the increase in money supply. Depreciation is reduced also if goods are close substitutes, since a small change in the exchange rate has a large effect on demand. Since choice of more leisure reduces the output response to the monetary shock and increases imports, welfare rises in both countries. There are permanent effects of a monetary shock through the current account and wealth accumulation.

The simple IS-LM with consumption as a function of income is an approximation, but so is the intertemporal approach with consumption as a smoothed function of discounted future wealth. Since the truth probably lies in between, both intuitions are useful.

Apart from optimisation over time, the building blocks include monopolistic competition for firms' price and output decisions, log-linear aggregation, use of the unit line so that the average is also the total and of symmetry to make the two-country problem tractable. The next chapter applies these building blocks to develop formal models for EMs and general insights from new open economy macroeconomics for monetary and fiscal policy.

APPENDICES

Appendix A.10.1
Labour elasticity and aggregate supply

Under monopolistic competition (Romer, 2012), firms producing differentiated goods, q_i, running from $1 \ldots n$, face constant elasticity, log-linear demand curves with elasticity $\eta > 0$:

$$q_i = y - \eta(p_i - p)$$

The supply side consists of n producer consumers, with production, consumption and utility, respectively, written as:

$$Q_i = N_i \tag{10A.1}$$

$$C_i = \frac{P_i Q_i}{P} \tag{10A.2}$$

$$U_i = C_i - \frac{1}{1+\varphi} N_i^{1+\varphi} \tag{10A.3}$$

There is increasing marginal disutility of work, so $1 + \varphi > 1$ where N is labour hours. Substituting Equations 10A.1 and 10A.2 into 10A.3 gives:

$$U_i = \frac{P_i N_i}{P} - \frac{1}{1+\varphi} N_i^{1+\varphi}$$

Maximising U_i with respect to N_i taking P_i and P as given (or setting P_i taking P as given) gives the FOC: $\frac{P_i}{P} - N_i^{\varphi} = 0$.
This can be written as:

$$N_i = (P_i / P)^{\frac{1}{\varphi}}$$

$$\text{or } q_i = n_i = \frac{1}{\varphi}(p_i - p)$$

222 *New open economy macroeconomics*

Giving aggregate supply as a function of relative price and the elasticity of labour supply, $1/\varphi$. Labour supply and production are increasing in relative price or optimal relative price is increasing in output. If the elasticity of labour supply is $\frac{1}{\varphi}(=0.1)$, the elasticity of price with respect to output is $\varphi \ (= 10)$. If one is low, the other is high.

AD can have larger real effects if φ is low, since relative prices are not adjusted and output adjusts. But elasticity of labour supply is normally low implying large price adjustment. In the NKE literature, additional features are used to deliver the required low elasticity of price (e.g. labour is off its supply curve or efficiency wages are paid).

Appendix A.10.2
Log-linearisation

To derive the log-linear form of the Euler Equation 10.15 (Galí, 2008), take logs, transfer all variables on the RHS, substitute $\rho = -\log\beta$ and $i_t = -\log Q_t$, open the brackets and take exponentials to write it as:

$$1 = E_t \left\{ \exp\left(i_t - \sigma \Delta c_{t+1} - \pi_{t+1} - \rho\right)\right\}$$

This follows, since $e^0 = 1$. In a perfect foresight, steady state with constant inflation π and constant growth γ, we must have:

$$i = \rho + \pi + \sigma\gamma$$

With the steady state, real interest rate being given by:

$$r \equiv i - \pi$$
$$= \rho + \sigma\gamma$$

A first-order Taylor expansion of exponential $(i_t - \sigma \Delta c_{t+1} - \pi_{t+1} - \rho)$ around that steady state with constant rates of inflation and consumption growth yields the log-linearised Euler equation.

Notes

1 Eichenbaum (1997) argues that agents are forward looking, and if they are not, dynamic macroeconomics should be taught to all high school students, who would then become forward looking! More seriously, such behaviour is a function of the stability and predictability of the environment. As this increases, so will the ability of agents to anticipate the future. Countercyclical fiscal policy gives a simple example of a new insight from the forward-looking approach. A stimulus today can more credibly increase demand if it is accompanied with a plan to reverse it.
2 See Blanchard and Fischer (1989) and Galí (2008).

224   *New open economy macroeconomics*

3 Another way to derive the Euler is to set up a Hamiltonian maximising consumer utility subject to a capital accumulation constraint. The MU from consumption is equated to the shadow price (also known as the co-state variable) of the constraint.
4 This is an example of a pure efficiency argument, which is compatible with any type of preferences or morals – it just shows how best to achieve those preferences. The difference is that it is an optimisation over time, when actions today affect outcomes tomorrow. An example of such an optimisation is the decision on hours of study today as a function of exam marks desired tomorrow. This example raises other interesting questions such as a change in the rate of discount or preferences over time. Self-one today may prefer to shirk, but self-two's preference tomorrow will be for self-one to study more today. The solution can involve types of binding for self-one, much like Ulysses' strategy when he bound himself to the mast of the ship to prevent possible temptation from the sirens.
5 For the simple case of producer consumers, it demonstrates the effect of the elasticity of labour supply.
6 * denotes advanced material.
7 The treatment follows and simplifies that in Obstfeld and Rogoff (1996), Chapter 10. See also Chapter 5, Sarno and Taylor (2002).
8 Aggregate global consumption can also be derived by adding the population-weighted averages of linearised demand functions. The relative price terms cancel out.
9 Technical strategies make money. These are basically bets against CBs in the short run, since CBs tend to 'lean against the wind'. Froot and Thaler (1990) found a strategy of buying US$, when US interest rates were higher and outperformed an efficient market random strategy.

References

Blanchard, O. J. and S. Fischer. 1989. *Macroeconomics*, Cambridge, MA: MIT Press.
Dornbusch, R. 1976. 'Expectations and Exchange Rate Dynamics', *The Journal of Political Economy*, 84(6): 1161–1176, December.
Eichenbaum, M. 1997. 'Some Thoughts on Practical Stabilization Policy', *AEA Papers and Proceedings*, 87(2): 236–239.
Froot, K. A. and R. H. Thaler. 1990. 'Foreign Exchange', *Journal of Economic Perspectives*, 4: 172–192.
Galí, J. 2008. *Monetary Policy, Inflation and the Business Cycle: An Introduction to the New Keynesian Framework*, Princeton, NJ: Princeton University Press.
Ghironi, F. 2000. *Macroeconomic Interdependence under Incomplete Markets*, Federal Reserve Bank of New York, New York, Mimeo.
Hau, H. 2000. 'Exchange Rate Determination: The Role of Factor Price Rigidities and Nontradables', *Journal of International Economics*, 50: 421–447.
Neumeyer, P. A. and F. Perri. 2005. 'Business Cycles in Emerging Economies: The Role of Interest Rates', *Journal of Monetary Economics*, 52: 345–380.
Obstfeld, M. and K. Rogoff. 1996. *Foundations of International Macroeconomics*, Cambridge, MA: MIT Press.

New open economy macroeconomics 225

Rogoff, K. 1996. 'The Purchasing Power Parity Puzzle', *Journal of Economic Literature*, 34: 647–688, June.

Romer, D. 1993. 'Openness and Inflation: Theory and Evidence', *Quarterly Journal of Economics*, 108: 870–903.

Romer, D. 2012. *Advanced Macroeconomics*, 4th edition, New York: McGraw-Hill Irwin.

Sarno, L. and M. P. Taylor. 2002. *The Economics of Exchange Rates*, Cambridge, UK: Cambridge University Press.

11 New directions for monetary and fiscal policy

> Teaching rational expectations to all high school students would make them forward-looking.
>
> —Martin Eichenbaum

11.1 Introduction

The new approach in macroeconomics has had practical implications for macroeconomic policy and has changed CB practice in many countries. Despite its rigour, simplifications reduce the closed economy DSGE model to an aggregate supply (AS) or Phillips curve and aggregate demand (AD) curve, which differ from the standard curves only in the presence of forward-looking variables. The latter follow from rigourous underlying optimisation by agents with foresight (Clarida et al., 1999; Woodford, 2003). These foundations make the parameters of the curves robust. In addition to straightforward policy analysis, the underlying optimising microfoundations also make welfare analysis feasible. Yet, the framework is simple enough to be used to form policy intuitions.

The AD curve relates the output gap or excess demand inversely to the real interest rate positively, to expected demand and to a demand shock. The AS curve shows inflation rising with the output gap, expected inflation and a cost-push or supply shock. The output gap is defined as the gap between actual and potential output. The CB's instrument is the interest rate, and sticky prices allow it to affect the real interest rate. Using the output gap rather than unemployment in the AS makes it easier to apply in EDEs because, even though it may be difficult to measure unemployment in dualistic labour markets, the output gap can be defined. First the idea of potential output and expected future changes in it are useful for an economy undertaking structural reform. Second, cost-push factors play a dominant role in inflation in EDEs. But major structural features of EDEs, such as dualistic labour markets, also have to be built in.

New directions for monetary and fiscal policy 227

Since our focus is the open economy, we start with a simplified version of a model that derives optimal monetary policy for a SOE. This links to the models in the previous chapter, since it has the same components. Then, we adapt the model and the approach by introducing some key aspects of an EDE, before discussing the general features of the new approach to policy and bringing out its new features. A discussion of inflation targeting and the Taylor rule (Taylor, 1999). Leads to the question of coordination between monetary and fiscal policy and whether a rule-based approach is also required for fiscal policy.

The remainder of the chapter is structured as follows: optimal monetary policy is derived for a SOE in Section 11.2 and for a small open emerging market in Section 11.3. Section 11.4 presents some practical implications of the new approach to monetary policy. Section 11.5 analyses a rule-based approach for fiscal policy, before Section 11.6 summarises and concludes. Some derivations are given in appendices.

*11.2   Optimal monetary policy in a SOE[1]

Gali and Monacelli (GM) (2005) derive optimal monetary policy in a SOE. Since this seminal paper generated a large amount of work, we present a simplified version of the paper. The economy is small, in the sense it does not affect foreign variables, but home and foreign disturbances affect the terms of trade. Foreign country variables, which are independent of home country action, are indicated by *. The blocks that build the model are similar to those used in the last chapter. There is monopolistic competition so that output is below the social optimal and money has real effects. Firms set Calvo-type staggered prices. There is CES aggregation over $i \in [0, 1]$ countries and $j \in [0, 1]$ product varieties. Intertemporal optimisation, by the representative consumer, gives the standard FOCs:

$$E_0 \sum_{t=0}^{\infty} \beta^t u(C_t, N_t) \tag{11.1}$$

C_t is derived from CES aggregation of C_H, C_F, with elasticity of substitution between home (H) and foreign (F) goods equal to unity:

$$C_t = kC_{H,t}^{1-\alpha}C_{F,t}^{\alpha}, \qquad k = \frac{1}{(1-\alpha)^{1-\alpha}\alpha^{\alpha}} \tag{11.2}$$

$C_{H,t}$ is an index of consumption of domestic goods derived by CES aggregation with elasticity of substitution $\varepsilon > 1$ over j domestic varieties.

228 *New directions for monetary and fiscal policy*

$C_{F,t}$ is an index of imported goods, derived by CES aggregation with elasticity of substitution $\gamma = 1$ over imported goods j from i countries of origin $C_{i,t}$, which is itself an index over j goods imported from country i and consumed domestically.

In the CPI price index below, which can be derived as in the last chapter, the share of foreign goods α is also the index of openness:

$$P_t = \left(P_{H,t}\right)^{1-\alpha} \left(P_{F,t}\right)^{\alpha} \tag{11.3}$$

11.2.1 *Deriving AD from consumers' optimisation*

Optimal allocation of expenditure across domestic and imported goods depends on relative prices and a scale variable:

$$C_{H,t} = \left(1 - \alpha\right) \frac{P_t}{P_{H,t}} C_t \tag{11.4}$$

$$C_{F,t} = \alpha \frac{P_t}{P_{F,t}} C_t \tag{11.5}$$

where $P_t C_t = P_{H,t} C_{H,t} + P_{F,t} C_{F,t}$

Specific CES form of separable utility function gives the log-linear FOCs[2] derived in Chapter 10:

$$w_t - p_t = \sigma c_t + \varphi n_t \tag{11.6}$$

$$c_t = E_t \left\{c_{t+1}\right\} - \frac{1}{\sigma}\left(i_t - E_t \left\{\pi_{t+1}\right\} - \rho\right) \tag{11.7}$$

The exchange rate creates a gap between domestic and consumer prices in an SOE, so it is necessary to derive the relationship between *domestic and consumer prices, terms of trade and the real exchange rate*. Log-linearisation of CPI (Eq. 11.3) gives:

$$p_t = \left(1 - \alpha\right) p_{H,t} + \alpha p_{F,t} \tag{11.8}$$

where p_t is the CPI and $p_{H,t}$ is the domestic price index. So, $\pi_t = p_t - p_{t-1}$ then is CPI inflation. Assuming the LOOP holds, the effective term of trade, for which a rise denotes depreciation, is:

$$Z_t = \frac{P_{F,t}}{P_{H,t}} \tag{11.9}$$

This can be written in log-linear form as $p_{F,t} = z_t + p_{H,t}$. Substituting this in the CPI Equation 11.8 gives:

$$p_t = p_{H,t} + \alpha z_t$$

$$\text{Or } \pi_t = \pi_{H,t} + \alpha \Delta z_t \tag{11.10}$$

where π_t is the CPI inflation and $\pi_{H,t}$ is the domestic inflation.

The real exchange rate, $Q_t = \dfrac{S_t P_t^*}{P_t}$, written in log-linear form is:

$$q_t = s_t + p_t^* - p_t$$

The relationship between Q_t and Z_t is derived assuming $P_{F,t}$ is the same in the definitions of Z_t and Q_t, that is, $p_{F,t} = s_t + p_t^* = z_t + p_{H,t}$. Substituting this and Equation 11.10 for p_t in the above equation for q_t gives:

$$q_t = p_{F,t} - p_t = z_t + p_{H,t} - p_{H,t} - \alpha z_t$$

$$q_t = (1 - \alpha) z_t \tag{11.11}$$

Without logs, this is:

$$Q_t = Z_t^{(1-\alpha)}$$

The consumption Euler Equation 11.7 gives the choice between consumption and saving in domestic bonds. Costless trade in foreign bonds or complete international risk sharing implies:

$$\beta \left(\frac{C_{t+1}^i}{C_t^i} \right)^{-\sigma} \left(\frac{P_t^i}{P_{t+1}^i} \right) \left(\frac{S_t^i}{S_{t+1}^i} \right) = \frac{1}{R_t} \tag{11.12}$$

That is, UIP will hold since the exchange rate affects the real return to bonds. Using the equivalent Euler equation for the home country, the definition of Q_t and integrating over $i \in [0, 1]$ countries to get C_t^*, gives:

$$C_t = \upsilon C_t^* Q_t^{\frac{1}{\sigma}}$$

Simplifying by assuming zero net foreign holdings, so that $\upsilon = 1$, gives:

$$c_t = c_t^* + \frac{1}{\sigma} q_t$$

$$c_t = c_t^* + \frac{(1 - \alpha)}{\sigma} z_t \tag{11.13}$$

230 New directions for monetary and fiscal policy

In the symmetric steady state with PPP, $C_t = C_t^*$ and $Q_t = Z_t = 1$. The system reverts to this steady state since external shocks are assumed to be stationary.

AD and output for the home country is given by domestic plus foreign demand for home goods, that is, home exports to all countries (*):

$$Y_t = C_{H,t} + C_{H,t}^* \tag{11.14}$$

By symmetry and substitution of the relevant indices (see Appendix 11.A.1), the FOC for the F consumer for home goods is:

$$C_{H,t}^* = \alpha Q_t \frac{P_t}{P_{H,t}} C_t^* \tag{11.15}$$

Substituting the FOCs for the home (Eq. 11.4) and foreign consumers (Eq. 11.15) in the equation for output equals aggregate demand (Eq. 11.14), and substituting out C_t^* using the risk-sharing Equation 11.3 and simplifying the AD-AS identity lead to Equation 11.6 for the case of $\sigma = 1$ (see Appendix 11.A.2):

$$Y_t = Z_t^\alpha C_t \tag{11.16}$$

The next step is to get the determinants of the *terms of trade*. Substituting risk sharing again (with $\sigma = 1$) in the aggregate demand = supply Equation 11.16 above, we get:

$$Y_t = Z_t^\alpha C_t^* Q_t$$

Substituting $Q_t = Z_t^{1-\alpha}$ and $C^* = Y^*$ gives $Y_t = Z_t^\alpha Y_t^* Z_t^{1-\alpha}$, which simplifies to:

$$Z_t = \frac{Y_t}{Y_t^*} \tag{11.17}$$

The determinant of Z_t is just the ratio of domestic to foreign output. If domestic supply exceeds foreign, foreign prices are likely to be relatively higher, so the domestic terms of trade is depreciated.

To get the *aggregate demand equation* from the consumption Euler, we need to substitute output for consumption in Equation 11.7. We can use the demand = supply Equation 11.16 to do so:

$$y_t = E_t\{y_{t+1}\} - \frac{1}{\sigma}\left(i_t - E_t\{\pi_{t+1}\} - \rho\right) - \frac{\alpha}{\sigma}E_t\{\Delta z_{t+1}\}$$

New directions for monetary and fiscal policy   231

Using $\pi_t = \pi_{H,t} + \alpha \Delta z_t$ to convert consumer into domestic prices leads to z_t dropping out if $\sigma = 1$, giving the AD as:

$$y_t = E_t\{y_{t+1}\} - \frac{1}{\sigma}\left(i_t - E_t\{\pi_{H,t+1}\} - \rho\right) \tag{11.18}$$

11.2.2   Deriving AS from firms' optimisation

The simple log-linear production function, which is the other common component of modern macroeconomic models, assumes output depends just on labour and its productivity, a_t:

$$y_t = a_t + n_t \tag{11.19}$$

From the firms' optimisation, marginal cost, mc_t, therefore depends on unit real wages net of productivity, plus any employment subsidy, τ, where $\nu = -\log(1-\tau)$:

$$mc_t = -\nu + w_t - p_{H,t} - a_t \tag{11.20}$$

Marginal cost adjusts $\hat{mc}_t = mc_t - mc$, depending on its distance from log of gross mark up in the steady state $mc = -\log\varepsilon/\varepsilon - 1 \equiv -\mu$, which falls with the elasticity of demand.

From the firm's optimal price setting:

$$\pi_{H,t} = \beta E_t\{\pi_{H,t+1}\} + \lambda \hat{mc}_t \tag{11.21}$$

Assuming the Calvo type of staggered price setting, where $(1 - \theta)$ per cent of firms change prices in a period ($\theta = 0.75$ is the standard calibrated value). This assumption implies that $\lambda \equiv \dfrac{(1-\beta\theta)(1-\theta)}{\theta}$ of the gap from optimal marginal cost is removed at any point in time.

Deviation of mc_t from its steady-state value $\widehat{mc_t}$ is related to the deviation of y_t from steady-state $\bar{y}_t$, because real wages can be substituted for output using the intratemporal FOC Equation 11.6. This relation is derived in Appendix 11.A.3. The output gap, x_t, is defined as $x_t \equiv y_t - \bar{y}_t$.

$$\hat{mc}_t = (\sigma + \varphi)x_t$$

232 *New directions for monetary and fiscal policy*

Combining the above with the price setting Equation 11.21 gives the AS or new Keynesian Phillips curve[3] as it is sometimes called:

$$\pi_{H,t} = \beta E_t\left\{\pi_{H,t+1}\right\} + \kappa x_t \qquad \kappa = \lambda(1+\varphi) \quad \text{if } \sigma = 1 \qquad (11.22)$$

The final form of the AD is also written in output gap space as:

$$x_t = E_t\left\{x_{t+1}\right\} - \frac{1}{\sigma_\alpha}\left(r_t - E_t\left\{\pi_{H,t+1}\right\} - r\bar{r}_t\right) \qquad \sigma_\alpha = 1 \text{ if } \sigma = 1 \quad (11.23)$$

$$\sigma_\alpha < \sigma \text{ otherwise}$$

$$\text{where } r\bar{r}_t = \rho - \sigma_\alpha\left(1-\rho_a\right)a_t\left[+\chi E_t\Delta y_{t+1}^*\right] \qquad \chi = 0 \text{ if } \sigma = 1 \quad (11.24)$$

The steady-state natural interest rate, ρ, is defined as the equilibrium real rate, consistent with a zero or target rate of inflation, when prices are fully flexible. It is also the time discount rate, since $\rho \equiv \beta^{-1} - 1 = -\log\beta$ where β is the discount factor. Shocks that change the natural rate open an output gap and affect inflation. The term $r\bar{r}_t$ that enters the AD, therefore, captures deviation of the natural rate from its steady-state value. The deviation occurs due to real disturbances that change natural output; $r\bar{r}_t$ rises for any temporary demand shock and falls for any temporary supply shock. Optimal policy requires insulating the output gap from these shocks, so that the CB's interest rate instrument should move in step with changes in the natural rate. Thus, the CB would accommodate positive supply shocks that raise the natural output by lowering interest rates. It would offset positive demand shocks that raise output above its potential by raising interest rates. Full stabilisation at the current natural output implies that $x_t = \pi_{H,t} = 0, y_t = \bar{y}_t$ and $r_t = \overline{rr}_t$.

To obtain optimal policy, a CB minimises a loss function, such as Equation 11.25, subject to the AD and AS Equations 11.23 and 11.24. The loss function is a weighted average of output, inflation and interest rate deviations from equilibrium values:

$$L = q_x x_t^2 + q_\pi \pi_t^2 + q_i i_t^2 \qquad (11.25)$$

The last captures smoothing preferences that prevent large changes in the policy rate, where i_t is the riskless nominal interest rate. The first term is the output gap and the second term inflation, which can be either consumer price inflation or domestic inflation $\pi_{H,t}$ if the

New directions for monetary and fiscal policy 233

inflation target is zero, or else it is deviations from this target. This is also known as gap analysis since the output gap plays a vital role, and the interest rate gap enters the AD.

The result of the maximisation typically requires policy to contract demand as inflation rises above a target, but with gradual adjustment because of a weight on output and on interest rate smoothing. In certain circumstances, it is consistent with a Taylor-type rule (Eq. 11.26) or commitment for the policy rate. With forward-looking price setting and a short-run output employment trade-off, there can be gains from commitment to a rule. The original Taylor rule equation was:

$$i_t = \pi_t + r_t^* + \phi_\pi \left(\pi_t - \pi_t^* \right) + \phi_x \left(y_t - \bar{y}_t \right) \tag{11.26}$$

where π_t^* is the desired rate of inflation, r_t^* is the assumed equilibrium real interest rate, y_t is the logarithm of real GDP and $\bar{y}_t$ is the logarithm of potential output, as determined by a linear trend. Taylor proposed setting $\phi_\pi = \phi_x = 0.5$. As long as $\phi_\pi > 0$, an increase in inflation of one percentage point would lead the CB to raise the nominal interest rate by $1 + \phi_\pi$, thus raising the real interest rate. The simple NKE models can imply a very low ϕ_x, since in forward-looking models with demand shocks response to inflation is sufficient to stabilise output.[4]

As the empirical Taylor rule literature developed, the estimated equation was simplified. Either the short policy rate was regressed on the deviation of output from potential and of inflation from target, or a constant term was assumed to include a constant inflation target and real interest rate. So, the short policy rate was regressed on inflation, on the deviation of output from potential and a constant capturing the inflation target. A lagged interest rate was included to capture policy smoothing.

GM find a flexible domestic inflation targeting rule (DITR) to be welfare maximising compared to targeting consumer price inflation (CITR), or an exchange rate peg. DITR targets the prices that can be sticky and cause distortions. Svensson (2000) found flexible consumer inflation worked best since as it allowed use of the exchange rate channel, which was the fastest channel of transmission, to reduce inflation. Strict CITR created too much volatility in the real exchange rate through vigorous use of the exchange rate channel. Flexible targeting involves considerable stabilisation of the real exchange rate, although unlike an exchange rate peg it does not prevent the CB from accommodating shocks to the terms of trade. The Taylor rule also works well but is not efficient since, especially in more complex economies, it disregards relevant information not captured in inflation and in the output gap.

234 *New directions for monetary and fiscal policy*

*11.3 Adaptation of the monetary policy DSGE to an emerging market[5]

Structural features have to be added to dynamic equilibrium models to capture key aspects of EM behaviour even while modelling individual behaviour. Large low productivity employment and dualism in labour markets is a feature of many EMs.[6] This feature leads to often expressed opinions that DSGEs cannot be applied to EMs. For example:

> The standard models taught in graduate schools in the U.S. and Europe are of limited relevance for developing countries. . . . more disturbing is that virtually all of the research uses full employment models, making the results of questionable relevance, e.g. in a country with 25% unemployment
>
> (Stiglitz, 2007).

But one way to work with equilibrium labour markets is by including two types of consumer workers with differing productivity. With no unemployment insurance or savings, the poor often cannot afford to be unemployed and work at low productivity jobs instead. These are the key differences in the small open emerging market economy (SOEME) model (Goyal, 2011), compared to the SOE of Section 2.

These are two representative households consuming and supplying labour: above subsistence (R) and at subsistence (P). The intertemporal elasticity of consumption ($1/\sigma_R$), productivity and wages (W_R) of R are higher, their labour supply elasticity ($1/\varphi_R$) is lower compared to those of P and they are able to fully diversify risk in international capital markets. Consumption of each type of good is a weighted average of consumption by the R and the P households, with η as the share of R. Aggregate intertemporal elasticity of substitution, $1/\sigma$, and the inverse of the labour supply elasticity, φ, are also weighted sums with population shares of R and P as weights. Figure 11.1 shows the structure of consumption and production.

The basic consumption Euler and household labour supply are derived for each type, with risk sharing only for R types. Payoffs D_t are taken as zero for P types, since they do not hold a portfolio of assets.

A smaller proportion of population sharing risks internationally make C_t, Y_t and Z_t more volatile. To solve for Z_t in terms of endogenous Y_t and exogenous variables, first substitute $C_{R,t}$ and $C_{P,t}$ for C_t in the aggregate demand equal to supply equation and then substitute

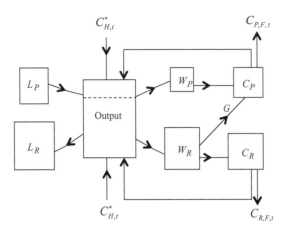

Figure 11.1 Nested structure of production and consumption in a SOEME
Source: Goyal (2011).

out $C_{R,t}$ using risk smoothing. As a result, a multiplier factor enters the determination of Z_t. The $Z_t = Y_t/Y_t^*$ in the SOE now becomes:

$$Z_t = \left(\frac{Y_t}{Y_t^{*\eta} C_{P,t}^{1-\eta}}\right)^{\sigma_D} \tag{11.27}$$

The multiplier factor $\sigma_D = \dfrac{\sigma_R}{\left(\eta(1-\alpha)+\varpi\alpha\right)}$, which affects the SOEME, is large because the existence of P types reduces the elasticity of substitution to $1/\sigma_D$. More openness moderates σ_D, however. If $\sigma_R = 1$, then $\varpi = 1$. If $1/\sigma_P = 0$, then $\sigma = \sigma_R/\eta$. It follows $\sigma_D < \sigma$. As α approaches 0, or the economy becomes closed, σ_D equals σ, which is its upper bound. In a fully open economy, α approaches unity and σ_D falls to its lower bound, which is unity. As α falls, σ_D rises.

The dynamic aggregate supply (AS) is now:

$$\pi_H = \beta E_t\{\pi_{H,\,t+1}\} + \kappa_D x_t \tag{11.28}$$

where $\kappa_D = \lambda(\sigma_D + \varphi)$. The slope for a closed economy is $\lambda(\sigma + \varphi)$ and for a SOE is $\lambda(\sigma_\alpha + \varphi)$, where $\sigma_\alpha = \dfrac{\sigma_R}{(1-\alpha)+\varpi\alpha}$, $\sigma > \sigma_D > \sigma_\alpha$. Although openness reduces the slope of the AS, the slope can be higher in the SOEME compared to a SOE, even though φ is lower for the SOEME, since $\sigma_D > \sigma_\alpha$. Z_t affects marginal cost through its impact on real wages.

236 *New directions for monetary and fiscal policy*

The dynamic aggregate demand (AD) equation for the SOEME is:

$$x_t = E_t\{x_{t+1}\} - \frac{1}{\sigma_D}\left(r_t - E_t\{\pi_{H,\ t+1}\} - \overline{rr}_t\right) \qquad (11.29)$$

where $\overline{rr}_t = \rho - \sigma_D\Gamma(1-\rho_a)a_t - \sigma_D(1-\eta+\Phi)E_t\{\Delta c_{P,t+1}\}$ (11.30)
$$+ \sigma_D(\Theta-\Psi)E_t\{\Delta y^*_{t+1}\}$$

And $\Theta = \alpha(\varpi - \eta)$, $d = \dfrac{1}{\sigma_D + \phi}$, $\Gamma = \dfrac{(1+\phi)}{\sigma_D + \phi}$,
$$\Psi = \eta(\sigma - \sigma_D)d,\ \Phi = d\big((1-\eta)(\sigma-\sigma_D)\big) \qquad (11.31)$$

In an EM, a change in c_p is an additional shock affecting the natural interest rate. A fall requires reduction in the policy rate, since it increases willingness to work *P*-type workers. The distance from the world consumption level also rises. The parameters of the other shock terms also differ from those for the SOE. Since productivity shocks, a_t, can be more persistent in EMs that are in transition stages of upgrading technologies, they change the natural rate less but potential output more. A temporary shock to c_p turns out to have the largest effect on the natural rate (Goyal, 2009). Table 11.1 shows the calibrations of the parameters.

Degree of openness, inequality and forward-looking behaviour affect the coefficients of AD and AS, including the relative size of inverse intertemporal elasticities $\sigma > \sigma_D > \sigma_R > \sigma_\alpha$. The interest elasticity of AD is lower in the SOEME. There is less affect of terms of trade on AD, more on AS (through changes in real wages). c_p decreases the impact of Y^*.

The slope of the AS curve is higher than for a SOE when Z_t is endogenous, especially in a low-income closed economy where η, α are low, but it is lower if Z_t is sticky, since this reduces the adverse impact of higher Z_t volatility (Figure 11.2).

Results and implications for policy from the model include: a temporary shock to C_p reduces the natural interest rate. Since such shocks are frequent, this gives a downward bias to interest rates. But shocks that raise wages raise the natural interest rate. Natural output is increased by C_p because of the potential labour productivity gap, but it is decreased by infrastructure constraints and technological distance. As η approaches 1, C_p approaches C_R and the SOEME collapses to the SOE.

Table 11.1 Benchmark calibrations

Baseline calibrations		
Degree of price stickiness	θ	0.75
Price response to output	φ	0.25
Labour supply elasticity of P type	φ_P	0.01
Labour supply elasticity of R type	φ_R	0.6
Elasticity of substitution between differentiated goods	ε	6
Steady-state real interest rate or natural interest rate	ρ or $\bar{i}$	0.01
Variations in the natural interest rate due to temporary shocks	$\overline{rr}$	± 0.01
Degree of openness	α	0.3
Proportion of the R type	η	0.4
The intertemporal elasticity of substitution of the R type	$1/\sigma_R$	1
The intertemporal elasticity of substitution of the P type	$1/\sigma_P$	0
Consumption of the P type	C_p	0.2
Consumption of the R type	C_R	1
Share of backward-looking price setting	γ_b	0.2
Share of forward-looking price setting	γ_f	0.8
Weight of output in the CB's loss function	q_y	0.7
Weight of inflation in the CB's loss function	q_π	2
Weight of the interest rate in the CB's loss function	q_i	1
Implied parameters		
Weighted average elasticity of substitution	$1/\sigma_D$	0.58
Discount factor	β	0.99
Weighted average consumption level	C	0.75
Log deviation from world output	κ	0.1
Philips curve parameter	λ	0.24
Steady-state real interest rate, discount rate	ρ	0.01
Labour supply elasticity	$1/\varphi$	4
Shocks		
Technology shock	a_t	
Persistence of natural rate shock	ρ^r	0.75
Persistence of cost-push shock	ρ^c	0
Standard deviation of natural rate shock	σ_ε^r	0.01
Standard deviation of cost-push shock	σ_ε^c	0.2

Source: Adapted from Goyal (2011).

238 New directions for monetary and fiscal policy

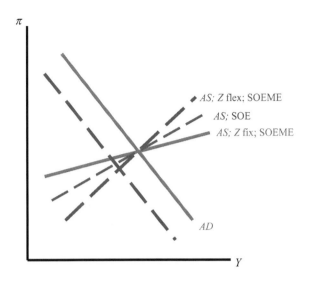

Figure 11.2 Aggregate supply with different slopes
Source: Adapted from Goyal (2011).

Dual or specific labour markets increase strategic complementarity ($\kappa_D < 1$), that is, there is a substantial effect of variations in nominal spending on output even if only some prices are sticky. But volatile terms of trade increase κ_D.

Weight on output as well as on inflation is required in the policy rule. Simulations show flexible DIT works best if CPI is lagged, otherwise flexible CIT is the best. But with Z_t credibly fixed, both DIT and CIT give similar results. A fixed Z_t implies that some exchange rate policy is used in addition to the effect of the policy rate on S_t, to affect S_t. CPI targeting performs almost as well as DIT only if Z_t is credibly fixed, since the AS then becomes flatter. With more openness, flexible CIT becomes optimal since monetary transmission lags are the lowest for the exchange rate, which changes the most under CIT, as in Svensson (2000).

So, loss from implementing DIT is minimal, as long as managed exchange rates are optimal. DIT with exchange rate intervention implies appreciation under a cost shock. This reduces the necessity to contract output to reach the inflation target. CIT can be volatile in some circumstances with excessive exchange rate movements nominal,

New directions for monetary and fiscal policy   239

although some exchange rate flexibility is required. DIT is more robust and has lowest volatility. If backward-looking behaviour dominates, a smaller policy rate response is optimal. It creates lowest volatility.

11.4 The intuition of the new approach to monetary policy

A simple analytical apparatus due to Romer (2000) shows the conceptual advantages and implications for policy of the new approach. The IS-LM is fully consistent only under fixed prices. When, as is the case in most countries, there is positive underlying core inflation with sticky prices, the IS-LM drawn in nominal interest rate and output space becomes inconsistent. Although the nominal interest rate is relevant for the money demand, the real interest rate is relevant for the aggregate demand components of the IS curve. With positive inflation, the curves will keep shifting. Inflation expectations, which are actually endogenous, have to be taken as exogenous to draw the curves.

Moreover, CBs today act to affect interest rates directly. Many of them follow interest rate rules.

The money market, therefore, is only relevant at a second level of analysis in analysing the determinants of changes in interest rates. Even here, money supply targets do not help, since the availability of close monetary substitutes has made money demand unstable. If the CB directly sets the short nominal interest rate, i_t, there is considerable simplification in the analysis, since it does not have to work through a change in money balances affecting i_t in the money market, and then i_t affecting demand. The other improvement with this analysis is that it works with narrow money or the money supply that the CB actually can control for stabilisation purposes. The LM curve – based analysis is forced to use broad money, for which the nominal interest rate is the opportunity cost.

CBs typically set a short overnight rate (e.g. the federal fund rate, in the United States) in response to inflation, that is, they aim to affect the real interest rate. Sticky prices are a precondition for CBs to be able to influence the real rate r_t, since with fully flexible prices P_t would jump with any change in M_t, i_t would adjust to expected inflation and r_t would be unchanged. With sticky prices, expected inflation does not adjust to i_t, and r_t changes instead. In an EDE, a larger percentage of prices are administered, and therefore fixed in the short run, making this effect stronger. It is, therefore, possible for the CB to change real interest rates as an intermediate or short-run target.

Romer draws the IS curve in the real interest and output space, replacing the LM curve with the MP or monetary policy curve. In the simplest analysis, inflation is taken as given at a point in time. MP then sets i_t as a function of this inflation. Given sticky prices, the change in i_t affects the real interest rate. Thus, MP is horizontal and shifts downwards as inflation falls. Therefore, lower inflation is accompanied by higher output, giving a downward sloping aggregate demand curve in inflation and output space. The causality is from inflation to the real interest rate to output. Since inflation is given at a point in time, the AS or inflation adjustment (IA), as Romer calls it, is horizontal at that inflation rate. If output is below full employment, both MP and IA will fall, as the CB lowers the interest rate, until full employment is reached (Figure 11.3).

Goodhart (1989, p. 293), in a wide-ranging survey of the actual conduct of monetary policy, writes: 'Academic economists generally

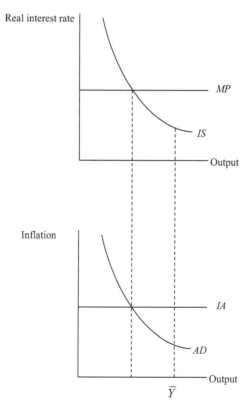

Figure 11.3 The monetary policy (MP) and inflation adjustment (IA) curves

New directions for monetary and fiscal policy 241

regard (open market) operations as adjusting the quantitative volume of the banks' reserve base, and hence of the money stock, with rates (prices) in such markets simultaneously determined by the interplay of demand and supply. CB practitioners, almost always, view themselves as unable to deny the banks the reserve base that the banking system requires, and see themselves as setting the level of interest rates, at which such reserve requirements are met, with the quantity of money then simultaneously determined by the portfolio preferences of private sector banks and non-banks.'

Thus, it is necessary to move from the LM curve, with its idea of a monetary aggregate, which is controlled, to the idea of monetary policy controlling a real interest rate. This is the variable that clears the money market in the short run and affects demand for goods. Actual operating procedures focus on interest rates and not on monetary aggregates.

In more complex models, the AS replaces the IA curve. Such an AS is derived, assuming a certain probability that administered and other prices will remain fixed in any period. When a price is varied, it is set as a function of the expected future marginal cost. A proportionate relationship is assumed between the output gap and marginal cost. A cost shock, then, is anything that disturbs this relationship. Such deviations can occur due to wage contracts or mark-up shocks.

11.4.1 Implications for monetary policy

Some relatively robust results for monetary policy, from the new approach,[7] are the following:

> *Result 1 (m)*: A short-run trade-off between inflation and output variability arises only if there is positive cost-push inflation.

Only current and future demand affect inflation, when cost-push is absent. The CB can then vary interest rates to set excess demand to zero for all time and lower inflation with no cost in terms of output, which remains at its potential. A fall in output is required to lower inflation only if cost-push is positive. The output sacrifice is larger, the more elastic the supply curve.

> *Result 2 (m)*: As long as there is cost-push inflation and deviations of output from potential may harm welfare, optimal policy would aim to achieve an inflation target only over the medium term.

Under a positive cost shock, forcing an immediate reduction in inflation would have a cost in terms of output foregone. Therefore,

242 *New directions for monetary and fiscal policy*

inflation should converge to its target only over time, if there is a positive weight to output stabilisation. These two results are especially relevant for a developing economy, where cost shocks tend to be major determinants of inflation.

> *Result 3 (m)*: Under certainty, when expected inflation is positive, optimal policy should raise real interest rates. While optimal policy should perfectly offset demand shocks, it should keep nominal interest rates constant under shocks to potential output.

Real rates should rise to contract demand when inflation is high because of a rise in demand, since there is no cost in terms of output in this case. That is, nominal interest rates should respond more than 'one-for-one' to expected inflation. If there is a rise in potential output, to the extent it is foreseen, permanent income and demand will both rise, so expected inflation will be zero and there will be no need to change interest rates. Policy must accommodate unexpected changes in potential output.

> *Result 4 (m)*: Under commitment to a rule, a CB will raise nominal interest rates relatively more compared to *Result 3 (m)*, when expected inflation rises.

The reason is that a tough credible policy today will decrease the output cost of lowering inflation tomorrow. Even if the CB is not trying to raise output above the natural level and there is no inflation bias, there is a gain from commitment to an inflation target, when agents are forward looking. Since it influences agents' expectations in the absence of perfect foresight, a rule can lower the costs of disinflation.

> *Result 5 (m)*: Since information is imperfect, policy rules have to be formulated in terms of forecasts of target variables.

All CBs work with imperfect information due to inadequate data or unknown policy lags. Good structural models are required to produce these forecasts. Prior to adopting formal targeting rules, an EDE CB must start producing regular forecasts of potential target variables and see how they perform.

> *Result 6 (m)*: Model uncertainty can lead to interest rate smoothing; the instrument is varied less than required by the optimal policy response.

New directions for monetary and fiscal policy   243

A more serious kind of uncertainty is imperfect understanding of the way the economy works – leading to parameter uncertainty in models. This problem is particularly acute in an EDE. Under uncertainty, neither expected inflation nor permanent income or potential output is perfectly foreseen, and it is difficult to distinguish permanent from transitory, supply from demand shocks, so that small changes are made while waiting for more clarity. Central bankers worldwide tend to smooth interest rates. Smoothing means that the desired interest rate change is not accomplished at one go, so that a series of small changes follow in the same direction. It is as if CBs add a lagged interest rate term, with a coefficient of about 0.8–0.9, to the optimal policy response function. This may be due to conservatism or 'status-quoism' caused by uncertainty or concern about the financial sector. The latter is particularly sensitive to variations in interest rates. Thus, model uncertainty leads to making less than full use of forward-looking behaviour in designing policy, in order to collect more information as well as lower asset price volatility. Excess volatility of asset prices, where forward-looking behaviour dominates, is partly due to rigidities elsewhere and also because asset portfolios cannot be fully diversified.

> *Result 7 (m)*: If inflation forecasts are within an acceptable zone, policy should target output; otherwise policy should bring inflation to the border of the zone, and then let it fall with favourable supply shocks.

Flexible inflation forecast targeting is suited to an EDE. It allows use of diverse information and the discovery of potential output. There is a high degree of uncertainty attached to the latter, and it changes more as reforms raise efficiency. With a medium-range inflation target, changes in potential output reveal themselves. If inflation does not rise even as output exceeds the expected potential, the potential must have risen. Inflation itself can be used as an indicator of potential output. Thus, flexible inflation targeting allows focus on domestic considerations and response to shocks. The earlier arguments for smoothing the nominal interest instrument also hold.

The measure of inflation targeted can be either core or headline inflation. The inflation rate – when excess demand is zero or output equals its potential – is called core inflation. It excludes headline volatile supply or commodity shock components. Using core inflation allows the first round effects of supply shocks to be excluded from the target and gives escape clauses for very large supply shocks. There are arguments for using headline inflation as the target in EMs

244　*New directions for monetary and fiscal policy*

since commodity, especially food price, inflation affects wages, and therefore has second-round effects. But if headline inflation is used, it is all the more important to target this only in the medium run and tighten only if there are second-round effects. It is difficult to forecast inflation under large oil or other supply shocks, but anchoring inflation expectations credibly can limit second-round effects and keep medium-term inflation low even under such shocks. As inflation becomes smooth, EDEs can gradually build up a reputation with forecasts that turn out to be correct most of the time.

In an EDE, a monetary conditions' index can be a precursor or complement to more formal inflation forecasting. It is a weighted set of variables that affect aggregate demand. The set and weights vary across countries, but include money and credit aggregates, short-term interest rates, exchange rates and their fluctuations, direct measures of domestic inflation, commodity prices, wages and even some real variables such as capacity utilisation. See Box 11.1 for the evolution of Indian procedures.

Box 11.1　Evolution of Indian monetary procedures

The basic objectives of monetary policy remained price stability and development, but in line with the recommendations of the 1985 Chakravarty Committee, over the mid-1980s till 1997–98, the intermediate target shifted from credit controls towards flexible monetary targeting with 'feedback' from inflation and growth. While M3 growth served as a nominal anchor, the operating target was reserve money. The cash reserve ratio (CRR) was the principal operating instrument, along with continued use of some selective credit controls.

But deregulation and liberalisation of financial markets, combined with the increasing openness of the economy in the 1990s made money demand more unstable and money supply more endogenous. There were repeated wide deviations from the money supply targets set. If money demand is unstable, monetary policy based on it would lack precision.

Flexible nominal money supply targeting proved inadequate under these changes, and interest rates were volatile in the 1990s. After the adverse impact of the 1990s peak in interest rates, the Reserve Bank moved towards an interest rate – based operating procedure, basing its actions on a number of indicators of

New directions for monetary and fiscal policy 245

monetary conditions, including forward-looking expectation surveys. It formally adopted a 'multiple indicator approach' in April 1998, following informal changes in practice from the mid-1990s.

The multiple indicators were the variables affecting future growth and inflation, which were the key objectives. The desirable rate of inflation was given as 5 per cent, with the aim to bring it even lower in the long term. Another objective was to reduce reliance on reserve requirements, particularly the CRR, shifting liquidity management towards OMOs in the form of outright purchases/sales of Gsecs and repo and reverse repo operations to affect interest rates. Operating procedures changed as well, with the policy rate becoming the operating instrument and the CMR the operating target. Table 11.2 summarises these changes.

The multiple indicator approach was criticised as list based. Flexible inflation forecast targeting, adopted in 2015, is a natural

Table 11.2 Monetary policy procedures

Monetary policy	1950s to end 1980s	Early 1990s to 1998–99	1998–99 to 2014–15	2015
Objectives	1 Stability 2 Development	1 Inflation 2 Credit supply for growth	1 Inflation 2 Growth	Flexible inflation forecast
Intermediate target	Priority sector credit targeting	Monetary targeting with annual growth in broad money (M_3) as intermediate target	Multiple indicator approach (rates, credit, external, fiscal variables and expectation surveys used for growth and inflation projections)	Variables affecting inflation
Operating procedure (Instruments)	Direct instruments (interest rate regulations, selective credit control, SLR, CRR)	Gradual interest rate deregulation CMR; Direct instruments (selective credit control, SLR, CRR)	Direct (CRR, SLR) and indirect instruments (repo operations under LAF and OMOs)	Repo

Source: Adapted and updated from Goyal (2014).

246 *New directions for monetary and fiscal policy*

progression that converts the multiple indicators from an omnibus list to action based on the determinants of inflation, even while retaining vital flexibilities coming from considering a range of information. The operating target chosen was headline CPI inflation, since that was the one most relevant for household inflation expectations. The aim was to bring it down gradually to 6 per cent by January 2016 and within a range of 4–6 per cent by January 2018.

More than a dozen AEs follow CPI-based inflation targeting, while among EDEs, Brazil, Chile, the Czech Republic, Israel, Poland and South Africa were early adopters. The 1990s, however, were a period of falling inflation and fiscal deficits for most countries, including those who did not follow rules. After Lehman, inflation rose even for inflation targeters like the United Kingdom and Brazil, while growth fell. In general, inflation targeters had relatively lower growth. This was a period of large commodity price shocks, also. Gelos and Ustyugova (2012) found their inflationary impact over the period 2001–10 more sustained in economies with higher food shares in consumption, fuel intensities and high pre-existing inflation. More independent CBs and better governance scores reduced the inflationary impact, but inflation-targeting regimes did not have much effect. Independence of the CB needs to be combined with democratic accountability. Variables, such as trade openness, financial development, dollarisation and labour market flexibility, were not significant.

The rhetoric of inflation targeting has disguised its reality; it is not really a rule, but allows considerable flexibility. It is actually constrained discretion, since it determines the behaviour of the interest rate as 'a predictable function of a few economic variables' (Allsop and Vines, 2000, p. 17) and is rule-like only in enforcing forward-looking behaviour. All the variables that affect inflation influence the decision. Since it is transparent, private sector jump variables, such as asset price expectations, help in its implementation. Since it is forward looking, it prevents the CB from taking actions with undesirable long-term consequences; the transparent discussion educates the public about these long-term effects, and therefore has political benefits. It forces both the CB and the public to understand the long-term consequences of choices made, and therefore to forego short-term opportunism and populism. But there is discretion to deal with unforeseen circumstances. It is not necessary to impose politically unacceptable

New directions for monetary and fiscal policy 247

short-term costs. Especially as the inflation target refers to a medium-to long-term range, it gives considerable opportunity for short-run stabilisation. If the floor is taken as seriously as the upper target, it implies stimulus must be given in order to raise inflation, if demand falls. Since a positive inflation rate is targeted for rather than a price level, real wages can adjust even if nominal wages are rigid.

A medium-term inflation target is consistent with short-run stabilisation and longer term saving, investment and external balance. In EDEs, the latter aspect is very important. Arrangements must facilitate a rapid rise in imperfectly known potential output and also disarm the political pressures that harm the future for the present.

> *Result 8 (m)*: In a SOE, the nominal interest rate instrument can be smoothed, and the intermediate target real interest rate can be achieved under a managed real exchange rate.

Although inflation targeting precludes using the interest rate to actively manage the exchange rate, since the focus is on inflation, the policy instrument can respond to the impact of the exchange rate on output and inflation and try to affect exchange rates through UIP. But, as we saw in earlier chapters, other instruments are available to manage the exchange rate, especially in an EM. Using these can help achieve the inflation target, since for CIT the transmission from the nominal exchange rate to inflation tends to be fast. A stable real exchange rate delivers lower inflation (Section 11.3). Varying the nominal exchange rate, in an implicit target band around the equilibrium, real exchange rate can make it feasible to smooth the nominal interest rate instrument and achieve the desired intermediate target real interest rate. But, this implies use of an active exchange rate policy independent of the interest rate.

11.4.2 Monetary policy transmission

Box 11.2 summarises the general channels of policy transmission, which comprise of the *aggregate demand, expectation and cost-push* channels.[8] The *aggregate demand channel* is the traditional channel, which is the focus of textbooks. It consists of the effect of the *interest rate, asset prices, exchange rate and credit* on demand. When CB action affects the price and amount of short-term liquidity, this affects the rate at which banks lend to each other in the short-term money market. For example, if the CB changes its repo rate at which it lends to banks in the short-term money market, this affects the cost of

248 *New directions for monetary and fiscal policy*

borrowing and works its way through a variety of market short-term interest rates. Transmission across the maturity spectrum affects long-term interest rates. Since prices are sticky, real interest rates change and affect investment and other interest sensitive components of aggregate demand. In the short run, aggregate demand affects output more than prices, as in the first channel shown in Box 11.2. This is the real interest channel.

The short-term interest rate mainly affects capital flows, exchange rates and other asset prices. It is the longer term interest rates that affect aggregate demand. Smoothing short-term interest rates can lower volatility in asset prices and yet allow the CB to directly affect demand through the long-term rate. If the short-term interest rate is expected to rise in the future, for example, the long-term rate will rise more. So, the long-term rate can be affected with a smaller current change in the short-term rate. This is especially so if forward-looking behaviour dominates, since then discounted future values determine current values of key variables such as exchange rates.

A change in nominal interest rates also affects exchange rates. A rise in domestic nominal interest rates raises the relative return to domestic assets attracting foreign inflows. The domestic currency appreciates in nominal terms and, because of sticky prices, in real terms also. This reduces the demand for domestic goods and raises the demand for foreign goods – exports fall and imports rise, thus reducing domestic output.

A rise in nominal interest rates makes bonds more attractive relative to equity, since both the expected dividend flow and their present discounted value will fall. Arbitrage reduces the value of other real assets, such as real estate, for similar reasons. This fall in wealth reduces household spending and output. This is the asset channel.

In addition to demand, price and liquidity or availability affects the generation of credit. Credit market imperfections, such as credit rationing, imply the quantity of credit as well as its price matters for aggregate demand. This is the credit channel. In an EDE with a large informal credit market, however, a change in the price of formal credit can have a magnified effect on the price and availability of informal credit.

In the short term, aggregate demand is expected to affect output more than price, but the traditional view is that in the longer term it affects only price. Money affects prices and its rate of growth affects inflation. Most economies, however, have ongoing positive inflation. Other monetary transmission channels can directly affect inflation, and therefore prices.

New directions for monetary and fiscal policy 249

The exchange rate affects traded goods prices, which directly enter consumer prices, as well as prices of key imported intermediate goods, such as fuel, depending on the pass through. If a rise in import prices raises wages and other costs of production, it leads to further rounds of inflation. This is the *cost shock channel* of transmission. Imported goods affect the CPI and CPI inflation, if there are second-round effects with a shorter lag than the aggregate demand channel. The impact of the exchange rate on the CPI rises in an EDE, once agriculture becomes a traded good. It is large, also, in an economy dependent on intermediate imports such as oil.

Apart from the effect of the interest rate on the exchange rate, CBs in EMs can also affect the exchange rate through different types of intervention and signalling. Movements in foreign interest and exchange rates that affect domestic exchange rates would also have similar effects on domestic inflation. Shocks to FX rates and prices are also part of the cost channel. An appreciation would directly reduce prices, apart from its effect through aggregate demand.

Box 11.2 also presents the *expectation channels*. The policy regime and its credibility will affect inflation and exchange rate expectations. Over time, inflation targeting regimes often succeed in anchoring inflationary expectations independently of aggregate demand.[9] Then, despite a rise in some relative price, such as oil or food, the second-round rise in wages does not take place and inflation does not rise. In inflation targeting regimes, aggregate demand is not allowed to exceed potential output.

The exchange rate is also an asset price, so capital flows, domestic and global fragility affect exchange rate expectations. A rise in country risk leads to expected depreciation. So, expectation-induced volatility can also have all the above cost-push effects. As costs rise, so can future inflation.

With a rapid pace of globalisation and financial innovations even in EMs, interest rates play a larger role in monetary transmission and become the natural instrument of monetary policy. First, interest rates become more flexible and responsive to CB intervention. Second, the interest rate becomes a more sensitive and fast signal of potential imbalances. As retail credit markets deepen, the interest elasticity of aggregate demand rises. Third, demand for broad money becomes unstable and enhancement in its supply from commercial banks more flexible, so that targeting monetary aggregates becomes difficult and the attempt causes high volatility in interest rates. Fourth, the size of foreign exchange, bond, equity and other asset markets rises. These are very sensitive to interest rates. Now, forward-looking behaviour

250 *New directions for monetary and fiscal policy*

becomes more important and markets are interested in guessing the CB's response to uncertainty and changes. Thus, transparency becomes a major issue. Even so, other channels of transmission, such as credit, continue to be important, although more open and unified financial markets lower the effectiveness of direct credit controls. Many backward sectors, less integrated with modern financial systems, do reduce the reach of monetary policy but more openness greatly raises its impact. First, since agriculture becomes a traded good, the nominal exchange rate affects agricultural prices; this affects wages and prices throughout the economy, since food is a major part of the consumption basket. Second, the exchange rate is an asset price that is very sensitive to interest rates and the expectations of domestic and foreign traders and arbitrageurs.

Box 11.2   Monetary transmission channels

- Aggregate demand channels
  - Real interest rate

$$re\uparrow \Rightarrow M\downarrow \Rightarrow r\uparrow \Rightarrow I\downarrow \Rightarrow AD\downarrow \Rightarrow Y\downarrow$$

  - Exchange rate (floating)

$$re\uparrow \Rightarrow M\downarrow \Rightarrow i\uparrow \Rightarrow NFI(i)\uparrow \Rightarrow S\downarrow \Rightarrow Q\downarrow \Rightarrow AD\downarrow \Rightarrow Y\downarrow$$

  - Credit

$$re\uparrow \Rightarrow M\downarrow \Rightarrow Credit\downarrow \Rightarrow AD\downarrow \Rightarrow Y\downarrow$$

  - Wealth

$$re\uparrow \Rightarrow M\downarrow = i\uparrow \Rightarrow \left.\begin{array}{l} \text{Equity prices}\downarrow \\ \\ \text{Asset prices}\downarrow \end{array}\right\} Wealth\downarrow \Rightarrow \begin{array}{l} I\downarrow \\ \\ C\downarrow \end{array} \Rightarrow Y\downarrow$$

- Cost shock from the exchange rate
  - Own exchange rate

$$S_t \uparrow \Rightarrow CPI_t \uparrow \Rightarrow \pi^e_{t+1} \uparrow$$

New directions for monetary and fiscal policy   251

- Exchange rate policy: intervention, signalling
- External rates

$$^{w} \uparrow \Rightarrow S^{w} \downarrow \Rightarrow S_{t} \uparrow \begin{cases} \Rightarrow \text{intermediate goods price} \uparrow \\ \Rightarrow \text{CPI}_{t}^{e} \uparrow \Rightarrow \begin{matrix} W_{t+1}^{e} \uparrow \\ P_{t+1}^{e} \uparrow \end{matrix} \Rightarrow \pi_{t+1}^{e} \uparrow \end{cases} \Rightarrow \pi_{t+}^{e}$$

- Expectations channel
  - Inflation expectations

$$re \downarrow \Rightarrow M \uparrow \Rightarrow \pi_{t}^{e} \uparrow \Rightarrow W_{t+1}^{e} \uparrow \Rightarrow \pi_{t+1}^{e} \uparrow$$

- Country risk

$$S^{e} \uparrow \begin{cases} \Rightarrow \text{intermediate goods price} \uparrow \\ \Rightarrow \text{CPI}_{t}^{e} \uparrow \Rightarrow \begin{matrix} W_{t+1}^{e} \uparrow \\ P_{t+1}^{e} \uparrow \end{matrix} \Rightarrow \pi_{t+1}^{e} \uparrow \end{cases}$$

Notation

AD: Aggregate demand; M: Money supply; re: Repo rate; r: Real, i: Nominal interest rate; I: Investment; Y: Output; NFI: Net foreign inflows; Q: Real exchange rate; S: Nominal exchange rate Rs/US$; S^{w}: World nominal exchange rate; i^{w}: World nominal interest rate; π_{t}^{e}: Expected inflation; W_{t+1}: Wage rate in $t + 1$; CPI: Consumer price index; WPI: Wholesale price index; P_{t+1}: Implicit GDP deflator in $t + 1$

In a large mature economy, the exchange rate channel of monetary transmission works through and is subservient to the interest rate channel. The mature floating exchange rate insulates macro-policy from the external sector. If the interest rate rises, higher capital inflows tend to appreciate the exchange rate and lower demand, thus contributing to monetary tightening. But in an EM, capital flows tend to respond to global risk factors not the domestic cycle. In thin markets, the CB has more ability to affect exchange rate expectations and risk perceptions.

The exchange rate can serve as an explicit nominal anchor fixing the inflation rate for traded goods. In particular, pegging the exchange rate of a high inflation country to that of a low inflation country can serve as a commitment to low inflation. But it would be credible only if fiscal policy is disciplined. Other disadvantages are: giving up autonomy of

252 *New directions for monetary and fiscal policy*

domestic monetary policy; transmission of external shocks as domestic interest rates change with foreign; real appreciation that harms exports; and suppression of feedback on the monetary policy stance from sensitive FX markets (Mishkin, 1999). A pegged exchange rate can encourage domestic firms to make excessive short-term international borrowing, resulting in financial fragility and crises. The perceived risk for foreign investors is also lowered. If EM currencies only depreciate over time as the pegged rate is adjusted downwards, this provides a safe one-way bet and encourages speculation. Exchange rate targets, such as a fixed or a crawling peg, have normally not done well in EMs (Chapter 9).

Managed floats, however, can help contribute to multiple objectives such as price stabilisation, maintaining competitive exports and preventing a currency crisis. If the exchange rate is managed in a 5 per cent band centred at the equilibrium real exchange rate, the nominal exchange rate could be varied in the short term, to stabilise CPI inflation as part of a flexible inflation target, while avoiding large fluctuations in both exchange and nominal interest rates.

11.5   Fiscal policy

There are different aspects to the relation between fiscal and monetary policy. First, they interact to determine output and interest rate in the short run. The IS (investment equals saving) and LM (equating the demand and supply of money) curves show how the two together affect aggregate demand and determine output and interest rates. Monetary policy affects aggregate demand through the short-term real interest rate and fiscal policy acts directly on aggregate demand.

Second, there are other aspects of coordination. In an open economy, interest rates have an immediate effect on demand, but they have uneven effects on different sectors. If, for example, exchange rates overreact, they put pressure on producers of traded goods. Fiscal policy can target these specific sectors. Fiscal consolidation often takes the form of reducing productive expenditure where there is more discretion, although this is precisely the type of expenditure that can reduce costs and remove supply bottlenecks. Lags in fiscal response and adverse changes in the composition of government expenditure could be reduced if some fiscal actions are appraised by a body outside the government (Wren-Lewis, 2000). For example, after experience with a 'regulator' responsible for some such actions, the United Kingdom created the Office for Budget Responsibility in 2010 as an independent fiscal council. The United States has a Congressional Budget Office.

New directions for monetary and fiscal policy 253

These watchdogs perform real time assessments of budgetary proposals against their own forecasts.

The third aspect relates to the financing of government expenditure over time. The government can finance an excess of current expenditure over revenue, either by borrowing money (issuing bonds) or printing money (seignorage). But either choice has implications for inflation, interest rates and government finances over time. The CB can change the mix between the two through OMOs. That is, if the CB buys (sells) government bonds in exchange for reserve money it issues, it increases (decreases) the stock of reserve money. If the CB prints money to buy government bonds held by the public, it monetises the debt and also increases the stock of money.

In a stationary equilibrium, where major ratios are not changing, the rate of inflation equals the rate of growth of money. Then, the gross fiscal deficit (GFD) is expenditure plus interest payments minus tax equals seignorage (reserve money balances multiplied by their rate of growth), which in turn equals the inflation tax (money balances multiplied by the rate of inflation). See Box 11.3 for definitions. Money balances are held by households and satisfy their demand for money. The rate of inflation is the cost of holding money; therefore, money balances held fall with inflation. From this analysis, a number of insights follow.

1   Zero inflation requires that the value of taxes in excess of expenditure over future successive time periods, discounted to the present, must equal current debt. Although the government need not do so immediately, over time it has to raise taxes to repay borrowings, thus satisfying its budget constraint.
2   A given gross of interest deficit can be financed by a high or low rate of inflation, since seignorage revenue can be the same with high inflation and low money balances or vice versa. Under high inflation, the cost of holding money is higher, so consumers hold less money. However, since money facilitates transactions, consumers have higher welfare when inflation is low and money balances held are higher.
3   In standard monetarist theories, inflation increases with money supply. This framework, however, shows a decrease in money financing together with an increase in bond financing in the initial period that unambiguously increases the inflation rate. This is because the steady-state GFD rises as interest payments accumulate. Sargent and Wallace (1981) derived this 'unpleasant monetarist arithmetic', which gives a fiscal theory of inflation. This result, however, holds only for the case where the government has to

254 *New directions for monetary and fiscal policy*

borrow to cover the fall in money supply, with fixed expenditures and given initial values of variables. If expenditures can decrease along with money supply or taxes can be raised to compensate for the fall in money supply, inflation does not rise. If, other things constant, the government commits to the level of seignorage or inflation, the only variable left free to adjust in the model is the initial price level. Then, this becomes a fiscal theory of the price level rather than of inflation. Monetarist theories argue that there is nothing to fix prices if money supply is endogenous, but here the price level is determinate even under an endogenous money supply with pegged interest rates.

Normally, if fiscal or monetary policy is active, the other must passively accommodate it in order to prevent instability. As we saw above, if large deficits are not monetised, rising interest payments and debt may enforce monetary accommodation down the road. The analysis of financing leads to the fourth major aspect of the relationship between monetary and fiscal policy, and this is politics. Political pressures may force particular types of fiscal-monetary coordination.

It is the government that has to face elections in a democracy. Therefore, fiscal policy normally functions as the leader to which monetary policy has to adjust. The government may force the CB to expand money supply to help finance a deficit, thus raising the inflation rate. But high inflation hurts the poor who have more votes, redistributing income from the poor to the rich. Therefore, accommodating the government normally involves squeezing the productive private sector (Goyal, 2014). This hurts growth. If deficits finance growth-enhancing expenditure, they can be absorbed as the economy realises higher potential growth (see Boxes 11.4 and 11.5).

The fifth aspect of monetary-fiscal interactions is their impact on government debt. The maturity value of nominal government debt $B_t P_t$ changes over time, as follows:

$$B_t P_t = (1 + i_t) B_{t-1} P_{t-1} + (P_t G_t - T_t) \tag{11.32}$$

B_t is the maturity value of real public debt; real government purchases are G_t and nominal net tax collections are T_t, so that real tax collections are $\tau \equiv T_t / P_t$. The real debt to output ratio is b_t. Dividing by Y_t and making other manipulations, Equation 11.32 can be written as:

$$\frac{B_t}{Y_t} = (1 + i_t) \frac{B_{t-1}}{Y_{t-1}} \frac{Y_{t-1}}{Y_t} \frac{P_{t-1}}{P_t} + \frac{G_t}{Y_t} - \frac{T_t}{P_t Y_t} \tag{11.33}$$

New directions for monetary and fiscal policy 255

Next, using $1 + g_t = Y_t/Y_{t-1}$, $1 + \pi_t = P_t/P_{t-1}$ and the approximation:

$$(1+i_t)/(1+g_t)(1+\pi_t) = 1 + i_t - g_t - \pi_t \qquad (11.34)$$

$$\text{Gives: } b_t - b_{t-1} = (i_t - \pi_t - g_t)b_{t-1} + \frac{G_t}{Y_t} - \frac{T_t}{Y_t} \qquad (11.35)$$

That is, the evolution of the real debt ratio. The latter rises with the debt level, nominal interest rate affected by monetary policy and primary deficit ratio (pd) or the excess of real government expenditure over taxation as a ratio to output. Therefore, both high debt levels and high nominal interest rates can imply unsustainable exploding debt.

Falling real interest rates and rising growth rates effectively reduce government debt. Inflation and growth rates do not affect the nominal value of public debt, $B_t P_t$, which increases in any year by nominal interest payments on debt plus the PD, $P_t G_t - T_t$. The latter is the non-interest budget deficit, while the fiscal deficit (FD) includes interest payments and is the total government-borrowing requirement to finance current and capital expenditure net of tax and non-tax revenue. The revenue deficit (RD), or deficit on current account, is the amount the government needs to borrow to finance its own consumption. If the real interest rate equals the rate of growth, the PD ratio alone would add to the debt ratio.

Box 11.3   Fiscal-monetary interaction concepts

Seignorage: Real revenue that accrues to a government from newly issued reserve money

Seignorage ratio: $\left(g_M \dfrac{M}{P}\right)\Big/\text{GDP}$, where g_M is rate of growth of reserve money, $\dfrac{M}{P}$ is real reserve money balances, P is implicit GDP deflator and GDP is real GDP at market prices

Inflation tax: Total capital loss made by holders of real money balances due to inflation

Inflation tax ratio: $\left(\pi \dfrac{M}{P}\right)\Big/\text{GDP}$, where π is the inflation rate

Gross fiscal deficit: Total expenditure minus total receipts (excluding borrowings) of the government: GFD = g − t + iB, where G is total expenditure, T is total revenue, iB is interest payments on debt, B

256 *New directions for monetary and fiscal policy*

Adjusted gross fiscal deficit: Subtracts change in G debt due to inflation from GFD

$$GFD(a) = GFD - \pi B$$
$$= G - T + (i - \pi) B$$
$$= G - T + rB$$

where r is the realised real rate of interest.

Another distinction used is to break up the deficit into its cyclical and structural components. After adjusting for the phase of the cycle that affects taxes and revenues, the latter captures any underlying imbalance between government revenues and expenditures. But it is difficult to do such an adjustment precisely.

Box 11.4 International experience

In the 1990s, the American budget deficit, which had mushroomed in the 1980s, was converted into a surplus while the economy prospered. How did they do it? Four factors made this achievement possible (Blanchard, 2000). First, an expansionary monetary policy complemented a restrained fiscal policy. Second, rules that bound government expenditure were adopted. Third, a cut in defence expenditure provided some leeway. Fourth, there was good luck in the shape of a booming economy. The good luck was, of course, helped by good policy.

Steep tax cuts by supply siders in the Reagan era were expected to stimulate output. But the expected increase did not occur, and since there was no equivalent cut in government expenditure, the deficit grew rapidly. It fluctuated around a peak ratio to GDP of 6.1 per cent in 1983. Volcker, the chairman of the Fedreal Reserve, had moved to a high interest regime to lower inflation by the late 1970s. Neither the rise in interest rates nor the cut in taxes had the desired effect of reducing government spending. The high interest rates led to capital inflows, strengthened the dollar and increased net imports, so that a trade deficit was added to the budget deficit. It, incidentally, also provoked the Latin American crises as capital flowed out of those countries to the United States. When Clinton came to power in 1992, there was consensus that the deficit had to be reduced – but the economy

New directions for monetary and fiscal policy 257

was just emerging from a recession. The new chairman of the Federal Reserve (Fed), Greenspan, implicitly agreed to support Clinton's measures to reduce the deficit, with an expansionary monetary policy. The latter would ensure that the economy was not plunged into a recession with the expenditure cuts. Average interest rates on one-year government bonds fell from 7.3 per cent in 1991 to 3.3 per cent in 1994. The economy entered a sustained expansion, which lasted through the 1990s. Inflation was also low. The deficit ratio fell steadily from 4.7 in 1992 and had turned into a surplus by 1998. Thus, this combination of monetary and fiscal policy worked, while the opposite tried in the 1980s failed.

Second, legislative rules helped reduce the deficit. The Gramm-Rudman-Hollings Bill, passed in 1985, set yearly ceilings for the deficit with a target for a zero deficit by 1991. It had some effect, but creative accounting – because of design flaws (including over strictness) – prevented the realisation of the target. The Bill also lost credibility because a very large deficit was required to fund the 1990 crisis in savings and loan institutions. Therefore, it was replaced by the Budget Enforcement Act of 1990, which corrected the design flaws shown up by experience. First, rather than restrict the deficit itself, constraints were placed only on spending. Caps that enforced small reductions in discretionary spending were set, but escape clauses were provided for emergencies. A 'pay-as-you-go' rule meant that new transfer payments to individuals could be made only if these transfers were demonstrated to have assured funding so that they did not increase deficits in the future. In a recession, as revenues fell, the deficit could increase, since restraints only covered spending. This macro-stabilisation provided another escape clause. Such flexibility lowered pressure to break rules, gave the Act more credibility and contributed to its success.

Clarida et al. (1999) point out that the Fed was highly accommodative in pre-Volcker years: on average, it let real short-term interest rates decline as anticipated inflation rose. Volcker and Greenspan took a proactive stance: systematically raised real as well as nominal short-term interest rates in response to higher expected inflation. The US experience suggests that monetary policy should use interest rates rather than monetary aggregates as instruments. Although clear articulation of the CB's goals

258 *New directions for monetary and fiscal policy*

is desirable, constraints that dictate how the goals should be achieved are not desirable.

McKibben and Vines (2000) argue that phased-in and preannounced fiscal contraction can have positive effects, since forward-looking adjustments dominate negative Keynesian effects. The US experience of the 1990s is one example of this. Blanchard (1997, 2000) gives another: the contrast between the two Irish deficit reductions in the 1980s. The first, which focussed on tax increase, did not lead to a credible belief in lower future budget deficits; growth fell and deficits did not improve. The second, which was based on cuts in spending and tax reform, had a favourable effect on expectations and output.

Another country that successfully coordinated monetary and fiscal policy for high growth was China in the 1990s. Although there were stop-go cycles, tax reform helped monetary policy accommodate huge government expenditure on infrastructure.

Source: Goyal (2002).

Ideal macroeconomic policy for an EDE should be robust to imperfect information about the economy and should be able to withstand political pressures that favour short-term populism at the expense of long-term growth. Fiscal rules, analogous to monetary rules, discussed below, should have this property.

11.5.1 Fiscal rules

A new feature of the 1990s was the adoption of fiscal as well as monetary rules. Countries following expenditure rules include the Netherlands and Sweden. The Euro area (under the 1992 Maastricht Treaty), Canada and Switzerland, follow deficit and debt rules, while the United Kingdom, Australia and New Zealand impose transparency requirements on governments.

In a democracy, it is the government which moves first, and therefore determines what monetary policy is feasible. Populist pressures fall more directly on an elected government. There is a strong temptation to give handouts in the short run, as well as huge requirements for productive government expenditures on infrastructure and the development of human capital in EDEs. Constraints on fiscal policy, which

New directions for monetary and fiscal policy   259

prevent the first, assure the latter and allow complementary monetary policy, are required.

> *Result 1(f)*: A Fiscal Responsibility Act (FRA) must restrict the RD.

Such an act would restrain unproductive populism, by curbing the tendency to increase government consumption and transfers for consumption on the basis of borrowed funds.

> *Result 2(f)*: If there already exists a large RD, backloaded reductions should be phased in.

A credible programme for reducing fiscal spending has even stimulated output in some stabilisation episodes, by inducing favourable private sector expectations (see Box 11.4). As conditions improve, tougher steps can be taken. Therefore, backloading, or imposing higher cuts in the future, allows maximum gain for minimum current pain. Hard to reverse structural reforms that remove fundamental causes of deficits should be preferred to excessively stringent macroeconomic policies that can cause a political backlash, and therefore cannot be sustained.

> *Result 3(f)*: Automatic non-discretionary stabilisers should be built in, with escape clauses for unforeseen large shocks.

If an FRA takes the form of phased caps on spending rather than on the deficit, the deficit could increase in case of economic slowdown when revenues fall, thus allowing automatic macro-stabilisation and increasing the political feasibility of the scheme. The deficit should be allowed to vary over the cycle, that is, it should be cyclically adjusted. Such stabilisers will reduce populist pressures and delays and both clauses will improve credibility. They will also improve transparency and communication, since the finance ministry will have to clearly explain and justify its actions and inactions.

> *Result 4(f)*: Capital expenditures that raise future revenue by increasing potential output should be protected from cuts and kept at maximum feasible levels, together with incentive-based reforms that improve the efficiency of such expenditures.

Such a rule would allow essential development expenditures to be met, improve their design and outcomes and favourably affect private sector expectations, since gaps in physical and social infrastructure are

260   *New directions for monetary and fiscal policy*

recognised as a severe constraint on development. Given the tendency for the government wage bill and interest payments to rise, pushing up revenue expenditure, a fiscal institution can also help protect capital expenditure, reduce the discretion to cut it, prevent lags and delays in projects and change the bureaucratic interface in public projects, in order to mitigate corruption.

> *Result 5(f)*: An acceptable zone should be set for the fiscal deficit, it should be brought to the border of this zone and further reductions allowed to occur naturally with the fall in the revenue deficit and higher growth.

If the Indian Fiscal Responsibility Act (FRA) is modified in these directions, it would allow optimal coordination of fiscal and monetary policies suited to Indian conditions. The existing 2003 FRBM, and its reset in 2010 by the 13th Finance Commission, does not satisfy these principles. It imposes reductions on both the revenue and fiscal deficit and on retiring government debt, without any backloading, automatic stabilisation or features to improve incentives. If the targets are not met, a pro-rata cut on all expenditures is to be imposed without protecting capital expenditure. Experience with the FRBM shows targets were met by cutting capital expenditure rather than from genuine reform. Moreover, they were reset when convenient, as after the GFC. State-level FRBMs that had incentives built in for compliance worked better. A fiscal council could be set up to discipline the Centre.

Box 11.5   Monetary-fiscal coordination in India

Both the reductive reasoning in Chapter 1 and the SOEME model of Section 11.3 imply the structure shown in Figure 11.4, for Indian AD and AS curves. AS is flat but a number of factors tend to push it upwards; apart from commodity and nominal exchange rate shocks and wage-price expectations, these factors include the complex of poor governance, infrastructure and public services that raise indirect costs. This is the sense in which the Indian economy is supply constrained and differs from the standard vertical supply curve used to indicate supply bottlenecks.

In such a structure, reducing demand to control inflation results in a large output sacrifice with little impact on inflation. Optimal

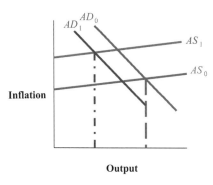

Figure 11.4 Aggregate demand and supply

monetary-fiscal coordination would involve working together to shift the AS downwards. For example, if the government is able to change the composition of public spending away from distorting subsidies towards improving infrastructure and other public services, the CB can afford to reduce interest rates in anticipation of a fall in future costs and inflation. While monetary tightening does reduce inflationary expectations, reducing food price inflation through a combination of agricultural reform and a stable nominal exchange rate can more effectively anchor expectations at less cost in terms of output and employment foregone.

India core inflation was below headline inflation over 2007–15, implying excess demand was not the major inflation driver. The aggregate demand transmission channel, therefore, was weak and counterproductive. Transmission had to work through the expectation or cost-push channels (Box 11.1).

11.6 Summary

This chapter brings out the importance of openness and of structure for monetary and fiscal policy and for their interaction. It moves from abstract principles to aspects of concrete application. The exchange rate channel is shown to be a major channel of monetary transmission in an open economy. The DSGE adapted to structural aspects of an EM is shown to collapse to that of the SOE as development occurs, implying that once some key modifications are made, similar analytical frameworks can be used to analyse EM issues.

262 *New directions for monetary and fiscal policy*

This chapter touches on new developments in macroeconomic policy and in CB practice, including the use of rules and other devices to constrain discretion, and obtain optimal fiscal and monetary coordination, in the context of EDE monetary transmission channels and the structure of AS-AD curves.

Among interesting insights from the new approach are that under sticky prices monetary policy they should respond more than one to one to any rise in inflation, in order to lower the total output cost of a disinflation. Since prices once set last for some time, lowering inflation expectations can abort a persistent higher inflation from setting in. Acting on expected excess demand policy can bring down inflation without any output cost, but there is a trade-off between inflation and output under cost shocks. This trade-off is higher, the more elastic the AS. Uncertainties and learning can reduce the required policy response, so that changes in the interest rate come in small steps.

In an open economy, the CB has to take into account the effect of the exchange rate on inflation and output. Moreover, the exchange affects consumer price inflation more than domestic inflation. A general result in the literature (Clarida et al., 2001; Gali and Monacelli, 2005) is that the AS and AD curves remain the same in open economies. There is only a change in the elasticities. We show that this result does not hold for an EDE. Although AS and AD curves continue to be isomorphic to those in an AE, the treatment of the real exchange rate can alter the variables entering the curve.

The real exchange rate is often far from equilibrium and cannot reach it in the short run. Policy can also affect its adjustment, since a float can be too volatile in a thin market. Under a managed float, the terms of trade become exogenous in the short run, unlike in an AE, where it is endogenous and can be substituted out from the AS and AD curves.

While this chapter developed a rigourous framework and applied it to EDEs, the next chapter will analyse specific differences in EDE structure and develop some useful frameworks of analysis, given that structure. Analysis of structural adjustment, including specific episodes, will bring out many aspects of monetary-fiscal coordination in practice.

APPENDICES

Appendix 11.A.1
Deriving the demand of home goods by the foreign consumer

By symmetry, the FOC for the F consumer, or demand for goods of the home country H, is:

$$C^*_{H,t} = \alpha \frac{S_t P^*_{F,t}}{P_{H,t}} \frac{P^*_t}{P^*_{F,t}} C^*_t$$

For example, $C^*_{H,t}$ could be US home consumption of Indian goods. The decision of an F country consumer to import from the home country depends on two price ratios. The first price ratio compares price of home goods $P_{H,t}$ to all other F goods in home currency, to decide whether to import from the home country. The second price ratio compares the foreign price index to the foreign price index of all F goods to decide whether to consume domestic or imported goods. Canceling $P^*_{F,t}$, multiplying and dividing by P_t and substituting for Q_t gives Equation 11.15 in the text.

Appendix 11.A.2
Deriving the AD equals AS identity

Substituting the FOCs for the home and foreign consumer in the output equal aggregate demand Equation 11.14 gives:

$$Y_t = \frac{(1-\alpha)P_t C_t}{P_{H,t}} + \alpha Q_t \frac{P_t}{P_{H,t}} C_t^*$$

Substituting out C_t^* using risk sharing: $Y_t = \frac{(1-\alpha)P_t C_t}{P_{H,t}} + \alpha Q_t \frac{P_t}{P_{H,t}} C_t Q^{-\frac{1}{\sigma}}$

And further simplifying:

$$Y_t = \frac{P_t}{P_{H,t}} C_t (Q^{1-\frac{1}{\sigma}})$$

$$Y_t = Z_t^\alpha C_t Q^{1-\frac{1}{\sigma}}$$

Since $1 - \frac{1}{\sigma} = 0$ if $\sigma = 1$, the aggregate demand supply identity reduces in this case to Equation 11.16.

Appendix 11.A.3

Deriving change in *mc* as a function of the output gap

To write $\widehat{mc}_t$ as a function of output, add and subtract p_t from the marginal cost equation (Eq. 11.20):

$$mc_t = -\nu + (w - p_t) + (p_t - p_{H,t}) - a_t$$

Substitute intratemporal FOC for real wages (Eq. 11.6) and the definition of s_t (Eq. 11.9) for relative prices:

$$mc_t = -\nu + \sigma c_t + \phi n_t + \alpha z_t - a_t$$

Substitute risk sharing $c_t = c_t^* + \dfrac{(1-\alpha)}{\sigma} z_t$ (σ in z_t cancels with that in c_t) with $c_t^* = y_t^*$ and $n_t = y_t - a_t$ from the production function:

$$mc_t = -\nu + \sigma y_t^* + \varphi y_t + z_t - (1 + \varphi) a_t$$

And finally, substitute $y_t^* = y_t - z_t$. If $\sigma = 1$, z_t drops out:

$$mc_t = -\nu + (\sigma + \varphi) y_t - (1 + \varphi) a_t$$

To get the output gap, first $\bar{y}_t$ can be derived from mc_t by imposing $mc_t = -\mu$, and then solving for y_t. If $\sigma = 1$, then:

$$\bar{y}_t = \frac{\nu - \mu}{1 + \phi} + a_t$$

266 *New directions for monetary and fiscal policy*

Subtracting y_t from $\bar{y}_t$, substituting for y_t from the mc_t equation and for $\bar{y}_t$ from the above give $\widehat{mc_t} = (\sigma + \varphi)x_t$.

Notes

1 * denotes advanced material.
2 Since GM assumes complete capital markets, the budget constraint is written with D_{t+1} and D_t instead of with B_t and B_{t-1}, as in Chapter 10, where D_{t+1} is the random payoff of a one-period portfolio. Price $1/R_t \equiv Q_t \equiv E_t\{Q_{t,t+1}\}$, where R_t is now the gross return on a riskless one-period discount bond or arrow security paying one unit of domestic currency in $t + 1$, so $1/R_t$ is its price.
3 AD written in output gap space will shift with every supply shock unless there is full forward-looking behaviour, so that output adjusts with potential. Else, shocks entering the two curves can be correlated.
4 The NKE literature calls it the 'divine coincidence' when the CB does not need to take fluctuations in the output gap into account when setting interest rates. While his work supported the Taylor principle, Woodford's (2003) differences with the empirical Taylor rule were as follows: First, the welfare theoretic loss function implies the inflation target should be zero in the pure frictionless model. Second, the output gap should be calculated using the natural output, not the past deterministic trend. All the shocks, such as technology and world income that affect the natural interest rate in Equation (11.2), affect the natural output. See Goyal (2009) for more details on natural output in an SOEME.
5 * denotes advanced material.
6 For example, in India in 2015, 90 per cent of the labour force was in the informal sector, with 53 per cent in rural areas, out of a total population exceeding 1 billion.
7 Condensed and adapted from Clarida et al. (1999) and Goyal (2002).
8 This section is taken from Goyal (2016).
9 After the GFC inflation did not fall in the West despite a slowdown. IMF (2013) attributes this partly to the better anchoring of inflation expectations.

References

Allsop, C. and D. Vines. 2000. 'The Assessment: Macroeconomic Policy', *Oxford Review of Economic Policy*, 16(4): 1–32.

Blanchard, O. 1997. 'Is There a Core of Usable Macroeconomics?', *AEA Papers and Proceedings*, 87(2): 244–246.

Blanchard, O. 2000. *Macroeconomics*, 2nd edition, New Jersey: Prentice Hall.

Clarida, R., J. Gali and M. Gertler. 1999. 'The Science of Monetary Policy: A New Keynesian Perspective', *Journal of Economic Literature*, 37(4): 1661–1707.

New directions for monetary and fiscal policy 267

Clarida R., J. Galí, and M. Gertler. 2001. 'Optimal Monetary Policy in Closed Versus Open Economies: An Integrated Approach', *American Economic Review*, 91(2); May: 248–252.

Eichenbaum, M. 1997. 'Some Thoughts on Practical Stabilization Policy', *AEA Papers and Proceedings*, 87(2): 236–239.

Galí J. and T. Monacelli. 2005. 'Monetary Policy and Exchange Rate Volatility in a Small Open Economy', *Review of Economic Studies*, 72(3): 707–734.

Gelos, G. and Y. Ustyugova. 2012. 'Inflation Responses to Commodity Price Shocks – How and Why Do Countries Differ?', *IMF Working Papers, No. WP/12/225*. Available at www.imf.org/external/pubs/ft/wp/2012/wp12225. pdf (accessed on August 2014).

Goodhart, C. 1989. 'The Conduct of Monetary Policy', *Economic Journal*, 99: 293–346.

Goyal, A. 2002. 'Coordinating Monetary and Fiscal Policies: A Role for Rules?', Chapter 11 in K. S. Parikh and R. Radhakrishna (eds.), *India Development Report*, pp. 157–176. New Delhi: IGIDR and Oxford University Press.

Goyal, A. 2009. 'The Natural Interest Rate in Emerging Markets', in Bhaskar Dutta, Tridip Roy and E. Somanathan (eds.), *New and Enduring Themes in Development Economics*, pp. 333–368. Singapore: World Scientific Publishers.

Goyal, A. 2011. 'A General Equilibrium Open Economy Model for Emerging Markets: Monetary Policy with a Dualistic Labor Market', *Economic Modelling*, 28(2): 1392–1404.

Goyal, A. 2014. *History of Monetary Policy in India since Independence*. Springer Briefs in Economics. India: Springer. doi:http://link.springer.com/book/10.1007%2F978-81-322-1961-3.

Goyal, A. 2016. 'Introduction: Unconventional Monetary Policy in Emerging Markets', *Macroeconomics and Finance in Emerging Market Economies*, Special Issue on *Unconventional Monetary Policy in Emerging Markets*, 9(2): 101–108.

IMF (International Monetary Fund). 2013. 'The Dog That Didn't Bark: Has Inflation Been Muzzled or Was It Just Sleeping?' Chapter 3 in *World Economic Outlook: Hopes, Realities, Risks*. April. Available at http://www.imf. org/external/pubs/ft/weo/2013/01/.

McKibben, W. J. and D. Vines. 2000. 'Modelling Reality: The Need for Both Inter-Temporal Optimization and Stickiness in Models for Policy-Making', *Oxford Review of Economic Policy*, 16(4): 106–137.

Mishkin, F. S. 1999. 'International Experience with Monetary Policy Rules', *Journal of Monetary Economics*, 43: 579–606, June.

Romer, D. 2000. 'Keynesian Macroeconomics without the LM Curve', *Journal of Economic Perspectives*, 14(2): 149–169.

Sargent, T. J. and N. Wallace. 1981. 'Some Unpleasant Monetarist Arithmetic', *Quarterly Review of the Federal Reserve Bank of Minneapolis*, 14: 328–350.

268 New directions for monetary and fiscal policy

Stiglitz, J. E. 2007. Remarks on Bank Research Evaluation. Available at http://siteresources.worldbank.org/DEC/Resources/84797-1109362238001/726454-1164121166494/JES-bankResearchReviewanjesfin.pdf (accessed on 12 January 2007).

Svensson, L. E. O. 2000. 'Open-Economy Inflation Targeting', *Journal of International Economics*, 50: 155–183.

Taylor, J. B. 1999. *Monetary Policy Rules*, Chicago, IL: University of Chicago Press for NBER.

Woodford, M. 2003. *Interest and Prices: Foundations of a Theory of Monetary Policy*, Princeton, NJ: Princeton University Press.

Wren-Lewis, S. 2000. 'The Limits to Discretionary Fiscal Stabilization Policy', *Oxford Review of Economic Policy*, 16(4): 92–105.

12 Structure, stabilisation and structural adjustment

Look for an object where it is lost, not where it is easy to search.

12.1 Introduction

In modelling macroeconomic issues for EDEs, it is important to keep in mind how differences in structure, institutions, government interactions and endowments affect outcomes. This chapter starts by bringing out these systematic differences in EDEs compared to advanced economies. Differences in endowments, such as whether a country is labour surplus or land surplus, can have persistent effects on the pattern of development. Institutions affect macro outcomes, but they themselves can change over time. It is also necessary to keep track of differences across individual EDEs and across regions. We will examine some of these aspects, and how they affect stabilisation and adjustment choices on the path to development.

Key institutions can be very different in Latin America, Asia, Africa or East Europe. Since the developing economy macroeconomics literature focusses more on Latin America, we focus more on Asia, and especially large densely populated countries like India and China.

This chapter develops specific analytical tools that are useful to analyse stabilisation and structural adjustment programmes and then examines specific episodes and shows how thinking on reform has evolved in the light of experience.

The structure of the chapter is as follows: Section 12.2 contrasts EDE structure with that of advanced economies; Section 12.3 develops analytical tools; Section 12.4 analyses select stabilisation and structural adjustment programmes in EDEs, before Section 12.5 summarises and concludes.

270 *Structure, stabilisation and structural adjustment*

12.2   The structure of underdevelopment

Table 12.1 shows the high share of rural population in lower income countries, the lower health, literacy and consumption parameters, so that development has to be understood as a transition in all these parameters. This validates the dual labour and consumption markets used to adapt the SOE to an EM in the previous chapter. Even though population growth rates are generally higher in lower income countries, output growth rates tend to exceed those at the high end, suggesting that convergence can occur. It is faster for some countries, while others are still trapped in poverty. The bracketed terms in Table 12.1 show progress in some parameters for the world as a whole in over 20 years.

Select parameters for India show that even by 2012 it was only a lower middle-income economy. Moreover, social parameters were still in the low-income category. In 2012, Indian GDP per capita was US$ 1,503. Although agricultural value added (as % of GDP) had fallen to 17.5, the share of rural population was above 60 per cent. Life expectancy at birth was 66.2, but even in 2006 the adult literacy rate was only 62.8. Because of the focus in this book, we first take up structural open economy features.

12.2.1   Open economy features

Exports from an EDE are normally a small share of total world output, so that changes in export supply do not affect world price. Therefore, such an economy takes P^* as given. This is the SOE assumption. In EDEs, it may be more appropriate to take both import and export prices – the terms of trade – as given, so that the real exchange rate can change only with changes in non-tradable goods prices.[1] Exports are often largely commodities. The average primary commodity share in DC exports was 71 per cent in 1991. In India, this was 27 per cent.

As country after country liberalised and moved away from the post-world wars import substitution-based paradigm of development, the share of trade went up. Over 1980–89, the average ratio of DC trade to GDP was 44.9, but for India, a late liberaliser, it was only 8.5. The share of Indian merchandise exports plus imports had risen, however, to 34.7 per cent in 2007–08. Its large population and the relative importance of domestic demand allow India to be characterised as a small open but large domestic economy.

Lower wage levels, and the large share of non-traded goods (40% in the 1980s), imply the exchange rate is normally lower in PPP terms.

Table 12.1 Comparison across income categories

Country	GNP per capita (PPP US$)	GNP per capita (US$)	Energy cons. per capita (kg oil equivalent)	Rural population share (%)	Life expectancy at birth (years)	Adult illiteracy (%)	Infant mortality rate per 1,000	Growth rate (%) 1965–92		
								Pop. (billion)	GNP per capita	Mfg. V-A per capita
Low income	1,523 (1,570)	380 (629)	370	73 (70)	63 (61)	40 (43)	60 (53)	1.7 (0.6)	3.6	2.1 5.6 India
Lower middle Y	3,001 (6,000)	807 (2,012)	622 (654)	61 (61)	63 (67)	35 (27)	63 (40)	1.9 (2.9)	2.6	12.9 Indonesia
Upper middle Y	6,188 (14,179)	2,859 (7,901)	2,185 (1,954)	33 (38)	69 (74)	18 (6)	40 (15)	1.4 (2.4)	3.1	14.00 Korea
High income	19,675	21,990 (38,274)	5,054	22 (19)	77 (79)	<5	8	0.5 (1.4)	2.7	5.27 Japan

Source: Compiled from World Bank http://data.worldbank.org/income-level/LMC.

Note: Columns for 1990 and brackets for 2014.

272 *Structure, stabilisation and structural adjustment*

The purchasing power of the local currency is much higher for local goods than it is for traded goods. As a DC liberalises and tariff and non-tariff barriers are removed, trade arbitrage implies traded goods prices approach border prices. That is, EP_T^* begins to influence P_T. Food also becomes a traded good and P_w^* begins to influence the local price of food. At low per capita levels, food is a large share of the consumption basket.[2] Therefore, traded goods prices begin to affect nominal wages.

While mature economies largely moved to floating exchange rates after the collapse of the Bretton Woods agreement in the early 1970s, DCs exchange-rate regimes continued to be closer to the fixed end of the spectrum; exchange rates were normally tightly managed.

Current accounts were liberalised and there was some capital account convertibility, for example, in Latin America and East Asia, but varying degrees of quantitative restrictions continued for the capital account. In India, for example, equity flows and FDI were partially liberalised in the early 1990s, but there were stronger restrictions on debt flows. Even in 2015, foreign holders accounted for only 5 per cent of India's bond market compared to 50 per cent for Malaysia.

Table 12.2 shows international debt for different regions in 1993. DCs average debt/GDP ratio was 70. India was moderately indebted at 29.3. The ratio of short- to long-run debt is also an important indicator of vulnerability to external credit crises, since repayment or rollover at onerous terms during a crisis can bankrupt firms, and through them the banks who have made the loans.[3] Remittances are classified as transfers in the current account, but NRI deposits are another kind of interest-sensitive inflows. Since equity shares risk, repayments are less during a downturn, when they are more difficult to make. That is the reason debt inflows continue to be restricted compared to equity flows.

Partial capital account convertibility in India also means that those who bring in funds can take them out, but domestic residents cannot freely hold foreign assets or adjust their portfolios. Even so, given the size of volatile interest-sensitive capital, sufficient arbitrage exists for international interest rates to influence domestic.

12.2.2 *Long-run supply behaviour*

The long-run supply behaviour in an EDE can differ from that in mature markets in systematic ways. For example, since public ownership of productive capital is higher, the public capital stock, its size and efficiency are important for the supply response. Government

Table 12.2 Financial sector indicators

Country	Debt indicators			1986–90	Monetisation ratios (% av over 1980–91)	
	Debt/GDP	*Debt service/ exports*	*Share of concessional debt in total debt*	*Private I/ total I*	*Narrow money ratio*	*Broad money ratio*
The United States					15.9	59.4
EDEs						
Nigeria	108.8	25.2	3.1	27.9	16.8	28.6
Asia						
India	29.3	30.7	41.6	52.0	15.8	42.9
Indonesia	66.4	32.7	28.3	59.1	10.9	26.7
Korea	14.4	7.1	11.6	78.8	9.7	36.7
Malaysia	47.6	8.3	12.1	61.2	19.8	63.6
Philippines	70.2	23.2	25.9	82.1	8.0	28.7
Thailand	39.0	13.1	13.2	76.1	9.6	56.0
Western Hemisphere						
Argentina	49.2	48.4	0.9	53.4	6.7	20.1
Brazil	78.8	30.0	2.5			
Mexico	36.9	30.9	1.0	74.2	8.3	25.8

Source: Compiled from World Bank (1993).

274　*Structure, stabilisation and structural adjustment*

spending cannot be regarded as just consumption and has major medium-term supply-side effects, especially spending on health, education and infrastructure. That is why Ricardian equivalence may not hold, and the appropriate composition of government expenditure can have persistent effects.

These economies emerged from an import substitution regime with protection and licensing. Pervasive government controls may have established corruption as a social norm, so liberalisation may result in more corruption unless institutions are improved.

12.2.3　Short-run supply behaviour

Short-run supply behaviour also differs. For example, imported intermediate goods typically account for half to 70 per cent of DE imports, so that imports are closely linked to exports. The net contribution of trade to aggregate demand may be low, and the exchange rate has a large effect on the costs of production.

Limited financial intermediation may leave small firms dependent on informal finance for working capital requirements. One consequence is that a monetary tightening may affect the supply side more than the demand side, especially if the interest elasticity of demand is low.

A large share of labour is in agriculture and in the informal sector. This can make labour supply elastic for unskilled employment in the short run and in general for the medium run, with sufficient time for skills to be acquired. A large population was earlier regarded as a liability, stretching resources available, but it can be a source of strength if capital is available to equip it, and skills can be expanded.

The institutional factors determining wage setting also influence the supply response. If the wage contracting process is such that nominal wages are rigid in the short run, a monetary shock can have real effects, affecting real wages and employment. For example, in the United States, nominal wages are normally set for a period of three years. If nominal wages adjust rapidly, as is typical in countries with high inflation or a memory of hyperinflation (Germany), a monetary impulse only affects the inflation rate. Cost of living adjustment giving automatic indexation of nominal wages implies sticky real wages. Economy-wide wage bargaining, as is common in the Scandinavian countries, tends to be in terms of real wages. In Latin American countries, because of the large share of imported goods in the average consumption basket, nominal wages are closely linked to the exchange rate.

In populous low per capita EDEs, such as India, despite limited indexation of wages in the large informal sector, wages tend over time

Structure, stabilisation and structural adjustment 275

to respond to the price of food. Political pressures in a democracy also imply inflation control has high priority and there are different kinds of interventions to repress the price of food for poor consumers.

12.2.4 Financial markets

Traditionally, in a capital-scarce environment, real interest rates are high. There is a large spread of interest rates, the difference between borrowing and lending rates being as much as 5–6 per cent. The reasons include not only inefficiencies in narrow financial markets and pricing power due to lack of competition or regulatory protection, but also due to the large share of government and forced allocation of credit to priority sectors. In general, more openness to foreign inflows has softened levels of real interest rates. But they still exceed international rates and can rise sharply in crises periods when the risk premium shoots up.

The Indian statutory liquidity ratio (SLR) for banks, which peaked at 38.5 per cent, was gradually reduced and was 21.55 per cent by 2015, but was still far from its eventual target of 10 per cent, especially since banks continued to hold 28 per cent of government securities. They lent only about 60 per cent of their deposits. The credit GDP ratio is very low in India. According to the 2015 Economic Survey, Indian credit GDP ratios grew from 35.5 per cent in 2000 to 51 per cent in 2013. Compare this to the Chinese ratio of 150 and the United States of 190! Government interventions keep corporate credit cheaper in China than it is in the United States, but the interventions have led to high NPAs in the Chinese banking sector. Prudential regulation brought NPAs down to single digits for Indian banks before the GFC.

However, the Indian corporate bond market was underdeveloped in the 2010–11, constituting only 2 per cent of the GDP. In China, it was 1 per cent. Corporate bond outstanding as a per cent of GDP was 49 in South Korea, 70 in the United States[4] and 147 in Germany. The money, FX and government securities market have seen considerable development, but more is required. Insurance is still dominated by the public sector Life Insurance Corporation. Domestic savings are high, but the large share of physical savings makes intermediation of financial resources poor. After reforms abolished the development finance institutions, long-term loans are underprovided. Informal credit markets are pervasive. Only 50 per cent of the population had bank accounts, even after years of expansion of the public sector banking system, although the 2014 Jan Dhan Yojana that combined

276 Structure, stabilisation and structural adjustment

bank accounts with a range of financial services had some success in expanding the number of bank accounts.

Even so, the Indian financial sector is well developed in some respects. The money stock/GDP ratios compare well with mature economies; stock markets are active; market capitalisation was second among developed economies, after Brazil, even in 1986; and the period since then has seen the establishment of the modern fully electronic National Stock Exchange, abolition of the old Controller of Capital Issues and its replacement by the Stock Exchange Board of India, which follows state-of-the-art practices in market regulation.

Financial reforms in India have reduced the earlier financial repression, where the government dominated the financial sector and interest rates were administered. But financial deepening is still required.

12.2.5 Government budget

The structure of government tax and expenditure tends to be different in an EDE. As Table 12.3 shows, compared to industrial governments, Asian governments spend much less on social security and more on infrastructure.

Taxes for social security are negligible. Taxes as a ratio of GDP are much lower. The share of income taxes in total tax revenue is lower and that of excise is higher compared to industrial countries.

Table 12.4 shows OECD governments tax, borrow and spend much more than Indian governments. Their spending on health care and pensions is much higher. India's budget documents show the share of Central social services expenditure in GDP to be 7 per cent in 2014–15. EDE governments generally have to spend on more areas with lower resources.

The low tax base has implications for the relationship between fiscal and monetary policies. EDEs tend to rely on seignorage revenue. Moderate inflation can be a lucrative tax, but the tax base shrinks at high

Table 12.3 Comparative government expenditure and taxes (1993)

G expenditure (% of total)	AEs	EDEs	Asia
Social security	37.7		7.1
Transport, communication	5.1		11.2
Income taxes	35.8	28.9	27.4
Excise taxes	29.3	30.4	34.8
Social security	28.4	6.2	0.2
Total taxes as % of GDP	31.2	18.1	14.8

Structure, stabilisation and structural adjustment 277

Table 12.4 India compared to the OECD average (% of GDP)

G interventions	OECD average	India
Expenditure (2013)	42.6	28.4
Revenue (2013)	36.7	20.3
Debt (2013)	107.6	66.7
Healthcare (2011)	9.2	4
Pensions (2009)	8.7	1
Education (2012)	4	3.4

Source: Compiled from OECD Survey, 2014.

rates of inflation giving rise to a seignorage Laffer curve. Countries in Latin America with income indexation and higher per capita incomes have tolerated high rates of inflation. China's stronger government has allowed it to follow stop-go macroeconomic cycles with sharp fluctuations in inflation, although lower per capita incomes meant inflation was never allowed to reach very high levels. India's low per capita income democracy, without indexation for the majority of incomes, meant inflation was normally suppressed to below single digit levels. This was done partly through administrative measures. Distortions, such as support prices and food subsidies, low user charges and low quality of public services, indirect and hidden taxes, raised costs, kept a positive chronic low inflation rate. Rising budget deficits were automatically financed during the initial plan years, but greater independence for the Central Bank meant government borrowed at higher interest rates.

A political business cycle, with more spending during election periods, is common, but the inflation bias (or surprise money creation) to reduce real wages and increase employment need not hold in a populous low per capita income country. In India, limited wage indexation in such a democracy implied an anti-inflation bias.[5] Wasteful populist schemes increase costs of production, while monetary policy squeezed demand to keep inflation low. Thus, controls, reforms and interest groups interact and affect policy in complex ways.

In EDEs, the representative agent of the benchmark macroeconomic model has to maximise utility subject to all the above constraints, to higher risk premiums and to poorer information quality. Thus, the above structure constrains macroeconomic outcomes and must be included in an analysis to get correct answers to questions posed. These constraints are not endogenous or affected by policy in the short macroeconomic horizon. EDEs often need to reduce macroeconomic

278 *Structure, stabilisation and structural adjustment*

vulnerabilities – that is, to stabilise – while preserving growth and strengthening institutions. Some analytical constructs useful for this exercise are discussed in the next section.

12.3 Growth, stabilisation and structural adjustment

When aggregate demand differs from aggregate supply, for any economy, internal balance (IB) does not hold. If the trade deficit exceeds the level that can be financed, or there are large continuous surpluses, external balance (EB) is absent. Stabilisation aims to restore macroeconomic balance. Policies to achieve stabilisation can be classified into those that change expenditure (or absorption) or those that switch expenditure (change prices). Substitution following price changes affects the pattern of output and expenditure. Fiscal policy, such as changing government expenditure or income taxes, affects absorption, while changes in the nominal exchange rate affect prices facing consumers and producers. The first is an example of an expenditure-changing policy and the second of expenditure switching. Absorption is total expenditure whether on domestic goods or on imports.

While stabilisation should be symmetric, it is most commonly applied in EDEs in the context of inflation and BOP deficits. BOP disequilibria are asymmetric since while a deficit will run into financing difficulties a surplus can continue.

Stabilisation measures, aimed at restoring macroeconomic balance and reducing inflation, focus on bringing the level of demand and its composition (tradable relative to non-tradable goods) into line with level of output and the financeable level of the current account deficit. Typically, reducing inflation requires a fall in both the public sector deficit and monetary financing of the government.

But in EDEs, stabilisation has to be combined with structural adjustment, that is, reform in policies and institutions to create a sustainable BOP, income growth and low inflation. In economies where markets were stifled, it may not only involve more market orientation, but also involves institutional reform for better governance and delivery of public services. Especially in labour-intensive countries, better education and skill formation, health and infrastructure are required to shift large populations to higher productivity work.

12.3.1 *Policy tools: absorption and switching*

In Figure 12.1, the full employment IB curve slopes downward in S and G space since an appreciation reduces demand, requiring a rise in G to restore demand to full employment levels. The curve gives the

Structure, stabilisation and structural adjustment 279

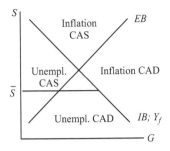

Figure 12.1 Internal and external balance

combination of S and G required for full employment. The EB curve gives the combination of these two variables that give a sustainable-BOP. It slopes upwards because a rise in G increases imports, requiring a depreciation to stimulate a compensating rise in exports. If there were no switching effects, the curves would be vertical. The figure shows the four regions of disequilibrium into which the two curves divide the space. Below the IB curve, there is unemployment, above it there is inflation. Below the EB curve, the current account is in deficit, above the EB curve it is in surplus. Similar curves would hold in absorption and S space.

Depending on the slopes and speeds of adjustment, it can be optimal to assign one policy instrument to achieving IB and the other to achieving EB. This is the *assignment problem*. Sometimes, two instruments are required to reach two objectives. For example, consider the economy to be in the bottom quadrant with unemployment and a CAD. The nominal exchange rate is fixed at $\bar{S}$ so that the only policy instrument is government spending. If the government increases spending to reduce unemployment, it worsens the CAD. If it decreases spending, it can reach external balance as imports fall, but unemployment worsens as it moves further away from internal balance. Even if there is no conflict and one instrument is working towards satisfying both objectives, changing the second may be necessary to reach the equilibrium point. Real depreciation can occur even with a fixed S, but will require a painful, and often slow, fall in wages and prices. The analysis of imported inflation below illustrates the flexibilities given by adjustment of the nominal exchange rate.

Figure 12.2 shows the effect on IB and EB of imported inflation. If P^* rises, there is a real depreciation of the home currency. S has to appreciate proportionally to the price change approximately by $\dfrac{S\Delta P^*}{P}$, to keep

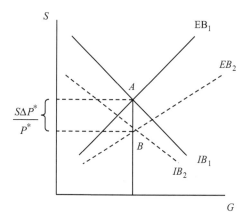

Figure 12.2 Importing inflation

the real exchange rate unchanged. This is the amount by which equilibrium IB and EB have shifted down in S space. If nominal exchange rate does not change, the old equilibrium will be one of inflation and CAS, slowly bringing about the required real appreciation. But if the nominal exchange rate were to appreciate, equilibrium could be restored at B without domestic inflation. Else, a rise in domestic prices proportional to ΔP^* would shift the curves back to A, but would take a long time (Krugman et al., 2014).

If perfect capital mobility makes the domestic interest rate equal the international and the nominal exchange rate is fixed, monetary policy freedom to change interest rates and affect domestic demand is limited. If the exchange rate is managed, more continuous changes are possible, and monetary policy can also affect aggregate demand.

Even if the flexibility of the nominal exchange rate is limited, the real exchange rate changes with prices in the longer run and switching works through this. The real exchange rate can be defined in different ways, so the relevant one should be used. EDEs lack market power in international markets, so they take P^* as given. The supply side of the MF model has a country producing a single composite export good, an imperfect substitute for the single composite good produced by the rest of the world. The latter is the country's import good. PPP holds in each good. The home economy is small in the market for the import good, but has some monopoly power in the market for the export good. Since P^* changes with domestic supply, so does the real exchange rate $Q = \dfrac{SP^*}{P}$.

Structure, stabilisation and structural adjustment   281

EDEs, however, are small in export markets also, so P^* is given. Since export demand is infinite, domestic demand or supply conditions have no effect on the price of the EM export good. So, adjustment in the EDE has to involve the non-traded goods sector. P_N has to change to effect relative prices. The Swan-Salter dependent economy model is useful to analyse such a situation.

The model has two domestic production sectors: exportable and non-traded goods. *Traded goods, exportables* and *importables* can be combined into a single category, because a perfectly elastic world demand for exports and a perfectly elastic world supply of imports makes their prices independent of domestic variables. Traded goods prices, P^*_T, are determined in world markets. The terms of trade or the ratio of export to import prices are exogenous. The key relative price to help the adjustment to full equilibrium becomes the real exchange rate, Q, defined as the ratio of traded to *non-traded goods* prices.[6] Consumption and production decisions across the basket of goods are made on the basis of this price. Non-traded goods do not enter world trade; internal costs and demand determine their price (P_N). Q is, therefore, the ratio of external prices to domestic costs.

$$Q = \frac{SP^*}{P_N} = \frac{P_T}{P_N}$$

The Swan-Salter model continues to be a useful simple approximation for policy analysis. Corbo and Fischer (1995) used it as the analytical underpinning for the 1980s adjustment programmes. Corden (2002) used it to analyse shocks and adjustments associated with East Asian crisis. He derived the exchange rate regime that would allow an easier approach to real targets and lower the probability of a currency crisis. The model is used to illustrate both structural adjustment and stabilisation (following Goyal, 2009) in the section below.

12.3.2   Structural adjustment

In Figure 12.3, the Swan-Salter model is drawn in the space of traded (Q_T) and non-traded goods (Q_N). The tangent of the price to the production possibility frontier gives the point of optimal production and its tangency to the indifference curve gives the point of optimal consumption. It can be used to demonstrate the process of stabilisation and of structural adjustment. An EDE needing adjustment could be consuming at point *a*, but producing at point *b* in Figure 12.3. The production of non-traded goods equals its consumption, but there

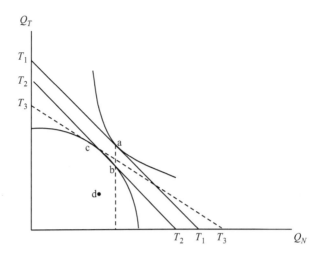

Figure 12.3 The Swan-Salter model in output space

is excess consumption of traded goods financed through a CAD. If the latter is unsustainable, stabilisation required to reduce absorption shifts the price line in parallel inwards so it is tangent to the production possibility frontier.

But typically, there would still be excess demand for tradable goods. The slope of the price line has to change to switch production towards tradable goods and reduce their consumption as they become relatively more expensive. Appreciation of the currency flattens the price line to reach the final equilibrium c where there is no excess consumption, the CAD is zero, consumption of both traded and non-traded goods falls and the production of traded goods rises compared to the earlier values. At the new price line, traded goods prices have risen relative to non-traded goods, so less of Q_T can now be bought compared to Q_N.

If the initial position was at d, where poor organisation wastes domestic resources, consumption can increase by shifting production out to the frontier. This illustrates the process of structural adjustment. Improvements in factor use and productivity can also shift out the frontier.

12.3.3 Stabilisation

The traditional Swan diagram has the real exchange rate on the vertical axis and real absorption on the horizontal axis. It can also be used to show the relationship between the real exchange rate and real wages.

Structure, stabilisation and structural adjustment 283

The schedule IB gives internal balance or the combinations of real exchange rate Q and absorption A, at which output demand equals full employment output (Y_f). A lower curve represents a lower level of output. The schedule is downward sloping because rise in demand and in foreign prices, relative to domestic, both raise output. As domestic absorption rises, Q must appreciate to reduce export supply (for which demand is not a constraint), and therefore total demand to the full employment output level.[7] Values above the schedule generate inflation as a more depreciated exchange rate and higher absorption raise demand than those below unemployment.

Schedule EB_1 gives external balance or the combinations of the two variables that yield an acceptable CAD that can be financed by a sustainable level of capital flows. The EB schedule is upward sloping because the CAD worsens with a rise in A as imports rise, but a rise in Q improves it as exports rise and imports fall. As A rises, Q must depreciate to raise exports sufficiently to keep the CAD unchanged. The BOP is in surplus above the schedule, since exports are higher and imports lower; it is in deficit below. The CAD is lower than capital inflows and can safely finance above and higher below the EB schedule. A curve above EB_1 represents a BOP, which is more in surplus. Absorption of both traded and non-traded goods rises with A, the first $(A_T$, which is imports) falls with Q, but domestic absorption A_N rises with Q as imports become more expensive:

$$A = A_T(Q, A) + A_N(Q, A) \qquad (12.1)$$
$$\quad\;\; -\;+ \qquad\quad +\;+$$

The external (Eq. 12.2) and internal balance (Eq. 12.3) can be written as below, where exports (Y_T) are a function of real wages in terms of traded goods (w), while the production of non-traded goods (Y_N) is a function of real wages in terms of non-traded goods (Qw):

$$B = Y_T^S(w) - A_T(Q, A) \qquad (12.2)$$
$$\qquad\quad\;\; -\;+$$

$$Y_N^S(Qw) = A_N(Q, A) \qquad (12.3)$$
$$\qquad\qquad\quad\; +\;+$$

$$w = W/P_T$$
$$Qw = W/P_N$$

284 Structure, stabilisation and structural adjustment

Labour market equilibrium requires:

$$N_T^d(w) + N_N^d(Qw) = \bar{N} \tag{12.4}$$

Substituting for w from Equation 12.4 in the equations for EB and IB gives the curves in Figures 12.4 and 12.5.

Since labour is the only domestic resource, non-traded goods prices equal *unit labour costs* or the nominal wage. Output is demand determined below the IB schedule and limited by available labour supply above it. So, output supply depends on absorption and on real wages. A rise in Q will make the production of export goods more profitable and labour will shift to this sector. In addition, domestic demand will shift away from tradables or the demand for imports will fall.

A negative relationship is assumed between Q and real wages. That is, a rise in real wages is associated with a real appreciation or fall in Q. P_N rises with nominal wages, if the price of the domestic good is

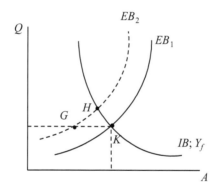

Figure 12.4 The Swan diagram: real exchange rate and absorption space

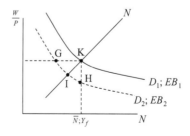

Figure 12.5 External balance and the labour market

Structure, stabilisation and structural adjustment 285

closely linked to unit wage costs $Q(= P_T/P_N)$ must fall as P_N rises. The deflator for real wages, however, is the aggregate price level, which is a weighted average of the prices of traded and non-traded goods. Wage earners spend on a weighted average of imported and non-traded goods. Since P_T is constant, the rise in P is less than that in P_N so that w also rises with W, giving the negative relationship with Q. If non-tradables are more labour intensive compared to tradables, also a rise in wages will raise P_N more.

The point of full internal and external balance is K, where the two schedules in Figure 12.4 intersect. The schedules divide the space into four zones of differing types of disequilibria. Even if an economy is in full equilibrium, a shock can place it in any one of the four quadrants. In analysing adjustment to equilibrium, it is useful to make a distinction between automatic forces of adjustment and policy responses. Prices of non-traded goods will rise with excess demand. This will not only reduce demand, but it will also appreciate Q, switch demand to tradables and deteriorate the BOP. Over time, labour will also shift to the production of non-tradables reducing the supply of exports and further deteriorating the BOP. But adjustment tends to be asymmetric since prices rise more easily than they fall. While Q will appreciate under excess demand bringing the economy back to Y_f, under excess supply, wages and prices would not fall so unemployment would persist.

Moreover, adjustment will be in the right direction only in the top quadrant. In the quadrant to the right, the BOP will move further into deficit as P_N rises. Policy intervention that reduces government consumption of non-tradables and depreciates the currency would be required. A similar argument shows that deflation of prices and wages in the lower quadrants would be equilibrating for the BOP only in the bottom quadrant. In the quadrant to the left, the surplus would tend to rise further, requiring policy intervention that revalues the exchange rate or raises government expenditure.

A combination of *expenditure-changing* and *switching* policy normally is required to reach *full balance* K. The first changes the level of the economy's total demand and the second the direction of demand, shifting it between domestic output and imports and shifting domestic resources between traded and non-traded sectors. The shifting of resources on the production side occurs over a longer run compared to the more immediate change in the direction of demand.

When *deflation* is required for automatic market-based adjustment, policy intervention is all the more necessary because deflation can be a very slow and painful process. In most economies, it is easier to raise

286 *Structure, stabilisation and structural adjustment*

prices and wages than it is to reduce them. A rise in nominal exchange rates achieves the required adjustment in relative prices with less pain. But this only works if there is nominal but not real wage rigidity. Real wages have to be flexible for real exchange rates or the terms of trade to change after nominal devaluation. Nominal rigidity and real flexibility is the normal assumption in Keynesian models.

12.3.4 *The real exchange rate and real wages*

If EB_1 shifts to EB_2 because a rise in global risk aversion has reduced capital inflows, real depreciation is required to reach the new equilibrium H in Figure 12.4.

In the labour market, with the negative shock, labour demand shifts from D_1 to D_2. The labour demand curve corresponding to the more depreciated exchange rate along EB_2 will lie below the demand curve corresponding to EB_1 (Figure 12.5), since demand for labour falls at the higher wage rate, which raises P_N and depreciates Q. For internal balance with employment still at N_0 and Y_f constant, real wages must fall to reach the new equilibrium H. This fall in real wages can come more easily from a rise in S. If labour supply is a rising function of real wages (the curve N in Figure 12.5) rather than fixed, then employment shrinks to I.

If $\bar{S}$ and if $\overline{W}$ or wages are sticky, the economy would shift from K to G (Figures 12.4 and 12.5). There would be a slow recovery in employment as nominal wages fall. If the exchange rate regime is FBAR (fixed but adjustable), a rise in S would raise P and decrease real wages, moving the economy much faster to the real target. Wages generally move upwards faster than they fall.

If there is full indexation and real wages are fixed, so N^S has a horizontal stretch over GK, then the economy would be stuck at G. Since nominal wages rise with prices, even depreciation does not work to decrease unemployment and achieve the real target if it cannot affect the real wage. Appreciation is not feasible if excess labour prevents real wages from rising. If the labour supply curve is flat at the efficiency wage until the full employment level is reached, real wages cannot rise. Some appreciation can be a part of the adjustment process, to the extent that minimum wages also rise with development so the horizontal stretch of the labour supply curve shifts up.

The analysis illustrates how adjustment depends not only on the slopes of the curves, but also on the types of shocks. Apart from changes in foreign inflows, other types of shocks are a rise in external prices or domestic excess demand due to fiscal profligacy.

Structure, stabilisation and structural adjustment   287

The framework can also be used to analyse the reverse case of higher foreign capital flows. The EB schedule shifts rightward from EB_2 to EB_1, and inflows now finance a rise in CAD allowing Q to appreciate and imports to rise. Absorption can be higher and the real exchange rate lower, at the new equilibrium K compared to the earlier equilibrium H, with unchanged employment. If the initial position of the economy is on the full employment IB curve at K, absorbing foreign inflows through a higher CAD will require a real appreciation. With an economy close to full employment, capital inflows must shrink the non-traded sector as appreciation transfers domestic spending to imports.

If, however, the economy is below full employment so that the initial position is G, expanding demand can raise employment and reach both internal and external balances at K, absorbing the larger capital inflows available without any policy conflict. Although a dependent EDE cannot affect world prices, demand for its exports is not infinite because of quantitative restrictions or problems of poor quality, so that unemployed resources persist. Demand lies below full potential output, and as demand rises with development, the production frontier also shifts out as more and more labour qualifies for inclusion in the modern sector.

12.3.5 Contributions of exchange rate policy

According to Corden (2002), there are three objectives that ER policy can fulfil: stabilise prices (nominal anchor function, NA), help reach equilibrium (real targets approach, RT) and improve market stability. The choice of exchange-rate regimes depends on the weight given to these objectives, and on various structural features and other conditions that influence outcomes.

S fix helps achieve NA. It implies S affects money supply and money supply leads nominal wages, but it can result in an overvalued Q. Flexible S helps achieve RT, and it automatically adjusts for inflation such that there is no real overvaluation and $Q = Q^*$. However, it implies that nominal wages are now the nominal anchor. They affect prices and then money supply. Low volatility of S benefits trade, as does $Q = Q^*$.

If nominal wage and prices are flexible, S fix performs better. If they are sticky downwards, a flexible exchange rate can bring about the required change in real wages. If real wages are fixed, however, S flexibility cannot help and a fix S does better.[8]

Under a fix S, money supply has to automatically adjust to money demand shocks in order to keep S fixed, but money supply is not

288 *Structure, stabilisation and structural adjustment*

independent. A flexible S automatically depreciates, thus moderating a negative demand shock, but money supply has to be adjusted to a money demand shock. Inflation targeting allows a more transparent response that helps the financial sector, automatically adjusts money supply and provides the required nominal anchor.

If fiscal policy is the problem, a fixed S will not be able to discipline it, although fiscal policy has a greater impact on output under a fixed exchange rate. The political economy issues, such as contests among groups or provinces for a larger share of resources, which are the fundamental cause of a fiscal deficit, need to be addressed first. Functional finance (fiscal policy as an instrument) is available under a flexible S, but is less effective because of appreciation working in the opposite direction to a demand stimulus. It can be used to counter the effect of foreign inflows. For example, if they are causing an appreciation, a fall in government expenditure can reduce demand, mitigating Dutch disease.

A fixed exchange rate work like a government warranty to firms encouraging UFB and building financial risks for domestic firms, but a flexible exchange rate can be too volatile in an EDE, enhancing the problem of original sin, that is, the inability to borrow abroad in own currency. Moderate flexibility, as in a managed float, is via media.

A flexible exchange rate offers an additional instrument under frequent supply shocks. For example, it could be used to neutralise changes in critical border prices that could otherwise trigger a rise in nominal wages.

The next section examines what combinations of variables were used and how well they worked in actual stabilisation programmes.

12.4 Varieties of programmes

The frameworks studied can help understand actual stabilisation programmes.[9] Most countries underwent adjustment after the Great Depression. The dominance of Keynesian ideas at the time meant that the majority of programmes were based on these.

Populist (Old Keynesian): The economy was closed, which allowed government spending to have the maximum impact on domestic demand, in the cause of state-led development. Import substitution was thought to be necessary to enhance domestic growth. Price-wage controls, low user charges and other administrative interventions aimed to reduce inflation and reduce income inequality. High taxes, land ceilings amd more aimed for redistribution, which was also thought to increase demand. With a fixed exchange rate and other prices also fixed, quantity adjustment had to dominate.

Structure, stabilisation and structural adjustment 289

But the focus on raising demand, supply-side inefficiencies and populist transfers resulted in high and rising inflation, especially after the oil shocks. Capital flows again became large as countries became more open. There were a series of currency crises in Latin America in the 1970s and 1980s. Now, orthodox stabilisation programmes were tried.

Orthodox: These focussed on fundamentals. Fiscal and monetary adjustment was to reduce absorption. Getting prices right was to bring demand and its composition in line with supply. The programmes were either of the sudden shock (cold turkey) type or based on more gradual adjustment. Typically, the sacrifice ratio or per cent of output decrease required for a 1 per cent decrease in inflation was about 10.[10] The cost was especially high if backward-looking staggered wage contracts dominated. Forward-looking wage setting allows quicker convergence to equilibrium wages, reducing the output cost. Stabilisations were either money based or exchange rate based.

1   *Money-based programmes* typically involve a sharp reduction in money supply or its growth rate to achieve internal balance, while variations in the exchange rate target external balance.

An example of such a programme was Bolivia in 1986. Since wages were set biweekly, with a strong effect of the exchange rate on wages, it was successful. Prices stabilised in a week and a half, illustrating the quick results possible when behaviour is forward looking. As inflation stabilised, monthly loan rates fell from 45 per cent in August to 21 per cent in December, and were at single digits the next year. Output costs are high when sticky wages and prices force output contraction to bear the brunt of the adjustment. Since structural measures were also undertaken in Bolivia, the output costs of the demand contraction alone were not clear.[11] Labour market institutions have a large effect on outcomes. Similar cold turkey stabilisation in Russia in the early 1990s caused enormous output cost and human suffering, since supporting institutions could not be created overnight.

Most episodes of money-based stabilisation involved high output cost. Apart from Chile in 1975, such stabilisations were undertaken in a number of Latin American countries in the early 1990s.

2   *Exchange rate-based programmes*: Costs were lower, at least initially, with gradual exchange rate-based adjustment. In the Southern Cone Tablita programmes in the late 1970s, the exchange rate was used as a nominal anchor to bring down inflation and inflation expectations, using strategies such as a preannounced devaluation. The conceptual base underlying these programmes was the

290   *Structure, stabilisation and structural adjustment*

MA to the BOP with continuous PPP, so that domestic prices were expected to be linked to international, as the nominal exchange rate affected domestic prices. A fall in the rate of depreciation could, therefore, be expected to lower inflation, while aggregate demand policy affected the external balance. Fiscal adjustment and trade liberalisation typically accompanied the programme. Supply conditions affected output growth.

An example of such a programme, which ended in a crisis, was Chile 1978. Real appreciation reduced demand; sharp rise in nominal and real interest rates triggered a financial crisis. Capital flowed out, in 1981 output growth was negative and the peso was devalued.

Calvo and Vegh (1999) list 12 episodes of such stabilisation of which only 4 did not end crisis. However, it must be remembered that many of these occurred during the 1980s, when a sharp rise in US interest rates was responsible for stress creating outflows from EDEs.

Comparing the two types shows some empirical regularities (Table 12.5) that Calvo and Vegh christen 'recession now versus recession later'. Real appreciation occurred because the fall in inflation was slow. With monetary tightening, the output cost was immediate and upfront. Harnessing forward-looking behaviour to interpret these regularities, they argue that an exchange-based stabilisation was not credible – the early appreciation was expected to end in a sharp devaluation. It, therefore, induced a rise in consumption and imports, raising activity and deteriorating the current account. The low credibility became self-fulfilling, leading often to crisis and recession.

Table 12.5 Comparing types of stabilisation

Money-based stabilisation	*Exchange rate-based stabilisation*
Slow convergence of inflation to rate of growth of money supply	Slow convergence of the inflation rate (CPI) to rate of devaluation (WPI relevant for tradable goods converges quite rapidly)
Initial contraction in economic activity	Initial increase in activity – real GDP and C – followed by a later contraction
Real appreciation	Real appreciation
No clear-cut response of TB and CA	Deterioration of TB and CA
Initial increase in domestic real interest rate	Ambiguous response of domestic real interest rate first decrease, but increase substantially later

Heterodox stabilisation was tried in the mid to late 1980s after the limited success of orthodox stabilisations. This combined an exchange rate freeze or a preannounced exchange rate path and income policies as either explicit wage-price controls or as a 'social contract', with correction towards fiscal, monetary fundamentals. The idea was to escape the deep recession that accompanied an aggregate demand contraction in the presence of wage-price rigidities and inflation inertia, due to backward-looking indexation and lack of credibility. The exchange rate and wage-price intervention was expected to address the latter problems and bring prices into alignment faster. It worked in Israel and Mexico, but not in Argentina and Brazil. As inflation fell, there was a temptation to slack fiscal discipline leading to a financial constraint and capital outflow.

In the early 1980s, Israel had a 14 per cent monthly inflation, with fast wage indexation. The exchange rate was also indexed through a PPP-based rule for the crawling peg.

There was a favourable start to the adjustment with devaluation plus a fall in wages in terms of tradable goods, facilitated by aid from the United States. Four stages were followed. In the first, the country moved from the dollar peg to a five-currency trade-weighted basket peg. After an 1987 devaluation of 10 per cent, cost of living adjustment was lengthened to six months from three. Annual inflation stayed at 20 per cent even after the removal of price controls, but growth was low at 2–3 per cent and did not recover its earlier robustness.

12.4.1 *The evolution of reform thinking*

A 1989 Washington meeting on reform in Latin America hammered out what came to be known as the Washington consensus, describing the reform measures that should be undertaken in liberalising adjustments. Much of the policy advice given to EDEs in this period followed the 10-point agenda below:

1 Fiscal discipline.
2 Reordering public expenditure to infrastructure, basic health and education (pro growth and pro poor)
3 Tax reform: broad base and marginal rates
4 Liberalising interest rates (financial liberalisation)
5 A competitive exchange rates: two-corner doctrine for exchange rate regimes
6 Trade liberalisation
7 Liberalisation of inward FDI

292 *Structure, stabilisation and structural adjustment*

8 Privatisation
9 Deregulation to ease entry and exit barriers
10 Property rights (especially in the informal sector)

Applications of this reform programme disappointed, however. In particular, it became clear that financial liberalisation should occur at different rates, together with improvements in regulation. The 1990s crises in Mexico, Brazil, East Asia, Argentina and Russia implicated high short-term private debt and outflows under full capital account convertibility. Under high interest differentials and implicit government warranties on currency risk from fixed exchange rates, firms had an incentive to borrow abroad, but the funds exited in a crisis. The focus on demand and prices alone in privatise-liberalise mantra neglected deeper drivers of productivity and performance.

A new group convened for a rethink. Williamson (2003) summarised the modifications to the Washington consensus below.[12] One of the main messages was institutions and incentives matter. For example, just saying reduce fiscal deficit is not enough. It is necessary to create incentives to make it happen.

1 Crisis proofing is required through:

- surpluses in good times to allow countercyclical deficits in bad
- subnational government's budget constraints and transfers to be made a function of government expenditure not the Centre's tax revenue, so that its anti-cyclical policy is not undermined
- accumulate reserves when exports are strong if subject to unstable agricultural cycles
- flexible exchange rate – depreciate under capital outflows and prevent overvaluation under excessive inflows
- minimise use of dollars or make banks hedge dollar liabilities
- flexible exchange rate plus monetary policy targeting a low rate of inflation, fiscal rules, government expenditure capped at the trend growth rate of the economy
- strengthen prudential supervision of the banking system

2 The major lacuna in first-generation reforms was the absence of labour market reforms.
3 Second-generation reforms should focus on improving institutions: the political system, governance, systems of accounting, including financial sector accounting, laws dealing with bankruptcy and creditor rights. Government should encourage innovation, research and development.

Structure, stabilisation and structural adjustment 293

4   Income redistribution:

- raise taxes on rich by closing loopholes, better collection, property tax
- improve opportunities for the poor: education, property rights, micro-credit

Compared to the above advice, where the focus continued to be largely to 'stabilise, privatise and liberalise', based on the experience of countries that had failed, a commission sought to extract lessons from countries that had succeeded – 13 economies that, since 1950, grew at around 7 per cent for more than 25 years. World Bank (2008) studied sustained high growth that leads to a doubling in size every decade: its causes, consequences and internal dynamics.

Nine of these economies were from Asia: China, Hong Kong, Indonesia, Japan, Korea, Malaysia, Singapore, Taiwan and Thailand. Their common characteristics included openness, macroeconomic stability, high savings and investment rates and market allocation of resources. Governments were capable – pragmatic and flexible rather than ideological. While willing to intervene in markets to promote exports through industrial policies and to manage exchange rates (with the use of selected capital controls and reserve accumulation), they were flexible enough not to get locked into distorting policies, such as permanent subsidies or price controls, to anticipate and change policies as required for growth.

An example of this 'crossing the river while feeling the stones' was Korea's evolution from labour-intensive manufacturing to a more knowledge-based and capital-intensive economy. Labour market reform, competition, resource mobility and urbanisation were all supported. For example, agriculture's share of employment fell from 40 per cent in 1975 to 15 per cent in 2000, in Malaysia. Public investment in infrastructure was emphasised. It accounted for 5–7 per cent of GDP or more. Specific contextual interventions and the microeconomic incentives created were important. External drivers alone did not create growth. And openness did not imply blind application of market-friendly reforms.

The report makes a specific recommendation for Asia to establish a mechanism to coordinate policies of the growing number of influential countries and to safeguard the stability of the IFS. Inflation targeting plus more flexible exchange rates plus fiscal rules seem to be working better, but the GFC has exposed problems from asset bubbles, capital flow surges and supply shocks.

294 Structure, stabilisation and structural adjustment

Repeated crises and higher growth volatility, especially in Latin America, gave rise to interesting model-based explanations such as that low credibility of stabilisation leads to excess consumption in good times (Calvo and Vegh, 1999), or that consumption is more volatile because policy uncertainty makes trend growth more volatile (Aguiar and Gopinath, 2007). But these generalisations do not hold for Asia where volatility is lower. Table 12.6 summarises some broad differences between Latin America and Asia. Individual countries may differ but broad comparisons are valid.

In China and India, non-standard growth-oriented adjustments gave more degrees of freedom. These large Asian countries with approximately two billion out of a world population of five billion underwent high catch-up growth. Gradualism allowed the public sector to shrink as the private sector grew. Higher growth in these countries reduced world poverty, but inequality grew – China reached Latin American levels of inequality starting from a system without private property. Given pervasive state interventions, it found it difficult to switch to a market- and domestic consumption-led rather than an export-led system.

Table 12.6 Comparing Latin America and Asia

Region	Latin America	Asia
Open economy	Primary goods trade KAC first S nominal anchor	Secondary goods KAC later; large FX reserves S competitive
Finance	Close to the United States Dollarisation GNS low	Relationship lending High debt/equity GNS high
Supply behaviour	M substitution G dominate G redistribution Inequality high W bargaining Liberalising reforms Corruption Land surplus	Export competition G helps private G infrastructure, education Inequality low flexible – food prices affect Productivity, regulations Connections Labour surplus
Government	Budget deficit Credibility low	Budget surplus Credibility high
Credibility high	High C, I, terms of trade, inflation	Low More smooth

Note: KAC: Capital account convertibility

Structure, stabilisation and structural adjustment 295

Macroeconomic vulnerability due to large double deficits in 2011 led to fears that India was going the Latin American way. But despite external shocks, macroeconomic stability was soon restored. Although growth fell much below potential, it was still one of the highest in the world. India is unusual in Asia in that it has a fiscal deficit, but high private savings compensate partly. Even so, consumption is a much higher share of GDP than it is in China. In some ways, India does follow a middle path between Latin America and Asia.

Although Indian opening out was calibrated, it unfortunately occurred in a period of major external shocks. Unlike China, domestic financial markets were deepened earlier in the reform sequence. Portfolio inflows, which were liberalised the most, were volatile. Although they would go out in periods of global risk-off, they soon returned since they were based on future growth, which remained attractive. Even so, India did too much of external liberalisation and financial reform, since it was easier to do, while neglecting hard domestic reforms such as improving governance, infrastructure, health, education and making India one market (Goyal, 2014). But, voters had started demanding these types of reform, which promises well for creating an economic inclusion while sustaining growth, and in 2014, voted in a majority government on a governance plank.

12.5   Summary

Development macroeconomics can choose among four different frameworks available: the monetarist school where prices adjust perfectly and clear markets; the RBC which introduces rational expectations so that perfect adjustment includes the future also; the structuralist school which emphasises politics and the conflict between groups in a short-run Keynesian framework; and the NKE which not only preserves the forward-looking approach, but also brings in price rigidities and various other frictions and imperfections. Since EDEs have many such frictions, this book takes the view that the latter approach is the most appropriate for EDEs. It also allows the use of modern tools and conceptual frameworks. But the frictions modelled have to be appropriate, for which knowledge of context is important. This chapter seeks to provide some of this context, especially for the Asian region.

It fleshes out details on the structure and institutions of typical EDEs, contrasting them with AEs and bringing out regional variations. For example, the Latin American region shows much more macroeconomic volatility compared to Asia.

296 *Structure, stabilisation and structural adjustment*

The concepts of stabilisation and structural adjustment are defined. The distinction between expenditure changing and switching is made. The latter works through changes in a key relative price – the real exchange rate. Since terms of trade are often exogenous for EDEs, changes in the real exchange rate occur through changes in the prices of non-tradable goods.

The Salter-Swan framework is useful to examine the achievement of IB and external balance in an EDE through changes in the real exchange rate and in absorption. The framework is developed and used to discuss shocks, adjustment paths and instrument allocation under different assumptions about price flexibility. It is also used to bring out the relationship between the real exchange rate and the real wage rate. A rise in the latter requires a real appreciation.

This chapter then analyses specific stabilisation episodes using theoretical frameworks developed, and the evolution of thinking on stabilisation and reform, as many of these programmes failed to deliver good outcomes. While the Washington consensus on reform could be summarised as 'stabilise, privatise and liberalise', the EDEs that achieved sustained high growth followed a pragmatic reform path that displayed knowledge of context, pragmatic flexibility, dynamism and use of both markets and government policy. Robust institutions and good incentives played a major role.

Notes

1 The SOEME model assumes monopolistic competition in each good, so that terms of trade can change.

2 In Japan, food budget shares fell below 50 per cent in the post-war period, and in Taiwan and Korea in the 1960s. China reached this stage by the late 1980s. They were at the latter levels for rural China in the 1950s. The total food shares for India were 63.2 and 54.7 for rural and urban households, respectively, even in 1993–94. Unlike India, most DCs were careful to moderate food price increases and focus on a rise in agricultural productivity as long as food budget shares were high. Food prices and nominal rate of protection in agriculture were allowed to rise only after that (Goyal, 2003).

3 After the ceiling on external commercial borrowings was liberalised, since the rupee was appreciating, risk premiums were low and domestic interest rates exceeded foreign, firms' borrowing abroad spiked. The share of corporate investment in GDP rose by 9 percentage points over the boom period 2003–08; a large portion of the less than half of this, not financed by corporate savings, came from external sources. By 2015, corporate borrowing abroad had exceeded 10 per cent of GDP and was considered as a large source of risk as the dollar began to appreciate with an expected rise in US interest rates.

Structure, stabilisation and structural adjustment   297

4 Source: www.ifmr.co.in/blog/category/long-term-debt-markets/page/2/. See also www.sebi.gov.in/cms/sebi_data/statistics/corporate_bonds/outstanding corpdata.html https://asianbondsonline.adb.org/indonesia/data.php.
5 Dr. Anjanavelu, an RBI officer, remarked that the RBI and the Ministry of Finance coordinate well together. Whenever the ministry has some other view, if the RBI convinces them that course of action would be inflationary, they agree to the RBI's suggestions.
6 The model of Chapter 10 assumes $(1 - \alpha)$ to be the extent of NT goods. Monopolistic competition gives some pricing power in each good. The real exchange rate is linked to the terms of trade through α.
7 In contrast, the goods market equilibrium IS* slopes upwards in S and Y space, because unemployment is assumed, output is demand determined and a depreciation raises output as exports rise.
8 Over 2008–13, the RBI reduced intervention in FX markets; fluctuating global risks created high volatility in S, but this only added to macroeconomic vulnerabilities, such as inflation, because high food inflation raised nominal wages at unprecedented rates. Real wages were rigid in terms of food prices.
9 The discussion of the programmes draws upon Calvo and Vegh (1999), Calvo (1996), Frankel (2011) and Chapter 10 of Agenor and Montiel (1999).
10 Okun in summarising research on the topic gave a range of 6–18 for the United States.
11 The same expert, Jeffrey Sachs, helped design both programmes. Sachs was a hero in Bolivia but a villain in Russia, where without the necessary market institutions big bang reforms collapsed.
12 Rodrik reviewing the World Bank's 'Economic growth in the 1990s: Learning from a decade of reforms' in 2006 called it 'Goodbye Washington Consensus, Hello Washington Confusion' (copy at http://j.mp/1ROcWqe). His point was that experience pointed to the importance of contextual policies and of pragmatism.

References

Agenor, P. R. and P. J. Montiel. 1999. *Development Macroeconomics*, 2nd edition, New Jersey: Princeton University Press.

Aguiar, M. and G. Gopinath. 2007. 'Emerging Market Business Cycles: The Cycle is the Trend', *Journal of Political Economy*, 115(1): 69–102.

Calvo, G. 1996. *Money, Exchange Rates and Output*, Cambridge, MA: MIT Press.

Calvo, G. A. and C. A. Vegh. 1999. 'Inflation Stabilisation and BOP Crises in Developing Countries', in J. B. Taylor and M. Woodford (eds.), *Handbook of Macroeconomics*, Vol.1, pp. 1531–1614. North Holland, Amsterdam: Elsevier.

Corbo, V. and S. Fischer. 1995. 'Structural Adjustment, Stabilisation and Policy Reform: Domestic and International Finance', Chapter 44 in J. Behreman and T. N. Srinivasan (eds.), *Handbook of Development Economics*, Vol. 3, pp. 2845–2924. North Holland, Amsterdam: Elsevier Science.

298 Structure, stabilisation and structural adjustment

Corden, W. M. 2002. *Too Sensational: On the Choice of Exchange Rate Regimes*, Cambridge, MA: MIT Press.

Frankel, J. 2011. 'Monetary Policy in Emerging Markets: A Survey', Chapter 25 in B. Friedman and M. Woodford (eds.), *Handbook of Monetary Economics*, Vol. 3B, pp. 1439–1520. North Holland, Amsterdam: Elsevier.

Goyal, A. 2003. 'Agriculture and Industry: Enhancing Mutual Gains', *Decision*, 30(2): 51–76, July–December.

Goyal, A. 2009. 'Swan Diagram', in Ramkishen S. Rajan and Kenneth A. Reinert (eds.), *Princeton Encyclopedia of the World Economy*. Princeton University Press. Available at http://192.9.13.155\e-library\coursemat\961.pdf.

Goyal, A. 2014. 'Introduction and Overview', in Ashima Goyal (ed.), *Handbook of Indian Economy in the 21st Century: Understanding the Inherent Dynamism*, pp. xxix–lxxiv. New Delhi: Oxford University Press.

Krugman, P. R., M. Obstfeld and M. Melitz. 2014. *International Economics: Theory and Policy*, 10th edition, Delhi: Pearson Education.

Williamson, J. 2003. 'The Washington Consensus and Beyond', *Economic and Political Weekly*, 38(15): 1475–1481, April 12.

World Bank. 2008. *The Growth Report: Strategies for Sustained Growth and Inclusive Development, Commission on Growth and Development*, Washington, DC: World Bank. Available at https://openknowledge.worldbank.org/handle/10986/6507.

13 Currency crises

> Those who cannot remember the past are condemned to repeat it.
> —George Santayana

13.1 Introduction

In Chapter 12, we saw that many EDE stabilisation programmes ended in currency crises. In Chapter 9, on fixed exchange rates, we analysed the effects of an expected devaluation – a sharp fall in FX reserves and rise in interest rates. These features normally accompany real-world currency crises.

Analysis of currency crises also again illustrates the interaction between facts and theories, which characterises macroeconomics. Theories of currency crises can be classified into first-, second- and third-generation models. Each captures the essence of and gives insights into the crises of the time. And each developed in response to new features of crises that earlier theories could not explain.

We start with the Krugman (1979) paper, which came to represent first-generation crises, although it built on other such attempts. This offers an abstraction and understanding of the repeated currency crises that accompanied the Latin American stabilisation programmes of the 1970s and 1980s. It implies a unique time of attack when reserves are still positive.

But countries in the exchange rate bands of the ERM leading up to the European Union sometimes experienced crises and sometimes did not, although fundamentals were similar. This required understanding possibilities of coordination between currency traders and led to second-generation currency crises models. The seminal paper here is Obstfeld (1996).

The Asian crisis of the late 1990s raised new issues – now currencies with strong macroeconomic fundamentals were attacked. The

300 *Currency crises*

weaknesses lay in the financial sector and balance sheet vulnerabilities. Third-generation crisis models explored these, including aggravations from cross-border flows and exchange rate policies. The model presented here is by Chang and Velasco (2000), which shows how a bank that runs in an open economy can make illiquid banks insolvent. The run-up to the Asian crisis and macroeconomic policy failures are also explored.

The structure of the chapter is as follows: Section 13.2 develops a first-generation crises model giving further insights into the Latin American currency crises discussed in Chapter 12. Section 13.3 presents an analytical framework for second-generation currency crises that occurred in countries with intermediate fundamentals. Section 13.4 describes the facts – background, triggers and outcomes – associated with the third-generation currency crises that occurred in countries with strong macroeconomic fundamentals. Section 13.5 presents a model to formalise and deepen understanding of such crises. Section 13.6 collects the lessons for policy from the large post-crisis literature, before Section 13.7 summarises and concludes.

13.2 First-generation crises: flawed fundamentals

The basic insight of first-generation crisis models is that, although an attack on a currency occurs when reserves are positive and draws down those reserves, the attack is the inevitable consequence of unsustainable macroeconomic policies. The responsibility for the attack, therefore, lies with those policies and not with those who attack the currency.

This can be seen in a simple model that assumes the government continuously runs a fiscal deficit, which the Central Bank finances by buying government securities. The economy initially has a fixed exchange rate, and the CB is committed to that rate as long as reserves are positive. When reserves are exhausted, it allows the currency to float.

The model draws on the asset approach to the exchange rate, with rational forward-looking currency traders. It has three blocks, the money market where money demand must equal money supply, purchasing power parity (PPP) and uncovered interest parity (UIP) in continuous perfect foresight form. That is, it uses the components of the monetary theory of exchange rates and the balance of payments, with flexible prices and markets that clear. Perfect trade arbitrage gives PPP and perfect capital mobility ensures UIP. The focus of the model is on short-term capital flows or arbitrage by rational traders, in response to profit opportunities, and therefore it abstracts from the real sector. Like all

Currency crises   301

monetary models, it assumes full employment. It draws on theoretical innovations, applies concepts learnt earlier in the book and demonstrates how to set up the simplest possible structure to address the question posed, while leaving out all inessential details.

Under a fixed exchange rate, from UIP, we have:

$$\dot{\bar{s}} = R - R^* = 0 \tag{13.1}$$

All variables except the interest rate are in logarithms and are therefore written in small letters. The world interest rate is normalised at $R^* = 0$. From PPP, we have:

$$\bar{s} = p - p^* \tag{13.2}$$

The world price level P^* is also normalised at unity, so its natural logarithm $p^* = 0$. Equation 13.2, giving the logarithm of the fixed exchange rate, therefore reduces to $\bar{s} = p$.

The money market clears. In logarithms, money demand equals money supply: $m^d = m^s = m$. From the MA to the BOP, the money supply must equal the CB's balance sheet.

$$m^s \equiv a + f \tag{13.3}$$

Since government securities, a, are continuously increasing, FX reserves f must be decreasing at the same rate, in order to keep money supply constant at the level determined by the fixed exchange rate. That is, the CB must be selling f to counteract the rise in a: $\dot{m} = 0 \Rightarrow \dot{f} = -\dot{a}$ where $\dot{a} = \gamma$. Since we are abstracting from output, we can normalise output Y at unity so that its logarithm $y = 0$. The money demand function, written in logarithms, then is:

$$m^d - p = -\lambda R \tag{13.4}$$

Substituting the PPP relation gives $m^d - \bar{s} = -\lambda R$. Substituting UIP, and remembering the change in the fixed exchange rate must be zero, reduces money demand to $\bar{s} = m^d$. Since money demand must equal m^s, we have:

$$\bar{s} = a + f \tag{13.5}$$

As reserves approach zero $(f \rightarrow 0)$ s must float, since it is no longer possible for the CB to defend the currency. As in the fixed exchange

302 Currency crises

rate case, the outcome must be consistent with UIP, PPP and money market clearing. So, from UIP:

$$\dot{\tilde{s}} = R - R^*, \dot{\bar{s}} = R \tag{13.6}$$

From PPP:

$$\tilde{s} = p - p^*, \bar{s} = p \tag{13.7}$$

Since $f = 0$, now $m^s = a$. Substituting in m^d gives $a - \tilde{s} = -\lambda\dot{\tilde{s}}$, or:

$$\tilde{s} = a + \lambda\dot{\tilde{s}} \tag{13.8}$$

This gives an expression for shadow exchange rate $\tilde{s}$ or the floating rate that would prevail once all reserves pass into private hands. Figure 13.1 (a) shows a steadily depreciating shadow exchange rate.

Let $\dot{\tilde{s}} = \gamma$, that is, the exchange rate depreciates at a constant rate. Substituting in Equation 13.8 gives:

$$\tilde{s} = a + \gamma\lambda \tag{13.9}$$

Differentiating Equation 13.9 with respect to time gives $\dot{\tilde{s}} = \dot{a}$ since these are the only two variable quantities. We know the rate of increase of government assets in the CB balance sheet $\dot{a}$ equals γ. The rate of depreciation assumed is now shown to equal the rate of creation of domestic credit, so $\dot{\tilde{s}} = \dot{a} = \gamma$. What was earlier assumed is proved. The money supply will be rising at the rate γ, once reserves are exhausted and the currency will float, depreciating steadily at the rate of expansion of money supply.

Log-linearity plus perfect foresight imply a unique timing of the attack. This occurs at T when reserves are still positive. It is possible to solve explicitly for T. Speculators make losses, if they buy reserves (sell rupees) at T' as shown in Figure 13.1 when $\tilde{s} < \bar{s}$, since after floating the spot exchange rate $\tilde{s} < \bar{s}$. Domestic currency sold would appreciate below $\bar{s}$, once all the reserves are in the market.

If the attack occurs at T'' instead of at T, the triangle from T between $\tilde{s}$ and $\bar{s}$ denotes unutilised profit opportunities. Rational speculators, however, would not allow profit opportunities to go unutilised. They attack, therefore, at the instant when $\tilde{s} = \bar{s}$ ruling out any jump in s, or unutilised arbitrage opportunities. A jump implies capital gains are instantaneously infinite.

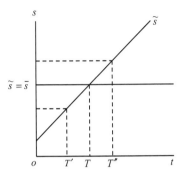

Figure 13.1 (a) Time of attack

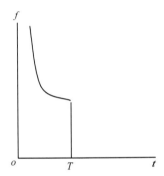

Figure 13.1 (b) Reserves

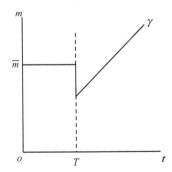

Figure 13.1 (c) Money supply

304 *Currency crises*

Once the exchange rate changes from fix to float and there is a positive rate of depreciation, demand for real money balances will drop sharply by $\lambda\gamma$. For continuous money market equilibrium, this requires a fully anticipated discrete rise in the exchange rate raising the price level. But the exchange rate jumping is inconsistent with rational speculators, so instead money supply must fall sharply at the point of attack. The required adjustment in real balances takes place through a fall in nominal balances, as speculators take out the remaining reserves in the course of the attack.

Once the floating exchange rate is established, credit and money supply expand at the rate γ. Since $\dot{s} = R = \gamma$, R jumps up by γ from UIP implying a fall in m^d by $-\lambda\dot{s}$. As authorities sell reserves in response to the attack, m^s also falls:

$$\Delta m^s = -\Delta f \tag{13.10}$$

For continuous money market equilibrium, the fall in money supply must equal the change in money demand. So, the fall in f through the speculative attack must be such that $\Delta m^d = \Delta m^s$:

$$\Delta m^d = -\lambda\gamma \Rightarrow -\Delta f = -\lambda\gamma \tag{13.11}$$

Over the period 0 to T, reserves must have been falling at the rate γ, in order to keep money supply unchanged as government securities rose in the CB's balance sheet. Therefore, at T:

$$f = f_0 - \gamma T \tag{13.12}$$

Since whatever is left is completely exhausted in the attack:

$$-(f_0 - \gamma T) = -\Delta f \tag{13.13}$$

This, in turn, equals the fall in money supply at the time of attack. It follows:

$$-(f_0 - \gamma T) = -\lambda\gamma$$
$$\gamma T = f_0 - \lambda\gamma$$
$$T = \frac{f_0 - \lambda\gamma}{\gamma}$$

There is, therefore, a unique time of attack depending on the parameters. Although this occurs when $f > 0$, it is not caused by speculative

Currency crises 305

activity, but is just the outcome of correctly forecasting the effect of government policies. The reserves can last longer making T large; if f_0 is large or γ, the expansion in credit is lower.

The model captures many features of Latin American crises of the 1970s, while giving fresh insights. A key insight is macroeconomic policies inconsistent with a fixed exchange rate are responsible for a crisis, not the action of speculators, even if the crisis occurs when reserves are positive. This explains the failure of the Tablita regimes due to persistent fiscal deficits. A fixed exchange rate could not discipline large fiscal deficits, which led to a steady increase in credit, making the fixed exchange rate unviable. The failure lay in the macroeconomic fundamentals.

Major criticisms for any model are failure to match data or internal inconsistencies. Actual Latin American crises, while driven by unsustainable macroeconomic policies, differed in that the predicted fall in money supply was not normally observed – governments would sterilise the loss in reserves. This failure came from a flaw in the model. While it assumes traders are strategic and forward looking, the government dumbly follows a fixed policy, waiting for the crisis to happen. This could be rationalised by interest group pressures or election driven short-termism. In reality, however, governments are also strategic and respond to expected trader actions. Moreover, new facts emerged, which the first-generation crisis model could not explain. This set the stage for a new framework of analysis.

13.3 Second-generation crises: intermediate fundamentals

In the early 1990s, the currencies of a number of European countries were attacked as they implemented the ERM currency bands on course for the European Union. The macroeconomic fundamentals of these countries were not obviously poor. In some countries or time periods, attacks occurred, but not in others. For example, when the ERM band was widened from 2.5 per cent to 15 per cent, there was no rise in depreciation in France, Belgium and Denmark. This should have accompanied weak fundamentals, such as the steady rise in fiscal deficits in the Krugman model.

Therefore, this was a new type of currency crisis. Obstfeld (1996) offered an explanation for these facts in a model with multiple equilibria. Models with these features came to be known as second-generation crises models. The example below, from that paper, illustrates the basic idea of strategic interaction between traders and a government that

306 *Currency crises*

continuously assesses its options comparing net benefits from defending the exchange rate to allowing it to change.

Consider two traders A and B; each has domestic currency resources of 8 units. Trader A has a choice between two strategies. She can either hold the currency (H) or sell it (S). Attacking the currency, that is, selling local currency, carries a transaction cost of one. If the attack is successful, the currency depreciates by 50 per cent.

Poor fundamentals take the form in the model of low reserves with the government, assumed to be 8. In this case, the payoffs are as in Figure 13.2 (a). If any one trader holds, she gets zero if she attacks and the other holds she gets 3 (= 4 − 1), while the other gets zero. If both sell, they share (4/2) − 1, each getting a payoff of unity. Therefore, the Nash equilibrium, where each does the best no matter what the other does, is for both to sell. An attack against the currency is certain to occur in this case, as in the first-generation crises model.

If, however, macroeconomic fundamentals are strong, the government will have a strong resolve and the means to defend the currency. This is the high reserve case where the government is assumed to have $R = 20$. Now, even if both traders sell, they cannot take out all the reserves and depreciate the currency, so the return to the one who sells, if one or both sell, is −1. The zero return from hold is, therefore, the strictly dominated strategy and (H, H) is the Nash equilibrium.

Nor consider intermediate fundamentals where the government has reserves $R = 12$ (Figure 13.2 [b]). The return to H is zero, as usual. A trader selling alone is unable to take out the government's reserves and has a loss of −1. But if both sell together, the currency depreciates and each gets a return of $(6/2) − 1 = 2$. Since the best returns for one trader

	Trader B	
	H	*S*
H 0 , 0		0 , 3
S 3 , 0		1 , 1

	Trader B	
	H	*S*
H 0 , 0		0 , -1
S -1 , 0		2 , 2

Figure 13.2 (a) Low reserves $R = 8$; *(b)* Intermediate reserves $R = 12$

Currency crises 307

changes with the other's strategy choice, both (H, H) and (S, S) are Nash equilibria. If trader A plays H, trader B gets the highest payoff from H and will play H. If trader A plays S, trader B gets the highest payoff from S and will play S. Hence, an attack will occur only if the traders are able to coordinate on selling.

Thus, now the responsibility for the attack cannot be put only on policy failures. Subsequent work (Morris and Shin, 1998) has shown that under a failure of common knowledge, traders would coordinate on the sell equilibrium, so that there is a unique outcome even in the intermediate fundamentals case. But transparency that alleviates the common knowledge failure can prevent the attack. The clear implication for policy is to encourage transparency.

When crises occurred under intermediate macroeconomic fundamentals, they required a further development of theory. A series of crises in Asia occurred in countries where the fundamentals were strong. So, how could they be explained? We first look at the facts in the section below, in order to show the evolution of theory in response to the facts.

13.4 Third-generation crises

The Mexican crisis in 1994 is regarded as the first of the third-generation crises[1] because of the key role played by a fragile financial system, although in this case government finances were not in a good shape so fundamentals were also weak. There was high short-term foreign government debt, so when demand shocks from an overvalued exchange rate and other adverse shocks, including wrong policy choices in an election year, triggered a currency crisis, the traditional defense of a rise in interest rates and devaluation did not work. It worsened the repayment burden and increased financial fragility.

Thailand was the country where the East Asian crisis started. Table 13.1 shows the magnitude of crashes in currencies and in stock prices in some countries in the region. The 1990s macroeconomic background was one of the high capital inflows, stimulating a (largely) asset price inflation, an increasing current account deficit (reaching 8% of GDP) and a tight monetary policy, which kept domestic interest rates high.

There were classic precrisis policy mistakes. Monetary policy sterilised inflows to maintain a nominal exchange rate target. But the resulting higher interest rates just attracted more short-term capital inflows through the banking system – the classic MF result. Exchange rate management moved away from the competitive exchange rate policy,

308 *Currency crises*

Table 13.1 Per cent changes in bilateral US$ exchange rates and local currency share prices

Countries	Per cent changes over 25 June–3 December 1997	
	Share price indices	*Exchange rates*
Thailand	–23.92	67.31
Indonesia	–43.9	61.6
Malaysia	–48.78	45.24
Philippines	–36.4	33.71
South Korea	–46.2	34.8
Japan	–19.8	13.16
Singapore	–16.19	12.59
Hong Kong	–25.61	–0.13
Taiwan	–11.77	15.77
China	–12.96	–0.12
India	–12.98	9.78

Source: Goyal and Dash (1998).

which was the cornerstone of the East Asian development strategy. Since Thai inflation was higher than that of its competitors, the fixed nominal rate implied real appreciation.

In a poorly supervised financial system, asset price inflation increased the demand for loans and vulnerability to a future fall in asset prices from a sharp rise in interest rates. But the disproportionate reliance on tight money and higher interest rates only encouraged the asset bubble compared to other investment. It is argued that low interest rates feed asset bubbles by forcing fund managers to take more risk. But at high interest rates, fund managers can get too comfortable. In addition, only high risk speculative investments tend to be viable. Those close to bankruptcy are more willing to take risks leading to adverse selection. There are problems at either extreme.

Among the triggers for the crisis were:

- Loss of competitiveness to China in the 1990s, worsened by the fixed nominal exchange rate.
- Stagnation of the Japanese economy in the 1990s reduced export demand.
- Export growth fell in 1996, but real appreciation and high interest rates intensified demand shocks.
- The dollar appreciated 35 per cent against the yen in 1995–96. Weakening of the Yen implied a real appreciation for countries

Currency crises 309

pegged to the dollar. The Baht appreciated when it should have depreciated with the Yen, as Japan was the major trade anchor for the region.

- There was a collapse in world prices of semi-conductors, a major export item. The worsening terms of trade constituted a transient real shock, but the classic policy response, a temporary nominal depreciation, did not occur.
- All these negative shocks implied the deviation of the real exchange rate from its equilibrium value increased. Moreover, falling asset values increased financial sector vulnerability.
- As the currency was expected to depreciate, speculators borrowed Baht to buy dollars, but the classic defense interest rate defense, raising interest rates against such speculation only increased financial vulnerability.

There were mistakes also in handling the crisis. It was one full year, from mid-1996 to July 1997, before the fixed exchange rate was abandoned. The reserves of US$ 38 billion were only nominal, since they were just equivalent to dollar liabilities in forward swaps. There were bailouts for the financial sector instead of restructuring, but high interest rates decreased asset values. Weak banks and financial institutions put pressure on government finances. The money given as bailouts was sent abroad. Only later were stockholders made liable while depositors continued to be insured. Moreover, the authorities reduced credibility by themselves, publicly doubting the value of the Baht.

In July 1997, the Baht was finally floated, but recovery was slow since interest rates were still high. The private UFB encouraged by the fixed exchange rate and positive interest differential created financial stress, but real wage flexibility due to rural migration somewhat mitigated the effects of the fixed exchange rate on industry.

The crisis had a major impact on three other Asian countries – Indonesia, South Korea and Malaysia – although as Table 13.1 shows, share prices and exchange rates were adversely affected in many Asian countries as capital flowed out of EDEs.

The spread and impact depended on local country conditions. Indonesia was plagued by UFB and crony capitalism. It suffered the heaviest and most prolonged effect on output and employment aggravated by incorrect post-crises advice on belt tightening.

In South Korea, the FX debt was hedged because of large exports, but asset bubbles contributed to financial fragility under high leverage. The debt/equity ratio of the top 30 chaebols was over 300 per cent by the end of 1996. In early 1997, NPAs were 15 per cent of total loans.

310 Currency crises

Malaysia also had asset bubbles, but capital controls on banks ensured there was no UFB. Tightening controls after the crisis hit allowed it to lower interest rates to revive the economy.

Although capital controls had not been able to save Malaysia from the crisis, they helped protect India and China. But falling domestic interest rates also mitigated spillovers to the two countries. China was in the middle of a soft landing, with falling interest rates, after a period of overheating. In India, policy rates were increased sharply in October 1996, precipitating an industrial slowdown. But a quick fall in policy rates prevented the vicious debt depreciation cycle setting in, although lending rates were sticky and remained high for quite some time. Capital controls meant there was very little short-term UFB. But high levels of domestic debt made firms very sensitive to a sharp rise in interest rates (Goyal and Dash, 1998).

Hong Kong had a very strong fixed exchange rate – a currency board, but it survived the crisis because of pragmatic fiscal policy that had built up countercyclical surpluses, and because of flexible real wages that could bring about the required adjustment in relative prices even without flexible exchange rates.

International institutions played a very negative role in the crisis. The IMF advised fiscal and monetary tightening in an unthinking generalisation from first-generation currency crisis. There was no appreciation of the sensitivity of highly leveraged societies to sharp rise in interest rates and to sharp depreciation if there was UFB. Moreover, finances of Asian governments were generally healthy compared to the unsustainable fiscal deficits that drove first-generation crises. There was scope for belt loosening instead of the belt tightening as advised. It advised a fiscal contraction for South Korea, but reversed it in one month – on a belated realisation that contraction is not effective unless there is a fiscal problem to start with.

Precrisis advice for monetary conservatism, together with financial liberalisation, in the context of limited exchange rate flexibility, set up the interest differentials that induced large foreign borrowing. Monetary policy was procyclical when countercyclical was required. The problem in designing a crisis response was that depreciation hurt the balance sheets of firms that held large foreign debt, but a rise in interest rates hurt those that held large domestic debt.

Even as the countries suffered, funds did not come from the IMF or came with large delays and inappropriate conditionality. Given its governance structure, the IMF was more attuned to financial interests rather than to providing a global public good by stabilising the global system. Democracy and transparency was lacking in its own working.[2]

Funds had been made available much faster in Latin American crises, perhaps because of the proximity of those countries to the United States and greater impact on US financial interests. The independent evaluation office set up for the IMF corroborated this assessment (IEO IMF, 2011).

Even so, most countries had recovered by 1998, except Indonesia where political unrest made a bad situation worse. Depreciation encouraged exports. But the V-shaped recovery suggests that fundamentals had been and continued to be strong, otherwise recovery could not have been so rapid. As in first-generation crises, the problems again stemmed from overborrowing, but now it was private borrowing rather than government debt. External shocks were aggravated through capital outflows and incorrect policy response.

There had been a lot of hype about Asian growth preceding the East Asian crisis. The World Bank had produced a book titled *The Asian Growth Miracle*. These countries had high savings and investment, education, good infrastructure and fiscal health. Therefore, with openness on the capital account, capital rushed in without proper evaluation.

But there were weaknesses such as inappropriate macroeconomic policy, poor bank regulation and legal framework. Krugman had been a lone voice casting doubt on the quality of Asian growth. He found growth to be driven by high investment with low productivity growth (Krugman, 1994). He noted the problems found in developing countries generally: government controls, fixed exchange rates, weak financial sector, laws, corruption and dominance of commodity exports (Krugman et al., 2014). But growth revived despite these issues suggesting the cause of the crises did not lie in domestic weaknesses.

Despite weaknesses, this crisis was not like the first- or second-generation crises. Asian countries had strong macroeconomic fundamentals: low budget deficits, low public debt, single digit inflation, high economic growth, high savings and investment ratios. There was large foreign currency denominated unhedged private foreign debt. Sharp currency devaluation increased the domestic currency value of the debt, implying further pressure for banks and firms, which suffered severe balance sheet effects as their asset values deteriorated. The rush to cover unhedged loans by buying future dollars put further pressure on the currency. These cumulative effects accounted for bankruptcies and large price and output declines. The implicit financial warranties implied large unfunded public liabilities, which emerged with the crisis. Financial crises, in turn, led to currency crises. Underlying causes were domestic financial fragility and problems in the international financial architecture.

312 *Currency crises*

13.5 Third-generation crisis: analysis

Third-generation models, therefore, needed to explain how financial imperfections could result in multiple interacting crises. Diamond and Dybig (1983) had an early model of such multiple equilibria where domestic bank runs occur if depositors lose confidence and seek to withdraw funds. In such circumstances, even a solvent well-run bank will exhaust cash reserves. Since most bank investments are illiquid, an attempt to liquidate them prematurely will diminish their value. Even strong banks, therefore, fail if a bank run (BR) occurs. Moreover, the failure of one bank can cause runs on others because of direct and indirect interdependencies among banks. Most governments provide deposit insurance as well as a lender of last resort (LOLR) facility to prevent such crashes. The first mitigates fear-driven bank runs and multiple equilibria and the second mitigates illiquidity.

Chang and Velasco (2000) apply the above model to a small open EM, to show the possibility of international BRs caused by illiquidity and banks vulnerability. With unrestricted capital markets, domestic banks are free to accept deposits from both domestic and foreign residents in both currencies. Then, any financial institution that issues short-term liabilities that can be converted into foreign currency can play a role in a currency crisis. If bank depositors seek to exchange their claims on the banks into foreign currency, but the bank liabilities are used primarily to fund long-term illiquid investments, an international BR can be the result. With a large amount of highly volatile short-term liabilities, such as interbank loans from foreign banks, rapid loss of reserves and extreme strain on exchange rates can occur.

13.5.1 *A stylised model*

Consider a SOE with a single perishable freely traded consumption good. Its price p^* is normalised at US\$ 1. Such a numeraire is equivalent to dollarisation of the economy. There are three periods – a planning period (0), a short run (1) and a long run (2).

There is a continuum of (measure unity) ex-ante identical individuals (depositors). Each is endowed with $a \geq 0$ at $t = 0$. Each maximises period 2 consumption. Each can lend infinite amounts, but can borrow only $f > 0$ at $r^* = 0$ from a continuum of identical risk-free foreign creditors (of measure unity).

Each can invest (lend) in a liquid asset b available in period 1 or in a long-term asset k maturing in period 2. There is a probability λ of a shock, which equals the proportion of the unlucky population. If it

Currency crises 313

occurs, an infusion $i < a + f$ will be required in period 1. The return in period 2 is Rk, $R(1 - \lambda) > 1$, but liquidation value of k at $t = 1$ is rk, $r \in [0,1)$. That is, the long-term asset is very profitable in the long run, but it is illiquid. There is, therefore, destruction of value if it is liquidated in the short run. The depositor's problem is to max period 2 consumption subject to the budget constraint $k + b \leq w$.

If the excess return from holding long-term assets to maturity exceeds the opportunity cost of holding liquid assets, it is optimal for b to be just sufficient to finance i. Since $R > 1$, there would be a loss if b exceeded i, so:

$$\tilde{b} = i$$

where ~ denotes autarky optimal values. It follows that:

$$\tilde{k} = w - i$$

and

$$\tilde{c} = R\ (w - i) + (1 - \lambda)\ i - f \tag{13.14}^3$$

This is the optimising tuple under autarky. Clearly, consumers could do better, if only the unlucky could hold the liquid asset to finance i and others could invest in the long-term asset.

Banks make this possible through the law of large numbers. They pool resources and maximise the consumption of the representative member. Their objective function is:

Max c
s.t
$k + b \leq w$
$i \leq c$ IC

An assumption is made that unlucky types cannot lie about their types, but the lucky can claim to be unlucky, obtain i from the bank and abscond. They cannot be caught, but once they get i they get no c. Therefore, c cannot be less than i to prevent such absconding. This adds the incentive compatibility (IC) constraint to the bank's maximisation. The optimal values are now denoted by a cap ^. The new optimising tuple ($\hat{b}, \hat{k}, \hat{c}$) turns out to be:

$$\hat{b} = \lambda i \tag{13.15}$$

314 Currency crises

Therefore, $\hat{k} = w - \lambda i$. The bank will hold only enough liquidity to shore up bad investments. It follows that:

$$\hat{c} = R(w - \lambda i) - f \tag{13.16}$$

Since $w = \hat{k} + \lambda i$,

$$\hat{c} > \tilde{c} = R(w - i) + (1 - \lambda)i - f \tag{13.17}$$

Since consumers now earn R on $w - \lambda i$ which exceeds $w - i$, so $\hat{c}$ raises c. Three kinds of assumptions underlie the results. First R is productive, second r is low and third the household opportunity cost of liquidity i is less than the loss due to early liquidation. Therefore, excess $(R - r)$ return from holding assets to maturity exceeds the opportunity cost of holding liquid assets (return foregone on i).[4] The CAD in this model is $k - a$. Since $\hat{k} > k$, the CAD increases under financial intermediation.

The optimal allocation $(\hat{c}, \hat{b}, \hat{k})$ is implemented through a demand deposit system, whereby depositors make their wealth available to banks, which then pay the depositors the return that finances consumption in period 2. Figure 13.3 shows the timeline and these transfers.

Two kinds of equilibria are possible. In an honest equilibrium by construction, the demand deposit system is feasible if depositors act honestly. The IC condition ensures that lying about shocks and absconding is not profitable for lucky depositors.

Since holding liquidity is costly, the bank may choose to become illiquid in the short run (period 1), that is, the international illiquidity condition (IIC) Equation 13.18 holds:

$$\hat{b} + r\hat{k} < i \tag{13.18}$$

The IIC implies the potential short-run obligations of the bank can exceed its liquidation value. IIC is necessary and sufficient for a BR to occur.

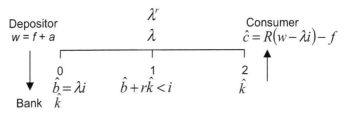

Figure 13.3 Timeline and equilibria

Currency crises 315

If IIC holds and depositors withdraw i, the bank is forced to liquidate all assets and close. Therefore, those who do not run will not be paid anything in period 2, so it is individually optimal for each of them to run on the bank. So, IIC ⇒ BR or IIC is sufficient for a BR to occur, that is $p \Rightarrow q$.

If $\hat{b} + r\hat{k} > i$, since the inequality holds for each depositor, so liquid resources exceed i for each depositor, even if all depositors withdraw. In a run equilibrium, the fraction of depositors reporting bad luck λ^r exceeds λ. Therefore, the bank liquidates $l = \dfrac{(\lambda^r - \lambda)i}{r}$ units of $\hat{k}$ in period 1 and has to pay $\hat{c}$ only to $1 - \lambda^r$ depositors in period 2. The bank is not forced to liquidate all assets. It will earn enough in period 2 to repay claims. Therefore, it is not individually optimal for depositors to participate in a run. So, $\sim$ IIC ⇒ $\sim$ BR. IIC is necessary for a BR to occur or BR ⇒ IIC, that is, $p \Leftarrow q$. If a BR occurs, it implies that IIC must have held.

Substituting $\hat{b} = \lambda i$ and $\hat{k} = w - \lambda i$ in the IIC condition gives:

$$r \leq \frac{[1 - \lambda(1 - r)]i}{w} \tag{13.19}$$

Bankruptcy occurs if r is low, that is, liquidation of long-term assets is costly. Therefore, self-fulfilling BRs are possible because the social optimum may imply international illiquidity. If so, runs are self-fulfilling precisely since they lead to insolvency. Costly liquidation turns an illiquid bank into an insolvent one.

Banks provide a service, allowing a rise in consumption compared to autarky, but they increase risk. Narrow banking where $b = i$ removes the risk of a crisis, but lowers consumption levels.

Third-generation crises are more closely integrated with the financial sector, compared to first- and second-generation models. Illiquid banks can suffer asset destruction and become de facto insolvent. Policy choices play a critical role. The basic model can be used to analyse a number of such choices. We briefly outline some of these issues before focussing on choice of exchange rate regimes.

Short-term debt was responsible for much of the aggravation in the East Asian crisis. Allowing depositors a choice between short- (d_s) and long-term (d_l) debt makes the term structure endogenous in the model. Since $r_s < r_l$, short-term debt is incurred because it is cheaper. There are many banks and each taking r_s as given and maximising gives $d_s = f \neq$ 0. All foreign borrowing can be short-term $f = d_s$. Each bank does not take account of the rise in country risk rating resulting from its higher

316   *Currency crises*

borrowing. But if depositors are risk averse, d_s should equal 0. Therefore, $d_s > 0$ is a market failure. Private and social incentives do not coincide. Therefore, controls or a tax on short-term debt is required to keep it low.

For crisis prevention, lengthening the maturity of debt through controls or taxes on short-term capital flows becomes necessary. But there is domestic short-term debt also, and it could serve a positive purpose, for example, as a commitment device, forcing banks to ensure access to liquidity. So, it cannot be eliminated.

For crisis management under short-term debt and coordination failure among lenders, bail-in, statutory debt reduction mechanism, collective action clauses, banks selling assets to FDI rather than liquidating, debt equity swaps and lending into arrears by international agencies can all help. The key to both successful debt management and future prevention is creditors must take a cut. They will then lend more responsibly in the future.

Bank regulation is important because banks maturity transformation increases welfare, but carries risks. Free entry and competition lowers franchise value, since it forces payment of higher deposit rates, increases short-term liabilities, and therefore risk of illiquidity. Since financial liberalisation increases competition margins are squeezed, $r\hat{k} + \hat{b} < i$ becomes more likely and bank vulnerability to runs rises. Deposit insurance is limited, so it cannot cover systematic risk.

Real exchange rate effects: As just liquidation of assets cannot cause a widespread crisis, the interaction with macroeconomic weaknesses is important. Changes in the real exchange rate have a major role. A steep depreciation occurs during a currency crisis. If non-traded goods producers have to pay loans in foreign currency – maybe intermediated through banks, as banks lend to them in domestic currency but then borrow in foreign – with real exchange rate depreciation, prices of traded goods rise relative to non-traded. Non-traded goods firms are bankrupted and unable to repay loans.

Policy should encourage foreign lenders to lend in domestic currency, thus sharing some of the exchange risk with local borrowers. During crises times, special credit lines should be made available to firms.

Government deficits lay at the heart of first-generation crisis models. But Asian governments did not run fiscal deficits making those models irrelevant. Even so, government's short-term debts decreased the overall liquidity position of the country's financial system. For example, the Mexican government's short-term *Tesobono* debt was a major cause of its 1995 crisis. Therefore, in measuring a country's

Currency crises 317

liquidity, account has to be taken of its government's short-term debts.

Since assets are destroyed with early liquidation in a run equilibrium, it is important not to impose fiscal austerity as conditionality in such a crisis.

Application to exchange rate regimes: To analyse the appropriate exchange rate policy, using the model, it is necessary to introduce domestic currency, foreign money and macroeconomic effects. We examine how successful the demand deposit system is in implementing the social optimum in different exchange rate regimes.

1   Dollarisation: If p^* normalised at one, the dollar price equals the domestic price. It is equivalent to a fully dollarised economy. The above analysis applies, and both the honest and run equilibria hold. Thus, a BR can occur in a dollarised economy.

2   Currency board: For all other exchange rate regimes, it is necessary to introduce the local currency (rupees) issued by the CB, Reserve Bank of India, (RBI). To introduce a demand for rupees, we assume a legal restriction such that domestic banks have to pay its depositors in rupees. Depositors need dollars to buy consumption goods in world market. This gives the dollar demand. They borrow f abroad in dollars. This gives the dollar supply.

Under a currency board, the rupee is fixed to the dollar. The RBI buys or sells rupees at dollar 1 (the exchange rate is assumed to be 1). Since it cannot print money, it can only give as many rupees as it has dollars.

Under a run equilibrium at period 1, or at the honest equilibrium at period 2:

a   Depositors withdraw rupees from banks in random order.
b   They join a second line at the RBI to buy dollars.
c   Commercial banks service withdrawals by liquidating foreign assets and selling the revenue received in dollars to RBI for rupees.

Figure 13.5 shows the swap of rupees for dollars. There cannot be a BOP crisis, given the timing of events. The RBI cannot run out of dollars since unless depositors get rupees i from commercial banks, they cannot buy i dollars from RBI, and the RBI would be holding the equivalent dollars it had earlier bought from the banks. But there can be a banking crisis, if the commercial bank liquidates all its assets in period 1; yet, there are still depositors in line, the bank becomes

318 Currency crises

bankrupt. If the commercial bank closes and does not pay i rupees, depositors cannot demand i dollars from RBI – there is no BOP crisis. The case brings out the close link between excess credit creation and currency crises.

So, a currency board is not a panacea. It does not prevent a banking crisis. A system that ties RBI's hands prevents it from printing money and also prevents it from rescuing banks in trouble. Since there is no domestic LOLR, a banking crisis can occur.

3   A fixed exchange rate: If the exchange rate is fixed, the RBI is able to print domestic currency, so it is able to function as a LOLR. If a run occurs, it gives a credit line to the commercial bank in return for the right to the remaining bank assets.

   a   As depositors withdraw i in random order from the commercial bank, it liquidates $\hat{b}$, then borrows from the RBI.
   b   Depositors sell rupees to (buy dollars from) the RBI.
   c   RBI sells dollars first with the dollars bought from the commercial bank, then by liquidation of the banks' long-term assets. It rises $r\hat{k}$ to maintain dollar sales.
   d   It runs out of assets, if $\hat{b} + r\hat{k} < i$. It shuts its window and there is a BOP crisis.

Since the exchange rate is fixed, if the RBI runs out of dollars it must shut its window or float the currency. It can print rupees but cannot print dollars. Loss of monetary independence implies a currency crisis can exist, since a fixed exchange rate ties the money supply, as in first-generation models.

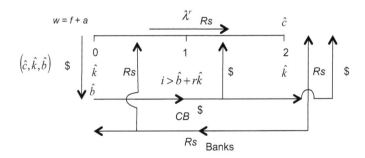

Figure 13.4 Rupee and the dollar flows

Thus, in this case, banks can be saved under a run equilibrium, but only through a currency crisis. The latter does not depend on the LOLR function but only on the IIC.

4 Flexible exchange rates: Now, there is an LOLR function and S is flexible. So, the demand and supply of dollars can be equated by auction of RBI reserves. There is no line at the RBI. If there is a run, the demand for dollars (supply of rupees) from depositors is $\lambda^r i$. The supply of dollars at the auction is λi. These are the dollars the RBI had previously bought from commercial banks. To convert the dollar supply into rupees, it has to be multiplied by the exchange rate S (rupees/dollar). Then, demand of rupees must equal supply or $\lambda^r i = S\lambda i$. So:

$$S = \lambda^r/\lambda$$

If $\lambda^r > \lambda$, S depreciates, so $S > 1$. The rupee loses value if more depositors are withdrawing i at period 1. But now, a run cannot occur since the lucky depositors withdrawing i will be able to consume only $i/S < i$. Since there is no early liquidation here $\left(r\hat{k} = 0\right)$, the bank will be able to pay $\hat{c}$ to each $1 - \lambda^r$ that does not run. Therefore, it is not optimal for lucky depositors to participate in a run. Only the honest equilibrium holds and $S = 1$. Figure 13.5 shows the demand and supply of dollars converted into rupees.

That is, flexible exchange rates implement the optimal equilibrium uniquely, with complementary LOLR or accommodative monetary policy. It will not work for a sudden depreciation after a fixed exchange rate, only for a floating regime. The latter will prevent inefficient liquidation of long-term assets. It is necessary that depositors be

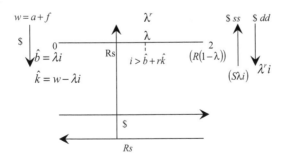

Figure 13.5 Equating dollar demand and supply with a flexible exchange rate

320 Currency crises

paid in rupees, since if they are paid in dollars nominal exchange rate cannot affect the real value of dollar demand. Therefore, dollarisation should be discouraged. Flexible exchange rates cannot deal with the panics of foreign creditors, since foreign loans are denominated in foreign currency.

13.6 Policy lessons

We survey some relevant literature in order to finally draw out policy prescriptions and lessons following the crises. Aghion et al. (2000) show how one type of crisis leads to another. They point out that many developing countries borrow abroad in dollars but produce for the domestic market. In their simple model with fixed prices and deviations from PPP, the rapid adjustment and overshooting of the nominal exchange rate hurts debtors. Bankrupt debtors can lead to failing bank assets and a run on the banking system. Credit supply falls and with it output, implying a reduction in money demand and further currency depreciation as net money supply rises. Self-fulfilling expectations of a banking cum currency crisis set in. Appropriate and balanced monetary policy is required before and during a crisis.

Calvo, in a series of papers with a number of co-authors, christened a sustained reversal of capital inflows a sudden stop (see Calvo, 2005). He shows that excessive volatility of capital flows, unrelated to fundamentals, is a special problem for emerging markets. The V shape of the typical EM crisis, the quick recovery after a steep plunge, implies fundamentals could not have caused the crisis – otherwise, recovery could not have been so rapid. Typically, during such an episode, spreads on debts rise even for EMs not undergoing a crisis. Indices, such as the Morgan Stanley emerging market bond index, show a sharp widening, implying the problem originates with creditors and their perceptions, not with the EMs.

He argues that as EM firms' productivity or its perception becomes more volatile, the returns to acquiring information rise. This increases price volatility, which causes further problems if firms are highly leveraged. He posits a production function f where productivity θ enters multiplicatively. Quasi rents $(w = f(k,\theta) - rk)$ are conditional on information i and the cost of collecting information is $N(i)$.

$$\left[f(k,\theta) - rk\right]/i - N(i)$$

$$f(k,\theta) = \theta k - \frac{1}{2}k^2 \tag{13.20}$$

Currency crises 321

In the no information case, the distribution of θ is known, so the maximisation is done with the mean value $\bar{\theta}$. Under full information, the realisation of θ, Eθ is known.

Quasi rents are higher with Eθ compared to $\bar{\theta}$, if θ is more volatile. Therefore, the returns to collecting more information rise with the volatility of productivity. It follows that relative price volatility is higher under full information. Analysis of sudden stops leads to a number of policy implications:

Domestic: The exposure to foreign currency denominated debt needs to be reduced, in particular the dollarisation of domestic liabilities, for example, banks borrowing abroad to finance long-term domestic loans. The problem is worse if short-term debt is used to finance long-term assets. One policy option is a tax on FX-based borrowing. Exchange rate fluctuations can encourage hedging, but excessive fluctuations can harm exports. Tight monetary policy can send the wrong signal to markets that the government is worrying about a possible mismatch, expansionary macroeconomic policy is better if the government itself is not subject to a sudden stop. Falling interest rates are possible under flexible exchange rates if inflationary expectations are not high.

Global: First, a global emerging market fund (EMF) can help stabilise EM bond prices or spread index. Markets tend to underprovide information since it has a cost and benefits others (it creates an externality) – some EMs and firms are sound, but the spread widens for all; the information provided by EMF support would be credible (unlike that provided by the alternative, a global information agency), since it would be backed with money. Second, underlending to EMs may occur during a crisis because of a failure of the international LOLR, which turns illiquidity into insolvency – the solution would be to improve that function of the IMF. But overlending to EMs may occur before a crisis because of assured bailouts and inadequate bail-in of creditors. Therefore, the latter needs to be strengthened. These reforms would help reduce procyclicality of markets.

Caballero and Krishnamurthy (2004) analyse the deeper structural problems that cause overborrowing abroad. Domestic firms underinsure reversals of capital inflow. This is partly due to domestic financial market imperfections. For example, they cannot sell insurance to those who need it. Bond issuance (domestic capital market deepening) would allow firms needing external resources to share their revenues with those with access to foreign funds. Therefore, while the IFS needs to improve, so do domestic financial markets. In the meantime, these imperfections justify common interventionist policies such as

322 *Currency crises*

holding international reserves, managing exchange rates, taxing capital inflows, imposing liquidity requirements and sterilising inflows to expand money supply under some conditions.

The overall recommendations are a relaxed monetary stance when a currency crisis is threatened to ease pressure on banks, to avoid a credit crunch and a fall in output. Liquidity risk should be reduced. Over the longer term, the aim should be to lower the probability of currency crises through systematic crisis proofing.

The large literature the East Asian crisis generated, some of which has been sampled above, tended to have sharply varying views of the causes of the crises and a differing emphasis for policy. Goyal (2002) classified these into the creditor and the debtor view. Roubini was an advocate of the first view, while prominent adherents of the second included Stiglitz and Sachs.

In the creditor view, the crises were due to fundamental causes. In this view, the weaknesses lay with the countries and their governments, as in the first-generation crisis, but for different reasons. Domestic financial weaknesses, including implicit and explicit government guarantees, led to debtor moral hazard and created asset price bubbles. Overborrowing abroad resulted in an accumulation of short-term unhedged liabilities. Tirole (2002) analysed the fundamental market failure to be sovereign risk, since governments cannot credibly commit not to follow policies that can harm creditor interests. In contract theory, it is well understood that unless the investor has residual rights he might underinvest. In international finance, many creditors have to contract with a single government. This multiple-agency causes an externality, since each creditor does not take into account the effect of his actions on others. These issues suggest that institutional arrangements have to be put into place to reassure creditors that they will recover their investments. The solution Tirole favoured is representation. The IMF must function as a delegated monitor and represent creditor interests. It is ironic, however, doing exactly that created and worsened the East Asian crises.

Real fundamental market failures could, therefore, be very different from the one Tirole identified. First, information failures limit capital market access for EMs. Second, global inequality in wealth and power prevents the adoption of balanced reform that would make global markets safer. And the solution, following from the representation principle, is also exactly the opposite: more democratisation of the IMF and a larger say for poorer countries.

The debtor view points towards multiple equilibria as in the second-generation crisis, and the possibility of self-fulfilling panics or bank

Currency crises 323

runs. A run can occur on solvent but illiquid banks and make them insolvent. Therefore, assessing financial health after a run is misleading. Failures in the IFS were an even more serious crisis cause, especially for EMs. Creditor or (reverse) moral hazard due to expected IMF bailouts could cause overlending before a crisis, and the failure of the international LOLR could cause underlending during a crisis. A reversal of capital inflows or drying up of foreign credit for an EM can occur independently of its fundamentals, due to safe haven effects in times of global financial fragility (known as risk-off periods). Contagion can affect EMs with sound fundamentals due to herd behaviour, portfolio rebalancing after a crises or competitive devaluation and trade links between countries. X withdraws because she sees Y withdraw, or margin calls activated in one market force liquidation in other markets. Exit is normally easier in more liquid markets. The debtor perspective suggests the fault lies with the IFS.

Some country weakness is necessary for a crisis, but the first view puts too much emphasis on this alone. The second view needs to establish why a particular equilibrium is selected or why there is a jump from one equilibrium to the other.

But both indict a fixed exchange rate and tight money when there is high debt.

The creditor view emphasised acceptance and implementation of international standards of good practice in financial sectors and in macroeconomic policy. It wanted transparency, legal and regulatory reform, a focussed LOLR and ex-post conditionality. The list from the debtor viewpoint included a managed exchange rate and market-based capital controls to deal with massive capital inflows for countries with liberalised capital accounts, strengthening prudential regulation and supervision of financial institutions and crises proofing domestic capital markets. Among measures to effectively manage a sudden reversal of capital flows was 'bailing in' the private sector to ensure that private creditors are involved in the resolution of crises, options such as debt-equity swaps or standstills, collective representation of creditors and majority action to alter contracted payment terms to allow quick, orderly debt restructuring and prevent a hold-up by a minority. Suggestions to improve crisis-time liquidity included special borrowing facilities, such as contingency credit lines in times of crises, complemented by regional financial arrangements with effective surveillance and conditionality. A careful sequencing of reform, and precautionary building up of reserves, was the lesson for countries with relatively closed capital accounts.[5]

Simple game theoretic examples of strategic interaction show how debt restructuring or standstills work. Holders of private or sovereign

324   *Currency crises*

country debt face a Prisoner's Dilemma if a country becomes illiquid, even though it is solvent. Each has to choose one of two possible strategies. She can either roll over the debt or ask for repayment – that is, grab whatever assets are available. If all creditors roll over, they maximise total welfare. If any one of the creditors is able to grab assets, she does the best for herself and the others are left with nothing. They will, therefore, try to grab assets. The EM firm is forced into premature liquidation or the country forced to devalue, assets fall in value and both the creditors are worse off. Bankruptcy procedures that give equal treatment to creditors of the same seniority can make holding on the unique Nash equilibria since the first to grab no longer gains. Therefore, both would play rollover.

But in the presence of short-term debt, those who agree to roll it over would lose out compared to those who refuse, as liquid assets are equally divided on bankruptcy. Then, instead of a Prisoner's Dilemma with a unique equilibrium, we have a coordination game with two Nash equilibria, since the payoffs are now different for the asymmetric strategies. Inefficient equilibria where both creditors grab, the country goes bankrupt and all are worse off can still occur. In such a case, a standstill, which gives protection against creditors, is required.

Consider the following example from Miller and Zhang (2000) showing the effects of the IMF's choice between bailing out or imposing a standstill. Figure 13.6 depicts the actions, equilibria and payoffs. The first number is the payoff to a creditor, the second to the debtor – that is, the country. Note that the payoffs are to the country, but the IMF takes the action. The face value of the debt is 10 units and the payoffs to the creditor are the fraction of the face value received. The payoffs to the country consist of earnings from the loan taken. Considering the first two columns of payoffs, the actions available to a creditor are to *roll over* the debt or to *grab* assets; the IMF either can *do nothing* or can make emergency funds available under a *bail out*. As the arrows show, there are two *Nash equilibria*, the first where there is debt *rollover* and the IMF does not have to take any action, and the second if there is

		IMF/Debtor		
		No action	Bailout	Standstill
	Rollover	(8,5)	(8,5)	
Creditor		↑	↓	
	Grab	(4,0)	(10,3)	(6,7)

Figure 13.6 Sovereign debt, bailouts and standstills

Source: Adapted from Goyal (2002).

grab and *bailout*. But if the creditor has first mover advantage, there is a unique *Subgame Perfect Nash Equilibrium* (10,3).

If a creditor moves first to *grab*, the IMF is forced to *bail out*, because the outcome with no action (4,0) damages both the creditor and the country too much. To undertake *no action* is not credible for the IMF, and therefore a creditor will always *grab* whenever the debtor is unable to service debt, though it may still be solvent. But if the third column is brought in or rules of the game are changed so that if creditors *grab* the IMF can impose a *standstill*, then creditors will prefer to *rollover* the debt. Since they are forced to accept a debt reduction under a standstill, creditors' payoff is relatively higher under a rollover. Now, the unique Nash equilibrium is (8, 5), with the creditor *rolling over* the debt and the IMF *doing nothing*. As the country has basically sound fundamentals, the lengthening of debt service under the rollover will give it time to recover. Both the country and its creditors are, therefore, better off.

Domestic bankruptcy laws in the United States have a provision for standstills. Even though bankruptcy laws lower the legal rights of individual creditors, they serve to help them because intercreditor conflict poses the greatest risk to asset values. Therefore, if reforms that bail-in creditors are adopted, the herd behaviour that brings on self-fulfilling crises would be discouraged. Otherwise, since protection from crises can never be complete, there will be a loss of profit-making opportunities for capital and a lower inflow to EMs. Even with bailout packages and other protective devices, all parties involved in a crisis make large losses. Moreover, if a standstill kicks in before a critical mass of creditors start leaving, they will not be able to escape by leaving first, and therefore their incentives to leave will fall, not rise. Such reforms will also not raise the cost of borrowing for EMs or make it more difficult for them to get loans, since combined with better monitoring and debtor selection they will lower the probability of default. Conversely, with *bailouts*, the near complete guarantee for creditors will encourage them to push loans without proper investigation or monitoring. Hence, the probability of default will rise.

Ex-post conditionality implies that cost of borrowing will rise only for countries with a poor record or prospects. Although creditors have not always in the past distinguished between EMs following good or unsustainable policies, this should change when they have to bear some penalty for not doing so. Incentives will improve both for recipients to follow good policies and for creditors to do more careful selection and monitoring.

326   Currency crises

Out of this large set of reform suggestions, the only reform implemented was a dilution of the collective action clause in international debt contracts, so as to prevent hold-up of restructuring by a minority of creditors. Tirole (2002) remarked that there are so many solutions, such as bail-in, standstill, which impose minimal costs. If they are not applied, it must be for deeper political reasons such as inequalities in global power.

The failure of reform contributed to the current reserve imbalances. In the absence of meaningful reforms, EMs were forced to go in for self-insurance through reserve accumulation and mutual aid through swap arrangements such as the Chang Mai initiative. Regional arrangements can eventually reduce the asymmetries in global power.

Gourinchas and Obstfeld (2012) construct a multicountry panel over 1973–2010 to study three types of crises: currency, banking and government debt default (Table 13.2). They find banking crises to lead other types of crises. Domestic credit expansion and real currency appreciation are predictors of crises for all countries; for EMs, high FX reserves sharply reduce the probability of subsequent crises.

The incidence of crises is much higher in EMs – they do need to improve institutions (Table 13.2)[6] – but it is clear they find much less support from markets and the IFS. For example, AE governments do not default because markets are willing to hold much higher levels of AE debt. The GFC points to problems in financial markets and the IFS, supporting the debtor view. The authors note that the EMs were 'remarkably resilient' in the GFC. This was partly because EMs showed more humility and reformed after the East Asian crises. But the many reform suggestions for financial markets were not implemented, leading on to the GFC. EMs also accumulated large FX precautionary reserves to compensate for failures in the IFS.

Table 13.2 Crises in advanced and emerging economies, 1970–2006

	Currency	Banking	Sovereign default
Advanced	43	5	0
Emerging	84	57	74
Total	127	62	74

Source: Adapted from Gourinchas and Obstfeld (2012).

13.7 Summary

This chapter explores the evolution of crises models in line with real-world currency crises in EMs. While Latin American crises of the 1980s were due to unsustainable macroeconomic policies, the 1990s currency attacks in Europe were due to coordinated attacks by traders under intermediate fundamentals. The East Asian crisis, however, where currency and financial crises interacted, pointed towards weaknesses in the IFS and the financial sector. Some financial weaknesses were specific to EMs, but others were more general.

Despite the damage they had suffered in the crisis, Asian countries were keen to participate fully in globalisation, which they regarded as inevitable and beneficial. It had given them rapid gains in growth. Therefore, they were willing to do whatever was necessary – adopt the best standards in transparency and in legal and regulatory reform. But they wanted more transparency for creditors also. In view of the GFC originating later in AEs, the paragraph below is prophetic:

> Recipient countries, however, would like similar requirements imposed on hedge funds, and stricter surveillance not only for emerging markets, but also for developed countries and offshore financial centers. Large investors should make their movements public. Korean President Kim Dae-jung (2000) proposed that a hedge fund monitoring channel be established at an appropriate multilateral institution, since ready exchange of information on the investment activities of highly leveraged financial institutions (including investment banks) would contribute to the stability of international financial markets. Scrutiny and surveillance were not adequate because regulatory structures lagged behind the increasing sophistication of financial instruments.
>
> (Goyal, 2002, pp. 184–212)

Many of these issues came up in the GFC.

Following such advice could have considerably moderated the GFC and reduced impact on AEs and costs the entire world has been forced to share. The reforms, including replacing external debt with risk-sharing equity, self-insurance and regional initiatives EMs followed did reduce the impact of the GFC on them.

328 Currency crises

Notes

1 The facts are drawn, among others, from Agenor and Montiel (1999), Chapter 16, Goyal and Dash (1998), Corden (2002) and Krugman et al. (2014); Roubini comments on Chang and Velasco (2000).
2 A telling picture from those times was of Camdessus, the then IMF managing director, towering over a shrinking Indonesian prime minister. The IMF's response to the United States was very different. Prior to the GFC, there was no action on US double deficits and proliferation of financial risks; after the GFC, it supported macroeconomic stimulus. The then MD, Strauss-Kahn, defended these actions saying one shoe cannot fit all countries. A major unstated reason for differential action was of course the US voting power in the IMF.
3 This follows since for the lucky $(1 - \lambda)$, $c = R\tilde{k} + \tilde{b} - f$ and for unlucky the λ, $c = R\tilde{k} - f$.
4 If $b = 0$, then $c = \left[(1 - \lambda)R + \lambda r\right]w - f$ since only the lucky earns R on w, the rest would earn r, the liquidation value.
5 More details are available in (Goyal, 2002), which this account follows.
6 To date EM currency crises, the authors use the Frankel and Rose (1996) criterion – a 25 per cent or greater nominal currency depreciation over a year that is also a 10 percentage point increase in the annual rate of depreciation. A more lax criterion is used to date AE currency crises, since their floats are assumed to be able to absorb greater volatility.

References

Agenor, P. R. and P. J. Montiel. 1999. *Development Macroeconomics*, 2nd edition, Princeton, NJ: Princeton University Press.

Aghion, P., P. Bacchetta and A. Banerjee, 2000, 'A Simple Model of Monetary Policy and Currency Crises', *European Economic Review*, 44: 728–738.

Caballero, R. and A. Krishnamurthy. 2004. 'Smoothing Sudden Stops', *Journal of Economic Theory*, 119(1): 104–127, November. Working paper version. Available at www.nber.org/papers/w8427.

Calvo, G. 2005. 'Crises in Emerging Market Economies: A Global Perspective'. Available at www.nber.org/papers/w11305.pdf.

Chang, R. and A. Velasco. 2000. 'Liquidity Crises in Emerging Markets: Theory and Policy', in Ben Bernanke and Julio Rotemberg (eds.), *NBER Macroeconomics Annual 1999*. Cambridge: The MIT Press, also *NBER Working Paper No. 7272*, July 1999, pp. 11–78.

Diamond, D. W. and P. H. Dybvig. 1983. 'Bank Runs, Deposit Insurance, and Liquidity', *Journal of Political Economy*, 91(3): 401–419.

Frankel, J. A. and A. K. Rose. 1996. 'Currency Crashes in Emerging Markets: An Empirical Treatment', *Journal of International Economics*, 41: 351–366.

Gourinchas, P. O. and M. Obstfeld. 2012. 'Stories of the Twentieth Century for the Twenty-First', *American Economic Journal: Macroeconomics*, 4(1): 226–265.

Currency crises 329

Goyal, A. 2002. 'Reform Proposals from Developing Asia: Finding a Win-Win Strategy', Chapter 7 in Leslie Elliott Armijo (ed.), *Debating the Global Financial Architecture*, SUNY Press Global Politics series, under the general editorship of James Rosenau, pp. 184–213. New York: SUNY Press.

Goyal, A. and S. Dash. 1998. 'Arbitrage: An Explanation for South-East Asian Crisis and Indian Immunity', *Economic and Political Weekly*, 33(31): 2098–2104, August 1.

IEO IMF (Independent Evaluation Office of the International Monetary Fund). 2011. 'IMF Performance in the Run-Up to the Financial and Economic Crisis: IMF Surveillance in 2004–07'. Available at www.ieo-imf.org/ieo/pages/CompletedEvaluation107.aspx (accessed on 2 September 2012).

Kim, Dae Jung. 2000. *Opening Address to the APEC Forum on Shared Prosperity and Harmony at the Onset of the New Millenium*, Hilton Hotel, Seoul, Ministry of Foreign Affairs, Republic of Korea, April 1.

Krugman, P. 1979. 'A Model of Balance of Payments Crises', *Journal of Money, Credit and Banking*, 11: 311–325.

Krugman, P. 1994. 'The Myth of Asia's Miracle', *Foreign Affairs*, 73(6): 62, November–December.

Krugman, P. R., M. Obstfeld and M. Melitz. 2014. *International Economics: Theory and Policy*, 10th edition, Delhi: Pearson Education.

Miller, M. and L. Zhang. 2000. 'Sovereign Liquidity Crises: The Strategic Case for a Payments Standstill', *Economic Journal*, 110: 335–362, January.

Morris, S. and H. S. Shin. 1998. 'Unique Equilibrium in a Model of Self-Fulfilling Currency Attacks', *American Economic Review*, 88(3): 587–797.

Obstfeld, M. 1996. 'Models of Currency Crises with Self-Fulfilling Features', *European Economic Review*, 40: 1037–1047.

Tirole, J. 2002. *Financial Crises, Liquidity and the International Monetary System*, New Jersey: Princeton University Press.

14 The global financial crises and the international financial system

> Power tends to corrupt and absolute power corrupts absolutely.
> —Lord Acton

14.1 Introduction

The queen of England was reported to have asked why economists did not foresee the GFC. There were a few who had warned of financial risks building up. But a large number had regularly predicted a dollar crisis. Large US double deficits were sustained by EM CBs investing their reserves in US treasuries. There was fear of a crash in foreign demand for these. Therefore, despite obvious financial sector failures, a section of the literature saw global imbalances as the fundamental cause of the GFC. The reasoning seems to be since precrisis what was predicted was a dollar crisis it must have been underlying currency stresses that caused the GFC! This chapter carefully examines this argument in a discussion of the causes of the GFC, including endogenous creation of leverage that aggravates booms. A simple model presented shows how banking can become unstable in the presence of factors causing cycles.

The IFS is supposed to ensure smooth working of the international system, but has shown repeated failures. A brief history of the IFS and the evolution of underlying rules of the game and institutions is a necessary background to evaluate proposed financial reforms and changes in institutions.

The weaknesses of these financial reforms are then taken up and several other sources of global risks examined, including the Eurozone and the Euro debt problem, competitive currency depreciation and continuing imbalances.

The remainder of the chapter is structured as follows: Section 14.2 discusses the factors that led to the GFC. Section 14.3 gives a brief

Global financial crises 331

introduction to the IFS, Section 14.4 analyses financial reforms and Section 14.5 examines current risks, including the European Monetary Union and Euro debt, reserve imbalances, currency wars and incomplete reforms to the IFS, before Section 14.6 summarises and concludes.

14.2 The global financial crisis

The GFC followed a global boom that had raised leverage to unprecedented levels. The resulting rise in risk and financial fragility, especially in AEs such as the United States and Europe, was the immediate cause.

14.2.1 The origin

The pro-market era weakened financial regulation both in law and in practice. The belief that markets were self-regulating while regulators could damage innovation had reduced the intensity of supervision. Regulatory knowledge was limited and they tended to raise costs or prevent activity. Ideology and interests led to legal changes that created perverse incentives to take more risks. The US system is rule based, but lawmakers relaxed the rules and regulators relaxed oversight to encourage competitive innovation. The United States' comparative advantage was largely in finance, generating political support for finance-driven growth. The share of the financial sector in US business profits had crossed 40 per cent.

After the US Glass-Steagall Act that separated investment and commercial banks was repealed in 1999, commercial banks also were able to underwrite and trade instruments such as mortgage-backed securities and collateralised debt obligations through structured investment vehicles that escaped regulation. The Commodity Futures Modernisation Act passed in 2000 exempted credit default insurance from regulation by calling them swaps. Swap dealers were granted exemptions from speculative position limits. The post-Enron 2002 Sarbanes Oxley Act allowed off-balance sheet activities so long as other entities held the risks and rewards, thus encouraging the 'originate and distribute' model of securitisation.

Amendment to the Community Reinvestment Act in the mid-1990s allowed securitisation of subprime mortgages to make home loans possible for low-income categories, since the Clinton administration wanted to expand home ownership. A laudable objective was driven to excess in the Bush era, where loans were pushed without documentation to parties with no collateral except rising housing prices.

332   *Global financial crises*

Tax breaks, such as deduction of mortgage interest payments from household taxable income, further encouraged leverage.

The US SEC was now the regulatory authority for securities and brokerage operations of investment banks. To escape threatened regulation in the EU, investment banks sought a bargain in 2004 that gave the SEC voluntary regulatory oversight over the parent holding companies, as well. In return, the SEC allowed higher leverage, relaxing the net capital rule that restricted borrowing to 12 times capital and letting investment banks use their own models to determine risk. Therefore, capital adequacy requirements, such as the Fed had earlier imposed on deposit accepting banks, were now severely diluted. A securitised loan required less capital adequacy than a loan originated and held in banks. There were no auditing requirements, so transparency was poor. The SEC had been given a window on the banks risky investments but never used it.

A consequence of light regulation was high leverage. Investment banks made money by borrowing short in the wholesale retail market, leveraging the borrowing many times and lending long. Leverage allowed by derivatives, multiplies this type of behaviour manifold. Large positions can be taken with little of own money at risk. Therefore, asset price bubbles can be created. These sustain for long before finally bursting when they depart too far from fundamentals. Moreover, this kind of strategy is extremely susceptible to a fall in asset values. Short-term funding, combined with high leverage, made institutions vulnerable to distress or 'fire' sales in the event of a rate rise. These destroy asset value.

The TBTF size of financial institutions meant they could effectively pass on risks to the taxpayer, who would be forced to rescue them for fear of spillovers. The structure of bonuses and other rewards encouraged excessive risk-taking, since payoffs in boom times were much higher than penalties in busts. No distinction was made between realised and unrealised profits, so that bonuses were earned on paper profits that would have collapsed if everyone tried to realise them. Rating agencies, paid by those they rated, had an incentive to soften ratings; those rated had an incentive to distort financial structures to earn high ratings. The ability to diversify risk through securitisation made banks less concerned with monitoring credit quality, and their specific knowledge on credit deteriorated. Since each entity felt it had passed on the risk, system-wide risk was neglected. This collective action failure aided bets on asset prices, despite so many experiences with asset price bubbles. Risk from interconnectedness and mushrooming growth or systemic risk was overlooked, although investors to whom

Global financial crises 333

the banks had sold subprime loans had, in turn, raised money from banks – so, the latter were still vulnerable.

Self-regulation based on the price of risk derived from models using market prices enhances procyclicality. Basel II allowed capital adequacy below 8 per cent through the use of internal risk models, based on market prices. Failed institutions were Basel II compliant, yet capital proved inadequate. Risk-sensitive models make the assumption of statistical independence, which does not hold. Since all players use similar models and market information, in the search for better risk-return trade-offs, volatility and correlation increases and prompts more model-driven selling. Modern mark to market accounting rules and dynamic hedging, designed for efficient markets, deepen these cycles. Incentives from features, such as bonuses and accounting rules, encouraged procyclical behaviour, as did no 'skin in the game' securitisation and market price-based risk models.

Opacity because of the chain of securities and structures financing subprime mortgages meant investors could not determine the location and extent of risk when housing prices began to fall. The lack of knowledge of where the risk lay led to worry about counterparties, a freeze in intra-bank markets and rippling crashes in the prices of structured products as banks were forced to sell them. This intensified after Lehman Brothers was allowed to fail. Valuation is difficult when markets collapse or are excessively volatile. In cycles of one-way buying or selling, the absence of diversity in risk assessments decreases liquidity.

Financial markets' useful contributions in price discovery, pricing of risk and enabling the laying off of risk were all compromised. It is necessary to create a diversity of views in markets as well as incentives to reduce procyclicality.

14.2.2 *Global imbalances and the search for yield*

Despite clear evidence of the overwhelming role played by lax regulation and excessive leverage, there is a view that blames the crisis on global imbalances and on low policy rates that forced advanced markets to take more risk.

Although US risk-free assets provided an insurance function to the rest of the world (Gourinchas and Rey, 2013), cross-border financial flows due to major saving-investment imbalances were thought to put stresses on financial intermediation that even sophisticated markets could not cope with (Portes, 2009). Caballero and Krishnamurthy (2009) argue that the large demand for safe US treasuries to park reserves in forced US financial institutions to leverage and increase

334 *Global financial crises*

their holdings of risky assets. Their argument is incomplete since they neglect the laxity in regulation, which allowed such leverage. As Blanchard and Milesi-Ferretti (2012) point out, regulation is expected to respond to excessive risk-taking.

Therefore, the alternative hypothesis to that of financial stretch to absorb excess savings is that an unregulated bubble developed. Moreover, the depth and capacity for expansion of US financial markets are the reason CBs buy dollar securities. US financial markets are so deep and liquid that their purchases do not disturb markets. There were no signs of stretch in US government securities markets themselves. They absorbed inflows many magnitudes higher than reserves, as funds returned to the United States after the Lehman Brothers crash. The huge volumes of post-crisis QE meant AE CBs became the biggest demanders of safe securities.

Numbers (Goyal, 2009) help to put these arguments in perspective. Notional amounts outstanding in derivatives grew from US\$ 100 trillion in 2002 to US\$ 516 trillion in April 2007 (BIS, 2008). Since 2000, the market for mortgage-backed securities exceeded that for US treasury notes and bonds. The 33 per cent compound annual rate of growth in derivatives occurred just over the period regulations were relaxed for investment banks. As a result, leverage shot up. When Lehman Brothers was allowed to fail, its leverage was 30:1 compared to 15:1 for a commercial bank.

Compared to this growth in derivatives and accompanying expansion in financial balance sheets, both the net ownership of US assets by foreigners and of reserves were trivial. The former grew by about US\$ 1.5 trillion in the period. Asian reserves were less than US\$ 3 trillion, while the US current account deficit grew from US\$ 200 to US\$ 700 billion. Such numbers should not disturb a well-regulated, deep and liquid financial system. Internally generated liquidity dwarfed any external source. US broad money supply growth averaged about US\$ 15 trillion, with an annual growth rate of about 6 per cent, nowhere near the growth in derivatives. Lax regulation gave financial markets large powers to endogenously create liquidity. After the 1980s, deposits were no longer the most volatile component of aggregate financial liabilities. Endogenous liquidity creation dominated.

14.2.3 *Asian oversaving*

Among other causes of the crisis, US monetary accommodation that kept short rates very low for extended periods is said to have encouraged excessive risk-taking. But in an attempt to again deflect

Global financial crises 335

responsibility to Asia, Bernanke (2005) argued the 'savings glut' was the reason long interest rates remained low, even after policy began raising short rates. Taylor (2009), however, pointed out the factual fallacy underlying the 'savings glut' argument. Since global savings were actually at a historical low in this period, high savings could not be responsible for low global interest rates. US dissaving overcompensated for Chinese savings invested in US treasuries.

Nor is it true that US savings fell because high Asian savings encouraged US deficits. Krugman (2009) argues Reagan-era legislation in the early 1980s started the decline in US savings. It removed New Deal restrictions on mortgage lending that required families to put a significant down payment for a home. Tax incentives and wealth effects from the real estate bubble, encouraged by the regulatory regime, accelerated the fall in savings.

Table 14.1 shows a steady fall in the US savings ratio from the peak level in 1984. The ratio and absolute level of savings had already fallen substantially before Chinese investment in US treasuries reached a critical mass. Until 2008, the Chinese investment was too low even to compensate for the large fall in US savings, let alone lower long-term interest rates. After peaking in July 2008, Chinese investment in US treasuries began to decline.

Low long rates probably reflected low inflation expectations and the underpricing of risk, rather than excess savings. Although after the GFC as high leverage reduced investment, savings may have been in excess.

Table 14.1 Chinese reserves and savings of US households

	US personal		Chinese (in billion US$)		Reserves	Investment in US treasuries
	Savings ratio		Savings (in billion US$)			
1984	11.2		1,259.2		17.4	
1994	5.3		997.8		52.9	
1999	2.5		634.2		157.7	54.6*
2003	2.4		699.5		408.2	135.8
2005	0.5		129.8		821	243.1
2008	1.8		770.6		1,946.7	767.9

Source: Calculated from Goyal (2010), US Department of Commerce, Bureau of Economic Analysis; IFS of the IMF; US department of the treasury.

Note: * gives the figure for M1 (January) 2000; in the column, other figures are for M1, except M6 for June in 2008.

336 *Global financial crises*

Moreover, the volatility of capital flows indicates they were investment not savings driven. Private foreign inflows to EMs fell in the period following the East Asian crisis, but more than doubled to an annual average of about US$ 200 billion over 2003–06. They peaked at US$ 617.5 billion in 2007 when the US policy interest rates, which had been held at 1 per cent over 2003–04, reached their peak of 5.25 per cent. So, it was not the interest differential or search for yield that drove flows to EMs as much as leverage in response to profit opportunities. There was procyclical expansion in US balance sheets. Finance-fuelled consumption booms and asset bubbles were responsible for the flows. CB investments are actually more stable compared to the private flows (Goyal, 2010). Bernanke later acknowledged (Bernanke et al., 2011) financial innovation-driven cross-border flows from Europe were exceptionally large in the post-2000 period. Asian CBs were not the only ones investing in the United States.

Interbank flows were the most volatile private capital flows to EMs, with the US and the UK banks dominating. Foreign bank branches borrow dollars from headquarters using their interoffice account or unsecured borrowing in the interbank market. Around 160 foreign banks raise about US$ 1 trillion of wholesale dollar funding in US capital markets to send US$ 600 billion to head office. These interoffice assets of foreign bank branches in the United States increased steeply since the 1990s. They dipped sharply in 2008, but rose again the next year (Shin and Shin, 2011).

In other economies, even if banking is mostly traditional, US liquidity creation affects balance sheets through foreign liabilities of the banking sector, and other types of dollar carry trade. The portfolio decisions of global banks that equalise returns across regions carry dollar liquidity across borders. The US dollar as the reserve currency is the funding currency for global banks. US monetary policy sustains cross-currency funding, because of these bank activities.

These spillovers, enhanced by successive rounds of unconventional QE, make US monetary policy the global monetary policy. Although the United States is the largest net debtor, it is a substantial net creditor for the global banking system. Its borrowing is long, as other central banks invest in treasury securities, but lending is short through commercial banks activities. Even for banks mainly funded by deposits, banks' liabilities to foreign creditors are not counted as money, but they expand balance sheets. Non-core liabilities, reflecting interconnections among banks, and FX borrowing of banks are special sources of cross-border risks. Shin (2011) argued for a tax on banks foreign and non-core liabilities, with a higher rate for short-term liabilities.[1]

Global financial crises 337

Thus, many features of the IFS create excess leverage, enhancing financial risks. Box 14.1 shows how some of these features make banks fragile.

Box 14.1 How banks can become fragile

Shleifer and Vishny (2010) show in a simple framework how banks' trading activity can make their balance sheets and project lending procyclical, enabling them to reflect and magnify market sentiment. There is an infinite supply of projects in period 1 and 2, requiring an investment of US\$ 1 and giving a payoff $Z > 1$ in period 3. All projects are financed through intermediaries (banks) that screen out $Z < 1$ projects. Entrepreneurs pay an upfront fee $f = \alpha (Z - 1)$, α lying between 0 and 1 implying banks and entrepreneurs share profits in excess of 1. Banks lend unity in period 1 and are paid back unity in period 3. They do not take deposits. Initial equity E_0 is invested in projects N_1 (long term) or kept in cash C in period 1, and invested in projects N_2 (short-term) in period 2, giving final equity E_t in period 3.

Project loans can be kept on banks books or they can be securitised (distributed). The mandated skin in the game when a loan is sold in the market is d. So, securitised loans kept in the books are dN. If $d = 1$, traditional lending (origination) occurs and all loans are kept on the books. Projects financed are $N = E_0$. Profits are $E_0 f$ (from fees charged).

Since $R = 0$, lending is smoothed over the two periods. It is not cyclical.

Now, let us see how banks can become fragile. If $d < 1$, securitisation occurs; $N = E_0/d$; $\pi = E_0 f/d = Nf$, so the balance sheet expands.

Although the fundamental payoff of securitised loans is the US\$ 1 repaid in period 3, prices in earlier periods can vary due to investor sentiment. Let $P_1 > 1$ and $P_2 < 1$. That is, there is a cycle with a boom in period 1. Securitisation can pay even though a bank knows $P_2 < 1$. A bank gains from securitising loans if $f > 1 - P_1$, covering the US\$ 1 it needs to supply to the entrepreneur. Assume the bank sells loans at $P_1 > 1$, collects and distributes $\pi = (P_1 - 1)$ $(1 - d) + Nf > Nf$ as dividends (equity cushion is not kept).

It is possible to make money in booms so the bank would expand its balance sheet procyclically using all capital at period 1.

338 *Global financial crises*

The condition under which it would neither want to hoard cash to securitise loans at 2 nor sell securities at 2 is $f < 1 - P_2$. If there is a capital injection of US\$ 1 in period 2, return from project finance is f, from buying traded securities it is $(1 - P_2)/P_2$; so the bank will trade securities instead of investing in primary projects as long as $f < \dfrac{(1 - P_2)}{P_2}$.

All expansions occur in period 1. It is cyclical, rising in good times. Propriety trading occurs until P_2 comes close to fundamental value of 1.

If leverage is allowed: Profits are all distributed so the bank needs loans to expand investment above equity. It would leverage equity by taking collateralised loans L_1 and L_2. The collateral available is Nd. For lenders security to cover costs of possible sale, there is a haircut h so $L_t = (1 - h)$ multiplied by collateral. If $h = 1$, $L_1 = L_2 = 0$. If the entire equity and loans is used for securitisation, the skin in the game condition with $P_1 = 1$ now implies $E_0 + L_1 = Nd$. The condition for the bank not to exceed its borrowing capacity in period 1 is $h = E_1/(E_1 + L_1)$ (i.e. equity covers borrowing). From the two conditions, substituting $E_0 = E_1$ gives collateral $Nd = E_1/h$ and balance sheet expansion as $N = \dfrac{E_0}{dh}$. If $d = 0.2$ and $h = 0.2$, $dh = 0.2 \times 0.2$ implies equity is leveraged 25 times. That is, leverage is $\dfrac{1}{dh}$ times equity. If P_2 falls, the bank can be forced to sell in a falling market to satisfy the haircut condition; it will have to sell more if h is small and the fall in P_2 is large. Table 14.2 summarises the timeline and alternatives available.

There is maturity mismatch and instability since banks give loans, which they securitise. They also borrow short term against their securities to finance long-term projects. Risk-taking is procyclical since that maximises long-term value. Among measures that can restrict procyclical bank balance sheet, expansion and contraction are direct restrictions on short-term borrowing and countercyclical capital requirements that fall in bad times. Such regulations would raise welfare, since they would restrain volatility of security prices above fundamental values. To the extent banks' investment in undervalued securities is reduced, project loans will rise. Haircuts, however, increase instability by forcing liquidation in bad times.

Table 14.2 Procyclical bank balance sheets

∞ ss	1	2	3
	US\$ 1 (LT projects)	US\$ 1 (ST projects)	$Z > 1$
All $Z > 1$ projects screened through intermediary bank for an entry fee	$f = \alpha(Z - 1)$ (profits split between banks and entrepreneurs)		US\$ 1 bank repaid
Price of securities	$P_1 > 1$	$P_2 < 1$	Payoff \$ 1
Banks short-term collateralised loans	L_1	L_2	
$d = 1$; No cyclicality	$N = E_0$ $\pi = E_0 f$ fees	$R = 0$ so lending smooth	
Securitisation: $d < 1$ Cyclical: good times	$N = E_0 / d > E_0$ $\pi = f E_0 / d > f E_0$	$P_2 < 1$; capital losses, but no liquidisation	US\$ 1 per loan; fundamental payoff
Leverage $E_0 + L$ Balance sheet expansion	L_1 $N = \dfrac{E_0}{dh}$	L_2 $h = \dfrac{E_2}{E_2 + L_2}$	
Haircut h	$h = \dfrac{E_1}{E_1 + L_1}$	$P_2 < 1 - f$ Forced to sell in a falling market	

14.3   The international financial system

A country's external balance adjustments impinge on other countries. The IFS was designed to mitigate such spillovers and ensure smooth and stable functioning of trade, payments and cross-border flows.

There were changes over time in the arrangements. Over 1880–1914, when the world was on the gold standard, the currency price of gold was fixed. CBs would sell gold at the fixed rate, and there was free import and export of gold. This price-specie flow mechanism led to automatic BOP adjustment. For example, if a country was running a CAD, it would lose gold. This would decrease the money supply and domestic demand, reducing the CAD.

340   *Global financial crises*

CBs wanted to decrease reserve movement. So, if they were losing gold, they would sell domestic assets to decrease money supply. If they were gaining gold, they would buy domestic assets since those were interest earning as compared to sterile gold. Moreover, capital flows were available to finance large CADs (e.g. reaching 6% of GDP). This was acceptable as long as gold reserves were not lost. The price level was stable because of the automatic adjustment. If money supply was increased, all prices would increase, including gold. The CB would have to sell gold to maintain its fixed price implying money supply would decrease.

There was also symmetric adjustment across countries. If any CB increased, money supply traders would sell domestic currency, as interest rates decreased. As they bought gold to buy currencies abroad, money supply would decrease.

Even so, there were problems. Availability of gold supplies restricted intervention to decrease unemployment. Fluctuations in gold prices created short-term volatility in price levels, giving power to mining countries. Bimetallism was tried as a way to reduce scarcity of mined gold, but the metal whose price rose would be driven out of monetary use. In practice, the burden of adjustment was on deficit countries that lost gold. Surplus countries did not face the same pressure to adjust.

CBs sometimes would sterilise reserve change, that is, buy domestic liabilities if they were losing gold to avoid the painful deflation otherwise required. Such flexibilities were what allowed the gold standard to survive as long as it did.

In the interwar period, there was a suspension of the gold standard. The float led to too much fluctuation in currency values and to competition for trade. Germany had a hyperinflation, the United Kingdom a deflation since it resumed the gold standard at the old rate. The Great Depression was linked to the gold standard – to deflationary policies it entailed to prevent reserve loss.

Over 1946–73, with the Bretton Woods agreement, the world shifted to the gold exchange standard. Now, only the US$, as the reserve currency, was fixed to gold – other currencies were fixed to it. The aim was to have enough stability to encourage trade, yet sufficient flexibility to allow focus on domestic unemployment. Short-term loans from the IMF gave some flexibility to finance temporary deficits, with export-stimulating devaluation agreed upon for persistent ones.

Adjustment was, however, asymmetric. The US Fed did not have to intervene to maintain a relative exchange rate. Since it was the Nth market, there were no restraints on its monetary policy. Discipline came only from maintaining the gold value of the dollar at US$ 35 an

Global financial crises 341

ounce. Moreover, other countries had to follow US monetary policy. For example, if US interest rates fell, other currencies would appreciate. To prevent that, CBs would have to buy dollars, increasing their money supply and decreasing their interest rates to match.

It was also asymmetric in that the United States was not free to devalue. As gradually the post-war US dollar shortage converted into a surplus, this became more of a problem. Other countries were holding US dollar treasury bills as reserves in excess of US gold stocks. The system, therefore, could work only as long as they did not want to convert these into gold.

The situation worsened after the US fiscal expansion, twin deficits and inflation following the Vietnamese war. There were speculative attacks on the US dollar and protracted negotiations. Finally, in 1971, the then US President Richard Nixon unilaterally removed convertibility, imposing a 10 per cent tariff on countries that did not agree to revalue against the dollar. By 1973, major countries were floating – this was thought to be temporary but it continued – and it helped adjustment to the oil shocks of that period.

The IMF's mandate is to promote the stability of the international monetary system and exercise surveillance over exchange rate policies. But after the United States abrogated the Bretton Woods agreement on fixed exchange rates in the 1970s, countries became free to follow what exchange rate regime they choose; there was no enforceable agreement on exchange rates with the IMF unlike in the pre-1970s system. It had some power over countries with CADs that needed to borrow, but none over countries running a CAS.

In 1976, the IMF article IV was amended to allow countries to adopt any exchange rate regime. The only constraints were policies had to be such as to promote stability and growth, with no manipulation of exchange rates to gain an unfair advantage. The IMF was reduced to a monitor with no clout against countries that did not need its loans.

While current account restrictions have to be approved by the IMF, it does not have jurisdiction over the capital account. Article VI, of the IMF's Articles of Agreement, gives countries the right to impose capital controls, if necessary. In September 1997, the governing body of the International Monetary Fund sought to extend the IMF's mandate to maintain free capital movements on the basis of Article VIII, which covers members' obligations to maintain payments systems for current account transactions, avoid discriminatory currency practices and allow convertibility of foreign held balances. But the repeated global financial crises made it difficult to force countries to open their capital accounts.

342 *Global financial crises*

As Chapter 9 discusses, each of floating and fixed exchange rate regimes have their advantages and disadvantages. Volatility followed the float. The dollar depreciated through the inflationary 1970s. But the Volcker tightening of the 1980s resulted in strong appreciation. The late 1980s saw coordinated intervention to decrease the dollar value, through the 1985 Plaza and 1987 Louvre Accord involving the G-5 countries. Policy coordination was found necessary to complement flexible rates.

The Iraq war led to the same problem of US twin deficits, now financed partly by Chinese reserve holdings, but culminating in a period of instability for the IFS. In the Bretton Woods period of fixed exchange rates, countries had turned inwards, but the float saw a revival of cross-border flows as AEs, followed by some EMs, liberalised and removed controls on their capital accounts.

Gains from trade over time: Trade in assets allows portfolio diversification, thus lowering risk as well as allowing exchange of goods and services for assets (claims to future goods and services). This intertemporal trade should raise welfare just as trade itself does. That is why it is a puzzle (as noted by Feldstein-Horioka) that domestic investment tends to be financed largely by domestic savings.

If markets were complete, it would imply world consumption was correlated, since income risk would be laid off or diversified through acquisition of foreign assets. For example, US FIIs that acquire Indian stocks would diversify risk if Indian stock markets were negatively correlated with US GDP. Such diversification is small but increasing with growth of international capital market since 1970. But it remains much less than required for full diversification (Table 14.3).

There are dangers, however, in financial liberalisation as repeated crises demonstrate. For example, banks played a major role in the GFC. It is not clear whose responsibility is a bank originating in one country, located in a second and accepting the deposits of a third. Collective action failure is highly probable. Countries are reluctant to pass up profit opportunities for their banks. This creates possibilities

Table 14.3 International risk diversification

	Foreign assets of US residents	*Foreign claims on the United States*
1970	6.2 % of US capital stock	4
1999	30	36
Full (= relve size of US econ.)	80	80

Source: Adapted from Krugman et al. (2014).

Global financial crises 343

for regulatory arbitrage. Deposits of currencies other than those of the country of bank residence are known as offshore banking. Such deposits can originate in trade or politics or regulations. In the 1950s, Russian deposited dollars in European banks that gave rise to the term Eurocurrencies. Petrodollars arose from the CASs of oil exporters.

In the 1950s and 1960s, foreign branches were a way to escape US banking regulations such as regulation Q interest rate ceilings. Eurocurrency center governments regulate local currency deposits more heavily, if they feel they can insulate the domestic financial system from shifts in foreigner's asset demands. For example, the United Kingdom imposes no reserve requirement on dollar deposits within its borders. To compete for business, the United States in 1981 exempted from tax only international bank funds for foreign customers.

Amounts are often too large for deposit insurance to cover. Coordination and convergence of regulatory standards is important, and for this, simple measures such as leverage caps are required. Although reforms are occurring after the GFC, they tend to be complex and too bank focussed. This encourages shadow banking and hedge funds, as we see in the next section.

14.4 Post-GFC financial reforms

While a pro-market stance was responsible for many regulatory weaknesses, overreaction leading to an anti-market stance also has to be avoided. Reforms need to preserve the energy and innovation of markets while reducing their tendency to take on too much risk. Regulation should aim to alleviate the fundamental failures to which finance is subject. These are asymmetric information, leading to exclusion and to arbitrage across asset types and markets; large systemically important financial institutions (SIFIs) that are too big to let fail; and spillovers that create excess volatility or procyclicality (Goyal, 2013). There are also regulatory failures such as delay and either laxity or overzealousness.

Improving transparency and reducing incentives for procyclical excessive risk-taking can reduce the probability of crises. Moreover, regulatory discretion should be minimised, to the extent possible.

14.4.1 Weaknesses in international financial reforms

Although more reforms were carried out than happened after the East Asian crisis, reform weaknesses include continuing gaps and exemptions that will invite arbitrage, enhance procyclicality and leverage. Delays in implementing reforms aggravate these features.

344 *Global financial crises*

14.4.1.1 *Arbitrage and shadow banking*

Incompleteness shows up in many dimensions. It affects institutions and transactions, and also appears over time. Any kind of incompleteness gives rise to arbitrage. The Basel III and Dodd-Frank regulations focus on banks is driving more financial intermediation to the shadow banking sector. Shadow banks include a broad array of institutions engaged in bank-like activities, among them hedge funds, private equity groups and money market funds. Reforms are in some ways too strict in allocating all risks to banks, but are too weak in leaving many gaps that enable escape from regulation. The IMF points out in its 2015 Global Financial Stability Report that replacing banks' contracting functions and a search for yield has raised hedge fund managers' securities turnover 40 per cent over 10 years to US$76 trillion. It suggests stress tests for hedge funds like those for banks.

There are proposals for more universal reforms. Hanson et al. (2011) suggested imposition of a minimum haircut requirement at the level of asset-backed securities for all investors, not just on banks. Such a measure can constrain short-term leverage for all investors taking a position in credit assets, thus restraining shadow banks also, although as Box 14.1 argues, it can increase procyclicality.

Transparency, including records of different types of transactions, is a prerequisite for broad-based regulations. Progress on reporting requirements includes creation of legal entity identifiers (LEIs). Overseen by the Financial Stability Board (FSB), these give a unique number to each registered legal entity globally. They have the potential to improve risk management for the individual firm and at the system-wide level. Since they identify counterparties, linkages among counterparties and all potential sources of default contagion, firms and regulators can take steps to reduce risk. By 2014, more than 320,000 LEIs had been issued to entities in 190 jurisdictions.

14.4.1.2 *Systemic risks and macroprudential regulation*

Since individuals do not take into account systemic spillovers from their decisions, risks build up cyclically. Countercyclical macroprudential regulations that increase the long-term cost of giving credit during booms and reduce these costs during busts are, therefore, required.

Traders cluster in activities that appear to be low risk, but the clustering makes the activities risky. This endogenous creation of risk is one reason why the own assessment of risk-based capital buffers of Basel II were inadequate.[2] But Basel III continues this approach. Risks

Global financial crises 345

also change for exogenous reasons – Euro sovereign debt had zero risk weights before the problems in Greece exposed underlying risks.

The primary purpose of capital adequacy or liquidity coverage-type regulation is often to provide a buffer to absorb shocks. While they should be countercyclical, loss-absorbing buffers are often built up in bad times, hurting recovery, and neglected in good times. De facto buffers tend to be procyclical. Shin and Shin (2011) argue the focus should be on preventing risky behaviour rather than on the loss-absorbing or shock-insulating role of buffers.

For this, the quality of capital matters. Prudential regulation can align incentives by putting the entity's own equity capital at risk. Admati and Hellwig (2013) believe in the importance of equity buffers that create own liability for risk taken and suggest that 20 units of equity must be held for 100 units of assets. In contrast, Basel III requires only 7 per cent of equity (core or tier I capital) against risk-weighted assets. The latter can be strategically chosen to be much lower than total assets, so that leverage[3] over equity can be very high, that is, a large amount of credit is created on a narrow base of own equity.

Basel III does for the first time restrict total leverage through a leverage ratio,[4] requiring 3 per cent of equity against total assets going up to 5 per cent for large banks. But 3 per cent is still generous in capping leverage at 33.3 times. A 3 per cent fall in asset values would wipe out equity, making the bank insolvent, or putting the burden on the taxpayer. Such a fall in value can come even from riskless assets such as government bonds as in the Greek case. Moreover, regulators allow repurchase (repo) transactions and derivatives to be netted out in calculating risk, when it is the gross value that more correctly measures the risk from a collapse of markets or counterparties. It is useful to remember that the leverage in Lehman Brothers was 30 and in Bear Sterns 33 when they collapsed. The Admati and Hellwig suggestion would restrict total leverage to five times.

A given level of leverage can be achieved either by mandating the asset cover (through a leverage ratio) or by restricting leverage itself. Thus, leverage caps can complement capital buffers, reducing their size, even as the share of high quality capital is raised. Caps also prevent risky behaviour, thus reducing procyclicality. Different types of broad pattern regulation, such as loan to value ratios, can cap leverage at a level below the ceiling derived from the level of assets and the leverage ratio. These measures can complement the use of a leverage ratio, reducing its disadvantages. For example, competition may force banks to acquire higher risk assets, if there is no risk-weighting in a leverage cap, since banks that do not follow such a strategy will be

346 *Global financial crises*

disadvantaged. Better measurement of leverage is also required since financial techniques can increase leverage without increasing borrowing. For example, knock-in options increase gain or loss conditional on some event.

A leverage cap may make the delays being negotiated in implementing full capital adequacy less harmful. Combined with more own capital at risk and sectoral restrictions on lending it would not lead to a shift to higher risk activities, even while avoiding cloaking of high risk or concentration on low risk activities that then become high risk, as happens with overreliance on internal risk assessments.

Since the potential rise in leverage is much larger for large banks, a leverage cap more effectively reduces the leverage in large banks that could otherwise create systemic risk (Goyal, 2013). Thus, it is another way of mitigating the risk from SIFIs, which has increased because of greater post-crisis concentration. There is an attempt to break them up by imposing higher capital adequacy requirements for SIFIs, but implementation has proved difficult. Some direct ways to restrict leverage are discussed below.

14.4.1.3 *Direct measures that restrict leverage*

Although the Basel framework continues to emphasise internal risk-based capital adequacy measures, there does seem to be some movement towards more universal measures and effective caps as part of macroprudential regulation. The FSB, in January 2015, set out a framework imposing minimum requirements on the *collateral* needed when firms borrow money from banks through short-term loans secured by stocks or bonds. The repo market is a key segment of the shadow banking world. A distress sale of assets used as collateral for repo loans could impact the wider financial system. Tougher rules on collateral for short-term lending proposed will affect both banks and non-bank players. They will reduce non-banks' build-up of excessive leverage and liquidity risk during peaks in the credit and economic cycle.

The FSB wants a minimum 1.5 per cent 'haircut' for corporate bonds with a maturity of between one and five years, and a 6 per cent haircut for equities. The latter implies a borrower would have to post US$ 106 of equity collateral for a US$ 100 loan. The haircut floors could in future be raised and lowered as part of efforts to lean against fluctuations in the financial cycle.

While the standards are also to apply to deals between non-banks, transactions that use government bonds as collateral are still exempt,

Global financial crises 347

in response to governments' worry about the potential impact on sovereign debt markets. There are also fears that restricting the repo market could affect liquidity in many financial assets.

Other potential tools that restrict leverage are *taxes* and *margin requirements*. They are automatically countercyclical since the tax base expands in good times, and they can be designed to fall more on highly leveraged activities, thus providing good forward-looking incentives. International harmonisation could perhaps be feasible for a simple universal tax. Its mobility made finance undertaxed, but new technology is changing that. A low tax that matches transaction fees charged would not be burdensome, since the same technology has substantially reduced transaction costs. Taxes would have to fall in EMs and rise in the major financial centers where they tend not to exist. A low financial transaction tax (FTT) is easy to impose, but is subject to severe political resistance.

Belgium, Germany, Estonia, Greece, Spain, France, Italy, Austria, Portugal, Slovenia and Slovakia agreed in 2013 to levy a FTT of 0.1 per cent on stock and bond trades and 0.01 per cent on derivatives transactions. The tax was to apply to financial institutions with headquarters in the tax area or who trade on behalf of a client in the tax area or for an instrument issued in the tax area but traded anywhere in the world. There were exemptions for the trades of CBs and pension funds. The move was, however, strongly resisted by the United States and the United Kingdom. Business groups feared double taxation.

Given resistance to a tax on transactions independent of profits made, a financial activities' tax that falls on profits, and therefore is not passed on to consumers of financial services, could be negotiated instead. From an EM perspective, an FTT has the advantage that it applies in the jurisdiction where a transaction is made and potential profits earned, while at present a profits tax earns revenues only for the country of residence or the country of source depending on tax agreements to avoid double taxation. Dominant tax by residence clauses favour AEs, from where the majority of portfolio investments originate.

The OECD model tax convention implied only profits of a non-resident company with a 'permanent establishment' could be taxed. The aim was to prevent double taxation of the increasing number of firms with cross-border business. Since this convention has been misused to escape taxes, there is a proposal to replace it by 'mutual agreement on place of residence'. This is part of the OECD and G-20-led initiative to counter base erosion and profit shifting (BEPS) in a necessary course correction. At the 2013 G-20 meet in Petersburg, it was

348 *Global financial crises*

decided: 'Profits should be taxed where economic activities deriving the profits are performed and where value is created.'

Financial services, which tend anyway to be undertaxed, are often also able to escape what taxes there are. It is easy to locate strategically, using treaties designed to avoid double taxation, to achieve double non-taxation. For example, the India-Mauritius Treaty allows tax by domicile. Mauritius accepts registration as domicile, so FIIs come into India through the Mauritius route, thus going against the spirit of the treaty. Another example is VAT on cross-border retail sales. Financial services are VAT exempt but self-assess input VAT; they are able to escape this using inputs from abroad or from related firms.

There is a requirement, therefore, for simple tax regimes that prevent both double taxation and double non-taxation. Thus, even if new taxes are not imposed, EMs should actively participate in the G-20 BEPS initiative to make sure foreign investors do not unfairly escape taxes. While one country acting alone can frighten away foreign capital, global coordination can reduce the undertaxation of finance, even while reducing the excess volatility that creates risk. G-20 has the potential to be very productive in such areas that require coordination across countries.

Margin requirements and position limits are also not uniform across countries. Regulatory coordination is required. There is evidence that short-term futures price bubbles were more pronounced in domains with lax regulation (Goyal and Tripathi, 2012) and contributed to the deviation of commodity prices from fundamentals.

QE, which consciously sought to drive up asset prices, also drove up oil prices, hurting importers such as India. As restrictions on bank's proprietary trade led to the large investment banks exiting commodity trades, commodity market speculation reduced. Moreover, high oil prices brought about a sustained rise in supply weakening OPEC's market power. Chinese demand also slowed, but was not the primary reason for the sharp 2014 fall in oil prices. Chinese growth had slowed to 7.7 in 2012 from 9.3 the previous year without reducing oil prices. Better prudential regulation in commodity markets could have mitigated the oil price bubble and its fallout.

14.4.1.4 *Measures to restrict leverage in India*

Leverage in EMs has always been much lower and use of macroprudential tools such as sectoral loan to value ratios that impose leverage caps much higher than in AEs.[5] The RBI seeks to preserve this regulatory comfort by prescribing a higher leverage ratio of 4.5 per cent,

Global financial crises 349

against the Basel III norm of 3 per cent. This allows a leverage of 22:1, but the leverage in 2014 was lower at 10:1 for Indian banks (5:1 in PSBs) compared to 25:1 average for AE banks (the Basel cap is 33.3:1).

Indian bank leverage is lower because of prudential broad pattern regulation such as countercyclical provisioning on credit to some sectors, position limits and limits on exposure to different types of risk, high SLRs to finance government debt and other types of taxation. Prompt corrective action that reduces regulatory delay is easier in response to sectoral cycles than aggregate cycles. India used a countercyclical rise in provisioning for bank housing and commercial real estate loans, when real estate prices rose, and found it to be more effective than changing risk weights, since provisioning affected the profit and loss account of banks. Rising risk weights could be escaped since average capital adequacy ratios were above the minimum (Sinha, 2011).

The broad-pattern regulations, outlined above, reduce risk-taking even without large procyclical capital buffers. They do not leave open the possibility of arbitrage through strategic use of risk weights. A better combination of financial stability and financial innovation then results.

Moreover, financial systems in EMs tend to be bank dominated, and banks and their lending has to expand with development, even as other legal, governance and market reforms occur. Therefore, a solely bank-focussed reform programme hurts them disproportionately, while the neglect of shadow banking and liquidity creation hurts them again through volatility in capital flows.

Despite domestic features that contribute to financial stability, Indian regulators implemented more than the required Basel III criteria and advanced the implementation schedule, since they were concerned about the reputation of Indian banks. Although Basel is a 'comply or explain' not a 'comply or else' framework, it was feared markets may regard any deviation unfavourably (Sinha, 2011). While burdening banks with these regulations, regulators also allowed cyclical risks facing banks to rise, raising interest rates to retain foreign debt flows in 2013, although structural features such as a larger share of loans in assets made banks more vulnerable to such risks.

There is a case, therefore, for reducing required capital buffers in view of these other types of regulation. The latter could fill gaps in global regulatory regimes, including risks from the delays and renegotiations, discussed below. Lessons from EMs, where simpler regulations successfully restricted leverage and acted countercyclically, should be followed rather than forcing them to follow international regulations that continue to have weaknesses. Trade-offs could be

350 *Global financial crises*

introduced between types of regulations, but not just for India as a special case. Similar standards are essential to prevent arbitrage in search of weak regulations. Empirical assessments, which are beginning, find that measures aimed at borrowers, such as caps, and limits are more effective in reducing the growth in banks' leverage, asset and non-core to core liabilities ratio compared to countercyclical buffers, although the latter also reduce leverage and assets (Claessens, 2014). EMs should articulate these issues in G-20 and in the BIS.

Regarding regulatory structure, the experience of the GFC made most countries give more responsibility for financial stability to their central banks. The United Kingdom had shifted to a financial sector funded unified financial regulator, focussed on supporting innovation. An Indian financial reforms commission wants to follow this experiment. But the United Kingdom found it to work poorly and returned powers to an independent Bank of England. It created a new bank regulator, the Prudential Regulation Authority, as a subsidiary of the Bank of England, and also established a systemic risk regulator – the Financial Policy Committee – within the Central Bank. This enables the necessary coordination between micro- and macroprudential regulation and monetary policy (Kohn, 2015).

The Volcker Alliance report has argued for a similar structure to plug continuing gaps and weaknesses in US financial regulation. It wants a new agency affiliated with the Fed to write prudential rules and perform supervision currently done by the Fed, the Office of the Comptroller of the Currency and the third bank regulator, the Federal Deposit Insurance Corporation. It points to poor incentives in the coordinating Financial Sector Oversight Committee and possible political short-termism in the treasury secretary chairing it. While countries are strengthening CB-based macroprudential regulation, Indian reformers want to weaken it, but are not able to establish the case for moving away from the current system, in which the RBI could implement innovative protective macroprudential policies, to a design that proved unstable elsewhere.

14.4.1.5 Delays

Apart from incompleteness and lack of international harmonisation, Basel III and other proposed post-GFC regulatory changes are inadequate also because of delays. Although enhanced capital requirements under Basel III are only to kick in from 2018, countries are actively negotiating to weaken the standards. The Dodd-Frank Act is passed, but its sheer size and complexity will create protracted legal wrangling

Global financial crises 351

aimed at expanding the ambit of the many exemptions given. It seeks to ban proprietary trading by deposit-taking banks in order to reduce their risk-taking. But exemptions include loans, spot FX or commodities, and also repo and reverse repo securities lending transactions required for liquidity management. It is inherently difficult to distinguish between trading on own account and that undertaken for clients.

In the European Union, the 2012 Liikanen report proposed milder ring fencing without full separation of investment and retail banking, in order to support the European universal banking model. Proprietary trading (with some exceptions to allow client servicing within narrow position risk limits) was to be hived off to a legally separate unit in the same bank holding company. But Europe is softening these proposals so banks do not have to separate out key market-making business. France and Germany are also diluting the capital requirements on their universal banks agreed under the Basel III framework. The calculations determining the liquidity coverage ratio and the quality of liquid assets banks have to carry, in order for them to survive a possible future short-term funding freeze, were moderated in 2013 and the implementation date further postponed. Apart from the government bonds and top-quality corporate bonds required in the initial draft, even equities, BBB-corporate bonds and discounted top-quality mortgage-backed securities were counted in liquidity buffers. This is a boost for the securitisation industry and has steeply reduced banks' liquidity shortfall. The collateral requirement for OTC derivatives was also softened (Goyal, 2013).

International harmonisation is difficult to achieve, and this failure also creates arbitrage gaps. The disagreements between the United States, the United Kingdom and the European Union originate from differing financial structures. The United Kingdom wants to preserve the current dominance of the city of London as a financial centre. The United States and the United Kingdom want reforms that do not hurt the market-based Anglo-Saxon model of finance. They are worried about competition from fledging Asian financial centers. Major EU countries have a more bank-based model and want to protect their banks, especially since the Euro debt crisis following the GFC has left them weak.

Simple regulatory or tax-based measures have a greater chance of being applied universally. Universal global standards and tax regimes are also necessary to prevent capital flight from individual country applying them. They can prevent one jurisdiction stalling regulatory reform in order not to lose competition to another jurisdiction with lax regulations. Reforms that are simple yet improve market incentives are preferable also, since the GFC demonstrated regulatory

352 *Global financial crises*

failure. Simple robust reforms are less vulnerable to regulatory capture, discretion and delays.

In addition to delays in the implementation and harmonisation of reforms, the new institutional structure being created may be inherently more subject to delays. Systemic concerns have been left to systemic councils where problems of regulatory discretion and coordination may lead to critical delays in response.

To summarise, changes in financial regulations may be in the right direction, they are too small, too slow, too narrow and too dependent on individual country and regulatory discretion. Dodd-Frank can force more transparency, information sharing, reporting and auditing in OTC markets, especially since suitable technology is available, only provided exemptions are not given. While teeth have been provided against SIFIs and the shadow banking system, there is no warrantee they will be used. The United States has favoured structural over countercyclical reform. The former tends to overregulate some sectors, leaving arbitrage gaps (Kohn, 2015). Non-discretionary direct rules, such as prompt corrective action against a troubled financial firm or leverage caps, or removal of all exemptions to transparent trading of complex financial derivatives can be more effective. Without these, for example, exemptions for FX swaps could be used to structure swap transactions to avoid regulation to expand shadow banking activity and create systemic risks. Large areas of discretion in addressing systemic failures and cross-border arbitrage by SIFIs imply a question mark over implementation.

Weaknesses in financial reform compound other sources of continuing risks. These include problems in the European Union, global current account imbalances and inadequate reform of the IFS. We turn to these next, beginning with a brief discussion of currency unions in general and the European Union in particular.

14.5 Continuing risks for the IFS

14.5.1 *Euro debt crisis and currency unions*

The theory of optimal currency areas (OCA) identifies conditions for such an area to succeed. Countries in an OCA should have symmetric shocks, free factor mobility, similar economic structure and trade links that are large with each other and low with the rest of the world.

Europe did not meet these conditions. Countries were at varying levels of efficiency and labour markets were rigid. The basic impetus for forming the European Union was political, to become large enough

Global financial crises   353

to effectively compete with the US, while resolving European distrust by creating common interests, and harnessing the trade advantages of one market. The trade benefits turned out, however, to have been overstated.

The process of creation was slow and elaborate, with a careful building of supporting institutions. The Maastricht treaty of 1991 and the Growth and Stability Pact of 1997 laid out strict convergence criteria. Government debt/GDP ratio could not exceed 60 per cent, the fiscal deficit 3 per cent; inflation had to be low and the exchange rate lie within a band.

The European Central Bank (ECB) was set up as the most independent CB, beyond the reach of any one national government. The European Parliament had no power to alter its statute. It was pan-European but German dominance, and the desire to gain from German credibility, made sure of monetary conservatism and commitment to low inflation. Decisions are made by votes of the governing council of the ECB – a six-member executive board and heads of national CBs. The only leeway for democratic accountability is that ECB's members are political appointments. But they have fixed non-renewable terms. The Maastricht treaty left exchange rate policy with politicians, but the ECB can overrule if it conflicts with price stability.

In an OCA where the conditions are not met, transfers are required through a fiscal or a banking union in response to shocks, since an independent monetary policy is given up. But Europe had strict national fiscal rules, and the European Parliament little power to tax and transfer to stagnating areas as is possible in a one-country federal structure. All this made the EMU fragile, especially after a large shock like the GFC.

Many European banks were exposed to subprime securities. Rescuing them added fiscal pressure. Even earlier, Maastricht criteria had proved difficult to implement. Agreements to cap debt ratios and fiscal deficits were violated even by countries like France and Germany. Despite this, markets were either not forward-looking or assumed bailouts would occur for sovereign debt. Flat spreads allowed a country like Greece to borrow at the same rate as Germany, even though the southern zone was not competitive with Germany at the same exchange rate. It, therefore, overborrowed. Investment bankers helped it disguise its deficits.

Euro debt crisis: As the extent of fiscal debt and the fudges, as well as constitutional limits on the ECB's ability to lend to sovereigns, became clear in 2011, there was a steep rise in spreads. The sharp rise in the cost of their borrowing made it difficult for indebted EU

354 *Global financial crises*

governments to borrow from markets, and they had lost the ability to print money to finance their debt. Fiscal discipline was a precondition for loans. Amounts available and transfers from the European Stability Fund were small.

A new ECB governor, Mario Draghi, found a way out by indirectly lending to banks that bought sovereign debt, through the LTRO (long-term refinancing operations for 6-, 12- and 36-month periods). His 2011 announcement that he would do 'whatever it takes' calmed markets. Despite the largest balance sheet expansion for the ECB,[6] Europe went through the most painful recession. The PIGS (Portugal, Italy, Greece, Spain) had to go through severe austerity to reduce deficits and suffered high unemployment rates that reached the twenties.

In 2015, the possibility of deflation because of a crash in oil prices allowed the ECB to start a broader QE, six years after US Fed, with asset purchases expanded to include Euro area governments, agencies and institutions bonds, with monthly purchases of € 60 billion, until at least September 2016 (this would add up to about € 1.1 trillion). They even made select interest rates negative in 2016 hoping to encourage lending.

Greece received many bailouts. But these did not bail-in the European banks that had given credit. Their rescue forced domestic taxpayers to bear a heavy burden, leading to political unrest. German insistence on the condition set in Eurozone negotiations that no Eurozone country taxpayers would have to bailout those in another prevented the debt forgiveness required for debt to become sustainable. The IMF had contributed heavily to the bailouts. But its constitution prevented it from lending to a country with unsustainable debt, making its participation beyond 2015 doubtful. That Greek exports were not competitive at Euro rates pushed it towards exit. The irrevocability of a monetary union was being questioned. But cohesive forces proved strong.

14.5.2 *Current account imbalances*

Large and sustained current account imbalances are a sign of poor adjustment and a source of stress in the IFS. Since the United States and China were the countries with the largest imbalances, there was a long-running debate between them. Each emphasised different factors as responsible for imbalances. The United States pointed to the Chinese exchange rate peg to the dollar, while China pointed to large US fiscal deficits and to the dollar's position as the international reserve currency. The United States downplayed the cheap imports for its consumers and China downplayed the contribution of US deficits to Chinese export demand.

Global financial crises   355

This illustrates psychological traps that prevent a resolution of international issues such as the global imbalances. First, *perceptions are distorted* – people tend to see their own losses and other peoples gains. This leads to *blame*. It is always the others' fault and it is always the other who should take action. Pushing the other to take action results in a final trap – *resistance*, or the 'don't tell me what to do' syndrome. Pushing may work if the advantages are all on one side, but in a more even situation only results in a stalemate.

The third trap is *fear*. There is a tendency to expect the worst outcome in any change, this can either bring on that outcome or lead to status-quoism.

This helps explain why imbalances have persisted for so long. But not all imbalances have to be removed. Blanchard and Milesi-Ferretti (2009, 2012) make the distinction between 'good' or required imbalances and those due to domestic distortions. Countries with aging populations need to run a CAS in anticipation of future dissaving. Those with a high return to investment need to run a CAD. Countries with deeper financial markets attract investors.

Distortions that create imbalances include high private savings due to a lack of social insurance or corporate governance, or the reverse of low private savings due to asset booms. Political pressures can lead to too high public borrowing and deficits. Investment could be low because of poor property rights or financial distortions. Policy should, therefore, act to reduce the underlying distortions. Blanchard and Milesi-Ferretti argue imbalances primarily reflected distortions from 2001 onwards. Apart from the United States and China, savings of oil exporters, German and Japanese CAS, an investment boom in East Europe and investment collapse in East Asia contributed to global imbalances. These aggravated domestic risks such as volatile capital flows and real appreciation.

But the GFC itself transmitted through US securities with European banks, not EM 'net' holdings of US securities. It was the gross not net external position that mattered when markets froze. CB demand proved more stable.

For adjustment of imbalances, the United States has to increase private and public savings, while China improves social insurance and corporate governance. Rising wages and more credit to households and small enterprises would help the shift from export-led to domestic demand-led growth. Rising wages would also allow equilibrium real appreciation. China instituted slow nominal appreciation since 2005, and in 2015 the IMF declared the renminbi was no longer overvalued, but was finding the transition to markets- and

356 *Global financial crises*

domestic consumption-led growth difficult. US savings also improved, but households were still going through post-crisis deleveraging. The fall in oil prices moderated surpluses of oil exporters. Thus, gradual adjustment is occurring without another crisis (Goyal, 2005).

14.5.2.1 *Valuation effects*

Since cross-border asset holdings are large, predictable valuation effects also affect BOP adjustment. These entail capital gains and losses. The international balance sheet (IBS) of a country determines its long-run solvency and affects the propagation of shocks. While net capital flows capture intertemporal transfer of resources across countries, gross capital flows affect IBS and the dynamics of NIIP. Net foreign assets = past assets + current account + valuation effects + errors, while the sum across asset classes minus sum across liabilities gives the valuation changes.

New data sets giving time series of assets at market prices allow these valuation effects to be calculated. US liabilities are in dollars and assets mostly in foreign currency, so under dollar depreciation there is no change in liabilities, but assets go up. These composition effects imply returns on assets exceed losses on liabilities. Gourinchas and Rey (2013) estimate that over 1952:1–2011:4 excess US returns amounted to 1.6–2.7 per cent of NIIP.

These excess returns are part of the 'exorbitant privilege' the United States enjoys as supplier of the reserve currency. But there is also an 'exorbitant duty'. Claims on foreigners tend to be riskier asset classes such as equities, which give higher returns, while liabilities are liquid government securities. This insurance function led to sharp capital losses in the GFC as risky assets fell in value. EMs survived the GFC well, partly since they had shifted their foreign liabilities from debt to risk sharing equity. They also increased their reserves. These helped build market confidence.

14.5.2.2 *Foreign currency reserves*

Post-GFC, low AE interest rates and QE have led to asset price booms and risk-on risk-off capital flow volatility. So, the precautionary function of reserves has become even more necessary. If the idea that investment of reserves in US treasuries reduces the world's supply of safe assets and leads to a risky search for yield is correct, then it is ironic that AE CBs are now the largest consumers of safe assets as QE expands their balance sheets.

Global financial crises 357

China accumulated above US$ 4 trillion of reserves with a large CAS, but not all countries with rising reserves had a CAS. In the post-GFC period, among the G-20 countries with rising reserves and a deficit were South Africa, Mexico, Israel, India and Brazil.

Annual data show that except for the United States, the United Kingdom, Euro Area, Chile and Argentina, reserves in G-20 countries have tended to increase steadily since the 1990s, the period of large inflows. All EMs had a substantial rise in reserves over 2009–11 (IMF, 2012, Table A13, p. 214). Goyal (2013) shows countries in the 0–50 US$ billion range of reserves to be Chile, Argentina, Canada and South Africa. Those in the 0–200 range were Thailand, Turkey, Mexico, Israel and Indonesia. India, Brazil, Korea, Hong Kong were in the 0–300 range and Russia, Saudi Arabia and Japan in the 0–1,200 range.

Only countries in an inner financial circle have ready access to US Fed swaps and other reliable international liquidity support. They did not raise their reserve holdings. Mutual vulnerabilities and interests are a precondition for availability of swap lines. Moreover, they are giver not user driven, are typically of short duration and limited by moral hazard considerations.

Reserve accumulation as a self-insurance mechanism, however, is expensive as well as has limited utility. Countries whose reserves were based on inflows did not use the reserves during the months of the GFC when outflows were large, preferring to depreciate exchange rates instead (Aizenman, 2009). The tendency to add to reserves but not to let them fall suggests a hoarding motive. Most countries fear market interpretations of a fall in reserves and the possible downward spiral it may set off. Rating agencies give too much weight to measurable aspects and tend to downgrade a country whose reserves fall, since the latter are regarded as a signal of strength. So, the precautionary use of reserves is limited then only to the signal. In addition, psychological pressures, such as bettering one's own past record, tend to keep raising the threshold for reserves. While reduction in precautionary reserve holdings is desirable, improvement in the IFS is a prerequisite for this to happen.

During a global slowdown, competitive currency depreciation is a temptation for any one nation, but can make all worse off as others follow similar strategies. Post-GFC, there were fears of competitive 'currency wars'.

14.5.3 Currency wars

A flexible exchange rate regime and appreciation of the Chinese currency were long seen as essential for correction of current account imbalances.[7] Extreme views wanted an appreciation of Asian exchange

358 *Global financial crises*

rates relative to the dollar large enough to compensate for lower Asian wages. But there are limits to appreciation in populous countries, since it requires a rise in real wages, which cannot occur unless surplus labour is absorbed or average productivity rises. Without that, wages and prices could be bid down to convert a nominal appreciation into a real depreciation. If wages were downward, rigid unemployment would rise. It follows exchange rates cannot bear the entire burden of adjustment. Part of the adjustment had to come from rising domestic absorption in Asia and reducing fiscal deficits and consumer demand in the United States.

Goyal (2005) argued during such a period of gradual adjustment that an attack on the dollar was possible but not certain. A unique Nash equilibrium required a collective action failure where all Asian countries sold their reserves. This was unlikely. Instead, there were multiple Nash equilibria with attack and hold both as possible outcomes. A coordination failure could result in an attack on the dollar. If the countries holding large reserves are talking to each other, the scenario where one sells its dollar reserves because it fears the other might do so becomes less likely. The probability of an attack rises under faster dollar depreciation. As it turned out, communication did improve with the setting up of the G-20 and gradual adjustment did remove the overvaluation of the Renminbi without an attack on the dollar.[8] In 2015, the IMF declared the renminbi was no longer overvalued.

A new fear in the post-GFC period was that countries would try to depreciate their currencies in order to boost exports and create jobs. The Brazilian finance minister, Guido Mantega, coined the term 'currency wars' in 2010 as QE in the United States and other AEs generated sharp inflows that appreciated the Brazilian Real. The Brazilian response was to impose market-based capital controls to discourage inflows. There was a reversal of capital account convertibility in many EMs.

Easy liquidity also contributed to a sharp recovery of oil prices, even though global demand remained low. This hit oil-importing EMs. For example, the Indian CAD widened. In addition, outflows of FPI that occurred in risk-off periods whenever global financial fragility rose, due to events such as the European debt crisis, made it difficult to finance the CAD. Episodes of rupee depreciation increased the import bill, given inelastic demand for commodities such as oil and gold.

Countries are forced to use a variety of measures to protect themselves from excess capital flow volatility. These are responses to inadequacies in the current IFS and should not be regarded as currency manipulation. At the very least, it is essential to distinguish countries

Global financial crises 359

with a CAD from those with a CAS. If a country has a persistent CAD, its exchange rate cannot be undervalued. Capital-account management policies that reduce short-term inflows can be a substitute for costly reserve accumulation. Any type of tax on inflows implicitly subsidises the costs of reserves held, funding the accumulation of reserves by the activities that create the need to self-insure by these reserves. The premise in the currency wars debate that all intervention is manipulation and all controls market distorting is, therefore, incorrect.

Talk of currency wars resurfaced again in 2012 when the Swiss and the Japanese[9] CBs took measures that reduced appreciation of their currencies. But risk-off capital outflows and the 2014 crash in oil prices led to a 40 per cent depreciation in the Brazilian real. A relatively better recovery in the United States led the dollar to appreciate from 2011. The US fed, concerned about the negative effect of appreciation on employment, reduced its pace of interest rate normalisation.

In the 2012 G-20 meeting, finance ministers agreed not to manipulate exchange rates for competitive advantage, but interest rate or liquidity boosting policy in response to domestic needs, which AEs typically use, was not to be regarded as manipulation. These measures are regarded as expenditure changing, not expenditure switching. But at zero interest rates, the primary impact of such measures is on the exchange rate. Then, measures such as intervention and controls that EMs with less developed markets are forced to use, in response to capital flow volatility, should also not be regarded as manipulation. A full float was adopted in mature economies after crossing a threshold of development, not before.

AEs also used communication to affect exchange rates. For example, Abe's campaign promise to aid export-dependent manufacturers, by bringing down the value of the yen, became self-fulfilling since traders acting in advance of expected action depreciated the yen. It is a stretch to fit these in interest rate or liquidity boosting policy, but G-20 interpreted it as a response to domestic needs. It follows domestic needs of EMs should also be recognised. But all countries should be aware of spillovers that reduce overall welfare and a possible race to the bottom in targeting exchange rates.

The AEs tend to take a view that whatever is good for AE growth will eventually be good for EMs. That is true; but slower EM growth, in turn, can reduce recovery in AEs, especially since they now have a larger share of global GDP and growth.[10] Action should be taken to moderate costs imposed on EMs, in order to preserve global import demand and help AEs. For example, the simple uniform types of financial regulation

360   *Global financial crises*

of Section 14.4 can moderate spillovers, such as risk-on risk-off capital flows and commodity price bubbles, from AE QE.

But such measures are still being avoided. Goyal (2002) tried to understand why creditors did not undertake financial reforms after the East Asian crisis. If rational creditors gain from bankruptcy procedures, they should be willing to adopt them. Potential reasons for their reluctance are first, discounting the probability of a future crisis, although the GFC has weakened this defense. Second, cognitive dissonance such that creditors are more concerned about a small current loss rather than a reduction in future losses, so that they do not minimise the expected value of crises losses. Third, the higher bargaining clout of investing nations leads policy makers to follow creditors' preferences and push to protect creditors in investing nations by ensuring they do not suffer a loss in case a crisis occurs, rather than by reducing the probability of crisis. This analysis implies that a loss in bargaining power could actually turn out to benefit creditors.

Such a loss would improve the nature of international financial integration, the credibility of global governance and confidence in the IFS. All of which would help reduce imbalances. Asia is keen to modernise and develop deeper financial markets. Some exchange rate flexibility decreases financial risk and furthers this objective. Reforms of the IFS and deepening of domestic financial markets would reduce the costs of global integration for EMs, allowing them to reduce controls and other defensive measures. Changes in the IFS continue to be inadequate, as we see in the next section, but improvements in bargaining power augur well for the future.

14.5.4   *Reform of international institutions*

There were many suggestions to reform the IMF and improve the IFS, even after the East Asian crisis. The creditor view wanted the IMF to focus narrowly on providing international LOLR services with strict preconditionality. This would require giving it power to create resources much as a CB can, with backing from world governments.

Debtors, however, suffering from incorrect advice and delayed funding, wanted an expansion of power to be accompanied by change in the governance structure to reflect current world economic strengths. The United States and European countries continued to dominate in a structure frozen as set post-World War II, with excessive political oversight. Moreover, they wanted quicker response and more sensitivity to the needs of poorer and debtor countries. They favoured ex-post conditionality, where countries following better policy are rewarded with

Global financial crises   361

better terms. This creates ownership of reform and better incentive to implement them. Criticism of IMF functioning led to a demand for the creation of an Asian Monetary Fund, which was shot down on the grounds that it would lead to a dilution of conditionality.

Post GFC, there were some improvements. The broader G-20 replaced the G-7. The membership of the Bank of International Settlement (BIS) and the FSB were made more representative. The G-20 came up with a comprehensive list of reforms. The G-20 (2009) report on regulation had 25 recommendations concerning a national focus on financial stability, oversight of all systematically important institutions, countercyclical macroprudential norms, comprehensive international standards to be applied consistent with the national context and micro-conduct regulation to improve incentives for financial stability. Prompt corrective action was to be mandated based on well-defined financial, prudential parameters. The G-20 stance is in agreement with EM emphasis on stronger regulation, eliminating tax havens, maintaining trade, transparency, global standards and funds for EMs to fight a crisis not of their making. EMs also wanted a fund to stabilise EM bond price or spread index, infrastructure spending to help revive global demand and contribute to development.

The G-20 was very successful in coordinating a global monetary-fiscal stimulus after the GFC. But conflicts between AEs and EMs, because of different speeds of recovery and a loss of focus on financial reform, made it less effective over time. Even so, regular dialogue among a broader set of participants did serve a useful purpose – in particular, preventing formal restrictions on international trade.

Most of the reforms, however, rely on the IMF-WB to oversee or implement. Therefore, they cannot progress without substantial reform of those institutions. Quotas, votes and voice of EMs all have to change suitably. Otherwise, the list will remain the wish list produced after the East Asian crisis, as financial interests regroup and persuade, and creditor countries support them. In April 2009, the G-20 trebled the IMF's resources. EMs made sizeable contributions, but representation in the fund's executive board remained incommensurate with their growing economic power as AEs resisted change. The IMF continued to have a European head, even as it focussed more resources on Europe. The WB did not deliver on a promised infrastructure facility.

After the GFC, IMF views towards the use of capital controls softened. The latter are now recommended in the face of volatile capital flows, but only as a last resort and if other macroeconomic fundamentals are in order (Ostry et al., 2010). It began conducting a regular Financial Sector Assessment Programme for all systemically

362   Global financial crises

important countries. A new Integrated Surveillance Decision aimed to make IMF surveillance more effective. Member countries' obligations under the IMF's Articles of Agreement could not be changed, but the existing legal framework was enhanced by making Article IV consultations a vehicle for multilateral as well as bilateral surveillance, to also cover spillovers from member countries' policies that may impact global stability. Even without legal commitments, this can bring peer pressure to bear on countries whose imbalances create spillovers on others.

A Pilot External Sector Report assessed current accounts, balance sheet positions, reserves adequacy, capital flows and capital account policies, in addition to exchange rates. It sought to go beyond cyclical factors to identify the impact of policy distortions, other structural and country-specific factors on a country's current account. It asked whether the home country's policies need to change or whether other economies should change course. An IMF staff discussion paper takes the position that while a country can give greater weight to domestic concerns over international spillovers, where the latter impose costs on other countries there is a case for multilateral coordination that can either ask for a reduction in capital controls or ask lenders to partially internalise the risks of volatile capital flows (Ostry et al., 2012). It says the latter is 'much thornier'!

Suggested reform of the IMF now favours a flexible and fast-disbursing facility with little or no conditionality for countries adversely affected by global shocks. Since March 2009, the IMF made a new flexible credit line available, without strings attached, to countries with a track record of sound macroeconomic policies and institutions. This proved useful for East and South European countries in distress.

It will be a major step towards symmetry if the onus for capital flow volatility is put on source countries also, instead of the current system where the entire burden of adjustment is borne by recipient countries. But it is not clear that actual adjustment will be symmetric. After the East Asian crisis EMs reformed, but AEs did not. Nor was the IFS modified. AEs continue to take the position that asset bubbles are not due to QE but to EM demand, again putting the onus on EMs.

While EMs allowed currency appreciation and stimulated domestic demand to correct global imbalances, deficit reduction in AEs was indefinitely postponed. In the June Toronto G-20 meet, AEs committed to 'at least halve deficits by 2013 and stabilize or reduce government debt-to-GDP ratios by 2016'. But at the 2012 summit in Mexico City, it was admitted this target would not be achieved. Moreover, it was said to be not advisable to reduce deficits, given continued global

Global financial crises 363

uncertainties. Instead, AEs only committed to 'ensure that the pace of fiscal consolidation is appropriate to support the recovery'. The argument that in a balance sheet recession when the private sector is deleveraging and there is a possibility of a debt deflation trap, the government must spend has some validity. Reducing debt and deficits is easier when growth is higher. But symmetry requires some action on EM concerns also.

In the absence of meaningful reform in the IFS and given dangers from volatile and poorly regulated capital flows, EMs are forced to continue with costly self-insurance and to undertake regional initiatives. Stonewalling of reform after the East Asian crisis resulted in many EM initiatives that have improved the bargaining power of this block, as has the post-crisis weakness of mature economies. The many Asian groupings can help maintain global power on an even keel and ensure that more reforms are actually implemented this time around and adjustment is more symmetric. Asian currency swaps, the AIIB and the BRICS bank can offer competition to the Bretton Woods institutions. Asian financial integration is much below trade integration, the new institutions can help reverse this and invest large Asian savings to meet their infrastructure needs. For example, CBs can invest large reserves in the region, reducing imbalances and investment in US treasuries. Market deepening is in EMs own interest, but more opening has to be calibrated and is conditional on a better IFS and market institutions.

14.6 Summary

This chapter analyses causes of the GFC, the subsequent financial reforms, the IFS and the process of change in the IFS, lacunae in the process and potential improvements and continuing sources of global risk. Although there has been some post-GFC improvement in the IFS and the institutions underlying it, it is far from adequate or complete. They have more voice now, but EMs lost an opportunity to improve global stability and contributed to a diffusion of the G-20 agenda by not insisting on a more even sharing of adjustment costs. They accepted strongly held AE positions without pushing for modifications that could moderate the spillovers from AE actions. Pressure from AEs also led to inappropriate macroeconomic policies in some EMs.

At present, financial reform proposals are more complex than necessary and subject to continuing dilutions and delay, while monetary and exchange rate policies imposed are often simpler than required in the EM context. For example, despite having robust financial

364 *Global financial crises*

regulation without the disincentives that full or no liability involves, India is imposing stringent, expensive Basel norms not suited to its bank-led system with underdeveloped credit. If, instead, some features EM investor-based prudential regulations were incorporated in global standards, financial stability would improve.

Understanding EM context and helping them to follow appropriate policies will help AEs. Lower growth in EMs harms recovery in AEs, as the global impact of the Chinese slowdown and market volatility illustrates.

After the East Asian crisis, EMs reformed but AEs did not, nor was the IFS modified. EM reforms, such as more flexible exchange rates, shift towards foreign equity from debt financing and rise in precautionary reserves holding helped them withstand the GFC. AEs did reform after the GFC but it was inadequate. AE CBs proved to be the largest consumers of safe assets and creators of global imbalances, as QE expanded their balance sheets. Competition from regional initiatives, regional financial deepening and competition, however, offer some hope for a more stable future IFS.

Notes

1 These non-core or non-deposit liabilities of the banking sector had also peaked in Korea before the financial crises in 1997 and in 2008 and were responsible for sharp depreciations of the won in 2008 and 2010. So, Korea imposed prudential taxes to reduce procyclical expansion of banks non-core liabilities.

2 The measure of risk can also be selected strategically. For example, one reason banks' capital varies widely for similar exposures is strategic use of number of years' data in their VAR models used to calculate risk. Accounting practices can be used to make banks' balance sheets inscrutable and non-comparable. In 2016, BIs put restrictions on banks own risk models.

3 Accounting conventions that affect the measurement of assets also affect leverage. Economic leverage is actually a broader measure. Off-balance sheet assets also need to be captured.

4 A leverage ratio of 0.03 implies 3 units of capital must be held against 100 units of assets acquired, that is, the accounting or balance sheet leverage is limited to 1/0.03 or 33.3 to 1. Accounting leverage is the inverse of the leverage ratio and is also known as the leverage multiple.

5 Claessens (2014) reports EMs used these tools four times more intensively compared to AEs before the GFC. The ratio fell to 3.3 after to GFC.

6 The IMF reported end December comparative balance sheets for major CBs in the December 2012 issue of *Finance & Development*. ECB's assets, comprising largely claims on banks, were € 5.5 trillion, a 241 per cent rise since August 2007; the Fed was at US\$ 3 trillion, a 221 per cent rise of claims against banks, the private sector and government; Bank of England at 400 billion pounds, a 380 per cent rise. Japan started its QE in 2012, a larger than the Fed programme for an economy with one-third US GDP.

Global financial crises 365

7 Since the Chinese currency was fixed to the dollar, it depreciated with the dollar against the Euro in the early stages of the GFC. So, if exchange rates were responsible for the US CAD, imbalances with China should have been large for Europe also. But many European countries did not run a CAD.

8 Since 2005, the renminbi peg was relaxed, allowing narrow daily movements. By 2015 the Chinese currency had risen 25 per cent against the dollar after more or less steady daily appreciation. In August, the formula used to fix the currency was tweaked to allow more room for market forces and USD-CNY depreciated from 6.21 in the beginning of the month to 6.34 by the end of the month. This biggest one-day movement since the mid-1990s again led to allegations of a currency war and fears of market instability.

9 The QE announced in April 2013 reversed earlier appreciation. By 2015, the yen had fallen 33 per cent against the US$.

10 In purchasing power parity exchange rates, developed countries share of global GDP was only 43 per cent in 2015 compared to 54 per cent in 2004.

References

Admati, A. and M. Hellwig. 2013. *The Bankers' New Clothes: What's Wrong with Banking and What to Do about It?* Princeton, NJ: Princeton University Press.

Aizenman, J. 2009. 'Hoarding International Reserves Versus a Pigovian Tax-Cum-Subsidy Scheme: Reflections on the Deleveraging Crisis of 2008–9, and a Cost Benefit Analysis', *NBER Working Paper No. 15484*. Available at http://www.nber.org/papers/w15484.

Bernanke, B. S. 2005. 'The Global Saving Glut and the U.S. Current Account Deficit', *Speech Delivered at the Sandridge Lecture*, Richmond, VA: Virginia Association of Economics, 10 March. Available at http://www.federalreserve.gov/boarddocs/speeches/2005/200503102/default.htm (accessed on May 2009).

Bernanke, B. S., C. Bertaut, L. P. DeMarco and S. Kamin. 2011. 'International Capital Flows and the Returns to Safe Assets in the United States, 2003–2007'. Available at http://federalreserve.gov/pubs/ifdp/2011/1014/ifdp1014.htm.

BIS (Bank of International Settlements). 2008. 'Foreign Exchange and Derivatives Market Activity in 2007', *Triennial Central Bank Survey*. December. Available at http://www.bis.org/publ/rpfxf07t.htm (accessed on 10 November 2008).

Blanchard, O. J. and G. M. Milesi-Ferretti. 2009. 'Global Imbalances: In Midstream?', *IMF Staff Position Note SPN/09/29*, December 22. Available at http://www.imf.org/external/pubs/ft/spn/2009/spn0929.pdf.

Blanchard, O. J. and G. M. Milesi-Ferretti. 2012. '(Why) Should Current Account Balances Be Reduced?', *IMF Economic Review*, 60: 139–150, April. doi:10.1057/imfer.2012.2.

Caballero, R. J. and A. Krishnamurthy. 2009. 'Global Imbalances and Financial Fragility, Papers and Proceedings', *American Economic Review*, 99(2):

366 *Global financial crises*

584–588, May. Available at http://pubs.aeaweb.org/doi/pdfplus/10.1257/aer.99.2.584.

Claessens, S. 2014. 'An Overview of Macroprudential Policy Tools', *IMF Working Paper, No. WP/14/214*. Available at https://www.imf.org/external/pubs/ft/wp/2014/wp14214.pdf (accessed on March 2016).

Gourinchas, P. O. and H. Rey. 2013. 'External Adjustment, Global Imbalances and Valuation Effects', in G. Gopinath, H. Helpman and K. Rogoff (eds.), *Handbook of International Economics*, also *NBER Working Paper 19240*, pp. 585–645. Amsterdam: Elsevier.

Goyal, A. 2002. 'Reform Proposals from Developing Asia: Finding a Win-Win Strategy', Chapter 7 in Leslie Elliott Armijo (ed.), *Debating the Global Financial Architecture*, SUNY Press Global Politics series, under the general editorship of James Rosenau. New York: SUNY Press, pp. 184–213.

Goyal, A. 2005. 'Asian Reserves and the Dollar: Is Gradual Adjustment Possible?', *Global Economy Journal*, 5(3): Article 3. Available at http://www.bepress.com/gej/vol5/iss3/3 (accessed on May 2009).

Goyal, A. 2009. 'Financial Crises: Reducing Pro-Cyclicality', *Macroeconomics and Finance in Emerging Market Economies*, 2(1): 213–223, March.

Goyal, A. 2010. 'Global Financial Architecture: Past and Present Arguments, Advice, Action', *Margin – The Journal of Applied Economic Research*, 4(2): 233–247. New Delhi: Sage Publication.

Goyal, A. 2013. 'Banks, Policy, and Risks: How Emerging Markets Differ', *International Journal of Public Policy*, 10(1, 2 & 3): 4–26.

Goyal, A. and S. Tripathi. 2012. 'Regulations and Price Discovery: Oil Spot and Futures Markets', *The International Review of Applied Financial Issues and Economics*. 4(3), September.

Hanson, S. G., A. K. Kashyap and J. C. Stein. 2011. 'A Macroprudential Approach to Financial Regulation', *Journal of Economic Perspectives*, 25(1): 3–28. doi:10.1257/jep.25.1.3.

IMF. 2012. 'Growth Resuming, Dangers Remain', *World Economic Outlook*, April, Washington, DC: International Monetary Fund.

Kohn, D. 2015. 'Implementing Macroprudential and Monetary Policies: The Case for Two Committees', *FRB Boston Conference October 2, 2015*. Available at http://www.brookings.edu/~/media/research/files/speeches/2015/10/frbboston-finalfinal.pdf (accessed on March 2016).

Krugman, P. 2009. 'Reagan Did It', *New York Times*, May 31. Print version on June 1: A21. Available at http://www.nytimes.com/2009/06/01/opinion/01krugman.html (accessed on May 2009).

Ostry, J. D., A. R. Ghosh, K. Habermeier, M. Chamon, M. S. Qureshi and D. B. S. Reinhardt. 2010. 'Capital Inflows: The Role of Controls', *IMF Staff Position Notes SPN/10/04*. February.

Ostry, J. D., A. R. Ghosh and A. Korinek. 2012. 'Multilateral Aspects of Managing the Capital Account', *IMF Staff Discussion Note*. 7 September.

Portes, R. 2009. 'Global Imbalances', in M. Dewatripont, X. Freixas and R. Portes (eds.), *Macroeconomic Stability and Financial Regulation: Key Issues for the G20*. London: Centre for Economic Policy Research. Available at http://www.voxeu.org/reports/G20_ebook.pdf (accessed on May 2009).

Shin, H. S. 2011. 'Global Liquidity', *Remarks at the IMF Conference on Macro and Growth Policies in the Wake of the Crisis*, Washington, DC, 7–8 March 2011.

Shin, H. S. and K. Shin. 2011. 'Pro-Cyclicality and Monetary Aggregates', *NBER Working Paper No. 16836*. Available at http://www.nber.org/papers/w16836.pdf.

Shleifer, A. and R. W. Vishny. 2010. 'Unstable Banking', *Journal of Financial Economics, Elsevier*, 97(3): 306–318, September.

Sinha, A. 2011. 'Macroprudential Policies: Indian Experience', *Address at Eleventh Annual International Seminar on Policy Challenges for the Financial Sector on Seeing Both the Forest and the Trees – Supervising Systemic Risk*, Washington, DC, 1–3 June 2011.

Taylor, J. 2009. 'The Financial Crisis and the Policy Responses: An Empirical Analysis of What Went Wrong', *NBER Working Paper No. 14631*, January. Available at http://www.nber.org/papers/w14631 (accessed on May 2009).

Index

abductive reasoning 3, 15, 23
accounting, basic 28–50;
  government and twin deficits
  46–8; intertemporal approach
  30–46; macroeconomic identities
  28–30
adjustment programmes, structural
  269
aggregate demand (AD) 2–3, 5–6,
  24, 28–9, 154, 156, 226, 230,
  234, 244, 247–9, 251–2, 274,
  278, 280; from consumers'
  optimisation 228–31; deriving 264
aggregate supply (AS) 221–2;
  from firms' optimisation 231–3;
  identity 264
asset bubbles 180–1, 193, 293,
  308–10, 336, 362
asset prices 123, 129, 160, 195,
  216, 243, 247–50, 308, 332, 348;
  flexible 128, 134, 166; inflation
  307–8
assets: long-term 312–13, 315,
  318–19, 321; safe 356, 364

bailouts 325
balance of payments (BOP) 24,
  28–50, 52, 124, 149, 317; current
  account, surplus 29, 36
Balassa-Samuelson effect 107, 114,
  116–21
bank regulation 316
bankruptcy 325
banks, large 80, 82–3, 345–6
bond issuance 75, 321

capital accounts 29–30, 36–7, 40–2,
  49, 51, 140, 149, 191, 272, 311,
  341–2
capital adequacy 90, 332–3, 345–6
capital markets, open 31, 179, 218
capital mobility, perfect 154, 157,
  175, 182, 193, 280, 300
cash reserve ratio (CRR) 244–5
Central Bank (CB) 36–7, 79–81, 86,
  96, 101–2, 126–7, 158–9, 174–9,
  184, 186–7, 189–95, 232–3,
  239–42, 246, 253–4, 261–2, 277,
  300–1, 317, 336, 340–1, 350
Clearing Corporation of India Ltd
  (CCIL) 87–9
collective action clauses (CAC) 316
commercial banks 9, 45, 174, 249,
  317–19, 331, 334
commodity exports, dominance
  of 311
consumer price index (CPI) 17–19,
  111–12, 114, 147–8, 228, 238,
  249, 251, 290; inflation 111,
  228–9, 232, 249, 262
consumption 9–11, 28, 30–4, 65,
  155–6, 205–9, 211, 214–15,
  220–1, 229–30, 234–5, 237,
  281–2, 294–5, 312–13
core inflation 239, 243, 261
corruption 260, 274, 294, 311
covered interest parity (CIP) 56–60,
  63–4, 69, 75–6; testing 58–9
creditors 74, 316, 320–7, 360
currency: domestic 61, 96, 159–61,
  169, 178, 248, 302, 316–18, 340;

Index   369

importer's 113–14; local 168–9, 191, 272, 317
currency arbitrage 52–5
currency board 186–8, 310, 317–18
currency crises 2, 12, 24, 252, 281, 289, 299–328; analysis of 299; domestic 321; East Asian crises 307, 311, 315, 322, 326–7; first-generation crises 300–5; global 321; Latin American crises 299–300, 305, 311, 327; Mexican crises 307; policy lessons of 320–6; second-generation crises 305–7; third-generation crises 307–20
currency markets 83, 99
currency unions 187, 352–4
currency values 69, 100, 124, 220, 340
currency wars 331, 357–60
current account balance (CAB) 39, 167–9
current account imbalances 354–7; foreign currency reserves 356–7; valuation effects 356

data sets, improvement 67–8
debt 30, 32, 36, 42, 199, 203, 253–6, 272–3, 277, 311, 315–16, 320, 323–5, 354, 356
debt/equity ratio 309
debt flows 42–3, 92, 95, 272
deduction and induction 3–11
delivery price 70
dollar deposits 53–4, 74, 343
dollarisation of domestic liabilities (DLD) 321
dollarised economies 317
domestic banks 312, 317
domestic credit expansion 326
domestic markets 85, 87, 96–9, 320
dynamic stochastic general equilibrium (DSGE) models 2, 4, 10–11, 24, 202–3, 218–19

East Asian development strategy 308
economies of exchange rates 24, 201, 225
electronic crossing networks 82
emerging and developing economies (EDEs) 1–3, 12–23, 95–6, 114–17, 141–9, 165–7, 180–1, 198, 226–7, 243–4, 246–9, 269–70, 276–8, 280–1, 295–6, 309; crises in 13–15; Indian growth and inflation 15–23; smoothing consumption in 32–4; stabilisation programmes 299
emerging market bond index 320
emerging market fund (EMF) 321
emerging markets (EMs) 2, 15, 183, 186, 200–1, 234, 236, 243, 249, 252, 320–3, 325–7, 336, 342, 347–50, 356–64
equations, fundamental 36–7, 125
equilibrium, goods market 125, 156–7, 161
equilibrium exchange rate 77, 141
equilibrium noise trader entry 103–4
Euro debt crisis 13, 24, 42, 87, 352–4
European banks 343, 353–5
European Central Bank (ECB) 353
exchange rate: bilateral 75, 81, 107, 110; bilateral nominal 52, 108, 110, 131; changes 113–14, 169, 183, 186, 304; channel 194, 233, 251, 261; depreciation 128–9, 131, 158, 179, 216–17, 220, 283, 286, 302; expected 54, 56, 59, 69, 77, 154, 159, 162, 175, 197; expected nominal 107, 134, 144; fixed exchange rates 155, 158–9, 170, 173–6, 179–82, 198, 288, 292, 299–301, 305, 309–11, 318–19, 323, 341–2; flexible exchange rates 12, 123, 125, 174, 176, 179, 181, 198, 218, 287–8, 292–3, 310, 319–21, 364; floating exchange rate 11, 49, 51, 304; monetary approach to 124–6; and purchasing power parity 107–18; real effective 109–10; spot 53, 56, 58–9, 70–1, 75, 136, 138, 302; volatility of nominal 111, 115
exchange rate, asset approach 51–77; currency arbitrage 52–5; discount bias, explanations 63–8; discount bias explanations 63–8; FX markets 68–77; market efficiency 55–63; uncovered interest parity 53–5

370 *Index*

exchange rate expectations: non-static 155, 159, 162, 173; static 155, 157, 164, 170
exchange rate management 180, 307
exchange rate mechanism (ERM) 7, 299, 305
exchange rate policy 79–80, 102, 117, 167, 173–99, 190–201, 238, 251, 287, 300, 317, 341, 363; active 193, 198, 247; automatic stabilisation 179–81; CB intervention 193–5; contributions of 287–8; fixed exchange rates 174–9; liquidity trap, solution 196–8; monetary approach and 190–1; portfolio balance channel, intervention 191–3; signalling and 195–6
exchange rate regimes 1, 12–13, 154, 173, 181–3, 191, 198, 200–1, 204, 281, 286–7, 315, 317, 341; application to 317; currency board 317; dollarisation 317; fixed 118, 318, 342; flexible 319; floating 63, 123, 129, 131, 135
exchange rate volatility 84, 96, 101, 117, 180, 183
expected depreciation 53, 55, 59, 64–5, 125, 129, 131, 145–6, 150, 159–60, 162–3, 249
expected inflation 131, 134–5, 144–5, 156, 197, 226, 239, 242–3, 251
external balance (EB) 278–80, 284

financial account 29–30, 36–7, 39
financial markets 76, 80, 166, 218, 244, 275, 326, 333–4, 355, 360
financial reforms 8, 96, 276, 295, 330–1, 343, 352, 360–1, 363
first-order conditions (FOCs) 202, 209, 214–15, 221, 230, 263–4
fiscal policy 4, 8–9, 23–4, 152, 154–5, 157–9, 161–7, 170–1, 173–4, 176–7, 181–2, 197–8, 226–36, 238–62, 288; fiscal rules 258–61
Fiscal Responsibility Act (FRA) 259, 260
flexible inflation forecast 243, 245

flexible price monetary approach (FPMA) 123–4, 126, 131–5; modifications in 144–7
food prices 10, 117, 244, 294; inflation 18, 23
foreign assets 2, 11, 30, 36, 59, 173, 175–7, 191, 193, 199, 272, 317, 342, 356
foreign currency: assets 43; exposures 89–90; reserves 14, 36, 174, 356
foreign debt 30–2
foreign direct investment (FDI): Indian vs Chinese 47–8
foreign exchange 12, 37, 53, 150, 224, 249; reserves 14, 30
foreign exchange (FX) markets 24, 68–77, 79–92, 95–102, 104, 150; counterparties/instruments/currencies 81–2; domestic markets, impact of measures 96–9; encouraging hedging 99–100; equilibrium 127, 155, 161, 175; functioning 84; Indian markets 84–91; institutional features 80–100; market microstructure 74–102; noise traders 100; and policy 100–1; regulation 83–4; structure 80–1; technology 82–3; types of intervention in 91–6
foreign inflows 42–6
foreign portfolio investment (FPI) 40, 42–4, 358
forward rates 56, 59–60, 64, 75, 87, 98
forward trades 88–90

G-20 countries 357
global financial crisis (GFC) 1–4, 9, 14–15, 40–1, 82–4, 90–1, 166–7, 187, 196, 326–7, 330–64; Asian oversaving 334–9; global imbalances and search for yield 333–4; origin 331–3
global imbalances 14, 24, 330, 333, 355, 364
gold standard, currency price 339
goods market 150, 154, 156, 160, 168, 180, 198; prices 154, 196

Index 371

goods prices: non-traded 114, 120, 281, 284–5; traded 114, 148, 249, 272, 281–2, 316
government bonds 253
Great Depression 1, 4, 12, 165, 340
greater generality 3
gross domestic capital formation (GDCF) 35–6
gross domestic product (GDP) 17, 19–21, 29–31, 40–2, 45–6, 255–6, 270, 275–7, 295, 307, 340
gross domestic savings (GDS) 35
gross fiscal deficit (GFD) 253, 255–6
gross national product (GNP) 30–2, 35, 271
gross national savings (GNS) 35–6

home currency 52, 60–1, 70, 73, 110, 263, 279
home currency value 69
home goods demand, foreign consumer 263

incentive compatibility (IC) 313
incentives 14–15, 74–5, 77, 81, 83–4, 100, 147, 260, 292, 325, 332–3, 345, 350, 361
Indian balance of payments 37
Indian banks 99, 275, 349
Indian FX markets 80, 84–6, 88, 101–2
Indian goods 52, 142, 263
Indian inflation 23, 117
inflation 6, 15–20, 24, 117, 131–4, 150–1, 166–7, 183–5, 223–7, 232–3, 237–49, 253–7, 260–2, 277–80, 287–94; headline 243–4, 261; imported 279; lower 16, 20, 240–1, 247, 256, 290; reducing 165, 278; sustain 117, 141
inflation adjustment 240
inflationary inertia 185
inflation differentials 109, 131, 185
inflation expectations 20, 22, 23, 128, 134, 239, 244, 249, 251, 261, 289, 321
inflation rate 133, 184, 210, 233, 240, 243, 245, 251, 253–5, 274, 290
inflation target 180, 185, 233, 238, 241–2, 247

interest payments 72, 253–5, 260
interest rates 18, 54–9, 96, 123–8, 131–2, 134–5, 145–6, 190, 195–7, 199–200, 208–9, 239–41, 243–7, 249–53, 307–10
intermediate goods price 251
international financial reforms: arbitrage and shadow banking 344; delays 350–2; leverage restriction, measures 346–50; systemic risks and macroprudential regulation 344–6; weaknesses in 343–52
international financial system (IFS) 14–15, 24, 293, 323, 326–7, 330–64
international illiquidity condition (IIC) equation 314–15
international institutions, reform 360–3
International Monetary Fund (IMF) 2, 14–15, 85, 88, 182, 199, 310–11, 321–2, 324–5, 335, 340–1, 344, 354–5, 357–8, 360–2
intertemporal optimisation, open economy 204–10; Euler equation, interpretations 207–8; optimal consumption and labour supply 205–6; simple variational proof 206–7; utility function, example of 208–10
intervention, sterilised 175, 191–2, 194
investment banks 14, 327, 332, 334
investment currency 61

labour, surplus 22, 358
labour elasticity 221–2
labour market reform 292–3
labour markets, dualistic 10, 22, 226
labour supply elasticity 222, 224, 234, 237
Latin American crises 299–300, 305, 311, 327
law of one price (LOOP) 107, 109, 111–13, 118, 212–13, 228
lender of last resort (LOLR) 312, 318–19
leverage ratio 345, 364
local currency pricing (LCP) 113

372 Index

log-linearisation 223
long-run impact, monetary approach 129–31

macroeconomic fundamentals 7, 77, 80, 305–6, 361; strong 299–300, 311
macroeconomics: modern 22, 123; structuralist 2
macroeconomic stabilisation, limits of 165–7
marginal cost equation 265–6
market efficiency 10, 52, 55–63; testing 59–63
market makers 80–1, 98
market microstructure 68, 74–102
market players 92, 199
market prices 40–1, 53, 55, 59, 64, 71, 76, 333, 356; sticky goods 123, 135, 180–1, 194
markets: perfect 124, 190, 195–6, 202; repo 346–7; stock 80–1, 84, 200, 276
market structure 83–4, 102
monetary and fiscal policy 154–71; directions for 226–62; Mundell Fleming model 157–9; output market equilibrium 155–6; relative effectiveness of 155–65; short-run price flexibility and 164–5
monetary approach 118, 123–9, 131–8, 140–2, 190; to exchange rate 124–6; flexible price 123, 131; sticky price 123, 126
monetary autonomy 23, 101, 176, 181, 187
monetary-fiscal coordination 260–2
monetary policy 7–9, 155, 157–8, 165–7, 173, 176, 182–3, 185–6, 197–200, 239–41, 244–5, 249–50, 252, 254–5, 257–8, 307; expansionary 256–7; implications for 241–7; optimal 227–33; transmission 247–52
monetary policy DSGE: adaptation of 234–9
monetary shocks 115, 118, 123–4, 128–9, 134, 152, 179–80, 186, 198, 203, 216–20, 274;

permanent 128; real effects of 123–4; temporary 128
monetary theories 107, 118, 140–52, 190, 300
monetary variables 140, 142–3, 154
money balances 126, 129, 146, 160, 239, 253, 255
money demand 127, 134, 160–2, 164, 176, 179, 190, 197, 216–17, 239, 244, 300–1, 304, 320
money demand shocks 180, 198, 287–8
money growth, higher 132, 146
money market 126–7, 134, 145, 147, 159–60, 175, 179, 190, 197, 239, 241, 300, 302; short-term 247
money market equilibrium 123–6, 128–9, 144, 157, 159–60, 164, 175, 216; continuous 304
money supply 126–32, 134–5, 142–3, 146, 158, 162–3, 173–80, 190–4, 197, 199, 217–18, 253–4, 287–9, 301–5, 339–41; domestic 160, 191; growth rate of 132; nominal 128, 142; relative 123, 125–6, 128, 134, 190
money supply growth 23, 131, 133, 143, 334
monopolistic competition 203, 209–10, 220–1, 227
Mundell Fleming (MF) model 154–5, 157–9, 162, 165, 170, 173, 175–6, 280; *see also* monetary and fiscal policy

Nash equilibrium 306–7, 324–5
natural interest rate 236–7
natural output 232, 236
net capital inflow (NCI) 35
net exports 29–32, 150, 155, 219
net income 31, 35, 39–40
net output 31–2
New Keynesian Economics (NKE) School 4
new open economy macroeconomics 51, 199, 203–20, 222, 224–5; building blocks 204–10; extensions 218–20
noise traders 100–4

Index   373

nominal exchange rate 107–9, 111, 113–16, 123–6, 128, 132, 134–5, 140–3, 146, 152, 178, 185–6, 247, 250–2, 278–80

nominal interest rates 60, 123, 131, 133–5, 144, 146, 210, 214, 232–3, 239, 242, 248, 251–2, 255

nominal wages 117, 119, 148, 247, 272, 274, 284, 286–8

non-deliverable forwards (NDFs) 73, 87, 99

non-static exchange rate expectations 159–65; permanent shock stabilisation 162–4; temporary shock stabilisation 161–2

non-tradables 37, 47, 114–15, 117–20, 149, 270, 281–3, 285

open economy 11–12, 300

open economy macroeconomics 2–3, 14, 24, 118, 123, 155; two-country 210–18

output cost 166, 242, 262, 289–90

output gap 8, 166, 226, 231–3, 241, 265

permanent shock short-run impact 128–9

peso problem 66, 193

policy rates 17–19, 55, 232–3, 236, 238, 245, 310

policy tools, absorption and switching 278–81

post-GFC financial reforms 343–52

potential output 15, 226, 233, 236, 242–3, 287

power parity and exchange rate 108–18, 120–1

price changes 168, 170, 278–9

price levels 107–9, 111, 115, 118, 120–1, 127–9, 133, 140–2, 144–6, 154, 178, 213, 247, 254, 340; relative 107, 134

price movements 68–9, 87

prices: consumer 164, 166, 228, 249; dollar 170, 317; domestic 37, 52, 113, 164–5, 170, 181, 231, 280, 290, 317; flexible 5, 123–5, 134, 138, 216, 300; import 113, 169–70, 181, 249, 281

price shocks, external 117, 194, 219

pricing to market (PTM) 113

private savings 8, 46, 295, 355

productivity 115, 117–18, 121, 128, 141–2, 149, 187, 198, 211, 231, 234, 282, 292, 294, 320–1

profits 31, 56, 58–9, 69–73, 75, 77, 83–4, 114, 193–4, 209, 332, 337–8, 347–9

programmes, varieties of 288–96; exchange rate-based programmes 289–90; heterodox stabilisation 291; money-based programmes 289; orthodox 289; populist (old Keynesian) 288–9

purchasing power parity (PPP) 107, 109, 111–15, 118, 123, 131, 134, 140–1, 144–5, 149, 199, 212–13, 271, 280, 300–2, 320; and exchange rate 107–18; LOOP and 111–12; trade arbitrage 108–11

random walk (RW) 63, 80, 112

rational bubbles 65–6, 124, 126, 136–8, 193

rational learning 66

real business cycle (RBC) 4

real exchange rate 107–9, 111–12, 114–15, 117–18, 120–1, 140–52, 156, 170, 198–9, 228–9, 280–3, 286–7, 296; broader determinants 141–2; emerging and developing economies 144–7; monetary approach and 142–4; and real wages 286–7; real wages and 147–51

real interest rates 143, 150, 152, 156, 196, 198, 214, 219, 226, 233, 239–42, 247, 250, 255, 275

real money balances 126–9, 145, 160, 163, 165, 178, 214, 304

real uncovered interest parity (UIP) 143–4

real wages 22, 116–17, 141, 147–8, 152, 167, 209, 231, 235–6, 247, 265, 274, 277, 282, 284–7; function of 283, 286

reform thinking, evolution 291–5

Reserve Bank of India (RBI) 317–18

rupee value 56, 141–2, 169

374 *Index*

second-generation currency 299–300
shocks, temporary 31, 33, 161, 163, 170, 173, 236–7
short-run adjustment 154–71
short-term debt 315–17, 321, 324
small open economy (SOE) 218, 227, 234, 247, 270, 312
small open emerging market economy (SOEME) 234–6, 238
speculators 56, 68–9, 73, 96, 178, 193, 302, 304–5, 309
spot market 56, 68, 73, 85
stability, financial 76, 349–50, 361, 364
stabilisation 282–6
statutory debt reduction mechanism (SDRM) 316
sticky goods prices 129, 138
sticky price monetary approach SPMA 123–4, 126, 131, 134–5: asset market and overshooting 126–31
sticky prices 4, 123, 129, 131, 134–5, 138, 157, 166, 199, 203, 216, 226, 239, 248; currency prices 129
structural adjustment 262, 269–70, 272, 274–96
supply shocks 20, 24, 33, 180, 199, 226, 243–4, 293
supply-side economics 8
Swan-Salter dependent economy model 281, 282

terminal price 72
Tesobono debt 316
tests, refining 63–4
trade arbitrage 108–14, 118, 140, 152, 219–20, 272; failures of 112–18; perfect 124, 140, 148, 300
traded goods 47, 111, 114, 117, 119–20, 140, 251–2, 272, 281–3, 316
transaction costs 58–9, 68–9, 82, 88, 90, 112–13, 118, 220, 306
turnover 82, 84–5, 92, 95, 97–8

uncovered interest parity (UIP) 300–2; expectations hypothesis 65–6; risk 64–5
underdevelopment structure, EDE 270–8; financial markets 275–6; government budget 276–8; long-run supply behaviour 272–4; open economy features 270–2; short-run supply behaviour 274–5
unhedged foreign borrowing (UFB) 309–10

wages 115–17, 120, 148, 150–1, 198, 234, 236, 244, 249–50, 274, 285–6, 289, 291, 355, 358
wholesale price index (WPI) core 16, 18, 20, 111, 112, 114, 116
World Bank 311